33

W9-CEB-141

**Illinois Central College
Learning Resources Center**

Inside the
New Europe

Inside the
New Europe

Axel Krause

Cornelia & Michael Bessie Books
An Imprint of HarperCollins*Publishers*

FIRST EDITION

Designed by Alma Orenstein

Library of Congress Cataloging-in-Publication Data

Krause, Axel.
    Inside the new Europe / by Axel Krause.—1st ed.
      p. cm.
    "Cornelia & Michael Bessie books."
    Includes bibliographical references (p.) and index.
    ISBN 0-06-039101-4
    1. Europe 1992. 2. European Economic Community. I. Title.
HC241.2.K698 1991
337.1'42—dc20   90-56379

92 93 94 95 CC/RRD 10 9 8 7 6 5 4 3 2

To Janine, Caroline, Anthony, and Nicolas

Contents

Acknowledgments

Were it not for a chance encounter with Beverly Gordey in the rue de Buci market in Paris on a bright Sunday in June 1987, this book would never have been written. As one of the leading American scouts in Europe for the book publishing industry (then with Collins), and aware that I was taking on new responsibilities at the paper, being an old friend she suggested I start putting an outline together for an eventual book on my experiences with Europe. Later that year, she put me in touch with S. Michael Bessie, who, with HarperCollins, saw the book through to publication.

Both provided steady, constructive help and criticism after the first draft of every chapter was written, which proved a blessing for a first book. Bessie, as my editor, deserves the main credit for having taught me what writing a book was all about, having enthusiastically guided me amid the dizzying pace of events and news breaking around us, which continued virtually nonstop.

This book would most certainly never have been possible either without the *International Herald Tribune* and my involvement with the paper as a reporter and editor. The *IHT*'s superb editorial quality and popularity among some quarter of a million readers in more than 160 countries helped open doors and, as much of the material for the book began accumulating, the *IHT*'s unmatched staff of editors over the years provided invaluable criticism, insights, and steady encouragement, which I drew on continuously. Most important, the affiliation provided me with the enviable, highly visible perch from which to record and assess what was happening.

A very special tribute goes to the paper's publisher, Lee Huebner, whose sense of history and vision transformed into immediate support and enthusiasm, which never ceased. His help and that of his kind, untiring, ever-available assistant, Linda Lamarche, proved invaluable under sometimes stressful conditions. My thanks, too, goes to Peggy Burns at Bessie Books in New York and to Miranda Book, Michael Bessie's assistant, for their cheerful guidance and help.

Many senior executives and press relations officers in companies, banks, law firms, governments, international institutions and universities, and fellow journalists also helped in providing guidance and in opening the doors to decision-makers, too numerous to list here. The following are those to whom I owe a special word of thanks, listed in alphabetical order: Samuel Abt, deputy editor of the *International Herald Tribune;* Philippe d'Abzac of Compagnie Saint-Gobain; C. Michael Aho of the Council on Foreign Relations; Joachim Bitterlich, European affairs adviser to Chancellor Helmut Kohl; P. F. J. M. Brouwers, retired deputy head of the Philips press office; John Crawford of Jones Day Reavis & Pogue in Paris; William Eberle of Manchester Associates; François Fontaine of the Jean Monnet Association; Professor Richard Gardner of Columbia University; Roland Glavany, retired general of the French air force; Elisabeth Guigou, France's minister for European affairs; Ella Krucoff, head of press relations, the EC Commission delegation in Washington; Pascal Lamy, chief of staff, the EC Commission President; Keith Richardson, secretary general of the European Roundtable; Véronique Saint-Geours, public relations consultant in Paris; Christian Sautter, Préfet of the Ile de France region; Greg Treverton, the Council on Foreign Relations; Bruno DeThomas, chief spokesman for the EC Commission; Pierre Uri, author and economist; and Richard Wilkinson, information counsellor of the British Embassy in Paris.

Scholars, diplomats, friends and relatives were also generous with their time and assistance in helping with the historical research, among them: Hans Ephraimson-Abt, of Saddle River, N.J.; Doctor Chantal Bozo-Bamberger of Paris; and Robert Korengold, minister counsellor for public affairs in the U.S. Embassy in Paris.

To Marie Cordoliani of Bastia, France, Philippe de Suremain, deputy director for European affairs in France's foreign ministry and his wife, Françoise, who generously lent their homes and warm hospitality during the difficult writing phase, I want to express my deepest thanks.

I accept full responsibility for any errors in fact and assessment of events and trends dealt with in the book, but they would certainly have been more numerous were it not for those who cheerfully read portions and provided invaluable suggestions, which I took into account, including the following: Michael Calingaert, European representative of the Pharmaceutical Manufacturers Association; Sheila Chevalier of the Institut d'Études Politiques in Paris and her husband, Bill; Robert Dilenschneider, president of Hill and Knowlton; James Elles, member of the European Parliament; Michel Glavany of Arianespace; Robert D. Hormats, vice chairman of Goldman Sachs International; J. Paul Horne of Smith Barney; Lee Huebner, publisher of the *International Herald Tribune;* Henry Kissinger; Anthony Krause of the École Normale Superieure; Thomas Niles, U.S. assistant secretary of state-designate for European and Canadian affairs; Jochen Thies, editor of Europa Archiv; and Elisabeth Vincentelli of the Rockefeller Foundation.

At HarperCollins, the exhaustive checking and suggested revisions in the manuscript made by copy editor Margaret Cheney greatly improved the final version.

Finally, for my wife, Janine, who helped most of all with her unflagging patience, steadying counsel, encouragement and understanding silence when the going became tiresome, there are no words to express the gratitude I will feel always.

AXEL KRAUSE

Paris
October 1, 1991

Introduction

The purpose of this book is to tell the story of contemporary Western Europe's slow, determined effort to become a more powerful and, above all, a united force in world affairs. It will attempt to explain how and why the Common Market, for the first time since its founding in 1958, is challenging the United States and Japan for dominance in world trade and high technology. The buildup of Europe's economic strength, however, is but the first step toward a more visionary goal: establishing Western Europe's global political power through modern and peaceful means. The movement has no precedent in European history, and that is why many observers predict the 1990s will be the Decade of Europe. Let us begin on a spring morning in 1981.

A chill wind was bending rows of yellow tulips outside the well-guarded headquarters of the giant multinational electronics company Philips in Eindhoven, Holland, a trim Dutch industrial town dominated by Philips just as the Eastman Kodak company in the United States dominates the city of Rochester, New York. Inside, hissing robots lifted television tubes onto a computer-operated conveyer belt, which zipped them to assembly stations operated by clusters of women amid disco music piped in from a local radio station.

The bustling atmosphere hid a grim reality: Philips, for three generations a showcase of European industrial excellence, was in crisis. Sales and profits were plummeting, its stock sagging on exchanges in Europe; Japanese competitors, with better management, lower costs, and strong government backing, were threatening to invade and conquer every major electronics market in Europe. As we wound our way around the work stations, Jan Linschoten, a Dutch engineer in his early thirties, said halfheartedly that the time required to produce a television set had been cut to less than four hours and would gradually be cut to just under two. "This is our first attempt to answer Japan, but we are not sure how—or even if—we will survive the next ten years," he said. "What we need desperately is clear—European leadership."[1]

I mention the visit, the first of many I was to make that year to European companies and political capitals on assignment for the *International Herald Tribune,* because Philips typified what was going wrong with the best and most technologically advanced of European industries. I was to return to Eindhoven, and to many other corporations on three continents, during the next decade to report on how they were responding to—and shaping—the new leadership Linschoten was seeking. The Philips visit demonstrated vividly—and early on—that the crisis went deeper and wider than any single European company or government realized, and that it would take more than management strategies to find a way out.

Reflecting Europe's general mood in 1981 were phrases of the 1970s still in fashion, such as "Eurosclerosis" and "Europessimism." Unlike the United States and Japan, most European countries had not even started to modernize their economies following the 1973 and 1979 oil-price shocks. Unemployment had reached record levels and was climbing. Double-digit inflation was widespread. Europe's heavily subsidized industries were faltering. American-inspired deregulation of Europe's hidebound industries, in particular airlines and telecommunications, was as yet unthinkable. European Community institutions, notably the Commission, its executive branch, were facing insolvency, caused by virtually uncontrolled subsidies for the Community's eleven million farmers, because of the Common Agricultural Policy, its controversial showcase program established in 1962 by Konrad Adenauer and Charles de Gaulle.

The consensus in Western capitals was that the Common Market, and other European institutions established in the postwar era, had failed to achieve prosperity and security through collective action—certainly of the federalist kind promulgated by Jean Monnet of France, widely considered to be Europe's "spiritual father," because of his role in establishing Europe's first federal organizations following World War II. Instead, national barriers and obstacles to the free flow of goods, services, and people were flourishing and growing. Many multinationals, including Philips, France's Thomson, West Germany's Siemens, Italy's Olivetti, and the European-based Americans, were already closing plants, and looking elsewhere to invest; Washington and much of America was gazing westward, to the Pacific. Young Europeans, particularly scientists and engineers, were migrating in ever-increasing numbers to the United States, while at home birthrates began to decline alarmingly, particularly in West Germany. In short, Western Europe appeared destined for permanent stagnation and decline.

Within a decade, the mood of Europe has been totally transformed, reflecting a fast-changing industrial, business, and banking landscape, an upheaval not seen since the early 1950s. A sense of excitement and revival is in the air, an upbeat, euphoric sense of confidence in the future that has penetrated virtually every corner of the twelve-nation Common Market with its 340 million inhabitants, and is spreading to far-flung corners of the globe. It has a name—1992. That date came to be known in much-publicized shorthand as the EC Commission plan to remove barriers to the free flow of goods, capital, services, and people by December 31, 1992. Most people called it the 1992 plan, or simply 1992. But it was but one blueprint for integration among many, trying to provide direction to Europe's quest for economic growth and power.

Starting in the late 1980s, new high-speed rail networks were also being built, or planned, crisscrossing in all directions. Airline deregulation was underway, spawning new regional airlines and somewhat cheaper fares. Banking was being thrown open to freer competition. Mergers, acquisitions, takeover battles were sweeping corporate Europe. Border controls and barriers to freer movement of goods, services, and people were disappearing. The Common Market, their member governments, in cooperation with corporations were launching multibillion-dollar civilian and military research-and-development projects. European symbols began sprouting everywhere: silver and gold ECU (for European Currency Unit) coins and ECU-denominated traveler's checks and postage stamps; identical maroon-colored EC passports for all Common Market citizens; blue twelve-star-studded flags fluttered at airports, hotels, camping sites, and homes. Flows of cross-border migrations, and a rush to learn additional European languages had begun; intra-European student exchange programs were flooded with applications.

Meantime, Europe's largest aerospace companies had made spectacular inroads in world markets against fierce American competition, while their engineers designed even more powerful planes and
spacecraft for the twenty-first century. And, equally important, economic recovery had begun, with higher growth rates than in the
United States, prompting many economists to predict that Europe
would become a locomotive for world economic expansion throughout the decade, rivaling both North America and Asia well into the
next century. Starting in mid-December 1990, negotiations had
begun for reinforcing the Community's political powers and developing a common approach to foreign and security policy, propelled by
Europe's humiliating failure to speak and act with a single voice
during the 1990–91 Gulf crisis. A draft treaty was expected to be
adopted by the EC heads of state and government in the medieval
town of Maastricht, Holland, during a crucial summit meeting in
December 1991, committing participants to political union with a
"federal character."

And, as if drawn by a gigantic magnet, more than a dozen countries were seeking closer ties with the European Community. Austria,
Sweden, Turkey, Malta, and Cyprus were actively seeking full membership; other neighbors—Norway, Finland, Iceland, and Switzerland—were negotiating closer trade, industrial, and regulatory ties
with the European Community. Hungary, Poland, Czechoslovakia
also were preparing for full membership, but in the late 1990s. And
the Soviet Union's and Yugoslavia's rebellious republics were seeking
ways of fitting into the magnet's economic field, raising the prospects
of a twenty-five-nation European Confederation, with a population
of well over 500 million people, the world's largest trade bloc. Investments were pouring into Europe from virtually every direction, particularly from the United States and Asia, with no letup in sight.
Europe, very simply, was in.

Why? What was the significance of this revival? Was Europe on the
threshold of a new era that would change the balance of global
power? How much of the European revival activity was economic and
industrial? How much was political, encompassing foreign policy,
military and security prerogatives? What if, as many observers predicted, Europe failed again? Who were the players in business, politics, and diplomacy? What about those who didn't fit in, or vociferously opposed what was happening? How do crime, drugs, and the
Italian Mafia relate to the opening of markets and elimination of

borders? Could the revival be stopped? Were there untold stories to tell? Finally, how will Europe look in the year 2000?

These were only the most immediate questions on my mind during the autumn of 1988 when I set out on what was to become a nearly continuous 123,000-kilometer working trip to more than thirty countries and dozens of cities, villages, and regions stretching eastward from California to Europe to Moscow, Singapore, and Tokyo. A year later, I began writing the first draft of this book, amid a predominating upbeat mood of "Europhoria"—the new buzzword implying Europe was on its way to becoming an economic superpower, with greatly enhanced political powers.

As I proceeded throughout 1990 and 1991, however, unpredictable cataclysmic events greatly jolted the schedule, and clouded earlier findings—the collapse of the Berlin Wall, the reunification of Germany, upheavals in the Soviet Union and Yugoslavia, the resurgence throughout Europe of nationalism, protectionism, organized crime, drug use, and racism, the impact of recession and worsening unemployment in the United States and Britain, and the Gulf War and its aftermath. Europe was now being buffeted and strained by external forces beyond its control. There were times when I seriously questioned whether this book would ever make any sense; I was constantly inserting, updating, trying to adjust to the dizzying, confusing pace of events. Had it not been for my publisher and editor, Michael Bessie, the book might have been postponed. It wasn't, because, I believe, we had correctly identified the sense of direction in Europe's contemporary history.

Where to begin? The choice of Brussels was prompted by Bessie, who, provokingly, early on told me he thought Belgium's largest and most international city could make a good book on its own. Not long thereafter, a friend suggested I talk to Ricardo Bofill, the Spanish architect, who had just returned to Paris, startled, from a personal briefing on Brussels given by Premier Wilfried Martens and Belgium's King Baudouin. Bofill told me that the plan for the development of Brussels was spectacular for size and scope, but that details of the plan, for mysterious and unexplained reasons, were being kept under wraps, as if it were a state secret. After many trips and talks with Brussels planners I began to understand why, and learned how the city was becoming the first modern "European" capital of its kind in the postwar era. The Washington, D.C., of Europe.

The main attractions of Brussels for me, described in Chapter 1, are not only the Community institutions headquartered there and its restaurants, art galleries, opera, and some sleaze, but its small army of lobbyists, consultants, association and company executives, lawyers, diplomats, journalists, artists, and urbanists. They now outnumber the Common Market's inner core of officials, with whom they interact through American-style lobbying.

The city's most prominent resident is the man who comes closest to being President of Europe—Jacques Delors, a self-made man, a Socialist, and a visionary, who since 1985 has served as president of the EC Commission. And because Delors is expected to continue playing an important role on the international scene after his second term expires at the end of 1992, I have devoted about half the first chapter to describing him. The combination of his ties to labor movements, his deep religious convictions, mellowed anti-Americanism, and driving ambition makes him one of the most intriguingly complex political leaders I have ever encountered.

Previous plans to unite Europe into a single power are worth recalling, for as historians have reminded us, although the word "Europe" first appeared in Greek mythology in the eighth century B.C., it only resurfaced in a political form during the eighth century A.D. with the dawning of the Carolingian era. Thus, as the eminent French scholar Jean-Baptiste Duroselle in his comprehensive history of Europe concluded, Charlemagne, the first king of Europe, is the "fascinating object lesson" for subsequent attempts to unify Europe. Duroselle's perception, which I share, partly explains why historical Chapter 2 begins with Charlemagne and a visit to his hometown of Aachen, or, as it is called in French, Aix-la-Chapelle.[2]

Distinguishing the contemporary movement from previous unification plans in the postwar era, such as the Marshall Plan, is that the leadership is being provided, not by Americans, but by Europeans themselves. It has taken the form of an unusual, loose, low-key alliance between business leaders, industrialists, and bankers, political leaders and statesmen, many of whom I interviewed, some of them, several times.

Among the prominent leaders interviewed for this book are: Henry Kissinger, Lord Carrington, Roy Jenkins, Valéry Giscard d'Estaing, Helmut Schmidt, Michel Rocard, Mario Soares, Simone Veil, Wilfried Martens, Gaston Thorn, Gianni De Michelis, Giovanni Agnelli, Carlo De Benedetti, Martin Sorrell, Robert Hormats, Felix

Rohatyn, Adam Michnik, Theo Sommer, Pierre Pflimlin, Wisse Dekker, Jean-Louis Beffa, Martin Bangemann, Edith Cresson, Vladimir Dloughy, Hisashi Owada, and Bernard Attali. In addition, four political heads of European states or governments provided a written answer to a single question: what is your vision of Europe in the year 2000—what will it be, and what will it not be? The leaders include Delors, Helmut Kohl, François Mitterrand, and Margaret Thatcher. Their written answers constitute most of the final chapter.

In some ways, Europe's revival most closely resembles what occurred in the United States in the late nineteenth and early twentieth centuries. Political leadership and ideas played key roles, of course, but much of the initial, driving force, the impulsion to build Europe's economic power base peacefully and democratically—like America's a century ago—has been generated by business leaders, individually and collectively. Why? Because the plan made both economic and political sense.

As I traveled and gathered or updated material and renewed contracts, I quickly realized nearly everyone had something to say on the subject, amid an explosion of articles, reports, pamphlets, conferences, seminars, film documentaries, special courses, and a dozen books assessing the new trends. Among them was a particularly negative, controversial, and best-selling book, written by a youthful, provocative Frenchman. He concluded that the 1992 plan was but an illusion, a myth that would have only one important consequence: domination by West Germany of a Europe stretching from the Atlantic to the Urals, which would ultimately lead to the "Finlandization" of all of Europe, because Europe lacked the will to unite politically.[3] The book, *La Grande Illusion,* by Alain Minc, contained elements of truth and errors of fact, and, although I disagreed with its conclusions, they deserve attention and testing.

Abroad, an ugly image of Europe spread rapidly. By early 1988, Tokyo, Washington, and other Western capitals began portraying the European Community as a fortified castle, its bridge drawn while nervous businessmen and political leaders were seen inside, peering out. Fortress Europe. That name summed up the widely cited image, which Europeans tried desperately to erase. Assertive or aggressive Europe might have been a more fitting description, because, despite more "pro-European" policies, the fact was that the Common Market remained the world's largest trading bloc, and a large export market for the United States. The Bush administration, divided on how to respond and under intense protectionist pressure from the U.S. Congress, threatened trade retaliation.

A crucial turning point—for the better—came during the July 1989 economic summit meeting of world leaders in Paris, where President George Bush took the lead in encouraging the EC Commission to immediately organize food aid and other forms of economic assistance to Poland and Hungary—on behalf of all the other industrialized nations of the world. The assignment was the first public recognition of the Common Market's growing influence in foreign affairs—even if to everyone's surprise it suddenly looked as if Bush were being more pro-European than Mrs. Thatcher.

The behind-the-scenes story of how President Bush overruled some of his advisers and shifted the administration's position came to light following interviews on both sides of the Atlantic, as did the story of how Bush adroitly snared Delors into coming to the White House for a memorable lunch several weeks before the summit meeting, recounted in Chapter 9.

But there was another deeper, more troubling reason for the Bush initiative, and later the restraint he showed in responding to Europe's painful, embarrassing disarray during the Gulf War. Partly, this stemmed from a trend dealt with in Chapter 6—the gradual erosion of American influence in Western Europe. Clearly, it seemed the United States was aggressively looking to the Pacific Basin and the Middle East, not Europe as in the past. The closing of the Atlantic Institute in Paris in 1988 was one example, among many, of the gradual erosion in transatlantic relations, coinciding with, and feeding into, a current of low-key anti-Americanism that had built up over the previous decade, and which became far more vocal and violent during the Gulf War. Not only was America no longer an idol and a model, particularly for European youth, but in some areas, such as television films, America had become a target for those determined to impose government-supported "European" cultural solutions.

Great frustration and jealousy over America's predominant political, diplomatic, and military leadership during the Gulf War only fueled the misgivings about American leadership, and forced the Europeans to argue for "European" diplomatic solutions in the Middle East, and a year later, in wartorn Yugoslavia.

While gathering material for this book, I was repeatedly struck by how determined and enthusiastic Europeans had become in asserting themselves against U.S. and Japanese competitors, even as they argued fervently against being called Fortress Europe. When asked to cite just one good example, I refer to Mitterrand and Felipe González, who in late 1988 jointly announced that $1 billion to modernize Spain's railroad system would be split between French and German companies as part of a "European solution," even though a Japanese company, Mitsubishi, asserted that its bid was 30 percent lower. This example, among others, appears in Chapter 4, which deals with Europe's global economic warfare being waged against the United States and Japan.

The first time I learned of the Tornado fighter-bomber project from German aerospace executives, I was genuinely surprised by two claims they made: First, that it was already Europe's largest joint industrial venture, grouping West Germany, Britain, and Italy, and which has been challenging America's latest fighter planes around the world. Second, that nearly 97 percent of its components were made in Europe. "There will never be a repeat of the F-16," I was told by a German official, referring to the highly successful and controversial sale of the U.S.-made plane to four NATO countries in the 1960s, widely known at the time as "the contract of the century."[4]

The development of the Tornado, whose British and Italian versions became famous during the Gulf War, is among several stories that warrant telling, because it illustrates how the Europeans are succeeding in areas previously dominated by the United States aerospace industry. The story of how Mrs. Thatcher helped sell the Tornado to Saudi Arabia, as part of a multibillion-dollar package deal, also appears in Chapter 4. Other examples demonstrate how in sector after sector—agriculture, telecommunications, transportation, high-definition television, banking, electronics, chemicals, automobiles—Europeans are battling to emerge as winners, despite extremely difficult odds and very heavy government and EC subsidization. In some cases, they run afoul of U.S. laws on defense procurement, antitrust and international trade regulations. Such clashes, where they have occurred, rather than triggering reform have greatly reinforced the determination by Europeans to capture markets and to reject American allegations of unfair play.

A related, reverse development, what I call the Great Leap Across the Atlantic, is the subject of Chapter 5. Here we encounter the rapidly growing wave of European acquisitions of companies, banks, and property in the United States and, to a lesser but surprising degree, in Latin America. The buying of U.S. firms and property has made Europe second only to Japan among direct foreign investors. This represents a total reversal of the trend made famous more than two decades ago in Jean-Jacques Servan-Schreiber's best-seller *The American Challenge,* in which U.S. multinationals were viewed as the dominating force in Western Europe, while European industry was portrayed as technologically dead, or going under, destined for extinction.[5] I particularly enjoyed discovering how a former East German company took over an American firm near New York City, the first venture of its kind in the United States.

But this book is not just about business and politics. By drawing on opinion surveys, writings by academics and colleagues, but above all through interviews and firsthand reporting, I have tried to show how the lives of average citizens are being affected, and why there is also hostility to European unity, fed by preoccupations with sovereignty, and by suspicion, fear, envy, disillusionment, skepticism, frustration, and resistance in every European country. This, hopefully, comes through with short interview-profiles with, for example, a poor French farmer, the mayor of a small village in Rhodes, an American educator, an Algerian unemployed worker, a Corsican businessman, a gypsy leader in Germany, a Spanish student, a Hitler-admiring bartender. They tell their versions of how the New Europe is affecting them, and what they are doing about it—if anything.

Four decades ago, Theodore White ended his memorable book on Europe, *Fire in the Ashes,* with a paragraph containing its title: "There is fire in the ashes of the Old Civilization. Americans can fan it to flame or smother it, but the flame cannot be fed from America. It must blaze from its own sources."[6] My conclusion is that, although Europe remains in the preliminary stages of attaining the status of the world's newest superpower, that status is slowly being attained, certainly in economic and trade terms. Politically, it may wind up taking an unusual form, probably a loose federation, more closely resembling multicultural Switzerland and Belgium than the United States. But it will occur, I believe, if for only one reason: the flame White described, despite opposition and deep national differences, is still blazing and shows no signs of going out. Let us head for Brussels on the first stop of this European journey to find out why.

Inside the
New Europe

Brussels:
The Washington, D.C.,
of Western Europe

I had no preference for such and such a place in Europe,
because what mattered was that the sole headquarters
for all the institutions to be created would be founded
on European territory, anticipating a federal district
of the future.

—JEAN MONNET
Mémoires

THE CITY AND ITS BOOM

Traveling on the Trans Europ Express to Brussels isn't what it used
to be. When I first began shuttling on the TEE between Paris and
Brussels in the early 1960s, hot breakfasts served with a smile still
startled some French travelers unaccustomed to such service. So did
the even more surprising discovery that for the first time in Europe
a new high-speed train was beating the plane, door to door. Once
aboard the sleek maroon-and-silvery cars, a sense of adventure and
excitement prevailed—until the French and Belgian frontier police
and customs officials strode down the aisles, vigorously inspecting
everything in sight.

Once in early 1982, a shapely, expensively dressed redhead was caught carrying a large sum of French francs in cash, clearly trying to circumvent strict exchange controls imposed, routinely, by the new Socialist government of President François Mitterrand. While being escorted to a guarded compartment for further questioning and searching, she furiously shouted in heavily accented English that her friends in high places back in Paris would hear about this.

Three decades later, the same crowded trains are still making the run from the Gare du Nord to the Brussels Gare du Midi, and hot breakfasts are still being served, but they are simply designated Eurocity trains, like nearly one hundred others crisscrossing the Continent. The floor carpeting has worn thin, the seat upholstery has faded, noise levels are higher, and the multilanguage recordings giving instructions sound scratched. But surprise: there are no more dreaded inspections of baggage and personal belongings, and frequently no passport checks either.

As we were speeding through scenic farmland and forests somewhere near the Belgian border, Jean-Jacques, a mustached French frontier policeman in civilian clothes, his automatic pistol holstered, began to explain. "This train, this entire Europe isn't what it used to be. Did you know that many border crossings between Belgium, France, Germany, and Holland aren't even manned anymore? That's because of the 1992 program. We, and particularly our colleagues in the customs service, are becoming federalized, just like our counterparts in the United States," he said. "Our future? Probably guarding entry points to the Common Market, which will be greatly reinforced as new, high-speed train networks spread all over Europe. It looks as if it will be more or less one, internal, frontierless zone—as I say, like America."

Slipping into Brussels's Gare du Midi 2½ hours later—after a trip evoking memories of a very similar run on the New York–Washington Metroliner train—I am struck by the rundown area around the station. It is a noisy, dreary place, impregnated by the odors of *frites*, or French-fried potatoes, and the sounds of pinball machines. The surrounding neighborhoods are a chaotic mixture of new office buildings, shabby hotels, bus depots, dimly lit movie houses, and sleazy bars. Is this the capital of the New Europe?

As our taxi swings onto the wide, tree-lined Avenue des Arts, one of the highways circling the city, another sight gradually appears: modern, well-designed glass-steel office buildings, luxurious high-rise hotels and apartment buildings, crisscrossed by a network of trolley and subway lines; nearby tidy parks and well-kept late-nineteenth-century town houses. The houses, many recently restored, radiate a decidedly upscale image and flavor, recalling the Georgetown district of Washington, D.C., and, farther north, suburban Maryland.

Listen to a resident American diplomat who knows both Brussels and Washington: "We love it here . . . this could be Montgomery County in Maryland," said Michael Ely, the seasoned professional minister-counselor in the American mission to the EC, whose sprawling four-bedroom house with swimming pool was less than a quarter-hour drive from downtown Brussels. "I know a lot of people complain, and true, this isn't Paris, but we do have good provincial opera, all the first-run English-language films, good food, safe, pleasant countryside, and, another thing, Brussels isn't all that socially competitive," Ely said. He and his wife were among some ten thousand well-paid foreigners who had been assigned to Brussels, and had happily plunged into the city's cultural life, including opera, its modern, well-stocked museums, antique shops, art galleries, restaurants, its somewhat provincial but comfortable suburban lifestyle, including international schools, clubs, and golf courses, with easy access to the surrounding countryside of Belgium, Holland, and West Germany.

A MELTING POT, BUT DULL

Brussels, with just over one million inhabitants, is a melting pot—again like Washington, D.C., with its population of just over 600,000. And of course foreigners such as the Elys come from somewhere else. But a large portion of each inner city's daily life is generally avoided by resident diplomats, businessmen, and other well-off foreigners. They rarely if ever venture into the city's black or immigrant ghettos and do not mingle with the "other" newcomers—lower-middle-class or poor immigrants, who in Brussels alone account for more than 27 percent of the population. Mainly, they are Turks, Algerians, and Moroccans. "Like blacks in Washington, a far greater proportion of the population, there is much of Brussels many foreign diplomats and residents never see, or want to," said Aislinn Dulanty, editor of *The Bulletin,* a popular English-language newsweekly that closely resembles Washington magazines catering mainly to the foreign diplomatic and business community.

The Brussels Dulanty refers to isn't pretty. Strolling from the well-appointed Amigo Hotel across The Grand' Place, surrounded by its elegant Flemish Renaissance buildings, crowded with tourists, to the wide Boulevard Adolphe Max beyond the Sheraton Hotel, we gradually come upon sex shops, nightclubs, smiling, buxom prostitutes seated behind windows of stores long deserted. Nearby, on corners of the seedy, rundown streets near the Gare du Nord, drug dealers work the neighborhood. But the visitor has to look for this side of the city to find it, and it has been shrinking in the path of bulldozers, making way for modern, respectable buildings.

Indeed, most of Brussels, an estimated 90 percent of the city, is calm, clean, residential, dull, and bourgeois, reflecting the city's Flemish spirit, its deep involvement in trade and commerce, dating back to the early Middle Ages. Its restaurants are first class, many on a par with the best in Paris and London. There is, as Ely noted, a good selection of theater and opera. Brussels, according to its fans, is a pleasant city in which to live, even though much of its charm has been badly mauled by the new modern nondescript office buildings that have sprouted everywhere and are crowding out much that is Old World in a city that built its first, fortified walls in the thirteenth century.

Starting in early 1988, everything, it seemed, was stirring, jolted every day by the bulldozers and work crews preparing the vacant lots for even more new buildings. Around the Gare du Nord, *les belles de nuit* have been eased away by the police to other neighborhoods to pave the way for what city planners describe as "a cleaner, business-like European role." "We are the emerging capital of Europe," boasted a city official. Other officials laugh when asked whether they could imagine their mayor in the same predicament as Washington's Mayor Marion S. Barry, Jr., who in late October 1990 was sentenced to six months in prison and fined $5,000 for his conviction on a misdemeanor cocaine-possession charge. "It just would never happen here," a French-speaking cab driver told me, shortly after Barry's sentencing. "We are very northern European, with our own troubles, such as corruption, but our officials would be afraid of drugs, because citizens here go along with authority, order, whereas Washington seems so uncontrolled and violent—*voilà la différence,*" he said.

That tidy image was shattered violently in mid-May 1991 during several nights of clashes between Brussels police and young North African immigrants, triggered by constant police checks of residents in the city's poor neighborhoods. The riots, which began near the

Gare du Midi, resulted in several hundred arrests and several injuries, as government officials tightened security in nearby neighborhoods. "This is still not Washington, because these riots were mainly directed against the police," commented Jonathan Kapstein, the longtime *Business Week* correspondent in Brussels, who in the summer of 1991 joined Carré Orban & Paul Ray, a large, American executive recruiting firm, which was expanding its activities as international business grew in Brussels. "Despite the riots, Brussels is a relatively quiet place, the traffic still flows . . . our major complaint—double and triple parking, which has reached epidemic proportions."

A NEW GOVERNMENTAL HEADQUARTERS

Nowhere has the change been more striking than downtown, on a four-hectare site near the elegant but rundown Gare de Luxembourg. Adjacent to it, one of Europe's largest development projects is taking shape. When completed in late 1992, it will include a complex of skyscraper hotels, luxury apartments, an underground shopping mall, restaurants, with connections to the city's subway system and to the new trans-European high-speed rail network linking Brussels to the Paris-Amsterdam line. Similar construction was underway at other sites throughout the Brussels area, as a flood of service and high-tech industries moved in, resembling the business expansion boom that hit northeast Virginia and Maryland in the 1970s.

In the midst of the new complex is a controversial building project, misleadingly named the International Congress Center. Belgian officials did not openly proclaim its real purpose as a home for the European Parliament for fear of arousing the jealousies of other major European cities, notably Strasbourg, which was fighting to keep the parliament there. Yet everyone in Brussels knew that this was no business center but is destined to become the site of Western Europe's largest, most modern European governmental headquarters complex. When completed, it will be available to accommodate the European Parliament, with seating for 720 deputies, far in excess of current needs, in anticipation of new EC members. Nearby, a new headquarters will be built for the European Commission, the Community's executive branch, and a new, modern home for the Council of Ministers, the EC's highest policy-making body, representing member governments.

Meantime, real-estate investors and developers from throughout Europe, Japan, and the United States have flocked into Brussels, investing heavily in a fast-expanding array of still more hotels and office buildings throughout the city and surrounding areas. This influx touched off the city's biggest speculative boom in nearly three decades. Property prices in traditionally low-cost Brussels surged, doubling in some cases, as city planners struggled to keep up with what one harried official described as "an absolute explosion of new interest, which could overwhelm us and ruin what charm is left in the city." Even Brussels' Zaventem Airport, strained for capacity and rundown since first it was opened for the 1958 World's Fair, is targeted for a major overhaul in order to bring it up to the level of other medium-sized European airports.

"What we are building here is something new that would surprise some of the founding fathers of the Common Market, because this is no purely governmental European district, nor some kind of European Vatican," commented the man who started the city renovation: Jean-Louis Thys, the jovial, stocky, bearded secretary of state in the Belgian government responsible for what he describes as "another, perhaps the greatest, modern European metropolis." Financed largely by private capital, led by the powerful Société Générale de Belgique, the country's largest banking group, the renewal project, including the International Congress Center, when completed will seek to rival similar sites in London, Paris, and a revitalized Berlin. Later in the 1990s, the expansion of the European Council, the Parliament, the Commission and new institutions alone will have brought the number of officials working for them in Brussels from about 13,000 to well over 25,000, Thys said. "Not counting all the others."[1]

LOBBYING EUROPEAN-STYLE

The "others" are the small army of lobbyists, consultants, lawyers, diplomats, journalists, business executives, and bankers, along with representatives from virtually every country in the world, who comprise the players in what has been called "the EC access game."

Consider the following:

■ Brussels is the headquarters for approximately twelve hundred professional associations. They range from the Union of Industrial and Employers' Federations in Europe (UNICE), representing just over thirty employers' and industrialists' associations throughout Western Europe, to the far smaller European Bureau of Consumers Associations, representing consumer-protection groups in virtually every EC member country, and the American Chamber of Commerce, representing several hundred U.S. companies and banks.

■ About 850 multinational companies have established their European headquarters or subsidiaries in Brussels, according to Belgian ministry estimates. Of these, 671 are American, followed by British (174), French (170), West German (162), Scandinavian, (93), and Japanese (84). That total is roughly double the number of foreign companies with comparable operations in the Washington, D.C. area.

■ Some 120 governments have permanent diplomatic delegations based in Brussels, accredited to the European Community organizations. They number about 4,000 men and women, and do not take account of some 1,300 officials assigned to the permanent staff of the North Atlantic Treaty Organization, which is headquartered in the city's outskirts. This compares to a larger contingent of 173 diplomatic missions in Washington, staffed by more than 2,000 professional diplomats, in addition to several thousand staff and secretarial employees assigned to the embassies.

■ A total of 555 journalists are accredited to the European Community, of whom 330 are from member countries; there are 30 accredited reporters covering for U.S. media. This compares to 4,700 reporters covering Washington, of whom 600 are foreigners from 75 countries, according to the U.S. Information Agency's Foreign Press Center; of that number, some 200 are covering for media based in one or several EC member countries. For newsmen stationed in Brussels and those shuttling from Paris and London, the EC is now rated as one of the most sought-after news assignments in Western industrialized countries.

Most of the business groups and diplomatic missions operate from within a radius of several kilometers of the EC Commission headquarters building on the Place Schuman—known as the Berlaymont Building.

A Brussels landmark for more than twenty years, housing some

3,000 Commission employees, the "Berlymonster" as it has become known, was scheduled to be torn down in late 1991 or early 1992, because of its rundown state and, particularly, carcinogenic asbestos insulation that permeates the corridors. As a result, employees will be temporarily housed in nearby buildings until the new skyscraper headquarters building is ready around 1996 while continuing their primary mission: to report on, assess, and, more important, influence decision making of European institutions.

With the acceleration of plans for developing the Community's internal market in time for its deadline of December 31, 1992, as well as plans for monetary and political union, the number of lobbyists, consultants, diplomats, business representatives, and others has swelled to an estimated 4,000 men and women. This is roughly equal to the influential hardcore group of civil servants and officials working for EC institutions in the city. And their numbers continue to grow, even though they have remained few compared to Washington: nearly 7,000 registered lobbyists and 500 political consultants now operate in the U.S. capital, according to *Newsweek* magazine.

Meet Steven Worth, contemporary American lobbyist. When I first interviewed Worth in his spacious office on the fashionable Avenue Louise in December 1989, he could barely contain his excitement. "It is happening, the momentum is really there . . . they are moving," he declared, as EC leaders at their summit meeting in Strasbourg were putting finishing touches on a sweeping agreement that would lead to establishment of monetary unity within the Community, including a central banking system. "It is only a step from monetary to political power . . . that's what it's all about, and what interests many of our clients," he said, noting that the list included forty blue-chip multinationals, such as American Airlines, IBM, Digital, Pepsi and Japan's Mazda, Hitachi, and Sumitomo.

From 1986 to 1990, Worth headed the Brussels office of Hill and Knowlton, the large New York-based public relations firm, which offers a wide range of services that range from complete monitoring services to arranging contacts with EC policymakers. "When we started out," Worth recalled, "we were five people . . . today we are twenty . . . hardly anyone knew what the Single Act (amendments to the Rome Treaty) was or meant; Americans were leaving Brussels as multinational companies turned their interests elsewhere." The most difficult obstacle in those days was the resistance of some EC officials to even meet with representatives of private companies, including Americans, he recalled.

NOT QUITE WASHINGTONIAN

Lobbying in those early days was not recognized. Even today registration is a far cry from Washington's strict methods, particularly as they apply to accreditation of non-U.S. citizens. In the United States, representatives of non-U.S. banks, businesses, governmental agencies and organizations are not only required to register with the Justice Department, but officials contacted should, for example, report telephone conversations with foreign lobbyists. Lobbyists of any nationality, including Americans, must register with the U.S. Congress. No such procedures exist in Brussels.

Yet some Brussels insiders, faced with an increasing number of arrivals, particularly of amateurs, neophytes, and even some disreputable operators, wish that the city were more like Washington. "In the good old days, back in the late 1960s, when we first moved into the Berlaymont headquarters building, we had an official directory like Washington, but gradually, no one knows why, it disappeared," said Claus-Dieter Ehlermann, the German director general of the Commission's powerful antitrust agency and formerly the Commission's chief spokesman. He added that with the mushrooming of numbers of consultants, lawyers, embassies, and representational offices of every kind, some form of registration procedure, with strict, U.S.-style rules of conduct, should be established. "It's true, control might help . . . talent is hard to find and there are now a lot of people running around in this business, including a fair share of charlatans," said Worth.

Nevertheless, Brussels's European-style lobbying is flourishing—loosely, and, in many cases, amateurishly, but flourishing. The main reason for the growth is that a rapidly increasing number of companies, businesses, trade associations, as well as state and regional officials from virtually every country in the world have been forced to concentrate—and to spend money—on finding out what the 1992 program and accelerating European integration mean to them. There now is a wide choice of consulting firms and lawyers available: McKinsey, Belmont, KPMG, Bernard Krief, Skadden Arps, Jones, Day, Cleary Gottlieb, Coudert Frères; these are only a few of the names on the roster. Fees for their services average around $250 per hour. That is still below the top rate in Washington—$400 per hour—but Brussels and U.S.-based consultants agree that the gap has been closing. Annual retainers now range as high as $400,000 for prestigious U.S. or British consulting firms operating in Brussels, and these annual rates also have been escalating.

The most recent arrivals are executive recruitment firms, known as headhunters. As the European Commission and multinationals based in Brussels have expanded and been faced with a shortage of qualified executives, they have turned to these firms that specialize in finding the right man or woman for the "Europeanized" jobs. "When we first started here in 1979, our assignments were mainly for Belgian blue-chip companies, but now with six full-time professionals, we are, for example, helping the Commission recruit officials to work in Eastern Europe," said Philippe De Backer, an American-trained partner of Carré Orban & Paul Ray, one of several large headhunting firms operating in Brussels. "We've also done a lot for the Commission on the banking side," De Backer said, adding that they helped recruit senior executives for the European Bank for Reconstruction and Development, the EBRD, which began operations in London early in 1991, and to which we shall return.

Hardly a day goes by without a foreign delegation coming to Brussels, seeking information, trying to make a deal, or attempting to change some provision in the vast, complex array of directives and regulations being prepared by the Commission, or being amended by the European Parliament, or being approved by the Council of Ministers.

Often the first stop for visiting foreigners is the home-government delegation. The U.S. delegation to the Community is one of the largest, and since 1989 its growing staff of about thirty-five men and women has been headed by career ambassador Thomas M. T. Niles, a low-key youthful diplomat, who previously served as the American envoy to Canada, and in the autumn of 1991 was appointed Assistant Secretary of State for European and Canadian Affairs in Washington. More than twenty-five U.S. states, cities, and ports maintain permanent offices in Brussels or in other European cities, mainly Frankfurt and London, helping their small and medium-sized homegrown businesses and banks find outlets for their goods, services, and investments, and, above all, establishing contacts within the European Community decision-making system. West German *Länder*, equivalents of U.S. states, maintain permanent offices in Brussels, as does Japan, through more than thirty diplomats and trade officials—all tracking the vast array of data and decisions being ground out by the EC machinery and trying to shape it.

Most of the lobbying is aimed at EC Commission officials. They are nonelected civil servants, who openly, actively seek advice and input from outside groups and business interests. In the U.S. capital, much of the lobbying is directed at Congress, whose members are, by contrast, elected. In Brussels, lobbying occurs very officially, and in an organized manner. A vast array of consultative lobbying committees, grouping management, industry, governmental, and labor groups, meet regularly with senior Commission officials to help shape EC legislation. Lobbying in Brussels and at the European Parliament is closely coordinated with similar efforts that are conducted in parallel in national capitals.

In growing numbers in Brussels, newcomers, particularly American and Japanese businessmen, have discovered that they require inside, specialized counseling. Worth recalls how shortly after he arrived, a U.S. multinational company was hopeful that EC standards then being established would be compatible with those of its products. The problem was that the top EC Commission official responsible refused to grant the company's chief executive an appointment. "The company turned to us, because they were getting nowhere; the EC official said they would deal only with European companies, even though we argued this multinational was deeply involved in Europe," Worth said. After many weeks of "harassing in a friendly way," the EC official's resistance broke down, and finally an appointment was arranged. "Not only did the standards issue become resolved in our client's favor, but he now deals with the officials involved directly," Worth added. "We have come a long way."

Typically, and like many of his colleagues and competitors, Worth brought a blended American-European background to the job: an attractive, French wife, a respectable knowledge of Europe's culture and languages; long experience in business and political lobbying, including a stint as press spokesman in the U.S. Senate, and critically important, he had acquired intimate knowledge of the inner workings of U.S. and European political institutions. "American methods, if applied correctly, with a feel for European sensitivities, can work here," Worth said over lunch at one of Brussels's posh downtown restaurants on the elegant Sablon Square, jammed with senior EC officials, diplomats, journalists, and lobbyists talking over the morning's events.

THE OTHER EUROPEAN CAPITALS

Not everything of importance in the European politicking game occurs in Brussels. Because the Commission and the European Council are still a long way from becoming a full-fledged European government, and because many major policy decisions are still made in national capitals, government officials and lobbyists regularly shuttle between their home bases and Brussels, Strasbourg, and Luxembourg. "The big difference with Washington is that the EC doesn't have a full-fledged political system, meaning a government, hence no political Washington-style lobbying—yet," said Richard McKean, a Geneva-based American consultant, who advises multinational companies on their EC strategies. "But what was a small trickle has now started to resemble what we saw happen inside the Beltway in Washington in the 1960s and 1970s. In its slow, very Continental way, lobbying has come of age in the European Community."[2]

Many Europeans agree with their American colleagues. "We must be operating virtually everywhere in Europe to influence Brussels, which means London, Paris, Madrid," said Patrice Alain-Dupré, who heads a Paris-based consulting-lobbying firm, with offices established throughout Europe and in the United States.[3] And following a narrow vote in the Bundestag on June 20, 1991, to relocate the German capital (338 to 320), the latest addition to the roster is the once imperial city of Bismarck, Hitler, and East German Communism—Berlin. Within less than a decade, the German government, its parliament, chancellor, president, and bureaucrats will move eastward to cosmopolitan Berlin from the small university town of Bonn, which has served as the country's "provisional" capital since the end of World War II. This does not mean that Berlin will necessarily regain its prewar European preeminence, although it is trying. "Being inside the New Europe means being in a lot of places at once, because of the decentralized nature of the system, and the fact that we still do not have a single European governmental system is undeniable," added Alain-Dupré. "But I agree we are slowly moving in that direction."

The controversy over how much national power in EC capitals has been shifted to Brussels—and we shall return to this issue in Chapter 8—is assessed forcefully by Peter Sutherland, Ireland's affable, pugnacious, pro-European former attorney general, who served as Delors's commissioner for competition policy from 1985 to 1989, and has wanted to return to Brussels ever since. "Our powers may not yet be comparable to Washington's," he told me during an interview in the autumn of 1989, as he was preparing to become chairman of one of Ireland's largest banking groups. "But keep in mind one simple concept—the basis of Brussels's power is the absolute, fundamental supremacy of EC law over national law in many key areas, such as competition, mergers and acquisitions, and the like." The EC law, he explained, meaning the Rome Treaty, which founded the European Community and the Single Act, which in 1986 amended the treaty, "is the equivalent of your American Constitution," he said. "And this is why what people call Brussels power is, in fact, real."

"MUSICAL CHAIRS" BECOMES FASHIONABLE

Even the very Washingtonian tradition of "musical chairs" has caught on in Brussels. That is the U.S. practice whereby senior officials of cabinet rank, upon leaving the government, routinely join private companies, banks, consulting or law firms—and, in the process, often double or triple their salaries. In Brussels this can be surprisingly expensive, considering that members of the EC Commission are among the highest-paid officials in Western Europe. Its president's base salary is higher than that of the president of the United States, totaling about $210,000. He and each of the sixteen other commissioners, who earn somewhat less, are also provided a chauffeur-driven car, plus an allowance, ranging from about $15,000 for the president to $7,000 for other commissioners, plus other perks, such as an exemption from paying Belgian income taxes.

The president of the United States earns an annual salary of $200,000, plus a taxable $50,000 for expenses and a nontaxable sum, not to exceed $100,000 for travel and an additional $20,000 for official entertainment. The vice president's annual base salary is $160,000, plus $10,000 for expenses. Cabinet members' annual salaries are $138,900. In other words, America's chief executive earns less, in terms of base salary, than the head of the EC Commission, but his greater allowances reflect a far more elaborate, demanding, and glamorous social life at the White House. The president of the EC Commission has traditionally lived in a rented apartment or house in Brussels, and some, like Delors, who works late regularly, shun many official dinners on the city's diplomatic circuit.

Until Delors's arrival in Brussels, EC commissioners were not exactly hot items on the executive job market. But this has changed. Lord Cockfield, a former British secretary of state, who was the author of Delors's 1992 plan for the single market and commissioner for the internal market, was one of the first to go. He was snapped up by KPMG, one of the Community's largest accounting-consulting firms, shortly after being removed from his job by Mrs. Thatcher for having "gone native," in the words of London diplomats, meaning Cockfield had lost his sense of national British priorities. Another former commissioner, Britain's Stanley Clinton Davis, who was in charge of transport and environmental and nuclear safety, joined Hill and Knowlton. So also did Alfred Kingon, the short, wiry, fast-talking former White House staff member under President Ronald Reagan, who served as U.S. representative to the EC until mid-1989. His opposite number in Washington, the lanky, effervescent Sir Roy Denman, retired to Brussels, joining a law firm as consultant, as did Kingon's predecessor once removed, George Vest, a former career U.S. ambassador. Sony, the giant Japanese consumer electronics company, hired the EC Commission's former director for telecommunications, a Dutchman, for its EC liaison work.

PICKING THE SITE

Historians comparing the origins of Brussels and Washington as sites, recall that Washington and the District of Columbia were not exactly on the top of the list of early American leaders seeking to establish their first capital. Indeed, it was only in 1790, after President George Washington signed the bill establishing the district on a marshy, no-man's land on the banks of the Potomac River, that competing sites were eliminated—Philadelphia and Wright's Ferry, both in Pennsylvania; New York City; and Baltimore. Each city had lobbied hard to be chosen, but the site that was to become Washington appealed strongly to the new president and, as many historians have noted, this was his choice, made in the face of intense competition, and support for other sites by other founding fathers of the young republic.

A similar predicament faced Jean Monnet in the early 1950s. In his memoirs, the legendary French leader, widely acknowledged as the dominant architect of postwar European unity, describes how the founders of the Common Market settled on their first capital. It was

July 1952. Recalling the American experience 162 years earlier, six European governments had been unable to agree on where to locate the headquarters of the European Coal and Steel Community, which, through subsequent reorganizations and mergers, evolved into what is now known as the European Community.

Monnet recalls how at 3 A.M. during the negotiations, French delegates, backed by the Italians, had argued for Strasbourg, the scenic Alsatian city near the German border. Belgium pushed for Liège, the industrial capital of the French-speaking part of the country. The Dutch government pressed for its capital, The Hague. Also considered were Brussels, Chantilly, near Paris, and Saarbrücken in West Germany. Monnet, however, had "no preference" for any of these sites, arguing that what mattered, above all, was that "all the institutions to be created should be founded on European territory, anticipating a federal district of the future."[4]

Thus, when one of the frustrated, tired delegates casually mentioned the group might consider Luxembourg, everyone jumped at the suggestion, which Monnet immediately supported. Within a year, Monnet was settled into the presidency of the European Coal and Steel Community, a post he occupied until 1954, in offices overlooking the capital city of Luxembourg.

Within a decade, two other European capitals had also emerged—all three with "provisional" status to avoid favoring one city over another: Strasbourg was designated as the site of the European Parliament and Brussels as headquarters for the Commission and the Council of Ministers. Even though Luxembourg also later became the site of the European Court of Justice and Strasbourg continued to host plenary sessions of the Parliament, Brussels acquired increasing powers and was designated as headquarters by other European agencies, organizations, trade associations, and lobbying groups. The Belgian capital also has become the permanent headquarters for the Parliament's influential committee meetings amid intense pressure from many legislators to move out of Strasbourg once and for all.

In many ways, but on a smaller scale, Brussels is comparable in its position to contemporary Washington in relation to New York City, Boston, Chicago, and Los Angeles. For Brussels also has plenty of competition. Berlin is feverishly rebuilding, following German unification in 1990, determined to regain its prewar status as a major cultural and political center. London, Frankfurt and Paris remain the Community's main hubs for banking and finance. Paris is headquarters for the European Space Agency and in a nearby city for Ariane-space, the European satellite launching organization. France's south-ern city of Toulouse is headquarters for the Airbus consortium, while Luxembourg has been carving out a role as a new European televi-sion and film center. Munich has become a booming high-tech city and headquarters for several of Europe's largest military aerospace projects. None of these developments would have upset Monnet, who died March 16, 1979, at the age of ninety.

"We were looking at a very federalized arrangement emerging, designed to balance everyone's interests, and this would have pleased him," recalled one of his closest advisers, François Fontaine, who edited his memoirs. Monnet, according to Fontaine, also would have felt perfectly at ease with the man who has come closest among his contemporaries to being the "president of Europe" in Brussels. The white-haired, soft-spoken Fontaine told me in his Paris office, where he works to keep the Monnet legacy alive, that "this man also works on Europe twenty-four hours a day, and Monnet, who faced a hostile de Gaulle, would have understood his struggles perfectly." The man called "le Président" by almost everyone in Brussels is another Frenchman—Jacques Delors.

THE ENIGMATIC MR. EUROPE

Not long after moving into his spacious office on the thirteenth floor of the Berlaymont, the apex of the Commission's power structure, Delors displayed one of his characteristically glum moods. He quipped that he had no power, not even a say, in choosing his fellow commissioners and that to make them work as a team he would be forced to pamper them like a nurse, or a psychiatrist. "I am Freud," he told French newsmen. Pascal Lamy, his tough-sounding, deep-voiced chief of staff, who followed Delors from Paris and is at his side frequently, said two years later that they had gradually discovered that running the Commission was totally unlike running the French fi-nance ministry. "This is not a government. It's a collegiate system, based on consensus . . . running it more closely resembles managing a corporation," said Lamy.

Within five years of assuming the job of Commission president, Delors was being described as the "Czar of Brussels," "Monsieur Europe," "Jacques the Ambitious," and the "President of Europe." Did these capsule descriptions fit?

Even his critics would readily concede that, between 1985 and 1991, Delors had almost single-handedly reactivated—and personified—a stronger, more united European Community and, more broadly, Europe itself. According to dozens of conversations with his friends and critics, this was his largest, most significant achievement. More specifically, he had engineered substantial reductions in the Community's chronic budget deficit by controlling the rapid growth in farm spending; he had helped double the amount of EC financial aid to developing regions of Europe; and by skillful lobbying and winning the confidence of the European business community, he contributed heavily to touching off a multibillion-dollar wave of private investment within the Community.[5]

On the diplomatic front, despite initial skepticism, he won respect and enthusiastic support for his efforts from the United States and the Soviet Union, while edging the EC Commission into areas previously off limits—environmental protection, transportation, science and technology, monetary union, new, tougher banking and merger controls, employer-worker relations, security and foreign policy. A major breakthrough came in July 1989 when the Commission was given a mandate from the world's seven leading industrialized nations to coordinate massive aid programs in response to the sudden, spectacular dizzying upheavals that were sweeping Eastern Europe.

Although Delors would never have succeeded without the active support of Chancellor Kohl, President Mitterrand, and, unknown to most Americans, of President George Bush, he was widely regarded throughout the world as "Mr. Europe."

Few European leaders are as difficult to describe succinctly as Delors. I realized in my travels outside France that his image was far weaker than at home, where he has studiously cultivated a path for an eventual return to national political power. Many Germans, particularly those in their early twenties, told me time and time again that they regarded him as technocratic, socialist and, above all, French. Many Italians, outside of the business and political elite, said they honestly had great difficulty citing his accomplishments. By contrast, Norwegians, particularly average workers and university graduates, repeatedly expressed enthusiastic admiration for Delors. Average Americans and Japanese I have approached on my travels usually appear genuinely startled, quickly conceding they have no idea who he is or what he does in Brussels. Some very senior diplomats in Washington and Tokyo consider him anti-American and anti-Japanese.

How do you describe Delors's personality? Pessimistic. Restless. Workaholic. Aggressive. Modest. Volatile. Proud. Supersensitive. Difficult. Tortured. Tireless. Temperamental. Obstinate. Conscientious. Honest. Tense. Rude. Impatient. Zealous. Domineering. Presumptuous. Pushy. Irritable. Regal. Theatrical. Deeply religious. These are some of the adjectives I have heard used to describe him. Many of those who have worked closely with him, including President Mitterrand, point to his Roman Catholicism as the key to understanding the complex nature of his personality. Others cite the mixture of his religious faith and commitment to trade unionism. I have always been struck by how he deliberately separates his inner, private feelings from what he says in public or even to visitors. But let us start at the beginning.

MAKING OF A PRESIDENT

Jacques Lucien Delors was born on July 20, 1925, in a tough, run-down, lower-class neighborhood of Paris, the only son of a minor bank employee at the Bank of France. Delors has always created the impression of someone struggling—for education, advancement, perfection, social justice in a modernized European society. He is marked by uncommon zeal and vision, stemming in large measure from his religion. "My parents encouraged me to go to mass Sundays . . . had I not wanted to, no one would have forced me. I went because I believed in God. Going to church has never been a struggle for me," he told Gabriel Milesi, a French journalist, who wrote the only biography of Delors.[6] Whether in Brussels or on the road, and however grueling the pace, he attends mass whenever possible. "You must understand one thing about him—he is a very devout Catholic," a mutual friend told me, "and this attribute, which annoys others, like Mitterrand, contributes to the aloof, suffering, somewhat mystical air about him."

For Delors, the last lap of the long, occasionally painful trek to the thirteenth floor of the Berlaymont began on a balmy June day in 1984 during a particularly tense summit meeting of EC leaders in Fontainebleau, south of Paris. Highly controversial, important issues were on the agenda, such as Britain's campaign to reduce its payments to the EC budget and the pending membership bids of Spain and Portugal. The succession issue also faced the EC leaders, because

Gaston Thorn, of Luxembourg, was ending his four-year term as Commission president and by tradition and consensus of the other governments would not be reappointed.

Yet, when the German delegates began circulating the name of their candidate, newsmen expressed total surprise. Kurt Biedenkopff? No one, with the exception of Bonn insiders, had ever heard of him. Apparently Chancellor Helmut Kohl was considering his old lawyer friend Biedenkopff, who had recently been replaced as the Christian Democratic party opposition leader in North Rhine–Westphalia and needed a job. We quickly learned this was but a trial balloon floated by Kohl, which was quickly punctured by other governments. And that was the last we heard of Biedenkopff at the summit, a reminder of how difficult it has been for Bonn, with a few notable exceptions, to find skilled, charismatic leaders willing to accept top jobs in Brussels.

Meantime, Kohl and Mitterrand began turning their thoughts to Delors, the one person they would both support for the top job in Brussels. He also had caught the admiring attention of Mrs. Thatcher—primarily for his rigorous, serious, middle-of-the-road approach to restoring France's economic dynamism while serving as finance minister. But Delors's thoughts were rooted in France, and he was still hopeful that Mitterrand would ask him to serve as the new prime minister in what was to be Delors's second crack at France's highest political post after the presidency. For the second time in just over a year, he was to be bitterly disappointed.

ALMOST PRIME MINISTER—TWICE

The first blow had come Tuesday, March 22, 1983. Two other candidates were also in the running, waiting to be called into the spacious, ornately appointed presidential office, overlooking the gardens of the Élysée Palace, Laurent Fabius and Pierre Bérégovoy, both Socialist ministers. Mitterrand first offered the post to Delors, who was to commit a fatal blunder, which he later said he regretted. Delors told Mitterrand, replying to the offer, that he would need control of the French Treasury in order to implement his policies, notably in the monetary field, a department that traditionally came under the control of the finance ministry.

Delors's mistake was asking Mitterrand for something he should have known would be rejected. There are several versions of what Mitterrand actually said to his then-fifty-nine-year-old finance minister, whom he had always regarded with a mixture of affection, admiration, and suspicion. The reply came within a matter of a second or two. Mitterrand, according to several versions, told Delors that he was asking for too much; Delors himself later said the French leader, whose face immediately glazed over, was offended by Delors's request for control of the Treasury, and that he was surprised by Mitterrand's reaction.[7] The incident revealed the deep contradictions within Delors's personality—his profound, perhaps blinding, ambition to lead France someday and his sincere, justifiable conviction that he needed control over monetary policy.

Within a year, Mitterrand was again about to name a new prime minister, and again, with Delors under consideration for the post, the final choice was someone else—in this case Laurent Fabius, one of Mitterrand's favorite young politicians, and one of those under consideration a year earlier. Yet, two days prior to the announcement, Delors was still vaguely hopeful of being named prime minister, or possibly foreign minister. His next job, however, was being decided in secret negotiations among the leaders of Germany, France, and Britain, who had agreed that, since there probably would be no room for him in the new Fabius government, his talents should be used for major tasks looming in Brussels. One of Delors's strongest backers was Kohl, who over the years had developed a warm, intimate relationship with the temperamental French finance minister, who spoke no German and only halting English. The announcement that Delors would be the next president of the European Commission in Brussels was made on the morning of July 18, 1984.

A "GOLDEN EXILE" BEGINS

Delors was not overjoyed. Commenting in one of his famous dejected moods, he told friends later that he considered the assignment a "golden exile," a bittersweet reaction to a strong hint from Mitterrand that Brussels, after all, wasn't far from Paris, and that Delors might be called back to Paris—someday. "Jacques has always considered his destiny to be in Paris, whereas Mitterrand had decided his destiny was in Brussels—and so the French president's will prevailed," recalled a friend of Delors, adding quickly, "None of us at the time realized Jacques was even thinking, or cared, about leading Europe."

Within several weeks, operating from his city hall office in the suburban town of Clichy, where he was mayor, the now President-designate Delors, accompanied by the ever-present Pascal Lamy, his tough, hard-driving chief of staff, made a swing to key EC capitals to sound out leaders on their priorities and suggestions for Europe. He had four possible topics on his draft agenda: first, persuading Community members to adopt a common, united security and foreign policy; second, strengthening EC political institutions; and third, establishing a Community economic and monetary union. By a process of elimination, following his talks, Delors had his answer: only the fourth agenda topic showed promise. This was a blueprint outlined in the Rome Treaty but never fully implemented—the completion of a frontierless internal market of some 340 million consumers, representing the world's largest single market and trading bloc. This marked the genesis of the 1992 plan.

"It was clearly a matter of eliminating what was unacceptable, and so I ruled out major reforms and initiatives that would radically change our systems of defense and foreign-policy cooperation, our European political institutions, and Europe's monetary system," Delors said.[8] No one in Brussels at the time, with the exception of Lamy and a few insiders, had the slightest idea of what he had in mind.

The world got its first look on January 14, 1985. The scene was the European Parliament's annual opening plenary session in Strasbourg. Every member present watched the unsmiling, tense, deadly serious Delors stride to the podium and begin speaking. Within minutes, hearing the blunt, tough talk, they realized this would be no ordinary speech and that this was not just another Commission president evoking platitudes and wish lists and preaching impossible, visionary goals.

Gloomily, he asked why the Community had failed. "I have often wondered why the Community with its committed and talented leadership has never got off the ground; why it has failed to attain the objectives enshrined in the treaty, objectives on which there was a measure of consensus; in short, why it has failed to bring about the economic, social, and monetary integration that is vital to the advancement of our ten nations." Gradually, he warmed up to the subject, and to the answer. Delors repeatedly emphasized that even pulling down Europe's frontiers would not be enough and that "economic convergence will be meaningless to people if we have not reversed the terrible rise of unemployment within the next two years." What was urgently needed, Delors emphasized, was endowing "ourselves with economic, technological, financial, and monetary strength."

SETTING A MAGIC DATE

As members of the Parliament, commissioners, ambassadors, journalists, lobbyists listened intently and from time to time applauded the new, vibrant message, Delors became more and more specific. "Europe will not modernize its production structures just because a large market exists . . . the search for the larger scale will call for the promotion of cooperation between European firms; it will call for the creation of a suitable framework; it will call for tax concessions to encourage business cooperation and financial incentives." What Delors was describing was, in effect, a new, pragmatic "step-by-step" approach to rebuilding Europe—starting with the economy. The organization would only be expanded and broadened later to cover political powers, along with establishment of a single European currency and a European Central Bank.

Few realized that one of his sixteen newly named fellow commissioners, Britain's Lord Cockfield—an owlish, sharp-tongued man, virtually unknown to the outside world—was already working on the details of the 1992 program that would bear his name: The Cockfield Plan, as it is also known. It contained nearly three hundred draft measures, or directives as they are called in Brussels parlance, to be buttressed by an unprecedented boost in EC spending on research and development, along with speedy deregulation of hidebound, subsidized, and protected sectors, such as telecommunications, banking, energy, and transport, including airlines.

Barely noticed at the time was a line in his speech that many later considered Delors's most masterful stroke—the December 31, 1992 deadline for completion of the program. The date will go down in history as one of the most successful public-relations tools in Europe's postwar history. The words used by Delors when he announced it sound awkward in English and not much better in French: "It may not be overoptimistic to announce a decision to eliminate all frontiers within Europe by 1992 and to implement it (that decision)," he said. "That gives us eight years, the term of office of two commissions." Instantly, the date became a powerful symbol, recognized throughout the world as a shorthand message, a somewhat gimmicky but galvanizing way of symbolizing Europe's future.

Other deadlines had also been considered. Only three days earlier, in a speech to the Center for European Policy Studies, Wisse Dekker, chairman of Philips and vice chairman of the Roundtable of European Industrialists, a lobbying group of senior business executives, suggested 1990 as the deadline for implementing a plan very closely resembling that of Cockfield; 1995 and 2000 were put forth by others. "All those dates were too soon or too far away, but 1992, well, it just sounded right and it fit the end of a second commission term—December 31, 1992—so we tried it out in that speech. And it worked!" Lamy explained.

Also virtually unnoticed at the time, a new, tough line on dealing with the United States and Japan on trade issues emerged in that speech. "The Community has been unable to persuade its two major trade partners and friends—the United States and Japan—to act in concert to remedy the glaring ills of the world economy," Delors said grimly. Thus, he urged, "Europe must find its imagination again and return to the attack. . . . We Europeans must tell ourselves each and every day: yes, we know how to do it, and yes, we can do it." He was to repeat that message hundreds of times and in dozens of different ways during the next five years, even though it contributed heavily to a new and ugly image of Europe—a fortified castle, its drawbridge up with menacing defenders inside. Fortress Europe.

THE MOUNIER INFLUENCE SURFACES

Another concept and buzzword, which raised enormous, bitter controversy and the ire of Mrs. Thatcher was Delors's strong commitment to what he called "Social Europe." It boiled down to a strong commitment to helping workers in Europe, as a reflection of his profound belief that the Europe of the future should not simply be built for business and nation states, but for employees, the average working man and woman. This was Delors's commitment to restoring a sense of balance to Europe's new growth patterns, which, in turn, stemmed from the strong influence on his thinking of Emmanuel Mounier, an influential Catholic philosopher and writer who achieved prominence in the 1930s by advocating a moderate, middle-of-the-road philosophy known as "personalism." Mounier argued for a "third way" between what he felt were the excesses of Marxism and capitalism, a way that he believed would restore the dignity of the individual at a time of worldwide economic depression and impending chaos.

The Mounier influence on Delors was to surface—in spectacular fashion—on a warm day in early September 1988 in the English town of Bournemouth. Delors delivered what was his hardest-hitting speech yet on the need to introduce a "social dimension" into the rapidly evolving plans for building Europe. The occasion was the annual meeting of the Trades Union Congress, whose members, like union leaders throughout the EC, had become deeply disillusioned with Delors's plans for an integrated market. Most viewed it as more than a blueprint for business growth, in which there was little, if any, room for labor's voice and predicted that the ultimate result would, in any case, be more unemployment.

When Delors strode to the rostrum, he was not exactly cheered by TUC members. The mood was glum, skeptical, even hostile, as he began to speak. Few European leaders had ever addressed them. But when Delors promised that labor would, in fact, have a legitimate place in the New Europe and that the European Community was counting on labor to participate and share in what was happening, the normally anti-EC, British trade-union members, surprised, began to warm up. As he finished, and as the applause died down, TUC members jumped to their feet and joined in singing the famous French children's song "Frère Jacques," to express their whole-hearted support. As Jean-Michel Baer, one of Delors's aides, said later, "It was one of those stunning moments in his life that stemmed from a crisis of conscience . . . a feeling that Europe was being built as industrial policy, for business only, and not for workers, which went against everything he had ever stood for, and so he reacted. What showed through perhaps more than anything else was Mounier."

The TUC episode, unlike most earlier statements, placed him on a painful, damaging collision course with Mrs. Thatcher, who had never addressed the meeting. Furious, she quickly denounced Delors's TUC speech as his attempt to bring to the EC "socialism through the back door." Now, more than ever, she was convinced that he was using his position in Brussels to pursue a leftist ideology that she not only did not share, but which she felt had no place in the future. The New Europe, according to Mrs. Thatcher, was almost totally economic in scope and open to outsiders—virtually unconditionally—providing, and this was crucial, that they accepted the ground rules of a free, liberal capital market and economy with virtually no strong political role for the Community. Delors disagreed, and told her so on many occasions later.

I mention these speeches and incidents because they showed his unusual approach to the job—being controversial in public, even if the ideas displeased member governments. Delors described this approach as follows: "I build houses. Sometimes they crumble. Sometimes they stand up. I think of myself as an engineer, a tactician, not so much a thinker or a philosopher or political leader, like Mitterrand. He has different responsibilities and is accountable to the French people. My task is totally different from anything I had undertaken before coming here. I keep going, with new ideas, initiatives, and that is what distinguishes the Community from other institutions in Europe. My job is to provide momentum, ideas, initiatives. I am not a politician."[9]

A SELF-MADE OUTSIDER

In the rarefied world of contemporary French business and public administration, getting ahead often begins with graduating from one of the prestigious French universities or elite *grandes écoles*, notably the École Nationale d'Administration (ENA), the graduate school supplying France with its top-ranking civil servants. Not Delors.

With only a high school diploma, for seventeen years, starting in 1945, he worked at the Bank of France—at the insistence of his father—studying at night. At the same time, he launched his second career as a union militant, working actively for France's large Catholic labor union, La Confédération Française des Travailleurs Chrétiens, the CFTC. "We considered him not as an economist, but as a [union] militant with an economic background," said one banker friend, adding, "He was at the time also trying to find his way in politics."

Yet, according to his contemporaries, Delors never fit into any of the main postwar political parties. This was to present an obstacle later. Because of his many hesitations and internal, ideological conflicts, he did not join the Socialist party until 1974, and for this and other reasons, he has been regarded with suspicion by other party leaders and leftist rivals ever since.

"When I first met Delors around 1954, he joined our fledgling

leftist party, Nouvelle Gauche," recalled Claude Bourdet, a World
War II resistance leader, and founder of *L' Observateur*, an influential, non-Communist leftist weekly, which later became *Le Nouvel
Observateur*.[10] "He certainly was difficult to characterize politically . . .
he was on the left, but not yet European, which was to come later,
much later. In any case, he didn't stay with us very long and went on
to other things and other parties, including the Gaullists."

Bourdet was referring to another delicate, painful phase of Delors's life, in which he became special adviser on social and cultural
affairs to Jacques Chaban-Delmas, the moderately left-leaning Gaullist mayor of Bordeaux. After Chaban-Delmas was named prime
minister in 1969, Delors helped the reform-minded Gaullists develop
a new program called "La Nouvelle Société." Chaban-Delmas's government, with Delors's guidance, established new, improved relations
between labor unions and employers and extensive adult-education
programs. But by helping the conservatives, Delors came to be regarded by many leftists and particularly the Socialists as a traitor to
their cause. Mitterrand was among the few who refrained from criticizing Delors in public.

Later, reflecting on this period and his ideology, Delors was
quoted by Milesi as saying, "My position was uncomfortable. . . . I will
always be right of the left and left of the right, rejected by one and
all. . . . My path is undoubtedly somewhat unrealistic." Mitterrand,
who has known Delors for three decades, believed he "committed an
error of judgment in thinking he could modify the system by integrating himself into it. He certainly did some good things, but it resulted
in a failure that took the concrete form of his own departure."[11]
Delors himself felt he might never live down the charges of "treason."

Yet, working with the widely admired Chaban-Delmas also placed
him in a strong position to appeal to France's center-right political
camp in the likely event that he entered the campaign to be successor
to Mitterrand, whose seven-year presidential term was due to end in
1995.

In July 1972, when a more right-wing Gaullist leader, Pierre Mess-
mer, took over as prime minister, Delors was eased aside. Two years
later, he joined the Socialist Party. He quickly found work—as a
teacher, researcher, think-tank leader, and starting in 1979, already
elected to the European Parliament as a Socialist, he was named
chairman of its influential committee on economic and monetary
affairs. This provided him the first taste of European institutions and

preparation for what lay ahead. He would not return to a government post until May 1981—as Mitterrand's finance minister, a job he held until moving to Brussels.

A FIRST ENCOUNTER

When I first met Delors in the spring of 1981, when he was fifty-six, he was seated in a cramped office in Socialist party headquarters on the rue Solférino on Paris's left bank. He told me in his low-key, reserved manner that he was but an "economic adviser" to the incoming government and that he would encourage international investments in France, notably from America. Only a handful of American diplomats knew much about him, but they had been tracking him for several weeks—with considerable suspicion and fear of what policies he might pursue in the event he became finance minister under a Socialist-Communist coalition government.

Within a year, with the franc under attack and confidence in heavy deficit spending collapsing, Delors argued for and obtained a dampening on government spending—an approach that was to help gradually bring down France's double-digit inflation and restore confidence in the franc. That also was to win Delors deep admiration and respect from Kohl in Bonn and Mrs. Thatcher in London. Because of his austerity policy, she became one of his most ardent admirers, although their relations cooled and gradually became hostile once Delors assumed the EC Commission presidency. Throughout the years in Brussels, Delors's ties to Mitterrand and Kohl have remained strong, for traditionally, without the support of Paris and Bonn neither the Community nor the Commission president can function effectively.

Consider the plight of Britain's Roy Jenkins, who was Gaston Thorn's predecessor as Commission president and is a longtime admirer of Delors. Jenkins told me in his office at the House of Lords in London that he had the unfortunate experience of not being supported by the majority of EC leaders—not even by his own government—and that the only member he could regularly count on for support in the Council of Ministers was Chancellor Helmut Schmidt. "My presidency in Brussels (1977–1981)," Jenkins said, was often bogged down "like a stagecoach in a quagmire," whereas Delors has generally been in the driver's seat, "sparking along—on a good, hard road."[12] Delors, Lamy, and other members of the presidential staff and their allies spend a great deal of time cultivating political leaders in most of the key EC capitals, lobbying for support, which, as Lamy notes, "does not come naturally . . . you have to work at it and we do, in Paris and Bonn particularly."

Stamina counts for a great deal. Delors gets by on about six hours of sleep and, following thirty minutes of physical exercise and breakfast, is at his desk at around 8:30. An intensely devoted fan of soccer and cycling, *L'Équipe,* a French sports daily, is among the publications he reads every day before plunging into his fast-paced twelve-hour routine. He delivers about fifty speeches a year, many of which he writes himself. Starting in 1989, as part of determined attempts to involve the Commission directly in economic-aid programs in Eastern Europe and in building better relations with the United States and Japan, Delors found himself traveling extensively. Wherever he went in Eastern Europe and Asia, enthusiastic but small crowds greeted him, curiously seeking a glimpse of this sober, conservatively dressed official getting red-carpet treatment.

STORMY COMMISSION MEETINGS

Delors's job involves running the Commission in Brussels and at the same time being "Mr. Europe." These tasks do not mix easily.

Although he appears at ease with most of his fellow commissioners, since their four-year terms began in 1989, it has been an uneasy, often tense and stormy relationship. This stems from a combination of the personalities involved and the diffusion of power within the Commission. It is both a civil service and the equivalent of an executive branch. The current seventeen commissioners, excluding Delors, are roughly the equivalent of U.S. cabinet officers, nominated by their governments and appointed by the Council of Ministers to four-year terms. The president and five vice presidents are chosen nominally for two years, and none of them can be removed before completion of their terms, except as a group by censure through the European Parliament—a power that has never been applied successfully. Most decisions are reached by simple majority vote.

We shall return in Chapter 8 to the inner workings of the Commission—its conflicts, failures, and successes—and examine in detail how Community decisions are reached. A major obstacle for the strong-willed Delors has been making this disparate group function as a team, and his first term was particularly tense and often explosive, given the fact that Delors's temper is short and he can be painfully direct and unpleasant when not getting his way.

Delors's tirades against some commissioners, undoubtedly reflecting the frustrations of the job, have become classics among stories circulating in the Berlaymont. During one particularly stormy Commission session, Delors told a Greek commissioner that he was so lacking in talent he couldn't run a taverna. He once accused a British commissioner of being a stooge for the Labour Party. Several commissioners have been deeply offended by Delors's verbal attacks on their performances; one described the French leader's tactics in the boardroom as "intellectual terrorism." This comment reflected clashes and deep splits over policy as well as over personalities.

There are several different, often-conflicting political tendencies within the Commission. The split, broadly speaking, is over the role of the states and governments in economic, trade, and social policy. Delors has traditionally been on the side of a strong interventionist role. Although it is difficult to generalize, the new Commission lineup announced at the end of 1988 reassured business leaders and EC trading partners for a simple reason: the incoming Commission included several longtime defenders of free trade and a reduced role for the Commission in the internal economic life of the Community, including in the highly controversial field of agriculture. Some proved formidable challengers to Delors's interventionist views, although in typical Brussels style compromises were found.

For example, Martin Bangemann, the stocky, outspoken former West German economics minister who succeeded Lord Cockfield and who has never hidden his free-trade views, has disagreed sharply with Delors over how flexible and open the Community should be with regard to restricting car imports from Japan. Bangemann is a key player in a group of so-called free-market liberals who oppose what they consider Delors's leftist, interventionist policies, and have not hesitated to challenge the president in the Commission's regular Wednesday meetings.

This group also includes the strong-willed Sir Leon Brittan of Britain, who succeeded Peter Sutherland and is responsible for the Commission's anti-trust policy; and Frans Andriessen of the Netherlands, who is serving a third term, and is responsible for the Commission's external relations. Andriessen, who is also a member of the so-called "Northern Liberal" group has often expressed bitter frustration with Delors's extremely active role in foreign affairs and, particularly, monetary questions. Brittan, Bangemann, and Andriessen, sometimes together, have challenged Delors, but have also managed to remain more or less immune to his volatile moods and occasional outbursts of anger.

Following completion of his first, highly acclaimed term as Commission president, I asked Delors what he planned to do next. "What do I want? I would like to be useful, to continue serving the Community or the general interest. I have held fourteen different jobs since my youth. I might be ready for a fifteenth. I have never been head of a company, for example." It was vintage Delors—who had indeed previously served as a banker, union leader, professor, writer, European parliamentarian, governmental adviser, and minister—but who deliberately disguised his personal motivations. Nevertheless, I and many others came to the conclusion that he would seek the French presidency, assuming Mitterrand did not run for reelection following completion of his second seven-year term in 1995.

Opinion polls have repeatedly shown him a strong second or third to Michel Rocard, a fellow Socialist, who resigned as Prime Minister in May 1991, and even, on occasion, ahead. But the Socialist party still has not displayed any enthusiasm for his ambition, even though Delors has cultivated his image in France, speaking out on domestic and foreign issues whenever opportunities have presented themselves, which on occasion has meant criticizing the United States, raising a controversial question: Is Delors anti-American?

BEING ANTI-AMERICAN PAYS

That question, while repeatedly raised in private conversations, particularly by European and American analysts and diplomats, is rarely, if ever, discussed in public. Until early 1989, the answer to the question would have been a clear and unequivocal Yes.

As General Charles de Gaulle and most of his successors demonstrated, playing an independent hand with regard to Washington is popular with the French, and Delors has been no exception. He began challenging American economic power early in his political career. Shortly after settling into his spacious offices in the Louvre Palace as finance minister in the spring of 1981, he firmly urged

Europe to work toward offsetting the power of the dollar; to pressure a fall in U.S. interest rates; to boost other forms of international liquidity and monetary cooperation built around the European Monetary System, possibly linked to the dollar and the yen. But such ideas, championed with equal fervor by Mitterrand, never got off the ground or found much support in Washington, Tokyo, London, or Frankfurt—where they mattered most.

Over the years, annoyed, frustrated, but undaunted, Delors pressed his cause in other areas. On many occasions this deeply annoyed Washington. Delors's highly controversial interference in France's "CGCTC Affair" in 1987 was a spectacular case in point.

At issue for over a year was who should be awarded control of France's second-largest and deficit-ridden telecommunications company, being privatized by the conservative government of Jacques Chirac, Compagnie Générale Constructions Téléphoniques. Five industrial groups were competing, three of them European, two from North America. On the grounds that it was necessary to boost Germany's role in EC cooperative ventures, Delors unexpectedly urged in an interview with France's leading daily, *Le Monde,* that control should go to Siemens, Germany's largest electronics company. Control would mean obtaining an industrial plum, because CGCT controlled about 16 percent of the French switching-telecommunications market, which within several years was booming as EC deregulation moved forward.

In Washington, the Reagan administration exploded with outrage. Reflecting the anger at Delors's move, senior cabinet secretaries and aides privately warned Paris and Bonn that the administration would retaliate against Siemens's business interests in the United States if control was awarded to the Munich-based giant on political rather than industrial grounds. More to the point, the front-runner in the competition for control of the ailing French company was the American Telephone & Telegraph Company, which had the strong backing of the White House and was favored by many insiders to win, mainly because its telephone-switching technology was, according to many experts, the best being offered.

In Paris, the Chirac government was deeply divided over whether to choose the AT&T-led venture or "the European solution," meaning Siemens or the "neutral" outsider, L. M. Ericsson of Sweden.[13] Embarrassed, angry, and determined to resolve the issue without further damaging relations with Washington, yet without appearing to capitulate, the generally pro-American, neo-Gaullist Chirac government felt itself obliged to award the contract to Ericsson and its French partner, the state-controlled defense contractor Matra, thus claiming a "European solution."

In New York and Washington, AT&T executives expressed shock, anger, and determination never to repeat their strategy, which had involved heavy-handed lobbying—relying almost exclusively on the Reagan administration in Washington and the U.S. embassy in Paris. One U.S. diplomat told me that AT&T officials, fearful of press coverage, insisted on total secrecy during their visits to Paris, to the point of entering through side doors and rarely venturing outside, much less to Brussels, while leaving media contacts to its Dutch partner, Philips, which at the time was still involved in telecommunications.

Meantime, in Brussels, Delors conceded he had failed in his immediate task of helping Siemens and had damaged his image in Washington. But, by the same token, he had clearly boosted his position in Bonn and with Kohl in particular. It was what Delors likes to refer to as his approach to diplomacy, the "step-by-step" way of doing things, even if that meant stepping on American toes.

But Delors remained suspicious of the Reagan administration. In Chapter 9 we shall return to this story and describe how President Bush masterfully handled Delors's prickly sensitivities, and why, to Washington's surprise, he reversed his predecessors' approach to the European Community, partly in recognition of the Community's emerging political role in world affairs.

The Plans That Failed:
From Charlemagne to Hallstein

> From Charlemagne through Napoleon to Hitler, soldiers
> and madmen have tried to hammer Europe together.
>
> —THEODORE H. WHITE,
> *Fire in the Ashes*

HOMETOWN OF "THE KING OF EUROPE"

The average tourist, unless passionately interested in the earliest
chapters of European history or in mineral baths, would do well to
avoid Aachen. It is a trim provincial West German industrial city in
the heart of Europe, with about 250,000 inhabitants, many of whom
have a well-deserved reputation for being haughty and difficult and
for knowing everything better than anyone else, particularly foreigners. Aside from visiting the town's casino and baths and attending
horse-riding events and two theaters, there isn't much to do.

But these are hardly reasons for avoiding what was once the
flourishing court and adopted hometown of Charlemagne, founder
of the Holy Roman Empire, which became known in contemporary
Germany as the country's First Reich. Here was the first successful
effort to create a united Christian Europe following the collapse of
the Roman Empire several centuries earlier. And Charlemagne is the

primary reason millions of visitors from around the world come—to catch a glimpse of what remains.

Mysteriously, his presence continues to haunt the city, and his legendary accomplishments still crop up in conversations about the future of Europe, recalling the way in which Thomas Jefferson, one of America's founding fathers, is still talked about in the university town of Charlottesville, Virginia, and at his nearby estate of Monticello, where he lived for nearly five decades.

Precious little that can be seen or touched remains of what Charlemagne accomplished in the ninth century—integrating the Christian lands of Western Europe into an area that, strikingly, corresponded roughly to the area covered by the six founding nations of the contemporary Common Market: much of France, West Germany, Belgium, the Netherlands, Luxembourg, Italy, plus Austria, Switzerland, and western Czechoslovakia. From his lively, heavily frequented court in Aachen, Charlemagne ruled a vast empire, the principal economic and political power in the West. It boasted a single, loosely organized administration, a single currency, a common language, and a monarchy that commanded allegiance from the ruling elites and from the papacy in Rome.

What remains of the original walls of the palace—fragments of stone—were incorporated into a fortified brownstone tower of the fourteenth-century city hall, which dominates the downtown area, the palace's former glory recalled by a metal plaque.

To discover more, one can stroll through narrow, cobblestone streets to the dimly lit cathedral, which was built by Charlemagne. The original octagonal basilica, resembling those of ancient Rome, was the first of its kind built north of the Alps. The marble columns were imported from Rome and Ravenna on orders of Charlemagne, who, as we shall see, was a meticulous, cultivated man. Inside on an upper floor, overlooking the altar, looms his unadorned, white marble throne, from which he ruled. Below, in a gold-and-jewel-encrusted tomb lie his remains.

I asked a twelve-year-old French student, as she listened to her German guide, to explain who she thought the great leader was. "Why, he was like us, French—king of the Franks," she replied without hesitating. The guide, a university student, hearing our French, insisted on commenting in German: "She is only partly correct. Here, we consider him German, our first emperor, and we call him Karl der Grosse, but we also see him as the earliest among modern Europeans." Both answers were correct, underscoring the complex difficulties of identifying and comparing previous European unification movements with contemporary Europe.

NAPOLEON, HITLER, AND THE OTHERS

Charlemagne. Napoleon. Hitler. Jean Monnet. Walter Hallstein, the first president of the EC Commission, de Gaulle. Can they, each with visionary goals and totally different methods, be grouped together? Perhaps not. But previous unification movements are worth recalling because they serve as reminders of how difficult, how costly the huge expenditure of human and material resources have proven in the many previous battles for unification. Yet in the end, in totally different historical contexts, these movements failed, or were crippled and stymied, as Europe repeatedly reverted to systems of governance dominated by nation states, or by regions within their borders, torn by deep nationalistic, linguistic, and cultural forces and barriers. Similar forces exploded with the dizzying, fast-paced collapse of Communist regimes in Eastern Europe that began in late 1989, raising the question whether or not European history wasn't repeating itself.

We begin with Charlemagne for several reasons. First, because in the years and indeed centuries, following his death, he became a prototype, a model, a symbol, a vision for other European leaders who also were determined to unify Europe, most of them bent on military domination. He also was a transitional figure, bridging Greek and Roman civilizations and the Middle Ages. The medieval kingdoms of Germany and France based their systems of rule on his monarchy and strove hard to keep those traditions alive following Charlemagne's death. From that point on, until 1531, when the coronation site was shifted to Frankfurt on the Main River, more than thirty German princes were crowned in Aachen.

Napoleon Bonaparte not only compared himself to Charlemagne but once toyed with the idea of also being crowned in Aachen. Adolf Hitler, similarly fascinated by Charlemagne, convinced he was one of the greatest leaders in history, gleefully accepted a replica of his sword during a tumultuous rally in Nuremberg in 1935.[1] But some Nazi ideologues criticized Charlemagne for having ruthlessly suppressed the Saxons on the empire's eastern frontier, and for having been a devout Christian and, in dress and manner, appearing more Frank than German. Nevertheless, during fierce battling for the city in the autumn of 1944, and despite impending defeat at the hands of the advancing U.S. First Army, Hitler ordered Aachen defended to the end, mainly because of its symbolic importance. On October 21, battered, smoldering Aachen became the first important German city to surrender to the allies.

FASCINATION WITH A LEGEND

Scholars also have been drawn to Charlemagne over the centuries.[2] During the Renaissance, writings about him resurfaced, and they were revived again during the nineteenth century, primarily by Victor Hugo and members of the Romantic School, who were actively promoting the idea of European unity following the 1848 revolutionary upheavals in France, Germany, and the Austro-Hungarian empire. In the early 1950s, another important scholarly wave of interest swept Western Europe, led by such scholars as Henri Fichtenau of the University of Vienna and by Louis Halphen of the Sorbonne.

This revival coincided with the more contemporary postwar European unification movements, such as the U.S.-led Marshall Plan, symbolized by the annual awarding of a Charlemagne Prize by the city of Aachen to a leader or statesman who had contributed to European unity. Since 1950, more than 30 recipients have included Winston Churchill, Konrad Adenauer, Jean Monnet, Walter Hallstein, George Marshall, Henry Kissinger, Helmut Kohl, and François Mitterrand; in 1991 the prize went to Vaclav Havel, president of Czechoslovakia. But what "nationality" was he? Why is Charlemagne considered "European"?

The young French student in the cathedral was, of course, correct in identifying Charlemagne as king of the Franks, and thus it is no surprise that he scores high in French surveys about personalities who have dominated European history. But young German students consider Karl their king and emperor and they, too, are correct. In a 1989 poll, an authoritative French history magazine, commemorating Napoleon, asked who in French history had contributed the most to building Europe. General de Gaulle scored highest (40 percent), followed by Mitterrand (18 percent) and Monnet (14 percent), but Charlemagne was next (9 percent)—well ahead of Napoleon (4 percent)—and he scored considerably higher among youth (14 percent), artisans (17 percent), and extreme right-wing groups (20 percent).[3]

Dr. August Peters, a German priest and scholar, has been for the past twenty years curator of the Aachen Cathedral. My wife and I were invited to lunch by Jean Barbey, the scholarly longtime head of Saint-Gobain in Germany, the giant French glassmaker, which has its German headquarters in the city. Aachen, incidentally, because of its developed industry and strategic location, nowadays is drawing a growing number of foreign companies, including Japanese, which increasingly use the area as a springboard to the rest of Europe. The region is also being developed to be a major hub for an east-west branch of Europe's high-speed rail network in the mid-1990s. But at lunch we were discussing history, not economics, and the reasons for the flow of 1.5 million visitors who make the pilgrimage to Aachen each year. "Today people come here to rediscover a man, a king, but also their European past," said Peters. "It is this searching, the quest for a past, which is particularly striking, both among Germans and the French."

On a hill overlooking Aachen, gazing toward its medieval walls, Peters and Barbey agreed that among the young Germans they meet, there is a sense of excitement about Charlemagne and what he accomplished. In contrast, the contemporary European Community, its institutions, treaties, directives, and leaders, including Delors, seemed far away, uninspiring, somehow irrelevant. In Peters's view, this reflected Germany's preoccupation with German problems, and, even more troubling, lack of knowledge about contemporary EC institutions and policies, particularly among German youth. "What we sense and feel here is that few people, particularly young people, look at Europe with a sense of idealism and belonging the way many of us did in the 1950s, after the war, or the way we still look at Charlemagne—as a strong European or universalist leader," added Barbey.

THE MAN AND HIS SYSTEM

Charlemagne, known also as Carolus Magnus, Charles I, Charles the Great, and Karl der Grosse, was born in 742, the eldest son of Pepin III, a Frank, who ruled a realm that had been on the point of breaking up, comprising mainly Germanic people who had penetrated into Roman Gaul. It was founded in the Meuse-Moselle region and covered an area roughly situated between the Loire and the Rhine rivers. Upon Pepin's death, the kingdom was split between his two sons. However, Charlemagne, because of the sudden death of his brother in 771, became sole ruler of the kingdom, which included most of contemporary France, extending eastward into what was West Germany. And, like some of his admiring successors later, he was bent on power and expansion.

Tall, robust, with a thin voice, large, piercing eyes, and a mustache throughout his adult life, Charlemagne relied on a combination of military force and diplomacy to attain his goals. Like Napoleon centuries later, he did not hesitate to place his family and friends in key positions of territories conquered, or to remove them when they fell out of favor. Partly because of weaknesses and divisions among his enemies, Charlemagne quickly extended his rule—southward to contemporary Bavaria and to Lombardy in Italy; eastward to Lower Saxony and to the Elbe River, which after World War II until Germany's unification in 1990, served as a strategic east-west border. This easternmost frontier, in turn, extended north to a fortified castle built by Charlemagne on a sandy promontory not far from the city of Hamburg, which became the northeastern border, providing the empire an outlet on the North Sea.

A NEPHEW IS KILLED

Advancing into Spain, however, in 778 proved disastrous. Charlemagne's army was forced to retreat eastward through the Pyrenees, amid fierce, rear-guard battling that led to the death of Roland, *préfet* of the Breton Marches, and a knight believed to have been Charlemagne's nephew. Driving toward the battle site today, two hours from Pamplona, Spain, on a winding road high in the Navarre Pyrenees, you can visit the tiny village of Roncevaux, where Roland was defeated by the Gascons and later died of his wounds. On the highest point overlooking the valley, embedded in a stone monument, there is a replica of his sword and an inscription recalling the poems and songs that kept the Charlemagne legend alive down through the centuries.

Historians continue debating whether or not Charlemagne had a master plan. Many believe he operated by instinct, on a day-to-day basis. But there is wide agreement that his primary goal was to unite his disparate regions, basing his policy on both political and religious convictions. His strong personality enabled him to enforce a new ruling system that gradually evolved into a pre-feudal system.

According to modern historians and the scholar Einhard, who spent twenty-three years in Charlemagne's service, the ruling system was, in effect, a primitive form of a European state, with a solid religious base. It took on legitimacy when Charlemagne was crowned emperor in Rome by Pope Leo III, an ally of the Frankish leader. The coronation took place in Rome on Christmas Day in the year 800, some fourteen years before he died. And, like Napoleon's coronation centuries later, the imperial title was enormously helpful as a symbol, enabling Charlemagne to pursue power and the buildup of his realm—economically as well as culturally.

At its height, Charlemagne's realm was far smaller and less power-ful than the first Roman Empire; in the second century A.D., the city of Rome boasted a population of nearly one million. And yet, at the time of Charlemagne's coronation, the population of the former imperial capital, weakened, corrupt, and overrun by invaders, had shrunk to the size of a town of around 80,000 persons, and had little relevance to the earlier empire.

CREATING "THE MISSI"

Even today, Aachen—located inland on hilly, fertile, nondescript land, surrounded by forests—hasn't changed much from what it must have been when Charlemagne first decided to settle there. Why did he? In those days, rulers traveled almost constantly, but Charlemagne had grown weary of holding court on a rotating basis. He also was a strong, avid swimmer, attracted by the warm springs in Aachen. Mainly for these reasons, he decided the site would become his future court, a permanent place of worship, and military headquarters from which he would run his European empire. The city's warm springs, like the cathedral and his throne, have remained a tourist attraction ever since.

Although power was tightly held by Charlemagne, his system of ruling was deliberately flexible and decentralized. He accomplished this by allowing regions' local administrations to keep their identities and local traditions. To maintain control and to generate revenues,

Charlemagne created a system of roving inspectors, known as *missi dominici*, who were sent throughout the realm to collect money; they represented a primitive and relatively efficient civil service.

The *missi* are viewed by contemporary French historians as forerunners in modern France to the *inspecteurs de finance*, the French finance ministry's elite service for policing government spending and revenues. Although most of those serving in Charlemagne's inner circle were either members of his family, clergy, or wealthy aristocrats, the *missi* represented the beginning of a *grand corps*, the elite group of senior engineers and civil servants, established in its modern form by Napoleon as the underpinning for his centralized administration.

DRESSING LIKE A FRANK AND SPEAKING GERMAN

Franks were the dominant people and Charlemagne made sure he looked the part. "He wore the national dress of the Franks . . . linen shirt and drawers and long hose and a tunic edged with silk," observed Einhard, the historian, who was Charlemagne's adviser and personal friend and who chronicled the leader's life.[4] "He hated the clothes of other countries, no matter how becoming they might be, and he would never consent to wear them. The only exception to this was one day in Rome when Pope Hadrian entreated him to put on a long tunic and a Greek mantle, to wear shoes made in the Roman fashion. . . . On ordinary days his dress differed hardly at all from that of the common people," Einhard recalled.

Determined to promote a more international spirit among his officials and others in his service, Charlemagne ordered that Franks mingle socially and professionally with non-Franks and other ethnic groups from throughout the empire; those less wealthy were urged to mingle with landowning aristocrats, in what became a system in which performance counted more than background. Charlemagne's goal was to establish a professional class of *fonctionnaires*, or bureaucrats, according to a leading scholar, to consolidate his power, and to justify the idea of a "Christian empire."

Foreshadowing what followed in subsequent centuries, a unified monetary system was established, comprising a common currency, with a silver mint established at Aachen—the coins being one of the most tangible signs of the empire's unity. This early single monetary system, similar to what the Romans had pioneered, embodied a primitive exchange-rate mechanism, designed and enforced by Charlemagne's central administration. A court and taxation system, which like the common currency was modeled on Roman precedents, was reactivated.

Although slavery had been gradually phased out since Roman times, daily life for the average man or woman was harsh and dangerous. In contrast to life in and around Aachen, peasants, comprising the majority of the population, were often serving their masters in a prefeudal, vassal system, suffering from poverty, sickness, famines, and wars—grim reminders of the severe limitations in comparing the ninth century with more recent periods of history.

Charlemagne, aware of his power limitations, also looked southeastward, specifically to Constantinople, the center of the competing Eastern Orthodox Church, with which he attempted to establish friendly, diplomatic ties. Just prior to his death, Charlemagne began studying construction of a canal linking the Rhine and Danube rivers, his visionary project for linking East and West Europe. Although his advisers warned that such a project was unrealistic, Charlemagne pointed to a success story that he viewed as a precursor of what he had in mind—a five-hundred-foot wooden bridge he had ordered built over the Rhine River at Mainz. The bridge, which Einhard said required ten years to build, inspired Charlemagne to undertake or study other major construction projects, such as the transcontinental canal.

Although he was illiterate, having made what Einhard described as "rather pathetic" efforts to learn writing, Charlemagne was passionately drawn to language as a potentially unifying force. Thus he called on Acluin of York, a scholar and grammarian, to cross the Channel to help in reviving Latin, which had deteriorated in use and form, as the main language of the empire. Charlemagne had learned Latin so well, Einhard said, "that he spoke it as fluently as his own tongue; but he understood Greek better than he could speak it." The leader also learned other languages in addition to his mother tongue: an old high-German dialect, which, Einhard noted, he also spoke "easily and fluently." The court at Aachen flourished, having become an international cultural and intellectual center, drawing many diplomats and scholars from throughout the realm, including from neighboring Spain and Britain.

Yet, for all his charisma, power, and determination, Charlemagne could not continue expanding much beyond the borders reached by his empire in the early 800s, for a major reason: lack of resources. He was unable to organize and finance a standing army, an efficient road and communications network, and a navy. And even during the height of his rule, raids by Norse and Danish pirates on the empire's seacoasts began to weaken his defenses. He also was unable to prepare a succession that would keep his empire united. Gradually, his power base disintegrated, along with his health. Following a series of attacks of fever and pleurisy, he died at 9 A.M. January 28, 814, at the age of seventy-two and was buried at the cathedral amid what Einhard described as "the great lamentation of the entire population."

His male and female heirs, weak, divided, or too inexperienced and young, were unable to govern effectively; revolts broke out amid continued intrigues and plots among his allies and family. When Charlemagne's last surviving son, Louis the Pious, died in 840, Louis's three sons, unable to agree, put together a succession plan the following year that partitioned the empire into three parts— roughly corresponding to contemporary France, Italy, and West Germany. Frontiers, national borders, had returned. The man whom a poet at his court once dubbed "the King of Europe," and his system of governance, had slipped into history, ending any immediate hopes for reviving the idea of a united Europe.

A CORSICAN ESTABLISHES
A FRENCH-DOMINATED EMPIRE

I was on an Alitalia flight from Rome on assignment for the *International Herald Tribune,* when a seasoned Italian steward leaned to the cabin window and pointed down at Corsica, one of the most scenic, colorful, culturally complex, and politically maddening islands in the Mediterranean. "That's where he was from, but the place, in many ways belongs to us, Italy . . . this is what makes Europe so crazy and difficult to understand, even for us," the steward said. "Some even consider him ours, because Corsica for many of us was, and in many ways still is, Italian."

The "he" was, of course, Napoleon, the second surviving child of Carlo Buonaparte, a lawyer of noble background, whose family had emigrated to Corsica from the Tuscan region of Italy in the sixteenth century. Napoleon was born a French citizen in Ajaccio, the island capital, on August 15, 1769, just over a year following the cession of the island to France by Genoa. Educated in French military schools, driven by determination to expand French power internationally, this high-strung military leader became emperor of what was known as *L'Europe Française,* French Europe. It comprised some ninety million people throughout Continental Europe, one-third being French. His reforms in the fields of law, education, government administration, and banking were to become a unifying force for modernizing not only France but, to a lesser degree, neighboring countries in Continental Europe his armies placed under French control or influence.

As Charlemagne had sought to establish a European empire, extending from contemporary France and Germany to surrounding areas, Napoleon's so-called "Continental System" likewise was geographically rooted in a core region—France, Germany, the Benelux countries, most of Italy, and Spain. Napoleon's system encompassed Charlemagne's former territories, which were absorbed into the "Confederation of the Rhine," and included some three hundred German states. Many historians have concluded that Napoleon came closer to establishing a united Europe than any other previous leader since Charlemagne. Indeed, Napoleon claimed he was Charlemagne's heir. But that greatly exaggerated link was to prove short-lived.

Once the Confederation was established in 1806 and the number of states reduced to about forty under Napoleon's ruthless style of administration, Francis I, emperor of Austria, renounced his title of Holy Roman Emperor. That title, incidentally, only originated well after Charlemagne's death, with Otto I. He was a German king who first assumed the title during his coronation in the Aachen cathedral in 962, claiming that the Roman Empire had never ended, but was only suspended with the abdication of the last Roman emperor in 476. German kings continued to use the title, but Francis's move ended once and for all what had become honorific and symbolic—the claims by Germany's kings through the centuries that they were propagating Germany's "1,000-year First Reich," a reference later revived by Hitler. The most important point about the disappearance of the title was Napoleon's determination to stamp his own imprint on history.

As has been amply documented, Napoleon's long-range ambitions were vast and grandiose, and they included plans for extending French power eastward to Russia, and southward and eastward to the Mediterranean. However, determined, increasingly fearful opposition to his expansion plans led Russia and England, with their combined forces, finally to defeat him. Indeed, Napoleon by training and instinct was, above all, a military leader, and just prior to the turn of the century had imposed a dictatorship on France, despite the promulgation of a constitution, on December 25, 1799. At the time, recent French military victories in Switzerland and the Netherlands enabled Napoleon to suppress opposition movements ruthlessly within France and in neighboring countries.

A tireless worker, and ferociously ambitious, Napoleon was also viewed by many of his contemporaries and allies as the defender of the French Revolution's ideals, the leader who would restore France's self-confidence and rebuild its economy. Not everything Napoleon accomplished was destructive or negative, for modernization was also one of his greatest obsessions. Some of his most important reforms have remained integral parts of daily French life.

For example, he established a centralized administration of *départements*, roughly equivalent to U.S. states, but run by *préfets*, officials named by, and reporting to, Paris. Judges, who had been previously elected, were named by the government to lifetime terms; powers of the police, already ruthlessly efficient, were greatly reinforced; he reorganized and centralized the government-run central bank, the Banque de France, which previously had been partly privately owned; higher education was greatly strengthened by the creation of *grandes écoles*, such as École Polytechnique, the MIT of France, and modernized universities. The franc was stabilized; roads, ports, communications systems were built or vastly improved. All are still flourishing.

Reflecting on his record while in exile on St. Helena, Napoleon tried to create the impression that everything he had done was for the unification of Europe. That Europe, in 1812 known as *Le Grand Empire*, stretched from Spain and France, south to Italy, but excluding Sicily and Sardinia; north to Germany and Prussia; eastward to Poland and the Austrian Empire, including Vienna and Budapest. "I wanted to make of all these people of Europe the same people . . . an agglomeration and a confederation of *grands peuples*.[5]

But like Hitler, conquering on behalf of Nazi Germany a century later, Napoleon was mainly working for his own country and the extension of its power.[6] In the final years of life he conceded as much: "My principle: France above all. If I conquered kingdoms, it was done so that France would have all the advantages," he said.[7] The plundering by Napoleon's armies of European museums and libraries for

French collections was another striking example of where his priorities lay. Even today, the pillaging remains a source of annoyance and contention between France and Egypt, Greece, and other European countries whose art treasures were carried off by his armies.

Napoleon's reforms and political institutions were also imposed outside of France, and to this day, vestiges remain in some countries. For example, simplified common laws and civilian codes were promulgated in areas under French control. Known as the *Code Civile*, it incorporated many of the Napoleonic principles and institutions already in place in France: the lay character of the state, a modernized and uniform taxation system, separation of the judiciary from the civil service, obligatory military service. The codes granted greater rights and freedoms to employers, but ignored workers. The right of divorce was broadened and reinforced for men, but women's rights were restricted. Throughout the German-speaking parts of the empire and to a lesser degree in Italy, local princes and high-ranking officials welcomed the reforms. Spain, however, fiercely resisted the Napoleonic reforms, reflecting the country's profoundly conservative traditions.

In contemporary Germany, vestiges of the Code are still reflected in the nation's civil-law system, which underwent its first complete modernization in 1900, and which until then had relied heavily on the imported Napoleonic law, notably in the western regions of Germany. A system of notaries, influential state officials who have far more power than their American counterparts, was also established by Napoleon, and they are still functioning in the Rhineland, Bavaria, Baden-Württemberg, Spain, and, of course, throughout France. In the end, however, Europe and, particularly France, paid a heavy price for Napoleon's ruthless ambitions.

Having mobilized a British-led coalition of Europe's major powers against him, Napoleon was soundly defeated during the famous battle of Waterloo June 12–18, 1815. Later, following his abdication and confinement on the island of St. Helena, even his friends acknowledged the heavy, tragic costs of his reign to France. Not only were the country's geographical boundaries reduced considerably from where they had been at the beginning of the French Revolution in 1789, but the Napoleonic Wars cost the lives of half a million men. Thus, despite glory and reforms brought to France and Europe, the loss of life caused by his conquests played a fatal role in depressing France's birthrate in subsequent decades.

A BORDERLESS ECONOMIC EUROPE REEMERGES

The date: August 21, 1849. The occasion: An international peace conference, known as Congrès de la Paix, being held in Paris. The agenda: A debate on how to translate the upheavals that had just swept France, Germany, and the Austro-Hungarian empire into a new, European push for unity. As a hush came over the audience, Victor Hugo, a delegate, whose father had served Napoleon as a general, and who had already emerged as one of the nation's most popular writers, began outlining how the European powers should organize themselves economically, politically, and, above all, peacefully. "The day will come when we will see two immense groups, the United States of America and the United States of Europe," Hugo said, immediately drawing sustained applause from the packed hall.[8]

Other European figures were to utter that thought in the subsequent century and a half—Napoleon III, the British legal scholar James Lorimer, the French historian Ernest Renan, France's President Édouard Herriot, Winston Churchill, French World War II Resistance leaders, the Swiss scholar Denis de Rougemont, Jean Monnet, and Helmut Kohl. But Hugo, if not the first, was certainly among the first prominent figures to have publicly called for a United States of Europe. For Hugo, an ardent European, the notion represented broad aspirations and admiration for what was happening on the other side of the Atlantic. He hoped that, somehow, the two continents would be linked. Hugo called for a modern transatlantic partnership between the two "United States," which he urged should encompass expanded trade and cultural exchanges. While the idea lacked political substance and European institutions, it reflected what was happening in Europe and Britain—in economic terms.

Led by an expansion-minded England, Continental Europe was moving into a period of extraordinary trade liberalization, providing the first example of a virtually free-trade zone extending from England to the Continent and eastward as far as Czarist Russia. Despite recessions and conflicts, such as the Franco-Prussian War, the European trading and monetary system was to become increasingly integrated and was to remain so until the outbreak of World War I. Some economic historians have concluded that trade relations among Western powers up to 1913 were freer than in the mid-1970s. "Before the First World War, there existed a world economic region, whose center was in Europe," commented a leading French historian.[9]

To be sure, as Europe and America entered the industrial era, customs barriers were deliberately raised high to protect new industries, but they were stable. Determined to protect homegrown industries, roughly eighty European cartels were organized in such sectors as steel, chemicals, oil, and textiles; transport costs were kept deliberately high in a fiercely competitive, nationalistic environment. Prussia, under the leadership of Bismarck, was, in the meantime, pursuing establishment of its own common market. Building on the Zollverein, established in 1834, this was Bismarck's vehicle for uniting Germany's divided states and, in the process, building a modernized and prosperous Second Reich, as it became known. By 1871, elimination of internal barriers and close economic ties resulted in a Prussian-dominated free-trade area encompassing not only modern Germany but the French regions of Alsace and Lorraine, brought under German occupation, which lasted until Germany's defeat in World War I.

Similarly, a decade earlier, England, which was by far the most open and liberal of Western economies, and a protectionist France had signed a trade agreement aimed at reducing French duties to a maximum rate of 25 percent within five years, while substantially lowering duties on French products, such as wines and luxury goods. At the insistence of France's leader Napoleon III, determined to stimulate recalcitrant, inward-looking French businessmen, similar agreements were signed with—and later among—nine European countries, all containing the most-favored-nation clause. This clause, still in use by the world's trading nations, binds a signatory to apply to its partner any lower rate of import duties it might grant to imports from some other country.

But this was only part of what was being called "Europe's New Economic Area," a name revived more than a century later by the European Community to describe the combined areas of the twelve-nation Common Market, plus the seven-nation European Free Trade Association, known as EFTA, including Norway, Sweden, Finland, Iceland, Switzerland, Liechtenstein, and Austria, as well as several Eastern European countries seeking EC membership.

In other words, Hugo's vision of a united Europe was already reality in several key economic aspects: capital circulated freely; Czarist bonds, for example, were successfully floated throughout Europe until the Russian Bolsheviks seized power in 1917. Currencies were freely convertible into gold, creating something of a common European exchange-rate mechanism, which was operated through flexible, informal arrangements between governments and central banks. In 1865, a fledgling monetary union was established among seven major West European countries, including Switzerland, plus Rumania. Balance-of-payments problems were minor. There were virtually no restrictions on movement of laborers and white-collar professionals.

Visas were suspended during much of this period, and for those who could afford it the Orient Express made its inaugural voyage October 4, 1883, and soon went into regular service—chugging out of Paris Tuesday and Friday evenings, arriving early in the morning in Constantinople eighty-two hours later. Although a far cry from modern high-speed trains, this first *grand express international* represented a time saving of some thirty hours compared to other available trains, and, like its modern, luxurious successor version, the Orient Express was generally booked solid.[10]

Looking westward, in a first, modern "leap across the Atlantic," English and Scottish industrialists and bankers expanded freely into a booming, capital-starved post–Civil War America; foreign capital as well as labor were actively cultivated and recruited. Scottish investment trusts, for example, played a key role in financing the building of American railroads and establishment of large cattle ranches in Texas. Meantime, other Europeans, led by the Germans, were moving eastward with investments and technology. Thus, well before the outbreak of World War I, Werner von Siemens, one of the founding brothers of the giant German electrical company bearing their name, designed and built long-range overland telegraph lines, laid deep-sea cables, and built plants in Poland, the Baltic states, and Russia.[11] In those days, Siemens operated out of three headquarters: London, Berlin, and St. Petersburg.

Today, executives at Siemens's modern headquarters in Munich delight in telling visitors that during this earlier period the giant company's sales in England far surpassed those in Germany and that once again, with Germany united, the company is looking eastward for markets in such huge, lucrative areas as state-of-the-art telecommunications and transportation systems and electronics products. Similarly, the large Frankfurt-based Dresdner Bank made a splash in the European media December 19, 1989, by announcing plans to reopen a major branch office in the East German city of Dresden, where the bank was founded in 1872. The move was only one among hundreds by leading West German banks and companies seeking to reestablish markets and business ties severed by the division of Germany following the end of World War II.

In some ways, the late nineteenth century was the precursor of the 1992, or the Cockfield, program—a European Community, dominated by Germany economically, while integrating its economies and banking systems and institutions into a loosely united single market. The 1878 edition of Baedeker's guide to Paris noted that the currencies of Belgium, Switzerland, Italy, and Greece were the same as France's, and the "obnoxious passport system was revived after the war of 1870–71, but has again been abolished." But as the British Economist magazine, tongue in cheek, noted: "Euro-harmonization had not yet reached the railroad clocks," because, the magazine said, quoting Baedeker, "the Belgian time is eight minutes, the German 25 minutes, and the Swiss 26 minutes in advance of French railway time."[12] Europe, with its distinct, sovereign habits and cultures would not integrate or harmonize soon, or easily.

The outbreak of World War I in 1914 dashed all hopes of maintaining Europe's unity, which had become strained and explosive. Subsequently, following Germany's defeat in 1918, protectionist measures proliferated in the 1920s, and yet, despite the growing threat of recession, the goal of establishing a United States of Europe remained alive. Édouard Herriot, for example, who became premier of France in 1924, urged creation of a West European union within the fledgling League of Nations, which would include England. French Foreign Minister Aristide Briand, who later succeeded Herriot, called for a European federative government, amid a proliferation of Pan-European movements among other victorious allies.

Belgium and Luxembourg, for example, established a free-trade area in 1921 modeled on the Zollverein, which was another step toward monetary union. These movements were to disappear quickly in the 1930s, with widespread unemployment, repatriation of American capital, worsening protectionism, devaluations, high inflation, and, finally, economic collapse.

The next chapter in Europe's experience with unity was already being diligently, ruthlessly prepared in Germany by Adolf Hitler and his allies. It would lead to the establishment of the powerful, destructive Third Reich, whose main goal in the early 1930s was already being uttered by the Nazi party faithful: *"Erst Europa, dann die Welt."* First Europe, then the world.

A PLAN FOR WORLD DOMINATION

Alongside the autobahn, some fifteen kilometers south of Munich, nestled among pine trees and flat farmland, rises a complex of modern buildings, heavily guarded by electronic gates and armed guards. A gate sign containing three black letters—MBB—provides the only hint of what goes on inside. The M stands for the family name of Willy Messerschmitt, the brilliant, flamboyant German airplane designer, who helped develop the Nazi Luftwaffe's most advanced fighters and bombers, and whose firm was gradually absorbed by Messerschmitt-Bölkow-Blohm, today West Germany's largest aerospace company and a division of the Daimler-Benz group. The scale models of planes on display in the MBB headquarters building recall, chillingly, how far Hitler had sought to extend his Third Reich not only eastward but westward and more specifically to the United States and Latin America.

For example, although it only flew fifty-two times in prototype form—in late 1942—one of Messerschmitt's favorite projects was a four-engine bomber developed on Hitler's orders, known as the Me 264. With an estimated range of fifteen thousand kilometers, this strategic bomber and others being designed were seen by Hitler as the means to bomb the United States into defeat and submission. Military experts and historians, scoffing at the Luftwaffe's chances for success and at the virtual impossibility of invading America, generally agree that had designers of the Me 264s been able to resolve the problem of refueling, they could have hit targets as far inland as the Great Lakes region.

They note that the distance from Berlin to New York is slightly under 6,800 kilometers, and that the prototype had successfully completed a total of seventy test flights. The designers had started work on adding two engines to avoid refueling. Captured Luftwaffe maps, made public in East Germany in 1972, showed that the targets included Boston, New York, and Washington, D.C., and industrial sites around the Great Lakes, notably Detroit.

The Messerschmitt bomber project was kept alive until the final days of World War II, reflecting what historians, such as William Shirer, have exhaustively described—namely, that Hitler was the latest of Europe's obsessive, visionary leaders who, by military might and oppression, succeeded in unifying Western Europe, and was convinced he could build on that unity for world domination.[13]

Although no single blueprint was ever published, it became clear from captured documents, speeches, and testimony in postwar Nazi trials that Hitler, like Napoleon before him, sought to dominate a vast area extending from the Atlantic to Russia, whose resources would be tapped for Germany alone—then numbering about 80 million people. Altogether, it would have meant a total of some 300 million people under total Nazi domination in what its leaders described as Europe's New Order, or "Fortress Europe." The latter term, its origins forgotten by many, resurfaced during the mid-1980s to describe the European Community's drift toward protectionist trade and investment policies.

The role of German industrialists, architects, and bankers who helped Hitler and profited from forced labor imported from conquered areas has been well documented, and I will not dwell on it here. Major German companies and banks, many today still bearing their original names, helped finance the Nazi buildup, starting in the early 1930s. They played a key role in buttressing Hitler's expansion, benefiting from captive markets, manpower, and ruthlessly captured human and financial resources. As Germany's prewar economy boomed and unemployment fell, admiring foreigners, including Americans, reported that Hitler's New Order appeared to be succeeding brilliantly, in sharp contrast to widespread economic depression spreading elsewhere in the West. Few people at the time had the slightest premonition of how the Third Reich would end. My mother was among those who sensed the emerging catastrophe.

LEAVING FOR AMERICA

A shiny, black replica of Hitler's convertible Mercedes limousine was one of my favorite toys. I remember carrying it to our last meeting in the summer of 1939 with my maternal grandfather, who was living in a country farmhouse nestled in the forested, hilly countryside near Vienna. He was a very devout Jew, but I didn't find that out until much later. My mother, convinced Germany was heading for disaster, told her father she planned on giving up her comfortable life in Berlin and that she would soon move to America with my younger brother and me. Furious, tapping his head with his index finger, he told my mother she was crazy. What would she do there? We left him shaking, puzzled, and angry about his headstrong daughter. I remember, somewhat sadly, saying goodbye, but also delighted that I had my Hitler car with me, and how tightly I held it.

The possibility never occurred to my grandfather, whose family owned a textile business in Melsungen near Kassel, and had served as an army captain in World War I, that within three years he and other members of our family would be arrested and sent to the Theresienstadt concentration camp in Czechoslovakia. Meantime, in Berlin my father, who also refused to consider leaving, told the American consul while my mother was applying for our visas that his own father, a former Prussian general, would turn over in his grave if he were to leave Germany. He, too, was convinced that the approaching war would end victoriously for Nazi Germany in six months and that we would return to Berlin. After all, he argued, Hitler would soon control all of Continental Europe through a system of militarily dominated satellite states, allied with Italy's Fascist leader, Benito Mussolini, and that, he said, was only a beginning.

NAZIS IN AMERICA

Less known at the time were Hitler's more nebulous, but related, plans for extending Nazi power across the Atlantic to the United States and Latin America. How? "Through bombing, and then, somehow, by uprisings led by fifth columns and German agents the Nazis were counting on—Nazi organizations, sympathizers, and local German populations in the United States, Chile, Argentina, and Brazil," said Jochen Thies, a West German journalist and scholar, who wrote a well-documented, highly readable book on Hitler's plan for world domination.[14] "It was madness, of course, but that was the idea—uprisings in the Western Hemisphere . . . that is what Hitler was counting on once the bombing of U.S. cities had succeeded," Thies told me, adding a bizarre note: Hitler's plans for America were partly inspired by Orson Welles's radio adaptation of H. G. Wells's *War of the Worlds*, broadcast to shocked radio audiences in America in 1938.[15]

I recall vividly our arrival in New York City in late March 1940, after sailing across the Atlantic on Italy's magnificent flagship, the *Conte di Savoia*, and the spectacular, sunlit view of the Manhattan skyline. Quickly we were escorted by boat across New York Harbor to Ellis Island, a gray, depressing place, compared to the fun life of luxury aboard ship. I recall shortly after arriving gazing for hours at the huge American flag hanging in the main hall. I had never seen one before. I complained to a guard in halting English about the tasteless quality of American food. He firmly assured me I would get to like it. I did.

Once cleared by health and immigration officials, and settled in suburban Yonkers, New York, among American friends, we caught a glimpse of how deeply the Nazis had actually penetrated America. My mother was repeatedly solicited by the German-American Bund, the quasi-military front organization of the Nazis in North America, founded in 1936. The Bund in those days was regularly sponsoring parades of its members in the Yorkville district of Manhattan and spectacular rallies at Madison Square Garden, which regularly attracted twenty thousand people. But these events, which, of course, we never attended, were only the visible, heavily publicized tip of the iceberg.[16]

The U.S. Immigration & Naturalization Service estimated the active membership of the Bund in 1937 at about 350,000 persons. The Justice Department figures were considerably lower. About 60 percent of Bund members were from low-income families and about half had remained German citizens after leaving Germany at the end of World War I. Scattered throughout the United States, and organized into "departments," women's clubs, and business associations, the Bund also maintained its *Ordnungsdienst,* an elite armed security unit resembling Nazi Storm Troopers, which were kept under close surveillance by the Federal Bureau of Investigation, particularly after the Bund was disbanded following America's entry into World War II in 1941.

I recall FBI agents regularly visiting our modest apartment in Yonkers during the early 1940s, checking to see if, for example, we had secretly installed a short-wave radio. Because we were considered "enemy aliens" until we obtained American citizenship in 1945, such radios were strictly forbidden. I wanted to change my first name to Bill, but my mother talked me out of it.

AIMING AT LATIN AMERICA AND RUSSIA

Meantime, in the Southern Hemisphere, particularly in Argentina, Brazil, and Chile, where Hitler as early as 1934 claimed Germany had "rights," German communities had also grown increasingly militant, supporting both Hitler and Mussolini. More than sixty thousand first-generation Argentinians of German origin were living in Buenos Aires alone, and many more settled in Rio de Janeiro, Santiago, and other South American cities.[17] German schools and cultural centers flourished throughout Latin America, generously subsidized by the Nazis. Later, Argentina's military dictator, Juan Domingo Perón, boasted that he had learned German in order to read Hitler's *Mein Kampf* in the original. His uniforms were modeled on those worn by Mussolini and Hitler. Understandably, Nazi penetration in Latin America raised considerable fear in the Roosevelt administration that Hitler would soon turn his military attention to Latin America. Nazi U-boats were regularly sighted off the Atlantic coast, while many other types of Nazi naval vessels operated menacingly throughout the South Atlantic.

Hitler's greatest single blunder, most historians agree, was his decision to turn away from Britain, the Mediterranean, and the Western Hemisphere and, instead, invade Russia—on the morning of June 22, 1941. This date, as Shirer noted, was the same day Napoleon crossed the Niemen River in 1812 en route to Moscow for a rendezvous that would also prove disastrous for him and his army.

Item: At the very edge of Moscow, alongside the Moscow-Leningrad highway, stands a stark, oversized, black steel antitank barrier. It marks the area where, in the dead of the 1941 winter, a fiercely determined Red Army turned back German troops. The rout not only saved Moscow but began the process leading to the defeat of the Third Reich. It had come into being January 30, 1933, and, according to Hitler, was destined to endure "another" thousand years, a reference to the Holy Roman Empire, which until its dissolution by Napoleon in 1806 had lasted just over a millennium. I stood at the Moscow monument on a balmy June day in 1989, en route to Sheremetevo airport, asking myself what might have happened if Hitler had followed the advice of, among others, Admiral Erich Raeder, his chief naval adviser and a brilliant strategist.

Raeder, as Shirer explains in his monumental work on the Third Reich, had already concluded, well before Germany's invasion of Russia, that British, U.S., and Free French forces would attempt to establish a military staging point in Northwest Africa. Therefore, he encouraged Hitler to take the area, starting with Gibraltar, urging that the Nazi effort be directed at driving Britain from the Mediterranean, while using the Canary, Cape Verde, and Azores islands as staging areas for bombing attacks on the United States, relying on the new Messerschmitt Me 264 bombers being developed.

Had Hitler followed Raeder's advice and that of other strategists, there might never have been a Soviet victory monument near Moscow. As Thies and another contemporary German author, Ralph Giordano, have noted, Hitler also planned to colonize Africa, starting at Gibraltar, and then move across the Mediterranean and southward to the Sahara.[18] Thies reports that Hitler had already ordered the training of crack marine units for duty in Africa, that light tanks were under development; language training programs were underway and dictionaries had been prepared in Swahili, the *lingua franca* of East Africa. The final stage of the plan, according to Giordano's best-selling book *If Hitler Had Won the War*, would have been to join Japan in blockading and bombing the United States with the new strategic bombers.

But the combination of refusal by Spain's dictator, Franco, to go along with Nazi plans to seize Gibraltar and Hitler's obsessive determination to attack Russia ended plans for bombing the United States and mounting a Mediterranean campaign. Thus the way was clear two years later for the allied invasions of Algeria and Morocco—and, ultimately, the ending of World War II.

I clearly recall my sense of shock in 1947 when, back in Europe, I set eyes on the war-scarred cities, the widespread use of rationing cards, the rubble, the sense of recent death and destruction, and how, with tremendous relief, we were reunited with my emaciated but good-spirited grandfather, who had turned up in a sanitarium in Lugano, Switzerland. He settled in Kreuzlingen, a scenic Swiss town on Lake Constance, where he enjoyed a new life for several more decades with his devoted Swiss companion, Claire Hurlimann, never to return to live in his native Germany. He rarely talked to me about life in Theresienstadt, and when he did, it was about how they managed without much food, or how he and fellow prisoners discussed philosophy and music to keep up their spirits.

Only after his death did Claire tell me about the extraordinary circumstances surrounding his release in February 1945, months before the war ended, confirmed by research in the United States by my cousin, Hans-Ephraimson Abt. My grandfather was among 1,200 Jews released by the Nazis under a secret agreement between Berlin, desperate for Swiss francs, and Jewish groups in the United States, determined to save as many Jews as possible even if that meant paying. The Nazis were also hopeful that what they described as "humanitarian gestures" might help them in the event the war was lost. A plan to establish a fund of five million Swiss francs never resulted in any payment to the Nazis because the U.S. Treasury Department refused. Washington's approach was to promise, but not pay.

The Nazis proposed the offer to inmates at Theresienstadt, which still stands north of Prague, and my grandfather was among those who, suspiciously, accepted. Thus, he and his fellow prisoners, now free, arrived by train in Kreuzlingen. The event was the subject of several articles in the Swiss press published February 8, 1945. But he never talked about the conditions of his release, nor about my grandmother who died in the camp, nor about his brother, who refused the Nazi offer, and I never asked.

My father, who never left Germany and remained a banker, remarried during the war and settled in Frankfurt.

These are but fragmentary, mundane recollections of one who survived, thanks to a courageous mother. But memories are among the vestiges of one of the most cataclysmic periods in modern history, which left more than fifty million people dead, two-thirds of them civilians.

HITLER'S LEGACY

Today there is little left to see of the Third Reich, and what remains is grim and chilling, conjuring up visions of horror, violence, and death: rusting, crumbling bunkers, the partly submerged hulks of American landing craft, tanks, and heavy German fortifications that still dot the French coasts of the English Channel and the Atlantic beaches; neat and well-kept U.S. and allied military cemeteries throughout Europe; sites of former Nazi concentration camps now converted into generously documented museums. There are also occasional public trials, or disclosures about former Nazis; the steady publishing of books about the life of Hitler and the Nazi period, reinforced by periodic surveys, which show German public opinion is by no means negative about Hitler.

One example: an elderly, proud German bartender at the Dreesen Hotel in suburban Bad Godesberg near Bonn, overlooking the Rhine, relished displaying his personal photo album, showing Hitler's frequent visits to the hotel before the war. "I used to feel uncomfortable about showing these, but no more," he declared during my last visit, proudly pulling the album out from under the bar counter, pointing to Hitler happily gazing out to the Rhine from the hotel's balcony. "I don't know about a Fourth Reich, but the Third was real, and we certainly were part of it, yes, even proud."

A Fourth Reich? Every time that phrase is uttered the Nazi period immediately springs to mind. The term was revived deliberately early in 1990 by critics of the Kohl government and by some of Germany's suspicious allies, notably the French and the Poles, fearful of a more powerful, nationalistic and unified East and West Germany. The chancellor repeatedly stressed this notion was absurd, even as Berlin stepped up lobbying to reestablish the former imperial capital as the revitalized political and cultural capital of the New Germany. As most observers now agree, Hitler's vision of Europe's future collapsed in the fiery ruins of Berlin, twelve years and four months after it began.

Thus, it was the shortest-lived of the three empires and by any measure the most savagely oppressive and destructive, not only for Germany but for a vast region stretching west to east from the Atlantic to the Volga River in Russia, and from the northern tip of Norway southward to the Mediterranean Sea. Hardly anyone I have interviewed believed it would, or could, be revived.

Yet, while a full-fledged revival appears remote, consider the following scene: a cavernous, noisy beer hall near Munich, a far-right politician and former sergeant in the Waffen-SS, Hitler's elite force, begins to address a boisterous crowd of several thousand supporters: "We are proud to be Germans. Now it is our turn," he shouts. It was mid-June 1989, not 1929, and the man was not Hitler but Franz Schoenhuber, the leader of the far-right Republican party, which had just won 7.6 percent of West Germany's votes in elections to the European Parliament in Strasbourg, to become Germany's fourth-largest party.

His hair closely cropped, his hands gesticulating vigorously, Schoenhuber has dissociated himself from his Nazi past, asserting repeatedly that the Third Reich was wrong, but proudly boasts about having volunteered for the Waffen-SS. "We are still always being beaten around the ears about our past. This must stop. Today's young Germans are just as innocent of what happened then as the sons and daughters of the Americans who committed the crimes at Hiroshima and Nagasaki," he was quoted as saying early in 1989. In a long interview with the *Wall Street Journal,* he provided a blunt answer to the question whether the European Community wasn't a venue for the revival of a new German empire.[19]

Schoenhuber's answer: "My God! I don't like the words 'German empire.' We had some bad experience with 'German empire.' We lost two wars—under a royal empire, under the Kaiser, and in a more devastating experience with the criminal empire of Mr. Hitler. We want no empire, we want only to see our national interests among others sensibly represented." Despite such comments, the Republicans talked enthusiastically about the "Germany of the Borders of 1937," meaning a return to the borders of the pre–World War II period, including East Germany and large portions of Poland.

By the time Kohl was overwhelmingly reelected chancellor December 2, 1990, not only had the Polish border issue been settled, but the Republicans had been decimated—they obtained only 2.1 percent of the total vote. But their activities, meantime, have shifted eastward to East Germany, where the Republicans established friendly ties with similar extreme right-wing parties, making similar outlandish claims. They actively joined in as hundreds of East German neo-Nazis, known in German as "skinheads," goose-stepped through Leipzig on February 5, 1990, shouting "Sieg Heil," smashing windows and disrupting a regular weekly demonstration for German unity. It was only a beginning.

At the time of Kohl's reelection victory, the Bonn government estimated that the number of neo-Nazis in what was formerly East Germany stood at thirty thousand and was growing. Many were identified as teenagers, who used Nazi slogans, to riot at soccer matches, and to commit street crimes in order, as Marc Fisher of the *Washington Post* noted, "to rebel against the new society." Most of the neo-Nazis, as in West Germany, have solid social backgrounds. Their fathers are often civil servants, teachers, professionals. Grouped in organizations with names like Fascist Storm Youth and Hitler Youth Schönfeld, referring to Nazi units, they dress in black and brown Nazi uniforms, singing Nazi songs. In the summer of 1991, painted swastikas appeared throughout the united Germany, notably in such cities as Berlin, Dresden, and even Bonn.

Although anti-Semitism and violent nationalism have resurfaced in Czechoslovakia, other eastern European countries, and Russia, it is the frightening fascination with Hitler in Germany that worries some political observers, citing his surprising popularity. A poll commissioned by *Der Spiegel* magazine, marking the centennial of his birth, April 20, 1889, showed that 25 percent of West German voters have either a positive or neutral view of Hitler, and that while only 3 percent of respondents said the Nazi period was "clearly positive," 43 percent thought it had both good and bad aspects; 38 percent said that Hitler would have been a great statesmen had it not been for his extermination of the Jews and starting World War II.

Meet Adam Michnik. historian, editor-in-chief of the Solidarity newspaper, *Gazeta Wyborcza,* Poland's first independent opposition daily, elected to the lower house of the new Polish parliament in June 1989. Chain-smoking, sipping a beer, stuttering slightly, he explains that he spent a total of six years in prisons and internment camps for his political activities and that he had just breakfasted with the man responsible for his suffering. "The man" was Poland's President, General Wojciech Jaruzelski. It was Sunday, February 4, 1990, and we were in Davos, Switzerland, for the annual World Economic Forum; both Polish leaders had been invited to speak about the New Europe. Jaruzelski had just reminded his audience that history had not been kind to Poland and that "we are still marked . . . by the past."

Michnik, born in 1946 and a product of postwar Europe, went further, warning of a resurgence of "Nazi elements," racism, and extreme rightist groups in East Germany, Czechoslovakia, and western Russia. "One of our fears is that Schoenhuber and his followers and allies in East Germany will dominate the unification process," he said during an interview. "There is uncontrolled chauvinism at work in many areas of Eastern Europe . . . yes, reunification [of East and West Germany] is inevitable, but many of us fear the new and dangerous forces at work." But, he quickly added, the general, his former enemy, was correct in telling twelve hundred business and government leaders from around the world attending the Davos meeting that "the New Europe must be different." And that, Michnik emphasized, meant looking to the West for leadership and help, more specifically and above all to the Common Market. Throughout 1990 and 1991, the Community's blue and gold star-studded flag was often seen fluttering alongside those of national flags in street demonstrations in Prague, Warsaw, Budapest, and Ljubljana, the capital of Slovenia, a rebellious Yugoslav republic.

STARTING AGAIN WITH THE "FATHER OF EUROPE"

If one person is to be credited with setting the course of the New Europe in this century, it surely would be, according to wide consensus, the slightly built, balding, mustached Frenchman Jean Monnet. From 1943 onward, Monnet, then an official in the exiled French liberation movement, who had served as deputy secretary general of the League of Nations following World War I, was convinced that Western Europe needed to undertake concrete plans and programs in order to avoid future conflicts. A brilliant organizer, with an extraordinary flair for convincing people that his ideas made sense, Monnet had already begun drafting plans for relaunching Europe before the defeat of Nazi Germany.

In a message to De Gaulle, Churchill, and other allied leaders, delivered August 5, 1943, Monnet declared that the warring nations of Europe, in peacetime, would be "too narrow, too small, to assure their citizens' prosperity . . . they [will] need larger markets . . . meaning that the states of Europe should form a federation, or a 'European entity,' encompassing a common economic unit."[20]

As we saw in Chapter 1, Monnet's first major achievement—it was essentially his idea—was the establishment of the European Coal and Steel Community. Indeed, when Robert Schuman explained the plan to newsmen in the Salon de l'Horloge in the French foreign ministry in Paris on May 9, 1950, Monnet was prominently seated to his immediate right.

But far more was involved than simply establishing Europe's first joint organization of the postwar era to manage coal and steel production. The High Authority, its executive headed by Monnet, was the precursor of the contemporary European Community, containing the basic structure of a future, federal European government, or what Monnet called an "embryo." It included the following: a Council of Ministers, coordinating the work of the High Authority and member governments; a Common Assembly, representing national parliaments with powers to fire the High Authority, and finally, a Court of Justice, with seven judges appointed to six-year terms. "With my colleagues, I established Europe's first institution with supranational powers . . . seeking common solutions to common problems," Monnet said later.

Monnet's dream of a peaceful, economically united Europe attained its culmination during glittering ceremonies held in Rome on

March 25, 1957. The occasion was the signing of a treaty establishing what has become known as the Common Market. Following months of difficult, tense negotiations, the six founding member governments of France, Germany, Italy, the Netherlands, Belgium and Luxembourg, expanded the Coal and Steel Community to encompass two new organizations: the European Economic Community and the European Atomic Energy Community, each with its own president. The latter two bodies were headquartered in Brussels on January 1, 1958, with the Court based in Luxembourg. Monnet, who had resigned as head of the Coal and Steel Community in 1954, continued to play a crucial behind-the-scenes role in the negotiations leading up to the signing of the Treaty of Rome, and thus was widely acclaimed as the "Father of Europe."

Eight years later, Monnet and his federalist supporters found themselves embroiled in a bitterly fought crisis, which came to be known as "the battle of the Holy Roman Emperor and the Pope"—conjuring up parallels with Charlemagne and Napoleon. The "emperor" in this case was Charles de Gaulle, then president of France, and the "pope" was a former West German university professor turned diplomat, who had been named the first president of the EEC Commission—Walter Hallstein. The majestic French leader won the battle, to which we shall return shortly. De Gaulle briefly paralyzed much of what some European leaders sought to accomplish, yet without resolving the complex, controversial question: how can Western European governments reconcile the goal of a federated, more politically powerful Europe with the deeply entrenched, grassroots forces of national sovereignty?

ANOTHER SELF-MADE FRENCHMAN

On a grassy hillside overlooking Lake Geneva, just south of Lausanne, Henri Rieben, who worked with Monnet for nearly twenty-five years, was telling me what it was like working with the man about whom President John Kennedy in 1963 said: "Under your inspiration, Europe has moved closer to unity in less than twenty years than it had done before in a thousand." I raised the subject of Napoleon and wondered if Monnet bore any resemblance. Gesturing toward an isolated, majestic oak tree, which dominated the field in which we were standing, Rieben, a professor, chuckled and explained that

Napoleon, en route to Italy, once reviewed his troops near the spot where we were talking. "What a contrast!" said Rieben. "Napoleon building Europe by domination and force, Monnet by persuasion and intelligence."

Monnet, like Delors, never attended a French university or a *grande école* and began working immediately after graduating from high school. And like Delors, Monnet began learning his father's business at the age of sixteen—in his case, trading in cognac from the Charente region of southwestern France. Slight, delicate, with a low, intimate voice that became metallic when raised, Monnet by temperament and training was the total opposite of previous European leaders we have mentioned; one can imagine him getting on well with Charlemagne, but uneasy with Napoleon and revolted by Hitler.

Determined, tenacious, a brilliant administrator, but modest, low-key, and always polite, Monnet, surprisingly, never aspired to a career in politics. Common Market buffs wonder why, for example, he never sought elected office following his three-year stint as president of the High Authority. Rieben, a professor at the University of Lausanne and director of a studies center dedicated to Monnet's life, explained that the reason may well have been his voice. "He thought about a political career a great deal after the war, but he did not have a strong voice that carried. . . . He realized that, partly explaining why he avoided a 'grand' career in politics," Rieben said. Monnet had grown up in an era in which addressing public meetings mattered for those seeking political careers.[21]

Nevertheless, Monnet's political voice—expressed mainly through writings—attracted the admiration and praise of world leaders with whom he became friends, including, among others, Churchill, Harold Macmillan, Kennedy, and Konrad Adenauer. For Monnet's close associates, such as Rieben, François Fontaine, and the prolific economist and writer, Pierre Uri, who also became an adviser to Mitterrand, Delors is probably the only contemporary European leader comparable to Monnet in stature, influence, and dedication to the establishment of an economically and politically united Europe. Separated by several decades and different contexts, such comparisons have obvious limitations.

THE BUILDUP TO CRISIS

Wartime destruction had created basic problems for European planners, which completely dominated the immediate postwar period and its priorities. These ranged from reestablishing democratic institutions to modernizing devitalized economies that were still paralyzed by the power of entrenched industrial and banking monopolies, inefficiency, and waste. Theodore White cited one particularly outspoken and perceptive American businessman helping the reconstruction effort in France who complained that "they've got the boards of these plants loaded up with marquises and counts, and all of them are tied together in one big combine. They're so goddamned cartelized, they wouldn't know how to go out and get business—even if it was there."[22]

No single reconstruction effort dominated the period as much as the offer of massive American aid to revive Europe's industry and agriculture made by Secretary of State George C. Marshall at Harvard University on June 5, 1947. From it blossomed not only funding but the first, visionary hopes for a peacefully united and prosperous Europe, amid considerable confusion and suspicion among Europeans and Americans, questioning what it would change in established European habits and structures. The Soviets, as is often forgotten, were also discussing their participation in the Marshall Plan.

But the Soviet delegation to meetings establishing the Marshall Plan, headed by the venerable foreign minister Vyacheslav Molotov, after six days of talks in Paris—embittered, convinced the Marshall Plan was but a plot aimed at U.S. domination of Europe—walked out and returned to Moscow. Even Andrei Gromyko, a more flexible and open-minded foreign minister, later described the plan as "expansionist," linked to the establishment of NATO two years later, and an instrument of the Cold War that was getting underway.[23]

Virtually all of Western and Central Europe, as White grimly noted, gave the impression of being "mortally ill." However, Western Europe's economies began reviving around June 1948, as the Marshall Plan swung into action and the disbursement of funds and loans began. American headquarters was established in borrowed offices on the second floor of a now fully restored American Embassy annex in Paris—the eighteenth-century Hotel Talleyrand, and formerly a Rothschild family mansion. The regular meeting point for the plan's American administrators was the bar of the nearby Crillon Hotel, which, like the Talleyrand, is located on the Place de la Concorde, where one official, or "an anonymous bard" as White described him, came up with the following ditty: "Reconstruction, integration, dollar shortage, liberalization, off with these old fashioned ties! Now's the time to harmonize."[24] The ditty always reminded me of similar lines composed, decades later, by EC officials who poked fun at their version of "harmonization," a greatly overworked concept contained in the EC's 1992 program.

The Marshall Plan, which funneled a total of about $13.3 billion in 1947 dollars to Western Europe (estimated at around $60 billion in 1991 dollars), was also the first in a series of U.S.-inspired measures aimed at gently forcing Europe to turn its back on prewar economic nationalism and work for the development of a large, liberalized, integrated market in Western Europe. One major result was the establishment in 1948 of the Organization for European Economic Cooperation, the OEEC, which was headquartered in another former Rothschild mansion in the 16th arrondissement of Paris. The OEEC's primary mission was assuring "efficient use" of Marshall Plan aid, which meant implementing specific plans for the opening of European borders, lifting exchange controls, removing trade and investment barriers, adopting modern accounting methods, and the like. Its members included nineteen West European countries, Turkey, and the United States, which remained its predominant driving force.

Some American and West European leaders also viewed the OEEC as a future political body, which might someday provide a permanent link among the Atlantic powers under a new, politically binding cooperative and consultative arrangement. But Britain, among others, strongly resisted giving the OEEC any enforcement powers and so it foundered. In 1960, the agency was transformed, and evolved into the Organization for Economic Cooperation and Development—the OECD. Operating from the same headquarters, the Château de la Muette, the OECD is an influential, highly respected, intergovernmental coordinating agency, aimed at promoting economic growth of member countries. It comprises twenty-four member governments from North America, Western Europe, and the Pacific region, including Japan, Australia, and New Zealand.

Meantime, other fledgling European integration efforts, long since forgotten by most people, also cropped up: France and Italy in 1949 tried establishing a tariff union called Francita; France and the

Benelux (Belgium, the Netherlands and Luxembourg) created something called Finebel that was supposed to emerge into a broader economic and financial association of Western Europe. Britain and Scandinavian countries established Uniscan in 1950. At about the same time, France and Italy considered joining and calling it Frita-lux—a "ridiculous" name, said Monnet; some half-jokingly said it conjured up the image of a Mexican potato chip. Gradually, thanks to Monnet and his allies, European integration efforts centered on the creation of the powers for the emerging Common Market and gradually moving members toward the goal clearly specified in the founding Rome Treaty signed in 1957: establishing a political federation. And there the troubles, which had been simmering, began.

THE "EMPTY CHAIR" TACTIC

By the middle of 1965, the EEC, as it was still known, was about to be plunged into its first major political crisis. Monnet was already bitterly at loggerheads with de Gaulle, who steadfastly refused to accept the idea that economic union should lead to political union. The general, whose hostility to Monnet and the EEC Commission in Brussels had been growing steadily, was already planning to withdraw France from NATO's integrated command. He did so the following year. According to John Newhouse, one of the most astute American observers who chronicled the crisis, de Gaulle was ready to "hatch a crisis from the first suitable issue which presented itself."[25] He did not have to wait long.

Confronting de Gaulle was Walter Hallstein, former law professor at the University of Frankfurt, who at the time Monnet met him was serving Adenauer as a state secretary in the ministry of foreign affairs in Bonn. Later, Monnet was to say that he was drawn to Hallstein because he was a leader with "political vision." However, once settled into the Commission presidency, Hallstein quickly developed a reputation for being intellectually brilliant but haughty, overbearing, and excessively impressed with the power of his job, which he planned to extend into hitherto forbidden, potentially explosive areas.

For example, in mid-March 1965, Hallstein visited the United States and, because President Lyndon Johnson wanted to display publicly his pro-European stance, Hallstein was not only put up in Blair House, the VIP mansion across the street from the White House in downtown Washington, but he held publicized talks with Robert McNamara, the U.S. defense secretary. Since the EEC Commission had no authority to act in defense matters, that visit alone was enough to infuriate de Gaulle. In addition, perhaps lacking sound advice, Hallstein was quoted by American reporters as saying that the EEC Commission president was "a kind of prime minister of Europe." Such comments, when they reached his desk, only further angered de Gaulle and paved the way for what was coming.

"It seems clear," wrote Newhouse, "that 1965–66 was fated to be the time of the decisive assault that would send spinning into irreversible decline the principle of integration, whether Atlantic or European."[26]

A central issue then—as now—was the political role of the Commission in Brussels and to what degree its powers should be expanded in relation to the Council of Ministers and the European Parliament. Hallstein was determined to increase the powers of the Commission as part of a complex package presented to the six EEC member governments, which would also have increased the voting powers of smaller members and of the European Parliament. Majority-rule voting in the Council also was due to come into effect January 1, 1966. Finally, Hallstein declared in the spring of 1965 that the unification of Europe was a prerequisite for Atlantic cooperation—not an alternative—and that consequently he planned moving the Common Market into the fields of foreign policy and defense. Negotiations aimed at resolving the issues contained in the Hallstein package went badly from the beginning.

Tense, exhausting talks went well into the night of June 30. To widespread shocked disbelief, de Gaulle's lanky, white-haired, and aristocratic foreign minister Couve de Murville told a news conference that a serious crisis had begun and that within several days France would withdraw its permanent representative from Brussels. It was the beginning of an unprecedented action: France would boycott all Community institutions in retaliation against the Hallstein proposals, determined to bring the EEC to a standstill.

This was the "empty chair" tactic of de Gaulle—paralyzing the organization until he got his way. In September, the EEC, its decision-making capacity blocked, de Gaulle denounced the Commission as "a technocracy, in large part foreign controlled, encroaching upon French democracy." He also emphasized that he would never accept majority-rule voting in the Council of Ministers. "He was not responding to the appeal of his five partners to return to his place in the institutions," Monnet concluded glumly.[27]

Six months after the crisis had begun, fearful of a loss to France of all that had been accomplished since the signing of the Rome Treaty, Paris agreed to a series of German proposals, which evolved into the Luxembourg Compromise. That complex formula mentioned majority voting as a principle only, urging its use wherever possible unless—and this was the key phrase—"the vital interests" of one or several member states were placed in doubt. The agreement thus assured the right of veto by any EEC member.

But, in suggesting a more flexible approach, the accord opened the way for qualified majority voting in the Council of Ministers two decades later. Monnet described it as "an ambiguous arrangement." In other words, de Gaulle had won. Hallstein and his fellow commissioners were, in Monnet's words, "sacrificed," meaning their power was weakened, even though they continued serving until the end of their term in 1967, the year in which the EEC, through streamlining, became known as the EC.

The crisis of 1965 marked the beginning of a period of chronic weakness for Community institutions, which was to continue for nearly two decades, as we shall see in more detail in Chapter 8. Major achievements were, however, realized, such as the establishment of the European Monetary System in 1979, which most observers agree would never have materialized had it not been for the dedicated work of two heads of government who knew and liked each other and who both were former finance ministers: Helmut Schmidt of West Germany and Valéry Giscard d'Estaing of France. Not until the 1984 EC summit meeting in Fontainebleau, as we shall see in Chapter 3, did the Common Market find a new approach, momentum, and a pragmatic EC Commission president to transform the new ideas into reality.

At around the same time, other new European initiatives and programs, totally independent of EC institutions, were beginning to make their mark on world opinion, sounding protectionist warning bells in other Western capitals and in Japan. Despite institutional weaknesses, Western European industry and political leaders were showing the first signs of moving, determined to reverse what had become universally known as "Eurosclerosis."

Economics Come First:
The Rise of Europe, Inc.

If the European Community can really act together, it
may well improve its position in the world, both
militarily and economically. If it does not—which, given
human nature, is the more plausible outcome—its
relative decline seems destined to continue."

—PAUL KENNEDY
The Rise and Fall of the Great Powers

MOVING AGAINST "EUROSCLEROSIS"

When contemporary historian Paul Kennedy wrote those lines in his
authoritative book on the world's great powers, there was much to
justify his pessimism and questioning of Europe's weakened capacity
to regain its postwar levels of economic growth and success. He
certainly was correct in also observing at the time his book appeared
in 1988 that little progress had been made on deregulating hidebound airline and financial services, that growth was stagnating,
unemployment had reached record levels, and that the European
Community, when it came to policy-making, was far more "splintered" than any individual member state.[1]

Agreeing with Kennedy was the man who coined the term "Eurosclerosis," German Professor Herbert Giersch, former head of the Kiel Institute of World Economics, who in 1988, the last time we met, praised the 1992 program as "a great opportunity," but also complained about Delors's "European socialism" and about what he termed excessive bureaucracy in Brussels, notably its more recent planned "intrusion" into social and environmental affairs. Five years earlier, one of Europe's wisest and wittiest journalists, Italy's Luigi Barzini, observed, more bitingly than either Kennedy or Giersch, that the Common Market amounted to "a fragile customs union, a mosaic of myopic, national, sacred egotisms badly harmonized, that any robust historical breeze or serious economic crisis could easily overwhelm."[2]

Yet Barzini, who died in 1984, would surely have expressed surprise, perhaps relief, at what ten determined European political leaders accomplished in June of that year during their Fontainebleau summit meeting near Paris: quite apart from moving on finding a new president for the EC Commission, they made a new start. Outgoing President Gaston Thorn, Luxembourg's short, feisty former prime minister, looking back on his four years in Brussels, told me in the summer of 1989 that "much of the groundwork for what was to follow had been laid, but when we met [at the 1984 summit, presided over by Thorn] we were completely blocked, nothing was moving. We were nowhere. Giersch and the others were right. Yet then, there at the summit . . . things began to move."[3]

Meeting near the scenic campus of INSEAD, the European Institute of Business Administration in Fontainebleau, culminating four years of bitter dispute and well over a decade of stagnation, the then ten EC leaders were defusing a problem that had assumed crisis proportions: Britain's contribution to the EC budget. Since 1979, Mrs. Thatcher had repeatedly insisted on a "lasting solution" to the discrepancy between Britain's position as the EC's second most important net contributor, after Germany, and the fact that its economy trailed the economies of France and Germany in terms of per capita gross national product.

Mitterrand, who was hosting the summit, quickly realized he was facing a crisis and a failure. The crisis had been provoked by Mrs. Thatcher's stubborn, repeated vetoing of plans to advance Community causes until Britain's payments to the EC budget were scaled back. The payments became widely known as "Maggie's check." Similar to crises that occurred later, Mitterrand, Kohl, and other EC leaders warned her that, if a compromise was not found, Britain would find itself isolated. That in turn triggered the first references to a possible two-tier, à la carte, multiple-speed Europe, which meant the European Community would move ahead on unity plans, without Britain. But change was stirring in her own mind and fear that her EC partners meant what they said. And, as she quickly demonstrated at the summit meeting, compromises were possible—if they suited British interests. In the end, Mrs. Thatcher's behavior bore out what Helen Wallace of the Royal Institute of International Affairs once wisely advised me: "Watch not what she says, but what she does."

I recall waiting with fellow reporters for Mrs. Thatcher's news conference to begin in INSEAD's crowded amphitheater. Radiating enthusiasm and good humor, Mrs. Thatcher praised the agreement that gave her an immediate and badly needed rebate of 750 million European Currency Units ($888 million in 1991 dollars) and established a system of reducing Britain's payments starting in 1985. The arrangement, she told us, was a "good deal" not only for Britain but for the Community.

The summit also cleared the way for assuring future financing of the EC's virtually empty treasury, drained by excessive spending on agricultural subsidy programs. The compromise agreement also permitted serious discussions to proceed on introduction of majority voting in the Council of Ministers, blocked since the 1966 crisis, and on the completion of negotiations for the impending membership of Spain and Portugal.

Most important, Mitterrand at his news conference, smiling and relaxed after two-and-a-half days of tense, acrimonious negotiation, made a startling disclosure: each of the ten participating EC leaders at the summit also had enthusiastically agreed to establish ad hoc committees for "relaunching Europe." These were to establish action proposals in the following key areas: liberalized flow of trade in goods, capital, and services within the Community, simplified border procedures, issuance of a single passport valid for all EC citizens, establishment of an EC television network, implementation of common standards for the EC telecommunications industry, and funding of research for building a European space station.

BUSINESS JOINS THE BANDWAGON

A clear signal had gone up that far more was at stake than "Maggie's check." Indeed, Mitterrand's announcement reactivated interest in what for years had been laconically, boringly described as the "strengthening and consolidating of the internal market." That was a strong, unmistakable rallying cry for support in "relaunching Europe" from another powerful community notable for its absence at Fontainebleau, yet with stakes every bit as important, if not more important, than those of the EC summiteers—European business.

Wisse Dekker is a balding, blue-eyed, soft-spoken Dutchman, who, despite major heart surgery in 1986, is anything but soft when it comes to fighting for the company to which he has devoted his entire life: Philips, Europe's largest electronics company and the world's second-largest after Matsushita Electric Company of Japan.

Dekker's lifelong commitment to one of the world's leading global multinationals gradually evolved into a visionary "Europeanizing" mission: to lead Western European industry back into a position of strength, armed to battle Japan, the United States, and other competitors, and to rekindle the dynamism and innovation that throughout the 1960s made companies like Philips models of success in the Western world.

Item: on the morning of November 19, 1990, a beleaguered, weakened Philips conceded to the world it was fighting for its life. The company had just announced a net loss for the year of $2.4 billion, the largest in its history, as Philips management prepared to fire, or lay off, nearly a fifth of its 285,000 work force around the world. Philips was not going under, but its difficulties were enormous and it wasn't the first time.

The situation reminded me somewhat of my first visit to Philips's Eindhoven headquarters in 1981. Then too sales and profits were plummeting, as gloomy financial analysts in Amsterdam and Dutch trade-union leaders predicted the company faced extinction. Executives complained bitterly about an absence of European political leadership. Dekker at the time was the company's executive vice president. What Dekker feared most was that Philips and perhaps other European companies in the same field, such as state-controlled Thomson of France, would go under in the wake of steadily intensifying Japanese and American competition, notably in consumer electronics.

Born in Eindhoven, son of a company employee who repaired cars for Anton Philips, one of the company founders, Dekker started with Philips in Indonesia in 1948. Like many of his colleagues who live in that trim company town, Dekker never worked for any other company. During our first meeting in the spring of 1981, Dekker created the impression that stress did not matter in his life. This outward calm reflected nearly twenty years' service in Southeast Asia, much of it among the Japanese, whose language he learned to speak—at about the proficiency level of a teenager, he says, which isn't bad for a Westerner. His plans for Europe—and his industry's role in it—were already taking shape in his mind.

Three years later, shortly after the Fontainebleau summit, Dekker was president and chairman of the board, and had started discussions to draft the outlines of a plan with several European colleagues and his staff at Philips. The talks led to a major speech, delivered by Dekker at the Centre for European Policy Studies in Brussels on January 11, 1985—with blockbuster effect. Its title: "Europe 1990—an Agenda for Action."

The speech was significant for two reasons. First, it was the opening, precedent-shaking appeal by the head of a leading European multinational company for support of what became the predominant political initiative for the incoming Delors EC Commission in Brussels—the bold and sweeping plan to remove the Common Market's barriers to the flow of goods and services by the end of 1992. For that goal alone—reinforcing Europe's capacity to better compete against Japan and the United States—Dekker pledged the wholehearted support of Philips and the European business community. Second, Dekker's speech, which attracted only passing interest from the Brussels-based news media, came just three days before Delors delivered his first major policy speech to the European Parliament in Strasbourg, announcing the 1992 plan. In many ways, it was similar to Dekker's. A coincidence? Certainly not.

"We knew what had to be done from our side, namely getting business behind Delors and the Commission and the other EC leaders," Dekker recalled several years later. "So we moved together, in parallel . . . you might say we were oiling the machinery, and we have been helping ever since, using our influence, because—well—the 1992 plan was good for European business, and our goal was to be sure Philips survived—this was also essential. It was teamwork and I really got to know—and admire—Delors for his commitment to the economic and, later, the political unity of Europe."[4]

A similar version of events, but with a different perspective, came from chief-of-staff Lamy, who on Delors's behalf had been working closely behind the scenes with all the other players. "The basic idea, the approach to building support—and action—on 1992, was to crack the nut," he recalled, "involving a formidable task, with business, the European Roundtable group, for example, on one side, and us—the Commission and the Council—on the other. We were, in effect, creating a new coalition." The "cracking" Lamy referred to was to prove a formidable battle, encountering deep resistance, skepticism, and downright ignorance in virtually every Western capital. As late as 1988, one could still ask well-educated Europeans, chosen at random, what 1992 meant. The responses ranged from the Cockfield Plan, the 1992 Barcelona Olympics, the celebrations of the five hundredth anniversary of the discovery of America, the 1992 Seville World Fair, to a puzzled stare or a shrug of ignorance. "We had competition on the date, and a lot of selling to do," added Lamy.

But Dekker and Delors were by no means acting alone. Helping prepare Dekker's speech was another key figure, Étienne Davignon, an affable, tough-talking, pipe-smoking Belgian viscount, known to his many American friends as "Stevie." He was completing eight years as an EC commissioner and vice president for industrial policy and by experience, high-level political and social connections, and charm, had become the Commission's most illustrious member. He later went on to become chairman of Société Générale de Belgique, the country's huge and powerful holding company, which in 1988 became the target of a bitter, highly publicized hostile takeover attempt by Italy's flamboyant financier Carlo De Benedetti. Also involved in the preparations for rallying business support for the 1992 program was Pehr Gyllenhammer, then head of Sweden's Volvo automobile group and president of the Roundtable of European Industrialists, which he had founded only a year earlier with about thirty chief executives from Europe's biggest companies.

What was happening, behind the scenes, discreetly and in unprecedented fashion—in a manner that might have made Jean Monnet uncomfortable, because he rarely felt at ease with aggressive, profit-minded industrialists—was the establishment of a new alliance. The alliance was never subject to a written agreement, but its basic purpose was to support the move toward economic and political integration. In almost every way, it was typically European: low-key, secretive, between men who for years had known each other—successful, powerful members of the European business establishment on the one hand, and on the other, Europe's political elite, including heads of EC governments and political parties and the EC Commission in Brussels. Many, like Delors, Mitterrand, and Felipe González, prime minister of Spain, are Socialists; others, like Kohl, Giulio Andreotti, prime minister of Italy, and John Major, prime minister of Britain, are tied through conservative, centrist parties.

And the alliance extends beyond Brussels and purely EC-related projects to other, increasingly powerful European cooperative ventures, which are also moving with fierce determination to turn Europe into a more united, world-class player. The most important ventures include the following:

- Airbus Industrie, the highly successful French-led consortium of West European aerospace companies, which since its founding in 1970, amid wide hostility and skepticism, had become the world's number-two manufacturer of wide-body passenger aircraft, after Boeing of the United States. By 1990, Airbus's fleshy, hard-driving, French general manager, Jean Pierson, was gently warning American aerospace companies that if they did not want to join Europe in building a new-generation supersonic plane for the next century, meaning a successor to the Anglo-French Concorde, Europe would again go it alone. Within a year, the French and British companies that built the Concorde and the Airbus were intensifying their joint studies for a new supersonic plane, as American, German, and Japanese groups expressed interest in cooperating.

- Arianespace, an eleven-nation space consortium, which since its startup in 1980 has captured 50 percent of the world's market for commercial satellites. Since then, Arianespace has become the main competitor to the U.S. National Space and Aeronautics Administration and privately owned U.S. launch companies. Meantime, under the auspices of the European Space Agency, a new, more powerful rocket for launching a manned, reusable spaceship called Hermès was being developed. Like Ariane, it would be lifted into space from the French-manned space center in Kourou, French Guiana, sometime in the late 1990s. American satellite users, seeking competitive prices and an alternative to NASA, are among Ariane's best customers.

- Eureka, a nineteen-nation cooperative research program started in 1985 at Mitterrand's initiative for virtually all European countries to develop high technology. Some 3,000 European companies and universities now participate in more than 500 projects covering fields ranging from biotechnology and semiconductors to mobile phones, robotics, and new materials, to high-definition television. Outsiders seeking membership have been kept at arm's length, particularly Japanese companies. "No question of allowing the Japanese in, and Americans will be invited into Eureka only if they already have solid R&D operations in Europe," commented a Eureka official from the agency's headquarters in Brussels. With the swift collapse of borders between Western and Eastern Europe, formerly East German, Polish, and Czech companies have been seeking membership in Eureka. "We know that we and our participants are a magnet for high tech in Europe," the official said.
- Two variants of Eureka:—An audiovisual Eureka program was established in 1989, comprising twenty-seven European countries, plus the Soviet Union, aimed at promoting and establishing European coproductions for television and the film industry. And Euclid, a military version of Eureka, was established in November 1990, during the height of the Gulf crisis by EC defense ministers, excluding neutral Ireland. Its goal: to develop about thirty advanced military technologies, ranging from avionics and surveillance satellites to advanced radar, artificial intelligence, and submarine detection.

Reflected in these programs is a new mood sweeping Europe, succinctly summed up by a Frenchman, Jean-Louis Beffa, a cheerful, hard-driving son of an engineer, who has risen spectacularly to become the youngest chairman of France's oldest private company—the three hundred-year-old Compagnie Saint-Gobain, Europe's largest glass and packaging group. "Everyone was writing off Europe a few years ago," he said, "but everything has changed with 1992, and now, with the accelerating events in Eastern Europe and the Soviet Union, we have new opportunities for markets there. The Germans have no monopoly in Eastern Europe," Beffa emphasized, "but what is significant is that this is Europe asserting itself. . . . If we can continue to harness our talent and diversity, we will be a much tougher competitor for Japan—and clearly, Japan is the biggest challenger we face."[5]

FIVE REASONS FOR REVIVAL

In the opinion of most of us following the revival, Delors and his allies would have failed had it not been for active support of business leaders like Beffa; Dekker; Davignon; and Karl-Heinz Kaske, the chairman of Germany's powerful Siemens group; Patrick Sheehy, chairman of Britain's B.A.T. Industries; and dozens of others. There was no doubting, either, that European business saw that it was in their fundamental interest to get behind what had become a bandwagon, rolling forward, amid wide publicity. One British bank asked a provocative question in an ad campaign: "Barclays is ready for 1992. Are you?" Thus, driven by a sense of urgency and missionary zeal, the Delors-led Commission was able to push ahead with its plans. There are five basic reasons why:

- The EC's previously disastrous economic performance. Starting with the end of the so-called Golden 1960s, real seasonally adjusted GNP began falling in EC countries from an average expansion rate of 4.8 percent to around 3 percent in the 1970s. Following the impact of skyrocketing oil prices, Western Europe had, by the second quarter of 1980, slipped into recession. From there growth inched up, to zero growth in 1982, and only then did it begin to rise to an average 1.6 percent rate of expansion in the period between 1982 and 1984, hardly a booming recovery. This rate was considerably below Japan's expansion, which averaged nearly 4 percent growth throughout the 1980s and was even under the U.S. average rate of growth of 2.6 percent. EC inflation in the 1982–84 period—averaging nearly 9 percent and double-digit levels in some member states—was more than twice the rate in the United States and in Japan. Meantime, the Community's share of world trade in manufactured goods fell to around 35 percent from 45 percent in 1973. Investments in the same period stagnated as gloom gripped European business leaders in virtually every EC state.
- The staggering costs of long-established barriers to trade within the Community. Example: A tourist traveling through ten member countries in 1991, changing money into local currencies, would wind up with less than half the original sum, because of commissions and other costs from making the exchanges. A more striking example: the costs of formalities and

delays at EC frontiers for trucks and other motor vehicles have totaled about $10 billion annually, in addition to an estimated $5.5 billion in lost transactions caused by paperwork and other forms of inefficiency. Still another example: only about 2 percent of contracts for government supplies and public works are awarded to firms in other member states, representing a huge, highly protected market—with sales estimated by the EC Commission to run as high as $600 billion annually.

- The equally staggering costs of wasteful government subsidies—equivalent to more than $100 billion annually. Direct or indirect government subsidies are poured into many sectors of member-country economies; some are healthy, others are ailing. Examples: Agriculture, which for several decades has remained the largest single—and highly controversial—item in the EC's budget; public transport, notably state-owned railroads; steel and coal industries; financial aid to regions and companies seeking to export, even though they are inefficient. David Henderson, chief economist of the OECD in Paris, startled colleagues in 1989 by publishing a research paper concluding that the European Community, as a whole, was more protectionist than fifteen to twenty years earlier and that, worse, EC protectionism in member states had become "more discretionary and less transparent, and hence less market-conforming" than ever before in postwar history.[6]

- The EC's weakened position in basic research and development. Although Europe, since World War II, has represented tremendous potential, with more than a million scientists and technicians, resources were widely dispersed, teams often working in isolation, amid considerable duplication. Many of Europe's best and brightest researchers have gone to the United States, drawn by attractive salaries and excellent working and living conditions. More troubling are relative expenditures: Western Europe in recent years has spent only roughly 1.9 percent of its GNP on R&D, compared to about 2.8 percent in the United States and 2.9 percent in Japan. And Japan, which started from a smaller base, has been growing faster than Europe and the United States, reflecting a widening in the gap between the EC and its main competitors.

- Stubbornly high levels of unemployment. The jobless rate in the EC averaged close to 11.5 percent in the early 1980s—more than 16 million people. That was three times as high as the 3.5 percent jobless rate in Japan and four times the 2.6 percent rate in the United States. By 1987 the rate had fallen only slightly, to 11 percent, compared to 6.2 percent in the United States and 2.8 percent in Japan. The combined unemployment rate that year in the entire OECD area, comprising North America, Europe, and the Pacific region, had eased slightly to 7.6 percent, which was well below the EC jobless rate. The dramatic dimension of the problem was driven home to Mitterrand in 1984 as angry, jeering French steelworkers, protesting imminent layoffs in the already ailing steel industry, burned effigies, blockaded the Lorraine region of eastern France, and ransacked government offices—only two months prior to the opening of the Fontainebleau EC summit meeting.

Indeed, one of the reasons the Fontainebleau summit succeeded—by no means the only one—was Mitterrand's determination to score a victory as he ended his six-month rotating term as president of the European Council. The momentum came partly from a need to respond to bitter attacks on his domestic program from conservative opposition parties throughout the country. In the end, however, even *Le Figaro*, a leading conservative, antigovernment daily, described the summit meeting as "an indisputable success," while Gaston Thorn told reporters that "we got rid of this poison now [the British-contribution issue] and this means we have a bit of time" to pursue building what Belgian foreign minister Leo Tindemans, described as "the beginning of a new Europe."

COCKFIELD DRAFTS A WHITE PAPER

As Delors, some seven months later in January 1985, was delivering his opening speech to the European Parliament in Strasbourg, that beginning was already underway—in a spacious office just down the corridor from his on the thirteenth floor of the Berlaymont. Inside, Lord Cockfield was working fifteen-hour days, six days a week, on the plan that would bear his name. Delors had been drawn to this studious, owlish-looking former secretary of trade, an accountant by profession and a favorite of Mrs. Thatcher, and had backed him for the Commission slot responsible for the internal market, financial institutions, and taxation. However, none of us paid attention when Delors, on a damp and chilly December weekend in 1984, at the thirteenth-century Royaumont Abbey near Paris, announced Cockfield's appointment.

Once settled into Brussels, however, Cockfield surprised the EC bureaucracy by the quiet, audacious manner in which he plunged into drafting the program—an approach and a zealous sense of mission that later was to exasperate Mrs. Thatcher, and cause his demise. He told Mark Nelson of the *Wall Street Journal:* "I decided [regarding the drafting of the 1992 program] that if you really want to get the job done, there was no sense in doing it in the piecemeal way it had been done in the past." He wrote the draft of the plan alone, helped by aides who deliberately ignored most of the conflicting national interests—and pressures—of member governments, with Delors's unflinching guidance and support.

The plan produced by Cockfield, the 1992 program, entitled "Completing the Internal Market" and published in June 1985, is divided into two sections—a fifty-page summary describing the many barriers to the free flow of goods, services, and people and an annex listing about 300 specific, highly technical measures, which later were trimmed to 282. There also was a suggested timetable for approval by the Commission, along with suggested dates for approval by the Council prior to submission to member states for implementation and, when necessary, follow-up by EC enforcement authorities. All the dates fell within the deadline Delors had announced in Strasbourg—December 31, 1992.

Several dozen guidebooks on the 1992 Plan have been published, and in the bibliography I have listed several considered among the best.[7] Basically the plan, as one of the American authors, Michael Calingaert, noted, drew heavily on work previously done under Davignon and others in earlier Commissions. But for the first time a plan divided the obstacles into detailed categories—physical, technical, and financial—and simultaneously suggested steps for removing them. The proposed remedies, or directives, covered everything from complex industrial norms and standards and border formalities, to air fares, taxation, subsidies, public procurement, and rules governing rights of migrant workers, asylum, and extradition. The Cockfield Plan was the most comprehensive listing of major obstacles to establishing a single market ever attempted.

However, by the time the report was published, Cockfield's zeal as

Nicholas Colchester and David Buchan in their authoritative book, *Europower,* also noted, had become "almost vindictive." He also had gone far beyond what Mrs. Thatcher considered acceptable. "They want an open internal market . . . well, they've got it," the British journalists quoted him as saying. Cockfield's plan, as he explained it, was but a first step in integrating the EC-member economies to ultimately establish a political union, which contrasted sharply with Mrs. Thatcher's objective: the creation of a liberal, deregulated free-trade area within Europe.[8]

COINCIDING WITH A RECOVERY

As the debate over integration gradually intensified and drew wide media attention, surprisingly few observers in the mid-1980s fully realized that the European Community had entered the new decade with an improving economy, which varied from country to country but on the whole spelled new growth. This revival provided the indispensable underpinning for much of what the Delors Commission and its allies were beginning to accomplish. Among the observers who spotted the trend first was J. Paul Horne, the seasoned Paris-based international economist of Smith Barney, the New York investment bank.

On the day Delors delivered his speech in Strasbourg, January 15, 1985, Horne published a penetrating article in a Smith Barney newsletter, headlined "Europe's Not So Bad Off."[9] It described the Community's stirring of recovery at a time when everyone had been portraying the Community as adrift, paralyzed, dominated by leftist politicians unable to cope with the crisis. Horne pointed out that "numerous European governments are making progress in dealing with problems," citing rigorous conservative, anti-inflationary fiscal and monetary policies that had started in Britain with Mrs. Thatcher's election in 1979 and had gradually spread—to Belgium, Denmark, the Netherlands, where center-right coalitions came to power between 1980 and 1982.

Within two years, left-wing governments began following suit in France, Greece, Italy, and Spain. The election of Kohl and Mrs. Thatcher's reelection in 1983—amid considerable euphoria—led to a decline in interest rates as inflation fell, helping touch off a major European investment boom. But there were other encouraging signs.

Government deficits began to fall, as conservative governments cut back on spending. Tax reform was in the air in France and Germany, whose governments had already announced major tax cuts for 1986 and 1988. Meantime, unit labor costs in the combined EC area, which had been rising at an annual rate of nearly 12 percent since 1980, had fallen to 3.7 percent in 1984, and were forecast to drop to 2.9 percent in 1985. As Horne, the OECD, and others noted, this would represent the lowest rate of increase in wage costs in more than fourteen years. Partly as a result, corporate profits were rising briskly and were approaching the levels of the early 1970s.

In addition, deregulation and privatization of state-owned companies and banks were beginning to spread throughout Western Europe, having started in Britain with a major privatization of capital and financial markets and the selling of shares in large, state-owned British companies, such as Britoil, British Airways, British Telecom. By the end of 1985, as the 1992 program was getting started, more than 14 billion British pounds in assets had already been successfully sold to enthusiastic buyers, and a sell-off of an equal amount in government assets was planned for the following year.

BLACK SPOTS AND A GRAY MARKET

A successful attack on the entrenched privileges of West European labor unions and their powers, many dating from the 1930s, also began in earnest. Mrs. Thatcher ended indexation of government worker salaries in 1980; Mitterrand's Socialist government followed in 1982; and the next year, Italy began overhauling its sancrosanct *scala mobile* system of indexing wages. In France, employers were allowed to lay off workers without first obtaining approval from the labor ministry, reflecting an EC-wide trend in favor of easing firing rules. Part-time work began to increase in commerce and industry throughout the Community, without, however, resolving what remained the black spot on Europe's record—worsening unemployment.

Yet there was little labor unrest, few strikes of long duration, and virtually no violence. Why? Surprising as it is to Americans and Japanese investors, the growing numbers of unemployed workers throughout Europe, due to eased firing rules, remain protected by generous insurance plans, and trade unions in Europe remain weak, particularly compared to their counterparts in the United States. We shall return to the unemployed and Europe's "new poor" in large cities in Chapter 7. There is a second reason: Europe's flourishing "black" or "gray" underground economy, representing vast and growing wage-earning activities concealed from government taxation.

Known in Britain as moonlighting, in Germany as *Schwarzarbeit,* in France as *travail au noir,* and in Italy as *lavoro nero,* the underground economies of Western Europe represent between 15 percent and 30 percent of member countries' GNP. Yet, as anyone living in Europe who has sought cut-rate plumbing, house painting, electrical work, or decorating knows, the illegal practice is generally tolerated by government authorities. The vast majority of jobless men and women between nineteen and twenty-five years of age I interviewed in my travels, many of them moonlighting, expressed a mixture of anger, frustration, and boredom with their political leaders and no sense of identification with what was happening.

For example, Lara Rachid, who had just turned twenty-two when I talked to him several days before the March 1986 presidential election in France, told me he had last worked as a night porter in a Marseilles hotel. We were in the French government unemployment office near the Paris suburb of Nanterre, and he was leafing through job offers. Dejected, he told me he had no interest whatever in the economic reforms being proposed by Socialist President Mitterrand and his right-wing, neo-Gaullist opponent, former Prime Minister Jacques Chirac. "I see little ideological difference between them," he said, "but what is worse, they do not address my problem of being unemployed. . . . I simply won't vote."

Rachid, whose family immigrated from Algeria in the 1950s, was among the 2.3 million unemployed French men and women, representing a record 10.5 percent of the work force. Most, like him, were under twenty-five years of age. Mitterrand himself conceded that the continuing surge in unemployment was "the principal failure" of his government since taking power in 1981 and that, if he lost the election, unemployment would be the reason. As it turned out, Mitterrand was reelected president for a second seven-year term, but a new power-sharing arrangement was established between President Mitterrand, who remained at the Élysée Palace, and Chirac, who took over as prime minister, reflecting a conservative victory in legislative elections and a grim outlook: unemployment was projected to continue rising. The number of jobless was not to fall below 2.5 million—and then only very slightly—until January 1990; it then resumed rising.

The picture was the same throughout the Community: with only Britain among the major EC powers facing a serious recession in 1991, the combined GNP growth rate for the EC countries for 1992 was revised downward to just below 2 percent from 3 percent growth in 1990—even after taking account of the additional half a percentage point of GNP growth from East Germany now incorporated into the German total. The EC's combined unemployment rate was projected to remain at just over 9 percent in 1992—a decidedly poor performance compared to the United States, with a projected 1992 unemployment rate of 6.7 percent and Japan of 2.3 percent. It was Europe's blackest spot, as Mitterrand had correctly noted and, according to most economists, despite moderate job creation in Europe, unemployment would remain chronically high.

A QUICK TRIP TO ROME AND MADRID

For Delors, positioning the Community for concerted action in order to promote economic expansion and reforming the Community's institutions meant lobbying at the highest levels of Europe's political and corporate leadership. Often, in his unusual post, he appeared resentful of having to cajole, argue, pressure, and charm leaders into action. Yet Delors also recognized that he needed their support, because being president of the Commission was not being president of France, or, for that matter, the national leader of any other important Western power. Brussels, as we have already noted, while bearing striking resemblances to Washington, D.C., was a long way from being a superpower capital.

This came through while I accompanied Delors on a one-day trip from Brussels to Rome and Madrid on a spring day in 1990. Flying high over the Alps in a borrowed U.S.-built Italian Air Force Gulfstream executive jet, I asked him about European business leaders and their role. Who really helped whom? "They were with us, of course, they supported us—from the beginning; some of them joined in later when they saw the way it was going." He credited the European Roundtable and other groups for supporting his efforts, but the answer also reflected Delors's conviction that the plan 1992 was in large measure his show, above all. This perception often created the inescapable impression that Delors was alone in his struggle, suffering silently as he cajoled others to move forward—in this case, as we were approaching Rome—making sure EC leaders were moving forward and keeping the faith.

Gradually, I discovered that gloom was a strong trait of Delors's personality, for when pressed, he admitted that he wasn't sure he could always count on Mitterrand and Kohl for support in pursuing European projects. At the time of our trip, he was mobilizing two prime ministers already friendly to his cause: Italy's Giulio Andreotti and Spain's Felipe González. His goal in Rome and Madrid was making sure that they would continue keeping the pressure on Kohl for the two key items on the Community's agenda—economic and political union—fearful that the Bonn government coalition might be overwhelmed, and distracted, by the unification of Germany.

As we were talking, I thought of Monnet. At that particular moment Delors reminded me of him—two Frenchmen, driven by a similar vision, separated by several decades, with relatively weak executive powers, seeking support among the politicians, amid complex European conflicts and interests, and shifting alliances and allegiances. The tall mustached Italian Air Force pilot strolled back to the comfortable, executive-jet cabin where we were talking. In response to my question, he told me the plane had been lent to Delors as a courtesy by Italy's prime minister. So why, I asked provokingly, had Italy opted for an American, and not an Italian or other European plane? "I don't know, but this plane is fantastic—nothing but the best," the captain replied, laughing. I turned to Delors, smiling sardonically, asking whether, at times, he didn't feel like Monnet— battling for the New Europe against difficult odds?

"Yes, sometimes I feel I am doing the work of not only Monnet but of [Robert] Schuman," Delors replied. It was a reference to the combined leadership of Monnet and Schuman, who skillfully engineered the creation of the European Coal and Steel Community. But the battling for European unity in the 1950s was different in scope and in substance, Delors emphasized. "Monnet and his allies were battling against Malthusianism [the controversial nineteenth-century theory postulating poverty and distress as unavoidable unless population growth was curbed] whereas today times are different. Let us not forget that today, in 1990, the most important is done—the economic renaissance of Europe has been accomplished, the decline of

Europe is finished, certainly in economic terms." But now a lot more remained to be accomplished, and hence the reason for the quick trip we were taking. Delors did not invite me to lunch with Andreotti, or to dinner with González, but that evening, on the flight back to Brussels, he provided some insights on how things work.

"You ask what did we accomplish? . . . I will tell you: first, I was able to place some doubt in the president's [Andreotti's] mind," regarding Kohl's intentions on supporting the reinforcement of powers for monetary union and for EC institutions. The Italians, who would hold the rotating EC Council presidency during the crucial Rome EC summit meeting in mid-December 1990, were confident Kohl would pledge wholehearted support; Delors was less certain and as we are to see, his instincts proved uncanny. Andreotti, who would be presiding, was a key link in the powerful network of centrist Christian Democratic politicians in Europe. "We need this kind of support—in Germany, Britain, Belgium, for example," added Lamy, sitting across the aisle, and so these kinds of quick trips become important, to keep the heat on." González, a faithful Socialist ally, needed only to be made *au courant* and "mobilized" to persuade friendly allies in other EC countries to support the launching of negotiations in 1991 aimed at establishing economic, monetary, and political union.

The message Delors was to repeat again and again in private and in public was clear and simple: Europe must capitalize on its economic gains, and move toward monetary and political union, particularly with a recession underway in the United States, followed, possibly, by further slowdown in Europe. We were speaking before Mrs. Thatcher resigned and before the American statistics showed the weakening U.S. performance starting in December 1990. Yet, even in hindsight, he appeared reasonably satisfied with the way European economies were performing and believed that the gains made were irreversible.

It was well after 9 P.M. as Delors, his blue eyes strained, reached across the aisle, took my notebook out of my hands, and began jotting down sets of numbers. One showed that the combined GNP growth rate of the twelve EC countries had grown from 1.6 percent in 1982–84 to 2.6 percent between 1985 and 1987, and to 3.6 percent in the period 1988–90. Another set showed that annual investments in the EC economies had risen to a 3.5 percent growth rate in 1985–87 from zero growth in the previous two-year period, and had

jumped to 7.5 percent in 1988–90. "You can see that in the beginning, when I made my first speech, we were only getting ready," he
said. "The rest came later, thanks to many people and actors in what
became a process . . . the 1992 process. And I must admit the business
actors mattered; they made a lot of it happen." By the end of the year,
at the Rome EC summit meeting, while even more worried about the
American recession and the possible failure of the talks on trade
liberalization, being held in Geneva under auspicies of the General
Agreement on Tariffs and Trade, known as GATT, Delors had not
changed his mind, particularly about the need for continuing support from business leaders and bankers. "I count on them," Delors
said.

ATTEMPTING A TAKEOVER IN BELGIUM

There are, as we have already seen, many examples in Europe of a
new breed of youthful, dynamic business leader. But, if I had to pick
one—and only one—European business leader who clearly had
demonstrated American-style boldness, agility, toughness, and imagination in the face of tough opposition, it would be Carlo De Benedetti of Italy. None of us will forget January 18, 1988, crowded into
the Paris office of his youthful, energetic French deputy, Alain Minc.
He and De Benedetti were explaining enthusiastically why and how
they had just launched the biggest, most spectacular, and what was to
become the fiercest corporate takeover battle in Western Europe's
postwar history. The target was Belgium's largest holding company,
lackluster, powerful, hidebound—and ailing—the Société Générale
de Belgique. Through a vast complex of industrial and financial
companies and family connections, Société Générale controls an estimated one-third of the Belgian economy, directly or indirectly.
When its top management learned what was happening, it vowed to
fight, touching off what quickly became known as the Battle of Belgium.

Appearing supremely confident and excited, and exuding un-
abashed confidence in his unique, brash brand of neo-European
capitalism, De Benedetti explained that the takeover battle was but a
first step in forming what he termed "a grand European holding
company"—and running it. "I want to create an alliance to compete
with Japan, the United States, and emerging economies like Korea,"

he told reporters, emphasizing that "Europe's survival is at stake. I am convinced that entrepreneurs can play a decisive role in integrating Europe."

In Brussels, EC Commission officials, when they heard about the takeover attempt, were delighted, barely able to contain their enthusiasm. One senior Commission official said it was "a day for Europe . . . this is exactly what we need . . . a concrete example of how the European market will operate after 1992." Financial analysts viewed the takeover as a catalyst, and a lively, indispensable ingredient for making the Cockfield Plan for deregulation work effectively. "I don't see Carlo as a U.S.-style raider, but as an industrialist with a strategy. . . . Europe needs more deals like this," said another highly enthusiastic Brussels banker.[10]

Unfortunately, things didn't work out as De Benedetti and Minc had planned. What was at best a disastrously mixed performance, in the end tells us a great deal about the difficulties in building the New Europe and something about the complex personality of one of its most dynamic players. By the time the Battle of Belgium died down, De Benedetti had spent nearly $2 billion buying up vast numbers of shares, and on hiring lawyers, public-relations consultants, and other general expenses. Renting a headquarters suite on the twenty-third floor of the Brussels Hilton alone cost $4,000 per day, prompting one Brussels banker to note, "It was, finally, like a U.S. operation, complete with raiders, power grabbing, influential lawyers and Wall Street bankers running around. . . . None of us had ever seen anything quite like it before. What a show it was!"

To their surprised embarrassment later, De Benedetti, Minc, and their allies had completely misjudged the strength, the breadth, and depth of the Belgian establishment, its political clout, family ties, and financial power, which predated the Belgian nation itself. The establishment, which portrayed De Benedetti as a menace to Belgium, closed ranks against him. Among their stalwarts was former EC Commissioner Davignon, a fellow Roundtable member and, until then, a friendly colleague and SGB director trying to stay neutral. Finally, he joined the battle—on the Belgian side. The newly formed Belgian coalition, backed by the government, quickly joined forces with France's powerful financial-banking group, Compagnie Financière de Suez, which in turn had the backing of the conservative Chirac government in Paris. The new group made a rival bid, supported by leading wealthy American and Japanese investors, who had rushed in to participate as the price of SGB's shares soared on stock exchanges throughout Europe.

At the end of the bitter battle, five months after it started, and following months of stalemate, a compromise agreement was negotiated. The French-Belgian group, which had spent an equally astounding amount, reportedly $1.9 billion, wound up with both financial and management control of SGB. De Benedetti's group, which had successfully purchased a respectable 43.5 percent share initially, sold a considerable number of the shares they had purchased, netting what De Benedetti later claimed was a "comfortable return," largely because of the inflated value of the shares. But he lost the battle for control.

Nevertheless, De Benedetti, whose share was initially reduced to 16 percent as part of what he termed a new "partnership" arrangement to run SGB, was named a vice chairman; he became a member of the executive committee, and had the right to name three directors to the board. Many articles and several books have been written on the subject since then.[11] Some authors portrayed De Benedetti's large-sized ego and powerful will as damaged, his image as a winner shattered. Others who know them both said Minc's blind confidence in his own abilities also contributed to the failure; he was removed from his post by De Benedetti in February 1991. At the same time, grave difficulties had arisen at De Benedetti's other vast European financial and industrial holdings, including at the crown jewel, Olivetti, Western Europe's largest maker of personal computers and office equipment. Its sales buffeted by a weak computer market and labor disputes, Olivetti announced massive layoffs in the late autumn of 1990, which followed similar, drastic restructuring moves announced by Philips, French computer maker Bull, and their arch-rival, IBM. To generate funds, De Benedetti sold off many financial holdings, including his shares in SGB.

So why pick him as an example of Europe's best and brightest business leaders?

For one thing, thanks to De Benedetti, SGB was forced into a full-scale reorganization and modernization against its will. This was the first step in rebuilding what had become a giant but greatly weakened and vulnerable European company. The episode also marked, thanks to him, the end of an era in Belgium. The son of one of the Société Générale's directors told Mark Nelson of the *Wall Street Journal* that he and other younger members of the Belgian establishment did not at all "view De Benedetti's raid as a bad thing." In fact, he said that like many younger Belgians they welcomed the change, even if it came forcibly and abruptly. Why? Because he hoped it would help Brussels become the capital of a united European Community, and that as a result the old rules would have to continue changing at SGB and throughout Europe. Davignon, who became chairman as a result of the operation and was now being called "Stevie Wonder," told friends later that the Italian financier had proven a necessary and welcome catalyst for sweeping changes that followed and that included bringing in a new, reform-bent banker as chief executive officer, and introducing further streamlining directed from Paris by the Suez group.

Many observers predicted that De Benedetti's example would touch off a rash of U.S.-style hostile takeovers in Europe. But analysts overlooked the fact that even in the United States, deeply immersed in "merger mania" in the late 1980s, hostile bids have never been numerous. According to several estimates, while hostile bids always attract lots of media attention, they have accounted for less than 5 percent of all acquisitions. A review of 150 hostile bids made in the United States since 1983 concluded that they accounted for only 2 percent of all acquisitions made or attempted, and that only half of them came from raiders. Moreover, the targeted companies, like SGB, were generally weak and ailing, or, as they are called in the M&A game, "underperformers."[12]

De Benedetti did set an unforgettable example for a rash of friendlier mergers and acquisitions beginning to sweep Western Europe, which would reach avalanche proportions around 1989; the wave eased in early 1990. But De Benedetti's boldness, brashness, call it what you like, riveted world attention on a point he has made repeatedly: only by converting old and tired European companies like SGB into modern, pan-European powerhouses could Europe emerge from what he termed its "arteriosclerotic" state. Reflecting a more mellow, low-key, and moderate approach, he told the French daily Le Monde in November 1990 that, although the 1980s certainly represented the era of "diversification," the 1990s would be the period of "concentration, reducing debt and protecting patrimony," a reflection of his determination to defend his vulnerable and shrinking $15 billion empire as tougher times approached. He also warned friends that there would be a shortage of liquidity in the 1990s.

Business leaders, he insists, have a primary responsibility to push forward, to lead and defend European interests, including through political lobbying in Brussels and working closely with EC leaders. He was among the earliest supporters of the European Roundtable, arguing vehemently for support of the 1992 program, placing his support behind the Delors drive for economic and monetary union and a common European currency; he was among the first European leaders to call for a "Marshall Plan" for Eastern Europe—on a French television show in early 1988—which he insisted should have a single goal: providing East European economies capitalist methods and, above all, modern management, not subsidized financial aid.

AT HOME IN IVREA

When I first interviewed De Benedetti on a sunny day in May 1980 in Ivrea, the small, quiet Piedmontese town where Olivetti was founded, he was forty-five, and tensed only slightly when I inquired about his bodyguards and armor-plated sedan, and about his family, whom he kept living in Geneva and visited only on weekends for fear of the terrorist attacks that had plagued northern Italy for five years. He was working sixteen-hour days, directing a dramatic turnaround at Olivetti, which had once been the world's most prestigious maker of elegantly designed typewriters, mechanical calculators, and office furniture. Two years earlier, Olivetti had been moribund; the company had not paid a dividend in several years and in 1979 had lost a record $100 million. Financial analysts predicted Olivetti was going under.

By cutting back drastically on manpower, investing in new, advanced technology, building alliances with foreign companies, including giant AT&T of the United States and Toshiba of Japan, while subjecting himself to a dizzying pace, De Benedetti was slowly achieving what *Time* magazine five years later headlined in a cover story as "A Dazzling Comeback." Sales that year had risen by nearly 22 percent from a year earlier to $2.2 billion while net profits were at $177 million, and rising. It had always seemed to me over the years that De Benedetti was trying to prove himself—prove that he was stronger, better, tougher, more talented in business than others, including Giovanni Agnelli, the suave, powerful chairman of his family-controlled Fiat automotive group, for whom De Benedetti worked briefly in 1976 as managing director before resigning over differences about how Fiat should be run.

What remained of the relationship is a sense of rivalry between the *avvocato*, Agnelli's nickname, which denotes his training as a lawyer, and the *ingegniere*, De Benedetti's nickname, denoting his engineering background.

But quite unlike the urbane, patrician, sociable, fun-loving Agnelli, De Bendetti always seems to be alone, somewhat tense, driven by some unknown force, always trying to prove that he is the best, and above all, a winner, even when it appears he is losing. There is a vague sense of sadness about De Benedetti I never sensed while talking with Gianni Agnelli or his younger brother, Umberto, who is expected to inherit the job of running the family empire when Gianni retires.

I once asked De Bendetti what for him was the ideal life. His answer: "Working in America. Sleeping in Italy."

Back in the small scenic town of Ivrea for the first time in ten years, and at our first meeting since the SGB battle, I found De Benedetti greatly mellowed, looking tired but exuding good humor and enthusiasm. If you had to do the SGB battle all over again, how would you? I asked. "Simple," he said in his deep, gravelly American-accented English. "I would have been more aggressive. . . . I played by U.S. rules by informing René Lamy (the SGB chairman at the time) that I had acquired 18.6 percent of his shares and would go for more . . . that was my mistake, because at the time I told him they had no idea who was buying up their shares—they did not even notice." Leaning forward, puffing on a cigarillo, De Benedetti noted that "twelve years ago, I did not exist. Today my group represents 10 percent of the private capitalization in Italy. . . . I am not always successful, but I exist."

De Benedetti was spending more time in Ivrea these days tending to Olivetti, but still engrossed in his other, widespread financial and business activities. At the time of our meeting he was battling flashy Milan-based television mogul Silvio Berlusconi for control of Arnoldo Mondadori Editore, Italy's biggest newspaper, book, and magazine publisher. But his main, immediate preoccupation was restoring Olivetti's slipping profits and market shares against increasingly fierce competition from Japanese, European, and U.S. competitors. A major, full-blown restructuring reminiscent of that of a decade ago was underway at Ivrea, but this time the leader was Vittorio Cassoni, a hard-driving American-trained executive, whom De Benedetti hired back from AT&T in 1988 as Olivetti's chief executive after he had launched the American company's computer business.

Born in Parma in 1942 and armed with an engineering degree, Cassoni was another, but less well-known member of the new, youthful breed of European managers, deeply committed to European integration. "EC-92 is stimulating all kinds of new demand for information technology products—we must be ready," he said.

Aside from directing a major restructuring of Olivetti, Cassoni led in the creation of a low-profile group of twelve major—and competing—electronics and telecommunications companies, which also included Thomson of France, Philips, and Alcatel, France's largest telecommunications group. Known as the Information Technology Roundtable, members of this group regularly exchange new products and sensitive information about their industrial competitors, and have pressed a hard-line approach to trading relationships with the United States and Japan, in close cooperation with the EC Commission in Brussels. "You must never forget that the competition is not just among single companies, but between industrial and economic systems. . . . It is Europe versus the United States and Japan," Cassoni said.

MERGER MANIA CATCHES ON

De Benedetti, while colorfully personifying some of the trends sweeping Europe, is by no means alone among European business leaders pursuing growth and opportunities within the European Community. Consider the following:

■ What was widely dubbed "Euro-merger mania" began in earnest during 1988, and continued to grow in the following two years. Of the total $119 billion spent worldwide on cross-border mergers and acquisitions in the benchmark year of 1988, EC companies accounted for about 54 percent, with the numbers of mergers and the sums being spent rising steadily to record levels in 1989. North American companies were the world's favorite targets in 1988, accounting for 64 percent of the total value of transactions. The EC was second, growing even faster in 1989—accounting for about $31 billion, involving a total of 753 transactions, according to KPMG, the large Amsterdam-based accounting-consulting firm. In North America during the same period, there were a total of 1,246 transactions worth about $75.5 billion. In late 1990, and continuing into mid-

1991, however, because of looming recession and the Gulf crisis, the mania began to cool and the volume of transactions began to fall.

- Approaching the U.S. level of transactions, the 1,246 cross-border mergers and acquisitions reported in Western Europe in 1989, occurred primarily in EC countries. They were worth an estimated $51.7 billion, according to figures published by Translink, a New York consulting firm. The record volume and value of the transactions reflected mainly acquisitions by U.S. companies, which totaled nearly $14 billion, and were made primarily in Britain. A study on EC takeovers, prepared for the British government in late 1989, showed that British companies were also by far the most attractive for hostile takeovers, accounting for twenty-three out of twenty-six hostile bids made in the Community. The volume and numbers of transactions began to fall slightly in 1990 and in 1991, but major U.S., European, and Japanese companies said they had no intention of stopping their buying in Europe, amid widespread expectations that the trend would revive in 1992.

- According to Translink's analysis, airlines, food retailing, banking, and insurance were the most active sectors for mergers and acquisitions in 1989, while electronics, telecommunications, transportation, and information technologies scored highest in 1990. France's BSN food and beverage group, led by its animated, tough-minded chairman, Antoine Riboud, has been among the most active. "The priority for BSN is Europe," he tells visitors. Next in line among active sectors were electronics, aircraft and airlines, insurance, banking, financial services, and automobiles. The star performers among large Western European companies included Siemens of West Germany, which under its chairman, Karl-Heinz Kaske, a former physicist, began acquiring companies in 1988, starting with the company's first hostile takeover bid. That was for Plessey PLC, a British defense and telecommunications group, in partnership with Britain's General Electric company; Deutsche Bank's acquisition of Morgan Grenfell, a leading London merchant bank, also swelled the numbers, reflecting the renewed appetite for EC expansion in Germany.

New reorganizations, shakeouts, and alliances began to appear on Europe's horizon. That prospect was given major impetus when, in

February 1990, Sweden's Gyllenhammar of Volvo and Raymond Lévy, the chairman of state-owned Renault of France, announced plans to merge their car and truck operations in a deal worth an estimated $4.1 billion. Many analysts predicted that, given a slumping market for cars in 1990 and 1991, a shakeout of European auto makers was in the making, and that by the year 2000 only four European car makers would remain, aside from Volvo-Renault: France's privately-owned Peugeot group and Fiat, with which Peugeot already had close industrial links; and West Germany's Volkswagen and Daimler-Benz groups.

But surprise moves, including among car makers, led to broad-gauged industrial alliances, not outright takeovers. Thus, on October 4, 1990, Fiat, Italy's largest privately owned industrial group, with less than half of its sales now generated by cars, announced that it was teaming up with Cie. Générale d'Électricité, France's largest electronics and telecommunications group, to create a new, French-Italian industrial powerhouse. By merging their railroad technologies under the control of CGE, which already builds the high-speed TGV train, *le train à grande vitesse,* and combining their competing telecommunications divisions, also under CGE control, the two companies directly challenged Siemens and other mighty German groups, including for new markets in Eastern Europe and in the Soviet Union.

HERE COME THE JAPANESE

Meantime, Japanese companies and banks, while initially shunning mergers and acquisitions, had by the mid-1980s become major players in Western Europe by virtue of direct investments in most EC countries. Large Japanese companies in key sectors, such as automobiles and electronics—Nissan, Sony, Toshiba, Canon, Sumitomo, Fujitsu, to name but a few—had grown fearful of EC restrictions on their exports. The conclusion reached by most Japanese and, increasingly, South Korean companies, was simple: here was "Fortress Europe" emerging fast. Thus, if you were not inside, investing, digging in, becoming part of the local scene, you would be locked out. A major goal for Japanese groups was obtaining access to bid on lucrative government contracts, one of the EC's most highly protected markets, encompassing both civilian and military business.

Although by 1989 and in 1990, the EC countries accounted for only about 17 percent of Japan's external assets, its outward investments were growing with great speed—rising to a total of well over $45 billion in direct investments in 1990, up nearly 39 percent from 1988, and up from a mere $5 billion as recently as 1985. Britain, encouraged by Mrs. Thatcher's policy of welcoming Japanese manufacturers, was by the far the most popular site for Japanese companies, but Germany, France, and the Netherlands were catching up. By the summer of 1991, despite economic slowdown in the Community, there were few indications that Japanese investors were slowing down, amid encouragement and funding from EC and local authorities seeking new investments and, above all, new jobs.

To police the new corporate merger wave, EC ministers several days before Christmas 1989 adopted a sweeping plan giving the Community wide powers to review all mergers and acquisitions within the EC in which the resulting company would have annual sales of more than $5.8 billion. The EC would maintain the long-established right to review cases under that amount. The agreement ended sixteen years of controversial debate over how much power member governments should transfer to the antitrust authority of the European Community. Sir Leon Brittan, the commissioner in charge of competition policy, termed it "a historic breakthrough in the creation of a single European market," estimating that the commission would now examine between forty and fifty large mergers each year, and, he indicated, U.S. and Japanese companies would be treated like EC companies.

That notion was, however, quickly challenged early in 1990 by several governments with important domestic automobile companies, such as France, Italy, and Spain, which insisted on "transitional" protection from Japanese cars, particularly those being exported from other EC member countries, notably from Britain. Several EC electronics groups sought increases in tariffs on imported Japanese components. This further fueled EC-Japanese tensions as the Community used the issue to seek easier access for Community products in Japan's highly protected and difficult markets. Undeterred, the Japanese investment wave in cars, car parts, and electronics continued.

AN ANSCHLUSS IN EASTERN EUROPE?

Meantime, the prospects of new acquisitions and joint ventures in Eastern Europe, following the collapse of the Berlin Wall November 9, 1989, further fueled optimistic scenarios for future growth, particularly among West German businessmen. A year later, looking eastward following reunification of the country, several dozen leading German companies and banks started discussions in East Germany and in neighboring countries, openly desperate for joint ventures and investments of all kinds. How soon would Eastern Europe become part of Europe, Inc.? Many of the participants cautiously cited enormous obstacles, such as the underdeveloped state of roads and telecommunications and the lack of managers and lawyers. Many French and British businessmen and bankers were nervously predicting that their big German competitors would, nevertheless, benefit most and perhaps monopolize the new business in Eastern Europe. My talks with East European planners provided a far different and more complex picture. I came to the conclusion that East Europe, Inc. would not necessarily be all German.

"We do not want a German Anschluss, or Annexation here—or anywhere else in Eastern Europe," declared Miloš Zeman of Czechoslovakia, a professor, head of an economics institute, and member of the Czech and Slovak Federal Assembly. We met for coffee in the elegant, recently restored Palace Hotel in downtown Prague on a cool evening in early October 1990, shortly after state visits to the country by Mitterrand, Mrs. Thatcher, and Delors, each of whom addressed the assembly. "We got encouragement, particularly from Mrs. Thatcher, to eventually become full EC members, and we welcome this. I have no fear of Germany, because here, in the capital of Central Europe, we will be seeking the help and participation of all our allies—in Western Europe, the United States, and yes, the Soviet Union."

Background talks with Czech ministers, high officials, journalist friends, and resident ambassadors convinced me that although the Germans certainly had an advantage, there was plenty of room for others; some were already taking advantage of the opening, notably French, Italian, and British industrial companies and banks. In late June 1991, senior Hungarian government officials in Budapest announced that France appeared to be closing in on Germany and the front-running United States as the country's third largest foreign investor.

Finally, economists and bankers on both sides of the Atlantic, late in 1990, began predicting that the EC's new trade and investment ties with Eastern Europe could add as much as a percentage point to the EC's growth rates, possibly two. The change in just one percentage point in the EC's GNP means an additional $50 billion in additional output of goods and services. Thus the combined EC growth rate—estimated at around 2 percent for 1991 and 1992—would put the Community slightly ahead of the recession-hit U.S. and closer to Japan with its 3.8 percent growth rate.

No one was writing off the United States, or a slow recovery in 1992, but Europe looked notably promising. Relaxing in his thirty-second-floor office on New York's Rockefeller Plaza on a sultry August day in 1989, Felix Rohatyn, the ebullient Lazard Frères & Company investment banker, said he was convinced that Western Europe was in many ways better positioned for future growth than even the United States. Not that the U.S. would lose its predominant position as the world's largest, dominant global power. Only a handful of the many people I interviewed, even before the Gulf crisis, predicted that America's power would decline in the 1990s and Rohatyn was certainly not among the pessimists.

"What I am saying," Rohatyn emphasized in his high-pitched voice, "is that Europe will be very powerful, and will grow faster than we . . . they are better positioned, and will have none of the obstacles to growth we, here in the United States, face going into the twenty-first century, such as integrating more and more poor people into this country." It was difficult for Rohatyn to contain his optimism about what was happening in Europe—and this was three months before the sudden, surprising tearing-down of the Berlin Wall. Vienna-born, fluent in French and German, with easy access to Mitterrand and other European leaders, he and his colleagues at Lazard offices throughout Europe had also become important players and intermediaries in arranging and financing mergers and acquisitions on both sides of the Atlantic, both for U.S. and European corporate clients; we shall return to the wave of European transactions in the United States in Chapter 5.

A PRUSSIAN COUNT AS MAVERICK

Meet Count Albrecht Matuschka, a wealthy, somewhat abrasive, and eloquent German aristocrat, whose intellectual energy and dexterity have enabled the company he founded in 1970 to emerge as Germany's largest independent nonbank financial-services group. He is widely considered by Germany's highly conservative, clubby banking establishment to be a brilliant, successful gadfly. In many ways, he might have fit better in the United States, where he attended high school as an exchange student. But he is very German, born in 1944, the son of a Prussian army officer, with family roots in the landed aristocracy of Silesia, who after the war became a priest in the industrial city of Dortmund, where young Albrecht spent his early childhood.

With money borrowed from friends, he and two associates established a small Munich-based asset-management firm, which provided the nucleus of his group. One of its subsidiaries pioneered venture-capital funding in Germany, in what has long been regarded as an unusual and direct, deliberate challenge to the powerful banks in Frankfurt, Munich, and Düsseldorf. He irritated many by attracting some of their best managers to join his group as partners; thirty-three of them, including Matuschka, own and manage the company, and handle accounts worth an estimated $4 billion.

What makes Matuschka unusual, aside from his personality and background, is his wealthy supporters—Germany's many small and medium-sized highly innovative firms, the celebrated *Mittelstand.* They turned to the Matuschka Group in 1989 to challenge giant German industrial firms in bidding on a major contract to supply mobile telephones to the Bundespost, the German government's post and telecommunications agency. "In that deal we failed against the giants, for many reasons, but we have been growing at 40 percent a year, with new, innovative methods of financing, and we are expanding around the world," Matuschka told me in his downtown Munich headquarters.[13] "And if it hadn't been for 1992, we wouldn't be doing what we are doing in the merger and acquisition field . . . 50 percent of our deals are cross-border."

The Matuschka Group, with branch offices stretching from Munich to Tokyo and Atlanta, Georgia, has also moved into East Germany, notably with his group's project for financing and building a mobile telephone network, based on the project previously proposed in West Germany. But he also has been among the first to urge creation of equity markets in East Germany, which, he believes, could be more efficient than those in Frankfurt and Düsseldorf, once privatization of East Germany's state-controlled companies is completed. In late 1989, Matuschka opened up his firm to six powerful partners, who purchased a 25 percent share of the firm. These partners included subsidiaries of General Electric of the United States, Japan's Nomura investment group, France's Suez investment group, and Charterhouse Bank of London. "This is our way of building Europe—through alliances and private initiative," Matuschka said.

Several of the newcomers in his group said they were motivated not only by the opening of markets in East Germany and Eastern Europe, but, above all, by the prospects of a more open and deregulated German financial market, as German authorities responded to 1992-related directives from the Community.

Senior West German bankers agreed that Matuschka, despite mistakes and disarray within his organization, deserves credit. "Say what you will about his brash style, his maverick approach," a senior executive of Germany's powerful Deutsche Bank told me at a year-end news conference in 1990. "But he has had the ideas, before anyone else, including us, and he did find Suez as a French partner . . . we are still looking for a bank to acquire in France, because of the way in which French banks are protected."

SURVIVING A RECESSION?

Even after discounting the hype, the claims for success, the colorful escapades of Europe's best and brightest, it was clear that Common Market countries were, relatively speaking, prospering. Some European-based economists, like Smith Barney's Horne, began making sweeping predictions about Europe's outlook compared to the world's other major trading blocs, the United States and Asia, primarily Japan. "The 1990s will be the Decade of Europe—for better or for worse—because of the Eastern European events and the EC's Single Market," he said.[14] Indeed, many economists and analysts around the world, like Horne, were rushing back to their earlier European forecasts and revising their figures—upward. A major new question was raised in the process, as recession loomed in the United States—namely, could the Community, on its own, survive a prolonged slowdown in the United States?

The 1970s, particularly following the first oil shock, shattered Europe's hopes for prosperity in the mid-1980s. But in two decades the Community countries have diversified heavily away from oil to nuclear fuel and natural gas; massive restructuring was undertaken, as reflected in the continuing high levels of unemployment. Equally important, EC member governments, regional authorities, cities, and private business established massive construction projects, creating a boom of unprecedented proportions.

American economists C. Michal Aho and Bruce Stokes, writing in *Foreign Affairs* in February 1991, termed Europe "a capital sponge," explaining that "the impending creation of a single market in Western Europe kept private European money at home and caused foreign capital to flow in." They predict that fixed business investment in Europe will have tripled between 1985 and 1995. The transformation of Brussels, as we saw in Chapter 1, is only one example.

The spectacular new rail-tunnel project under the English Channel, for the first time linking Britain with the Continent, to which we shall return in Chapter 6, is only one major component in a vast, complex network of rail, air, road, water, audiovisual and telecommunications systems being built in every EC member country—without taking into account the vast, multi-hundred-billion-dollar reconstruction programs being planned for East Germany, Hungary, Poland, and Czechoslovakia. Taken together, they represent a new, mammoth effort to modernize a Europe stretching from the Atlantic to the Urals, now being estimated at well over 500 million consumers—120 million more people than when the 1992 program began, and including several million former Soviet and East European citizens now settled in the West.

The costs of building new infrastructure in the EC countries alone, from 1991 to 1995, is conservatively estimated at $150 billion, the costs of rebuilding Eastern Europe at well over $200 billion. Analysts in London, New York, and Paris confidently predicted that as a result of such staggering projected expenditures, Europe would prove to be a major new growth center of the Western world.

In a study by the Bank for International Settlements which surprised financial analysts, the European Community for the first time since the late 1970s attracted more direct investments in 1990 than the United States. Reflecting the slowdown in the United States and the attractiveness of the Community, investments rose to a record $72.2 billion in the six largest EC countries, a slight increase from a year earlier, according to the BIS, which is based in Basel, Switzerland. The flow to the United States, however, fell sharply in the same period to $25.7 billion, from $72.2 billion in 1989, according to the report published in June 1991.

What this reversal in the trend meant, according to many analysts, is that the EC economies, taken together, are in the strongest position since the postwar era to survive a recession in the United States—on their own and decoupled from North America. Leading U.S. economic analysts told my colleague Lawrence Malkin in New York early in 1990 that an American slowdown or recession would have to become truly severe to pull down Europe with it; a mild recession, they concluded, might even help Europe by easing inflationary pressures. Many, surprisingly, also reported that the European economies were lessening their trade dependence on the U.S. market, which in 1991 represented less than 10 percent of the Community's total exports; 62 percent of the Community's trade is with its EC partners, meaning a strong majority of its exports and imports.

Just how wealthy was the European Community bloc in absolute terms? According to the most recent statistics compiled and compared by the OECD in June 1991, the EC's GNP, at current exchange rates, ranks ahead of the United States: $6.02 trillion, compared to $5.32 trillion for the United States and $2.89 trillion for Japan. The Soviet Union's GNP, calculated on the same basis, was estimated at $1.5 trillion, thus ranking it fourth, behind Japan, the EC, and the United States.

Not everything was rosy in the EC outlook, however. A grimmer reality lurked behind the upbeat aggregate forecasts, widespread hype, and overly upbeat statements by some politicians, which even the carefully controlled, optimistic drive of Delors could not hide: throughout Europe, there was considerable doubting, hesitation, and even growing opposition to the 1992 program and monetary and political union, to which we shall return in Chapter 7. Polls and conversations with many businessmen showed that while most now knew what 1992 was they were fearful of how approaching deregulation and removal of barriers would affect—or threaten—their businesses. As the Gulf crisis worsened in early 1991, many companies began to shelve investment plans, halted hiring, and just waited, citing the overall uncertainty.

As the war ended and the economic outlook brightened, many leaders predicted that EC unemployment would continue to rise, rather than fall, because of the necessity to continue cost cutting, and despite large-scale job creation throughout the main EC countries, equal to about 1 percent of Europe's labor force in 1990. Many economic leaders expressed skepticism about whether the 1992 plan could significantly improve the capacity to expand, particularly small and medium-sized firms in Germany, Italy, Spain, Greece, and Portugal. Many businessmen feared growing Japanese and South Korean investments sprouting throughout the Community, even though they were creating new jobs and generating local business. Influential business and political groups throughout the Community, particularly those in regions with high unemployment, even argued for restrictions on foreign investments and imports, as part of an EC-wide revival movement to "Buy European."

American and Japanese diplomats on assignment in Europe began worrying and warning their business communities of the dangers and risks involved. The U.S. Embassy in Paris, for example, in a background paper leaked to the press as early as 1988 warned that "American business, especially small and medium-sized firms, needs to move quickly to educate itself to the changes taking place in France and in Europe, related to the completion of the internal market. U.S. companies will need to position themselves to take full advantage of the commercial opportunities that 1992 will offer . . . the U.S. government and American industry [also] need to be on guard that American firms are not excluded from access to or participation in the unified market."

Acting on the recommendations of perceptive ambassadors, such as Kingon in Brussels, whom we met in Chapter 1, the Reagan administration established an interagency task force in Washington, headed by Carla Hills, the Special Trade Representative, aimed at protecting American business interests as the 1992 program took shape. "We are not going to sit by and watch 1992 go by—we will be lobbying for U.S. interests," commented a senior U.S. diplomat in Paris. "What we see emerging in industry and agriculture amounts to European deeply rooted protectionism, and we don't like it!"

Kingon, himself a somewhat abrasive, tough, but personable executive, was among the first senior U.S. ambassadors to warn Washington that not everything was going America's way in the New Europe, and he went public with the message early. Writing in the first of a series of special supplements on 1992 published by the *International Herald Tribune,* Kingon warned: "I hope that those who guide the course of development of many pan-European industries and financial institutions do not yield to the temptation to benefit existing European companies in an unfair way. . . . Were it to happen, the Community would soon find itself cut off from the free flow of information and technology, and on its way of losing further ground."[15]

While not yet a direct threat, the warning clearly implied retaliation was being planned against the Community—if and when American interests were threatened by what Washington regarded as unfair competition. The message, which was to be repeated many times, was anchored in economic and industrial reality. Aggressive, expansion-bent European leaders were indeed now reaching—dangerously—into realms where American global political interests and economic stakes were considered vital, notably in areas of high technology such as aerospace.

Global Economic Warfare:
Trying to Outsmart the United
States and Japan

This plane will never sell, and certainly not to us. It reminds me of the definition of a camel—a horse designed by a committee.

—SENIOR EXECUTIVE OF A MAJOR U.S. AIRLINE

That quote had become so commonplace in the late 1960s no one today can recall who made it first. But it succinctly summed up the prevailing attitude among American aerospace executives when they first heard of work underway on a "European camel." Many predicted disaster for what was billed as the world's first wide-body passenger jet, called Airbus. Aviation writers joined in to scoff at the idea that a new jet capable of transporting three hundred passengers over two thousand nautical miles could be powered by only two engines, and that somehow three disparate European countries could join forces to make it happen. Yet, with engineering teams of different nationalities working round the clock in scattered locations in Britain, France, and West Germany, and with generous funding from the French and German governments, the new plane, designated A300, began testing successfully. On December 18, 1970, another new animal—a Pan-European management company—was quietly set up in modest offices in downtown Paris, and called Airbus Industrie. But not a single plane had yet been sold, the first test flight was two years off, and the predictions of doom continued.

CAPTURING A MARKET

Twenty years later, in what had become Western Europe's most spectacular industrial success story of the postwar era, Airbus Industrie had captured 52 percent of the world market for wide-body jets and more than 26 percent of the world's total jetliner market, previously dominated by America's two main aircraft manufacturers: Boeing and McDonnell Douglas. Airlines from around the world—in America, Western Europe, Eastern Europe, and the Soviet Union—were ready to buy the new, high-technology jet planes being offered by the consortium, which came to include the leading aircraft companies of France, Germany, Britain, Spain, the Netherlands, Belgium, and Italy. It had settled into a sprawling modern headquarters complex just outside the historic southern French city of Toulouse.

On a vast, flat site near the city, Airbus planes roll off the assembly line at the rate of 15 per month. In mid-1991, firm orders from about 100 airlines around the world stood at a record 987 planes, worth more than $68 billion. Executives confidently predicted that Airbus would attain its long-cherished goal within a few years: 40 percent of the world market for jet aircraft with 100 seats or more. Indeed, as *Aviation Week,* the industry's authoritative magazine, editorialized April 11, 1988, Airbus Industrie had come of age.

Airbus is the most controversial example of how West European governments and their domestic aerospace industries pooled resources to attack—and then ended—the virtual monopoly of American companies in this key and strategic area of high technology. Responding fiercely and doggedly, successive administrations in Washington, pressured by worried U.S. aerospace companies led by Boeing and McDonnell Douglas, have sought to slow, stop, and eliminate what had emerged as a major source of competition and a challenge to U.S. aerospace power around the world. Yet even the Bush administration, which displayed somewhat more flexibility than the Reagan White House, has been unable to stop Airbus.

One major reason is subsidies and other forms of government aid, to which we shall return, and effective politicking by the Europeans— at home and abroad—arguing that U.S. aerospace companies were receiving as much in government financial assistance as the Europeans, if not more. Yet transatlantic trade warfare has never broken out, despite years of skirmishing. Why?

It isn't publicized in Washington, nor in Seattle, and St. Louis, Missouri, but as much as one-third, or more, of the equipment and technology that goes, or can be put, into an Airbus is American, notably the engines, electronics and the radar. And most U.S. airlines that have bought the Airbus are satisfied. But most important, the industry outlook is relatively rosy.

As Boeing entered the 1990s, it estimated that worldwide sales of commercial jets between 1990 and 2005 would attain a record $617 billion, including $15–$20 billion in orders from Eastern European airlines seeking to modernize their dangerously outdated fleets. Airbus Industrie said it would double production by 1995, and in the autumn of 1990 inaugurated a new $200 million plant near its present site in Toulouse, the largest, most modern aeronautical plant in Europe. But Jean Pierson, Airbus's managing director, predicted at his January 9, 1991, news conference in Paris that, because of the Gulf crisis and the dangers of war, the year would be one of "turbulence" and "uncertainty." Six months later, at the Paris air show, he declared that Airbus remained in "pretty good shape," and that his forecasts remained optimistic.

Despite such seemingly contradictory, complex scenarios, battles for billions of dollars in orders have been waged behind the scenes— relentlessly, fiercely, amid charges and countercharges that each side was using unfair, allegedly illegal inducements to obtain business, such as government-backed subsidies, padded economic-aid packages, bribery, and even political blackmail. This meant, for example, accusations of tying generous economic-aid packages for developing countries to purchases of planes. American and European executives have told me how their competitors regularly arrange for electronic surveillance of their hotel rooms and telephone conversations; search their luggage and other belongings while they are traveling abroad, particularly during the Paris and Farnborough, England, air shows, the traditional gathering points for the world aerospace industry.

RELYING ON SECRET AGENTS

Other executives, diplomats, and aviation writers I have talked to played down the frequency of these techniques, noting they are difficult to verify, but conceded that the practices were spreading in all fields of high technology. In a spectacular case brought to light by the French magazine *L'Express* in the spring of 1990, France's intelligence service, Direction Générale de la Sécurité Extérieure, attempted to collect industrial secrets at foreign offices of the U.S. computer companies IBM and Texas Instruments in an effort to help Bull, the ailing French government-controlled computer group.

The operation, run between 1987 and 1989, was uncovered by the Central Intelligence Agency and the FBI, whose investigators only confirmed the *L'Express* report in late November 1990, adding that, while France was among the most aggressive, Britain, West Germany, the Netherlands, and Belgium also use their intelligence services to support domestic industries.[1]

"It used to be only the Soviets that used these notorious methods," commented a senior Boeing executive during an unusually frank talk, "but now, with the Europeans, anything and everything goes, including the use of agents and real professionals to get at our marketing information. . . . It is global economic warfare." Do Americans hit back? "Outside the United States, you better believe it," the executive, a vice president for marketing, told me, on the condition he not be identified. "The CIA and the State Department know all about the sales methods used, the photographs taken of our documents left in hotel rooms and the like. We have our own methods of retaliation. . . . The CIA generally refuses to get involved, but we hire private security agencies, and we do get sound advice from our overseas embassies," he said.

In the autumn of 1990, amid charges and countercharges regarding allegedly "dubious" Airbus financing for a major purchase of A-320s by Northwest Airlines, I asked a very senior French trade-ministry official whether all the talk of spying and bribery didn't bother him. He shrugged, and with a slight smile leaned forward, a cigarette in his hand. "My friend," he said, "we are living in a difficult, complex world as both our governments and our companies recognize. We do what we must do—to survive in a very competitive business."

Charges and countercharges are common, but rarely proven and often deliberately blurred. Thus, two weeks after the February 14, 1990, crash of an Indian Airlines A-320 while landing at Bangalore, killing ninety-two people, Indian authorities charged Airbus Industrie with having bribed eight former Indian officials to cancel a previously signed deal with Boeing in favor of the European planes— thirty-one A-320s, worth $1.2 billion. The allegations over bribery had nothing to do with the dispute over the cause of the crash; Airbus Industrie claimed Indian pilots were careless during landing, while pilot groups suggested there was a "design problem" with the plane.

The Indian government charges regarding bribery, in fact, went back to 1985, when it was alleged that bureaucrats in the Civil Aviation Ministry and two former managing directors of Indian Airlines were paid to rig technical and financial data to make the Airbus proposal look more attractive.[2] Airbus Industrie vigorously denied the allegations, and insisted that the A-320 was chosen over the Boeing 757 because of "superior technology, not because of occult interventions." The same charges had surfaced in 1985 in Washington, as the Reagan administration began its first major assault on European strategies regarding airliner sales.

That year, Airbus sales practices were being studied at the sub-cabinet level in the Reagan administration, with grounds being sought for possible retaliation under Section 301 of the U.S. Trade Act of 1974. A senior U.S. trade official told my colleague Warren Getler that the Indian Airlines cancellation of the Boeing order had raised the administration's concern about so-called "inducements" to jet sales, and that it was but one example of unfair trade practices used by Airbus, which, if proven, would violate international trade agreements. A list of these alleged practices was presented to European governments, citing the following: promises of French technical assistance in cleaning up the Ganges River; European support in the World Bank for securing soft loans for India; French support in the United Nations for India's goal of a nuclear-free zone in the Indian Ocean; and acceleration of delivery schedules of Mirage jets— charges brushed off by Airbus Industrie and the French government as untrue.[3]

A year later in Washington, I learned that the official Getler interviewed was a friendly source of mine, who told me that Boeing had made the allegations in a letter and other written materials, but they were never proven, nor pursued under U.S. trade legislation. "These kinds of inducements are part of the business, because everybody is fighting for orders," the U.S. official emphasized, his voice rising, "but we know the Europeans are more aggressive, and go a lot farther than our people. . . . U.S. companies start with the airline and work up, Airbus starts with the government and works down, but the deals are never proven." Several weeks later in Paris, I asked my friendly French trade official for his reaction. He laughed. "Look, our embassies are not exactly asleep, in places like India," he said. "Do you think we don't know what's going on? Do you think we, Dassault, Aérospatiale, Boeing, and Douglas don't pull out the stops? . . . Everybody uses every technique they can to sell, and if they, or we, can get the president, the prime minister or our most senior officials involved, believe me, we do."

SELLING TANKS IN SWITZERLAND

In fact, U.S. embassies, the White House, and visiting American congressional delegations often become involved in encouraging major sales of U.S. export items, such as planes, telecommunications systems and, in one memorable case, American tanks in Switzerland.

This was billed as the largest single purchase of military equipment in Switzerland's history. General Dynamics and Krauss-Maffei, one of West Germany's largest arms makers, and now part of the Daimler group, were battling in 1983 for a contract worth more than $1 billion to build 420 sophisticated tanks for the Swiss army. Unprecedented and startling for the Swiss was the unusual salesmanship of a very unusual saleswoman, the attractive and very determined U.S. ambassador to Switzerland, Faith Ryan Whittlesey.

Convinced that the American M-1 Abrams tank was superior to Germany's Leopard-2, Mrs. Whittlesey had herself widely photographed test-driving the M-1; she made dozens of speeches throughout the country promoting it, including at her farewell talk before joining the Reagan White House staff. But she shocked a lot of Swiss citizens. As the editor of one leading Zürich newspaper commented to me, "This high-powered U.S. salesmanship was bad enough. But it did seem a bit incongruous to see a mother selling a tank, even if she was a very effective, professional ambassador."

In the end, despite enthusiastic backing from Washington, the Germans won, because as one senior Swiss army officer evaluating the two tanks in Bern told me with a laugh: "The final decision really had little to do with your lively, likable lady ambassador. . . . Our military people are very German, and well, the Leopard reminds them a bit of a shiny Mercedes, whereas your tank resembles—a mean, dark weapon." He quickly added that Krauss-Maffei also offered a better industrial subcontracting package to recession-hit Swiss industrial companies, which were determined to benefit from an attractive licensing and coproduction arrangement proposed by the German arms maker.

HOW "STAR WARS" PRODDED EUROPE

Europe's drive to challenge American and Japanese predominance began in earnest during the early 1980s as most European governments became convinced that they would have to either restore viability in a wide range of high-technology sectors or allow them to go under. The reasons were compelling; as the somewhat panicky strategists pointed out, Japanese industry had already dealt a mortal blow to many companies in the United States, notably in consumer electronics. The priorities set by governments and the EC Commission, led by Belgium's hard-driving Davignon, while serving as EC commissioner for industry policy, were protecting existing jobs in sensitive defense-related industries, while creating new jobs wherever possible; boosting Europe's balance of payments by reducing dependence on growing imports, particularly in computers, electronics, and telecommunications equipment; and most important, keeping scientists from moving, as they did in the 1960s and 1970s when Europe's best and brightest were attracted to the United States by generous research budgets and, above all, by better salaries.

It isn't that Europe lacks scientific or technological ability or talent. According to EC estimates, more than one million scientists and technicians work on research projects throughout the Community, and Europe over the years has won a respectable proportion of Nobel Prizes for research. But their resources have been dispersed, laboratory teams isolated, and research work uncoordinated with manufacturing and marketing. In other words, there still is no full-fledged European version of California's Silicon Valley. As a knowledgeable Japanese ambassador to the EC, who preferred anonymity, put it to me in his spacious Brussels office in 1986: "The problem with the Europeans," he said caustically, "is that they do not want to grow the plant first. They just want to pluck the fruit."

Within several years, the mood—and the action—began to change directions as, gradually, governments, the EC Commission, European industrial leaders, the European Roundtable, and UNICE, the Union of Industrial and Employers' Federations in Europe, began to shift their energy and resources toward launching cooperative R&D programs in the twelve-nation EC area. Venture-capital firms, thanks to new, liberalized tax laws, began to spring up throughout the Community, along with small science cities, or "Euro-technopoles." These sites, for the first time, linked R&D laboratories and local universities in relaxed, comfortable surroundings. Sophia-Antipolis, established near Nice on the French Riviera in the mid-1970s, was one of Europe's first such centers, but several dozen are now functioning in Britain, Germany, Spain, Belgium and the Netherlands. "Silicon Glen," a high-tech area in Scotland, is another example.

The EC was also strongly urging at first, and by the late 1980s insisting, that Japanese companies flocking to Europe invest in high technology and advanced manufacturing in such vulnerable sectors as automobiles and electronics. Starting around 1989, Japan was being told that it would not be enough simply to set up assembly, or "screwdriver" operations, based on cheap imported components. We shall return to the role of Japan in Europe in Chapter 7. What Europe needed most in this period was shock treatment. It finally came from an unexpected quarter—the United States. Its name: the Strategic Defense Initiative.

When President Reagan first proposed the SDI, or Star Wars, in 1983, few Europeans realized its potential impact, but gradually it became painfully obvious to most European leaders that if Europe were to be excluded, it would only further aggravate Europe's predicament and possibly seal its fate as a technological backwater. Among those who saw the danger early was President Mitterrand who, following the recommendations of his close Élysée Palace adviser Jacques Attali, proposed during the Versailles summit of industrialized nations he was hosting that the summiteers establish a working group to jointly develop eighteen advanced technologies as a way of bolstering the European and U.S. research efforts.

But President Reagan had other priorities, notably stopping the Europeans from building the trans-Siberian gas pipeline in the Soviet Union, and thus he and his advisers ignored the Mitterrand-Attali idea. Refusing to be brushed off, France gradually won support for its own plan from Germany, Italy, and the EC Commission, which it was hoped would trigger a revival of European R&D, perhaps as a complement to SDI. But few outside of a handful of European officials and the Élysée Palace yet knew what the American plan, known as the Strategic Defense Initiative, was supposed to be, who would be involved, and what it would accomplish.

SDI, however, appeared to promise precious little direct fallout for the Community. Hubert Vedrine, Mitterrand's adviser on strategic affairs and Élysée secretary general, was among the insiders who immediately grasped the technological implications of SDI for Europe, and quickly obtained approval for a confidential crash study. Mitterrand was fond of recounting how at the 1985 seven-nation economic summit held in Bonn, he heard Reagan use the word "subcontractors" to describe European involvement in SDI, which the French leader said only "confirmed my intuitions," namely, that the leadership and control of R&D activities would remain with the United States.

In other words, Europe would never be a full-fledged partner in SDI, nor share in developing the most sensitive technologies. This only confirmed what European industry and government officials had been complaining about for years—namely that the U.S. market for their civilian and military aircraft and space-launch facilities had been highly protected and that the Reagan administration was heavy-handed in its dealings with the allies over transferring sensitive technology.

Several weeks following the Bonn meeting, during a crowded news conference in the gilded Salon de l'Horloge at the foreign ministry in Paris—the same room in which the Schuman Plan was announced in 1950—German foreign minister Genscher told reporters that the U.S. effort to enlist European support for the SDI program amounted to "Americans going through Europe with their checkbooks," adding that "we cannot afford to lose our best brains." What few of us realized at the time was that Genscher and his opposite number, France's foreign minister Roland Dumas, along with Kohl and Mitterrand, were secretly drafting a plan that would become Europe's answer to SDI.

That plan was Eureka, a European collaborative R&D program, aimed at challenging the United States and Japan in a wide range of civilian sectors, such as computers, telecommunications, robotics, biotechnologies, new materials, advanced manufacturing systems. The political impetus came from President Mitterrand at the first Eureka conference held in Paris July 17, 1985. He announced that France would immediately contribute $125 million; political and financial support was also pledged by Britain's foreign secretary, Sir Geoffrey Howe, and Kohl, who emphasized that Germany would most certainly participate. Ten pilot projects were immediately launched, including production of a standard EC microcomputer for education and personal use, development of a laser for cutting cloth in the European apparel industry, design of membranes for water filtration that could be used to desalinate sea water, development of a diagnosis kit for sexually transmitted diseases, and a project for advanced optic electronics.

Five years later, seven of the original ten projects were still under development, but three were completed, which along with others produced what Eureka's Brussels-based secretary general, Olaf Mayer, described as "concrete results, meaning they have led to sales." The list has been vastly expanded to 500 projects, involving 3,000 institutions in 19 European countries. In early 1991, cautiously admiring Japanese diplomats began portraying Eureka as a European version of their MITI, the powerful Ministry for International Trade and Industry, which had forged Japan's formidable links between industry, research, and government.

That comparison with MITI is highly exaggerated, but, as Mayer noted, some of the Eureka projects have been converted into profitable, commercially viable operations and some of the companies supported by Eureka have demonstrated how a Pan-European approach can work in practice.

One example is an unusual company known as ES2, which stands for European Silicon Structures. Virtually unknown outside the industry, ES2's uniqueness lies in its advanced technology and Europe-wide organization. The company developed a new chip-etching process that permits the production of custom chips in less than half the time and at less than half the price of its American and Japanese competitors. The $18-million-a-year company was incorporated in Luxembourg and headquartered in Munich; its research facilities were installed in Scotland and the manufacturing base in Rousset, a town near Aix-en-Provence in southern France. English was adopted as ES2's language and the ECU, the European Currency Unit, the EC's fledgling money, as its currency. Among ES2's founders were a

group of executives who formerly worked for the European operations of Motorola, the U.S. electronics company. One of them,
Frenchman Jean-Luc Grand-Clément, is fond of telling visitors that
partly because of ES2's involvement with Eureka, the company projects a "European image," meaning that French companies have
come to believe that they are dealing with a French company, the
British with a British company, and the Germans consider it German.

GAINING IN R&D, BUT A MIXED RECORD

Europe was gradually showing signs of reversing Professor Giersch's
"Eurosclerosis" scenario. Consider, for example, U.S. government
and industry spending on R&D, excluding military expenditures. The
United States still spends more than any of its global competitors—in
excess of $130 billion, which is more than Japan, Britain, West Ger-
many, and France combined. Yet the three main EC member countries now devote a far larger share of their GNP to R&D, and have
been gradually closing the gap with the United States. Germany, for
example, during recent years has gradually increased expenditures,
corresponding to roughly 2.8 percent of its GNP spent on R&D;
Britain has moved upward to 2.4 percent, France to 2.3 percent,
Japan to 2.9 percent, while U.S. spending has leveled off at 2.6
percent. The National Science Foundation in 1990 reported that for
the first time in fourteen years U.S. spending on corporate research
and development had not kept pace with inflation.

However, as leading European research experts have also noted,
Japan began from a smaller base, and has been growing faster than
EC countries; thus, the gap between the EC and Japan has been
widening, particularly in such sectors as electronics. Yet Europe also
was holding its own in some sectors and battling hard in others and
even gaining in some. Consider the following:

- Pharmaceuticals. Of the top ten drug companies in the world,
  six are European. In 1989, the EC Commission proposed reinforcing its patent-protection laws to bring them in line with
  those of its EC competitors. The basic idea is to extend the
  effective protection of patents, because of the long time that
  elapses between the issuance of patents and the clearance for
  marketing products. The proposed extension was not supposed

to exceed ten years, but that would, the EC hoped, strengthen EC pharmaceutical companies' positions, particularly with regard to U.S. competitors; American laws had been amended in 1984. Additionally, the EC moved to allow ten-year extensions on expiring patents to reinforce further the position of EC-based companies, particularly with regard to R&D.

- Telecommunications. Of the world's six leaders, three are European: France's Alcatel, West Germany's Siemens, and Sweden's Ericsson. The EC Commission, as part of the 1992 program, has initiated widespread deregulation of EC markets for equipment and services. While modest in scope compared to individual company research programs, the EC Commission accelerated R&D spending under a five-year program known as RACE, involving expenditures of $1.5 billion for such projects as developing data transmission and video telephones. One goal is to reverse the EC's growing trade deficit with the United States and Japan for telecommunications equipment. AT&T and IBM were also establishing marketing beachheads, in some cases with local, European partners.

- Semiconductors. Europe has been making slight headway in this critical sector. In 1985, Western Europe represented 18 percent of the world's semiconductor market. By 1990, the share had grown to 20 percent and optimistic EC estimates place the share at 22 percent by 1995. According to officials at JESSI, a $4 billion cooperative European program designed to develop a new generation of memory chips, Europe's semiconductor industry now spends 20 percent of its sales on new plant and equipment, compared to 15 percent by Japanese producers and 13 percent spent by American competitors. Early in 1990, JESSI began cooperating with SEMATECH, a similar, U.S.-government-backed project, and allowed IBM and Japan's Fujitsu to participate in several projects in response to U.S. and British pressure on European authorities.

- Industrial Electronics. In this related field, Thomson, Siemens, Olivetti, and others are fighting to maintain strong leads in several categories, notably high definition television, office automation, software, and advanced military radar. Fears that European electronics would not survive Japanese competition, particularly in high-definition television, spurred EC governments to boost financial support for research to small high-tech companies, as well as to the industry giants. The French government was the first to pledge—$550 million to state-owned Thomson to develop its technology in HDTV. Other EC governments were considering following.

- Biotechnology. Of the world's top ten chemical companies with heavy involvement in biotechnology, seven are European and they have been pressing hard for expansion, notably through acquisitions in North America. Standouts have been West Germany's Bayer and France's Rhône-Poulenc. Japan, lagging in basic R&D, has launched a bid to overtake the United States and Europe in applied biotechnologies, and it has touched off interest in even the smaller EC countries. For example, Danish, British, and Belgian firms have provided their own modest, but significant, success stories by developing new products.
- Railroads. An emerging high-speed rail network crisscrossing Europe has started a rush to sell new powerful high-tech locomotives and modern passenger cars and rail infrastructure throughout the world.

In a major breakthrough in late May of 1991, France's TGV train was awarded a franchise to build a 970-kilometer, high-speed route that would link Dallas, Houston, and San Antonio, Texas, by 1998. The Texas High Speed Rail Authority rejected a competing bid from a German-led consortium, whose West European participants had proposed the InterCity Express, known as the ICE. This high-speed train only entered service in early June 1991, a decade after the TGV. But the competition illustrated that Europe, not the United States, and not Japan, is the leader in this field. Nevertheless, all the contenders were planning to compete for high-speed rail systems being planned in Taiwan, South Korea, and elsewhere in Europe. One of the reasons Fiat and CGE, its name changed to Aleatel Alsthom, pooled their rail business, for example, was to prepare for submitting a joint bid for the first high-speed rail link between Lyon and Turin that would cross the Alps.

GOVERNMENTS THE PROVIDER

Without generous subsidies, government-backed loans and orders, most of Europe's high-tech industries, notably those in aerospace, electronics, and nuclear energy, could not survive. The Europeans insist that the same holds for their American and Japanese competitors. But Americans have repeatedly made the perfectly justifiable point that much of what happens in Europe is deliberately shrouded in secrecy, reinforced and nurtured by close alliances between defense-related industries, many state-controlled, and their governments. And there is far less transparency in many key sectors, compared to the United States and Japan. Thus, for example, Airbus Industrie publishes no consolidated financial results, yet argues it competes fairly.

Pierson, Airbus managing director, at his January 9, 1991, news conference announced that for the first time since its founding the consortium earned an operating surplus in 1990, estimated at around $125 million on revenues of $4.6 billion, adding he expected an even larger surplus in 1991. But he produced no published report.

U.S. financial and intelligence analysts, challenging those assertions, have estimated that more than $13.5 billion in government-backed funding has been provided unfairly to the consortium's partners for building its planes, mainly by France, Germany, and Britain. In November 1989, the Kohl government approved an additional $2.2 billion in subsidies to write off MBB's outstanding debts and to provide Daimler, the controlling parent company, protection against low dollar exchange rates through the year 2000—a move the Reagan and Bush administrations challenged as illegal under international trade rules. Responding to the criticism, a compromise agreement was reached between Bonn and Daimler, reducing the subsidy by about $680 million, but the plan has remained intact, to the great annoyance of U.S. industry and Washington.

Retaliating verbally in the spring of 1991, Henri Martre, the gregarious president of France's state-owned Aérospatiale and a key, founding Airbus shareholder, told newsmen that Boeing's complaints were caused by fear of competition. He was referring to plans announced during the Paris Air Show in June 1991 that Airbus was planning a new jumbo jet, a 650-seat aircraft that would compete directly with Boeing's 747, the American company's most profitable plane, which has no direct competitor. Aérospatiale also released estimates purporting to show that U.S. competitors, including Boeing, Lockheed, and McDonnell Douglas, had received more than $26 billion in indirect financial aid from the U.S. government between 1978 and 1987.

But Airbus Industrie bears a closer look because it is but the tip of a much larger European iceberg. Consider the following:

MBB, now merged into Daimler-Benz, Germany's largest industrial group, maker of the Mercedes-Benz, the world's best-selling luxury car, as well as missiles and electronic products, owns 37.9 percent of Airbus. British Aerospace, Britain's biggest defense high-tech group, which controls the ailing automaker Rover, owns 20 percent of Airbus. And Aérospatiale, France's largest aerospace group, heavily involved in building the French nuclear striking force, rockets, missiles, and helicopters, also owns 37.9 percent of Airbus, while Construcciones Aeronauticas of Spain (CASA), Spain's largest defense and airplane manufacturer, owns the remaining 4.2 percent share. Altogether these four groups and their affiliated companies employ about 900,000 people. In other words, the Airbus consortium is but one highly visible member of this European high-tech family, and its planes are examples of its product range.

There is Ariane—a family of rockets designed and built under the auspices of the Paris-based European Space Agency, established in 1975 by eleven West European countries with a single goal: achieving European autonomy in space. This meant development of Europe's own rockets for manned and unmanned transport into space and, eventually, an independent manned space station. Ariane was the successful response to the first priority, following a string of failures by Europe to establish a united front in this field in the 1960s. Despite the fact that the United States still spent roughly ten times as much on space as Europe, there was wide agreement that the Europeans entered the 1990s with the infrastructure and resources needed to build and operate most advanced space systems.

Thus, despite the sudden explosion and destruction in February 1990 of an Ariane rocket carrying two Japanese communications satellites, executives responsible for the rocket employed by its marketing company, Arianespace, were proudly proclaiming their intention to continue building on an already impressive base, resembling that of Airbus—more than 50 percent of the world market for launching commercial satellites, worth an estimated $37–$45 billion through the year 2000. It was Ariane's fifth failure out of 45 launches since December 24, 1979. That was the date of Ariane's first, successful launch from its pad at Kourou in French Guiana, which is undergoing massive expansion and which American space experts say is easily on a par with America's most advanced test sites.

Here again, as with Airbus, the competition was mainly American, in the form of NASA and a handful of leading U.S. private aerospace companies, led by McDonnell Douglas, General Dynamics, and the Martin Marietta Corporation, and the competition was fierce. "Ariane has captive European customers and shareholders, who are told to buy European," a senior General Dynamics executive complained bitterly during the June 1989 air show at Le Bourget near Paris. "We are fully competitive with our Atlas launcher, but they are killing us," the American said.

Responding energetically, a European space executive, asked: "How many satellites can we launch for NASA or the U.S. Air Force? None. Why do we succeed? Because we are commercially competitive, and yes, we have committed considerable resources to Ariane so that it succeeds, but we do compete fairly." At its tenth-anniversary celebrations in Paris December 11, 1990, Charles Bigot, Arianespace's chairman, predicted the battling would continue and that his American competitors indeed had the advantages. "It is a protected market, which means the U.S. military and the government get the priority."

Consider another spectacularly costly example of how EC governments support their industries. In 1985, the defense ministers of Britain, Germany, Italy, and Spain agreed that their companies—British Aerospace, MBB, Aeritalia, and CASA—would join forces to build an even costlier plane, the European Fighter Aircraft, EFA, Europe's largest single cooperative project to date. It was to be developed at a record total cost of $37 billion, and the first flight of the first prototype was scheduled for early in 1992. Four years later, assuming governments approve, production of the new combat fighter would begin and compete directly with advanced U.S. and Soviet fighter planes also being developed, despite disarmament plans for Europe. "We want to keep the technology, and compete for the export market," a senior British aerospace official said, adding, "We certainly don't want to leave the market to the French."

France, which initially was a member of the EFA consortium, broke away in 1985 during a bitter dispute and decided instead to build the Dassault-designed Rafale, a similar, competing fighter project. The decision to go it alone, thus assuring French design leadership, was taken by Mitterrand, heavily influenced by the Dassault family, one of the most powerful and wealthy business dynasties in France, with close connections to both conservative and leftist parties, as well as the Élysée Palace. Although the prospects of reduced defense spending in Europe raised the question whether Rafale and EFA would go into full production in the mid-1990s, European defense planners are confident that EFA's development will proceed, probably under British leadership, even if Germany dropped out under political pressure. Meantime, Dassault, hard hit by the collapse of export markets for its military planes, has shown greater willingness to cooperate with other major European aerospace companies in other projects, but has continued the Rafale. The sleek twin-engine fighter made its public debut on the opening day of the Paris Air Show, June 13, 1991, with an intense, admiring Mitterrand looking on.

SEEKING AUTONOMY IN AEROSPACE

Attempting to win against the United States has been the driving force for the biggest projects. "When we started out with the Tornado fighter project, well before EFA, the Americans did everything possible to discourage us," recalled Folkhard Oelwein, spokesman for the West German aerospace industry association. "Why? Because we were building a new plane, which after its maiden flight in 1974 looked as if it would succeed, and, as they soon began to realize, it would contain very, very little American technology . . . only 3 percent to be exact, in the radar."[4]

The Tornado fighter-bomber, Europe's largest collaborative aerospace program, is expected to continue well into the 1990s with total anticipated production of more than 1,100 planes, including exports to Saudi Arabia. Tornado fighter aircraft sent by Britain and Italy to Saudi Arabia during the Gulf crisis belonged to, and were manned by, the Royal and Italian air forces. But the Saudis were counting on getting more Tornados under terms of a multibillion-dollar package deal between Britain and Saudi Arabia announced in 1988, and actively, enthusiastically supported by Mrs. Thatcher.

I once asked Sir Raymond Lygo, before he stepped down as British Aerospace's chief executive, who did the deal, and his answer was unequivocal. "She did it," he snapped, referring to Mrs. Thatcher. The deal was important because it was the single largest arms deal in postwar history, and because it allowed Britain temporarily to replace the United States as the Arab kingdom's primary arms supplier. Consideration of Europe's future role in space was also fueling the ambitions of industry as cutbacks of major defense programs began in many EC and Nordic countries, including in Germany, where parliamentary pressures grew to withdraw from the EFA program.

Similarly, in space, I recall watching proud, expressionless Hans-Arnt Vogels, president of MBB, stride to the podium at the headquarters near Paris of Arianespace, the European company responsible for operating the Ariane space project, and begin praising what Europe was doing in space. "We can be proud of what we have accomplished," he said, his voice quivering with emotion, as he gestured to five gleaming-white models of Ariane launchers standing nearby, and then turned back to his audience of European aviation-industry officials and observers. "We must be ready to continue competing with the United States, and be aware that Japan is also entering the space field, but we can hold our noses high—as Europeans—because the next century will be the century of space," he declared, as the room erupted in two minutes of sustained applause.[5]

BUYING EUROPEAN

Europe was relying on more than just subsidies and government financing to bolster its global strategy. A "Buy European" dimension was also being built into the EC's emerging rules on procurement practices, which clearly favored EC-based companies in bidding on government contracts. Some European planners justified this approach on the grounds that strong "Buy American" legislation discriminated even more unfairly against foreign suppliers bidding on federal and state contracts in the United States.

Coming into widespread use were selective quotas and the imposition of "voluntary" restraints on the importation of Japanese cars, television sets, copiers, and electronic components. The goal was obtaining "reciprocity," and "symmetry" with regard to elimination of trade barriers in Japan. Despite strenuous objections by Washington, Tokyo, and Seoul, European planners were also determined to legalize "transition" periods for sectors facing allegedly unfair competition, notably automobiles and electronics, the periods being proposed ranging from five to ten years.

When I first interviewed Cornelius van der Klugt in early 1986 as he was about to become chairman of Philips, he told me: "I am not a patient man, and the company has to grow a lot more than it has."

At sixty-one virtually unknown outside the company, he was tense, volatile, aggressive; he lived up to his image as "a street fighter," as portrayed by a Dutch magazine. He pledged to increase Philips's profits by cutting costs and boosting the company's involvement in R&D, including EC-financed projects. "As a Philips man, I keep a sense of our history around the world," van der Klugt said with a mischievous smile on his tanned face. "We intend to get help from our authorities in our strategy, which means protection if need be." A bit surprising, I thought, for the man who replaced the charismatic, unflappable, publicity-minded Dekker in the top job at Philips, He like Dekker was a self-made man without a university degree and had joined Philips at the age of twenty-five, believing, I thought, in liberalized trade.

Three years later, a tense and angry van der Klugt began addressing a conference on EC industrial policy in Brussels. Looking out at the audience, comprising members of the European Parliament, trade unions, industry groups, and the EC Commission, he held out a domino in his hand. "Do you know what this is?" he asked. He quickly came to the point. "The bad news about electronics is that a global war is going on for supremacy over this technology. . . . If one or more of these sectors were to fall, it could have a domino effect on the other sectors," he said, warning that Europe's survival would depend on its ability to develop both "offensive and defensive" strategies at the same time, emphasizing that EC governments and the EC Commission must continue playing a major role. Many of the speakers agreed that temporary protection would be needed more than ever to meet Japanese and U.S. competition. In three years, the Japanese had made important headway, and van der Klugt's days, although he didn't know it yet, were numbered.

Faced with an unexpected plunge in profits, a hostile board, and skeptical investors, van der Klugt was forced to resign as chairman July 1, 1990. His policies and strategies were immediately accelerated by the new chairman—Jan Timmer, nicknamed "Hurricane." As the former, highly successful head of the company's consumer-electronics division, Timmer launched his own sweeping reorganization and cost-cutting program, which involved slashing nearly 20 percent of Philips's work force of some 285,000 men and women. We will return to Philips in Chapter 7. But it had become clear that more battling was in store for the Community's high-tech industries, and that additional help from governments and the Community would be needed.

In fact, battling in these fields has become so necessary, that heads of state and government become personally involved in helping support their industries and even in selling—at the highest levels, particularly when government contracts and state-controlled companies are involved. Former French President Giscard d'Estaing, Vice President Bush, Mrs. Thatcher, President Mitterrand, Chancellor Kohl, Prime Minister González—each has used his or her influence to help push through major contracts for their industries. Sometimes they work on each other, sometimes for and against each other, and on several occasions they have joined forces.

What some observers considered one of the most revealing examples of Fortress Europe occurred in Spain. In late November 1988, Prime Minister González's government had come under considerable pressure from Paris to buy France's new high-speed train, *le train à grande vitesse,* the TGV, as part of a massive modernization of Spain's antiquated rail system. Competing for the same contract, worth nearly $1 billion in rail technology, financing and equipment, and enormous prestige in world markets for the winner, was Germany's Siemens, leading a consortium of other German and Swiss companies led by the Zurich-based ABB. A third contender was also competing—Japan's Mitsubishi.

It looked as if the Spanish leader were caught hopelessly between two of his closest allies and Japan, which held out the promise of other, vast investments in Spain. But this time, in contrast to the earlier fighter deal, a "European" solution was found.

To keep Mitterrand and Kohl and their industrial allies happy in the interests of what Spanish officials described as "European harmony," the González government split the contract between the French and German groups, giving French groups virtual control of the Spanish rail-building industry and orders for twenty-four high-speed trains; the Siemens-led consortium sold seventy-five high-speed locomotives. But the third alternative was rejected: a bid by Tokyo's Mitsubishi Corporation to supply a modernized version of its Shinkansen, or Bullet Train, at a price Mitsubishi said was thirty percent below the French and German bids.

Several weeks before the decision was announced at the end of 1988 by González and Mitterrand, the large Japanese conglomerate, sensing the outcome, in an unusual move issued a terse, tough-sounding statement to the Spanish news agency in Tokyo. Mitsubishi warned that Japanese investment in Spain would suffer if the decision was made on political, rather than economic grounds. And, the giant group added angrily, an unfavorable decision would "demonstrate that the Spanish government does not respect Japan."[6]

Later, in Madrid, I asked the youthful, fashionably dressed chairman of RENFE, the Spanish state railway company, why the Japanese had not been chosen. He did not like the question. "There were many considerations, including where we could obtain the best technology," said Julian García Valverde. "But first, Mitsubishi was more like 20 percent under [the competing bids] and they were trying to sell us a nonexisting locomotive for a nonexisting train." In other words, Spanish officials told me later, the French Alsthom-built high-speed trains and the Siemens locomotives were already operating successfully, and most important, as one official put it, "We wanted a European solution . . . and that's what we got. Besides, have you ever tried to sell a Western locomotive in Japan? Forget it!"

Mrs. Thatcher's behind-the-scenes salesmanship in the Saudi Tornado deal was another case of how involved heads of state become, and in this case, the stakes were even greater. The contracts, which could reach an estimated $15 billion, will stretch into the twenty-first century, providing work for several thousand British employees of Aerospace and its subcontractors. According to British press accounts and industry sources, Mrs. Thatcher worked hard on the deal and even once interrupted a badly needed vacation to help push through agreement with Prince Bandar bin Sultan, a key member of the royal family, who at the time was Saudi ambassador in Washington. That was but one of many meetings she and senior British officials had with him, because what was happening in Washington had become critical: Congress had refused to approve the sale to the Saudis of forty F-15E strike fighters in 1985 and eight hundred Stinger missiles in 1986, infuriating the Saudis.

As the negotiations were ending, a Saudi official in Washington told the *New York Times* that "American technology is generally superior. But we are not going to pay billions of dollars to be insulted. We are not masochists." The consensus of many officials I have interviewed, including Sir Raymond Lygo of British Aerospace was that without "herself" actively involved in the selling, the deal would probably have fallen through.

Left unanswered was the question whether or not British or European political influence was being enhanced by such deals, compared to American influence, and if so, for what purpose. The preliminary answer was that British and French influence in the region was enhanced, but a coordinated, common "European" policy in the Middle East was also emerging, as we shall see when we return to the Community's foreign policy during the Gulf War and its aftermath in Chapter 9.

Oil was another key ingredient in the deal, which the United States had difficulty matching. To help the Saudis pay for the 72 Tornados and several hundred other aircraft, including Hawk jet trainers and helicopters, as well as minesweepers, and provide training for the Saudi's 45,000-man army and 15,000-man air force, while building base facilities, Britain negotiated a complex oil-barter arrangement. According to industry sources in London and in the Middle East, Royal Dutch Shell and British Petroleum during 1989 and 1990 were taking delivery of about 400,000 barrels per day of crude oil from Saudi Arabia, and paying the proceeds into a defense ministry bank account, which was set up to pay for the equipment and services specified in the agreement, plus commissions.

AMERICA REBOUNDS, HITTING BACK

Gradually, America began to hit back in other areas of the globe, reinforced by legislation that made it easier to meet foreign "inducement" competition outside the United States. This took the form of amendments to the Foreign Corrupt Practices Act adopted in 1988.

The original law, enacted in 1977, reflected the determination of the Carter administration and Senator William Proxmire to crack down on bribery and other practices that surfaced in the wake of the Lockheed scandal; the case was so named because the Lockheed Corporation was found to have paid large sums to political leaders and parties in Italy, the Netherlands, Japan, and other countries, to buy its aircraft. A Senate report, based on investigations by the Securities and Exchange Commission, revealed that "corrupt foreign payments [had been made] by over 300 U.S. companies involving hundreds of millions of dollars. . . . The image of American democracy abroad has been tarnished. A strong antibribery law is urgently needed to bring these corrupt practices to a halt and to restore public confidence in the integrity of the American business system."[7]

But several years later, as the memories of the Lockheed scandal receded, and at the urging of major U.S. multinationals, notably in the aerospace field, amendments were felt to be needed to allow

American business to be more "flexible." As a top U.S. corporate lawyer for many of the companies told me, "the amended language has one key provision—it, in effect, keeps bribery illegal, but exempts U.S. executives from prosecution if they do not have 'direct' knowledge of what is going on regarding sales of aircraft, for example. . . . It has helped many American companies." The new provisions, supported by the Reagan and Bush administrations, also made it perfectly legal for American businessmen to pay or offer gifts or anything of value that is lawful under the "written laws and regulations of the foreign official's, political party's, party official's, or candidate's country." It also legalized payments to foreign clients for bona fide travel or lodging, or for expenses related to the promotion, demonstration, or explanation of products or services.

What this meant was that Washington was ready to help American business meet, head on, the increasingly aggressive methods of the Europeans in key sectors, and would make use of the new laws and the administration's support in fighting back.

Consider the case of AT&T's comeback in Europe's telecommunications scene, following its disastrous, humiliating failure to win in France during the "CGCT Affair" in 1987. Senior AT&T officials told me afterward that if ever there was a next time, they would do things differently—and win. The next time was a year later in Italy in what was widely regarded as one of the nastiest, hardest-fought foreign business-political battles ever seen in Italy. The central question was which group would be allowed to become the privileged partner in a joint venture with state-owned Italtel, and join in supplying some $30 billion in telephone and telecommunications equipment to modernize Italy's backward phone system through the year 1992. It was America versus Europe, with AT&T on one side and on the other a lineup that closely resembled the earlier players: Sweden's Ericsson, which had won in France; Siemens, whose executives were still smarting over their losing to a "neutral" European, and finally, Alcatel of France.

By the end of November 1988, *Business Week*'s Rome correspondent John Rossant, who covered the story closely, and other observers, tentatively concluded that intense political pressures from Paris and Bonn would again force a "European solution." But this time, AT&T was determined and geared up to avoid what happened in France, because this effort might represent the giant American company's last chance to become a major force in the European Community.

Separate interviews with Italian, U.S., German, and Swedish diplomats, including two cabinet ministers, confirmed how AT&T did it. First, rather than avoiding resident diplomats and friendly government officials, as they did in France, for fear that reporters would get wind of their strategy, AT&T enlisted the active support of the U.S. Embassy in Rome. As a result, with Washington's blessing, a team was assigned to help with the negotiations and lobbying of influential Italians.

Meantime, in Washington, President Reagan and President-elect Bush strongly encouraged a "U.S. solution" during a visit in December of that year by Prime Minister Luigi Ciriaco De Mita and former Socialist Prime Minister Bettino Craxi. The counterpressures were building.

An Italian minister and several U.S. sources, who insisted on anonymity, confirmed that AT&T Chairman Robert E. Allen had approached De Mita during the December trip and proposed making some of the planned new investments near Naples, his political base. An AT&T official, quoted by Rossant, said that proposal "gave him something he could take back to Italy."[8]

Allen, in a letter published by *Business Week* several weeks later, and other AT&T executives in conversations with me, denied having proposed investments "as a political incentive," and said the agreement was, as Allen said, "clearly based on its commercial and technological merits."[9] Rossant and other U.S., Swedish, and French sources reconfirmed the story of the AT&T proposal, following signing of the final agreements in Milan June 5, 1989, which ended nearly eighteen months of negotiations.

Responding to questions at a news conference following the signing, Allen repeatedly insisted that there were no plans for AT&T to invest in a new plant near Naples. But a new, powerful industrial alliance was formed, greatly strengthening Italtel in Europe, and providing AT&T its foothold in the European Community. While visiting Italtel in Rome in the spring of 1991, the state-owned company's chairman, Salvatore Randi, explained that the two companies were jointly developing and marketing new telecommunications products for export markets and, together, had recently established a joint venture in the Soviet Union to modernize the country's rundown telecommunications network. A plant in Leningrad to begin producing equipment for the venture is due to start operating at the end of 1992.

"The deal in favor of AT&T helped them as a company and the United States government, and it helped us," a senior Italian ambassador involved in the negotiations told me several months later, "because—and please don't underestimate this point—it helped Europe somewhat reduce its ugly image in the United States of being a fortress, closed to Americans . . . and this image in the mind of the administration had become very dangerous."

To help erase that image by providing some tangible proof of Italian intentions, an important secret tradeoff was negotiated. In July of that year, Airbus sources said that Alitalia, Italy's state-owned airline, would be the first to place a firm order for the new A-321, Airbus's latest single-aisle, wide-body jet. Deliveries of twenty planes worth $1 billion were to begin in 1994, thus breaking the virtual monopoly in Alitalia's fleet held by Boeing and McDonnell Douglas, which had been supplying the Italians since the end of World War II, with generous subcontracting for Italian companies.

The Airbus deal, easily offsetting the "U.S. solution" in telecommunications, was viewed as a major victory for the European partners in the consortium. But there was more to it, because the turnaround in Italy's position on Airbus also represented a victory for the feisty, gregarious French political leader, who in May 1991 became France's first woman prime minister—Edith Cresson. I recall how she complained vigorously, in her excellent, American-accented English, about the Italians having shunned joining Airbus. She then was minister for industry and trade and was completing a one-day trip to Milan and Rome, promoting French business and European industrial cooperation. It was early autumn 1984, and we were flying back to Paris from Rome in a French government Mystère 20 Dassault executive jet and she was angry, following a long talk with Prime Minister Craxi. "Do you know that man is not a European?" she said. Why, I asked. "Because we have been talking aerospace, and why Italy has never joined Airbus," she said, her voice rising. Why not? "Because," she told me firmly, "you Americans have the Italians tied up like this," she added with a smile, holding her arms forward with crossed wrists.

Several months later, I was in Rome doing a profile on Alitalia, whose executives were very anxious to respond to the Cresson quote that had appeared in my *International Herald Tribune* article about her. They told me, with considerable emotion, how Airbus approached them in 1970. "Everything was done by the French and the

Germans, everything . . . they had decided who would build what, from the wings to the cockpit," one executive said, his voice rising. "And do you know what they proposed we build? We, Italy? The toilets! Now that was unacceptable, particularly in light of all the work Boeing and McDonnell Douglas have provided our industry over the years, with subcontracted work."

This time, Airbus had learned its lesson. By early 1990, it appeared certain that Aeritalia, Italy's state-owned aerospace company, and already a partner in Tornado, EFA, and a regional airliner with Aerospatiale, would participate in helping build the A-321, which competes directly with the Boeing 757, a twin-engine narrow-body airliner in which Aeritalia has no involvement.

Aeritalia, its name changed to Alenia, would, therefore, become another in a roster of some 1,400 companies throughout Western Europe that supply components for Airbus planes, and by the 1990s they will be directly employing a total of some 40,000 people. Yet Airbus only employs 1,400 people directly, and has the unusual, mind-boggling job of not only designing, selling, and servicing the planes, but coordinating production of components in eight main plants in four countries. The worksharing arrangement reflects the financial shares held by Airbus owners and a broader dilemma: how to make such ventures work. British Aerospace builds the wings in Britain; MBB makes most of the fuselage sections in West Germany, while Aerospatiale makes the cockpit and the wingbox, with responsibility for final assembly when finished components are flown to Toulouse on swollen-bodied transport planes, known as Guppies, which regularly shuttle between the various plants.

Was this an efficient system? The answer depends on how one defines "efficient." In the view of most experts, shareholders, and the four governments, many reforms would be needed before Airbus could be considered a model for any future venture of its kind.

The central issue of the consortium has been how to overhaul the management system so that costs and prices of components can be identified and, above all, controlled. Under the existing system, once work is assigned each partner negotiates a fixed price for its share. But since no single partner knows the exact amount of costs or prices charged by the others, the practice is to set high charges, according to industry managers. Although Airbus publishes its figures on sales and orders, profits and losses are shrouded in secrecy. Since the consortium was founded, the net loss or profit figures are made known only to the individual shareholders and never published on a consolidated basis for the consortium as a whole.

There are many problems with Airbus's organizational setup. The members of the five-man supervisory board, for example, are the chief executives of the partner companies, and they take all major decisions, not Pierson and Airbus Industrie's management; similarly, about half the group's 1,400 employees are on loan from the owner companies, which creates a two-tier employment system, a quota system for nationalities.

BUILDING EUROPEAN TEAMWORK

Yet there was wide agreement that one of the most positive consequences of joint research projects and Pan-European companies, such as Airbus Industrie, Arianespace, and ES2, was that they provided what had always been lacking—a sense of teamwork, irrespective of national borders and cultural and linguistic differences. "Until these EC-backed programs got started, many of us hardly knew our colleagues, the total opposite of how things work in the United States or Japan," recalled George S. van Houten, responsible for research at Philips in Eindhoven. Today, because virtually all EC-funded programs are in the non-, or pre-competitive research area, companies cooperate actively. "Researchers in these programs—and there are hundreds—pick up the phone and call each other, because they know each other . . . that is the important result, and it's completely new for Europe," van Houten said.

A similar sense of European identity was building up on campuses of the leading business schools, such as INSEAD in Fontainebleau, the London Business School, the International Institute for Management Development School in Lausanne, and the Lyon ESC Graduate School of Business in Lyon, France. These and a handful of others were increasingly sharing professors and students, developing and using purely European cases in classrooms—thus breaking the virtual monopoly held on international-management education methods by such leading schools as Harvard Business School, MIT-Sloan, Northwestern University, and the Wharton School of Finance. Nine of Europe's leading business schools, led by l'École des Hautes Études Commerciales, the HEC the graduate school of business in France in December 1990, created a joint master's degree program. Dozens of student-exchange and scholarship programs also were operating, or expanding, some funded by the EC Commission.

MOVING INTO EASTERN EUROPE

As Europe struggled to find its sense of identity and common purpose, two new—and related—chapters had opened in the New Europe's quest for global economic power, and both posed enormously complex and difficult issues. The first revolved around the expected gradual winding down of defense expenditures within Western Europe and the impact this would have on many of the industries we have been examining; the second centered on prospects for new trade and investments in Eastern Europe and in the Soviet Union.

The two issues were closely linked in the minds of European strategists, who saw in expanded East-West trade the ideal way of cushioning cuts in their defense spending—assuming, of course, they could succeed—by converting their defense industries to civilian purposes, while also establishing a predominant European business beachhead in Eastern Europe and Russia. That meant outsmarting the United States and Japan with more generous, more appealing economic and political conditions for trade, while relying on long-standing built-in advantages, such as proximity, the predominance of the German language, and a common history.

Even before the Berlin Wall was battered away, joint U.S.-Soviet arms-reduction programs had dampened the outlook for many high-tech industries with heavy involvement in aerospace and defense. European corporate strategists were also straining to adjust to sharp cutbacks in export markets, fueled by austerity-driven governments in the Middle East and Latin America, amid intense competition from relative newcomers to the business, such as China, Brazil, South Africa, and Israel. But the deepest worries stemmed from the impending withdrawal of as many as a third or more of U.S. armed forces stationed in Europe and the new, highly popular political pressures in Germany and neighboring countries—except France—to scrap weapons programs and slash defense spending.

Yet even Daimler, Europe's leading aerospace and defense group, was shaken by the wave of pressure in West Germany to cut arms spending, particularly funding for the EFA tactical fighter project, in which Deutsche Aerospace had a 33 percent share. But Edzard Reuter, the trim, hard, tennis-playing, intellectual chairman of Daimler, stated repeatedly that his goal was to continue diversifying and developing high-tech involvement of all the group's divisions, which he described as "the glue" for future growth.

As antitrust officials in Berlin and Brussels said they were monitoring the company's evolution closely, Daimler announced a string of new foreign ventures in early 1990—with Aerospatiale in the field of helicopters; with United Technologies Corporation of the United States to cooperate in building jet-engines and possibly in automobile components. Two weeks earlier, Daimler had announced the startup of wide-ranging talks with Mitsubishi, which a German spokesman in Stuttgart said was aimed at "enabling us both to better compete world-wide and cooperate world-wide."

The emerging ventures showed how blurred the lines between Europe, the United States, and Japan had become, as complex global alliances spread among the competing camps; few executives involved could tell me how they thought the alliances would look in a decade. But they agreed on one essential point: Europe could be a winner.

Meantime, prospects that the Soviet Union's leadership might change its pro-Western stance and that a return to the Cold War could not be ruled out prompted European defense leaders to begin expressing new support for defense projects, such as EFA, and research programs, such as Euclid, which we touched on in Chapter 3. This program, established by twelve European NATO governments, was aimed at reducing the transatlantic gap in R&D spending on military research—the United States spends about $10 billion annually, compared to about $3 billion by European powers, led by France, Britain, and Germany, which account for about 90 percent of the total.

Covering sectors ranging from modern radar to modular avionics, satellite surveillance and underwater detection, Euclid is designed to boost cooperation in development of European military technology, and was described by *Aviation Week* as another example of Fortress Europe, because it deliberately excluded the United States and Canada. "One never knows how things might work out, but one of our underlying goals was autonomy—from the United States," a senior German defense planner said.

GERMANY TAKES THE LEAD

Many German companies and banks preferred concentrating on the East, and during the first three-quarters of 1990, Germany accounted for 59 percent of the joint ventures signed in Eastern Europe and the Soviet Union and 38 percent of the acquisitions, followed by France with 13 percent and 18 percent, respectively, according to a survey published at the end of the year.[10] The United States was in third place, but with a mere 3 percent of the acquisitions and only 14 percent of the joint ventures in Eastern Europe and the Soviet Union. And of the thirty-four joint ventures, fifteen were in the Soviet Union. Summing up the U.S. attitude, Jonathan Fuerbringer of the *New York Times* concluded that Americans were "being cautious, if not timid," which should not have come as a surprise to anyone examining the track record of U.S. business in the area, and of its main competitors—namely, Western Europeans, notably Germans, French, and Italians. This isn't to say Americans were sitting around with their arms folded.

The list of American companies that were striking important deals in Eastern Europe was impressive: General Motors was sharing in building a $300 million auto-parts plant in Hungary; General Electric established a $150 million joint venture there to make light bulbs. Other ventures throughout Eastern Europe and the Soviet Union included McDonald's, Coca-Cola, PepsiCo, Levi Strauss, Schwinn Bicycles, Chase, Anheuser-Busch, and Boeing, among others.

Some deals contained unusual twists. For example, in Czechoslovakia, Anheuser-Busch, the giant American brewer of Budweiser beer, was negotiating with a small Czech brewer—formerly known as Budweis—to gain access to the entire European market. The problem posed was a 1939 trademark dispute, which had kept Anheuser-Busch from selling Bud in most of Europe, while locking the Czech brew out of the United States. But both sides were determined to find a solution, because an agreement would open up the entire European market for the American brewer for the first time and allow Budweis, being privatized by the new Czech government, to expand worldwide with Anheuser-Busch as its partner. The unusual twist was that despite predictions that Germany would wind up dominating the area, here was a case of another, popular American beverage cracking Eastern Europe.

Item: In Prague, the medieval Charles Bridge spanning the Vltava

River is jammed with tourists. Two Dixieland bands are heartily playing American numbers; nearby, young couples in blue jeans are
strumming guitars, singing Czech songs; the languages being spoken
are Slovak, English, German, French, and Italian. An American ac-
quaintance, passing through from Vienna, tells me he is now convinced that Central Europe's cultural center will be here, not in
Berlin. It is a balmy autumn day in 1990, and only the evening
before—exactly at midnight, October 2—we watched the somber,
funeral-like ceremonies merging East and West Germany, televised
live from East Berlin, followed by violent clashes between young
radical right-wing militants and police. Where was the all-powerful,
the Bismarck-like Kohl in all this? Were the Czechs afraid that pre-
World War II history might be repeated?

That afternoon, we enter the Presidential Palace overlooking the
sprawling baroque city. President Havel is recuperating from a whirl-
wind one-day visit by the youthful, hard-driving president of Brazil,
Fernando Collor de Mello; earlier in the month he had received,
successively, the visits of Mitterrand, Mrs. Thatcher, and Delors. "You
must understand, and can see perhaps, that we do not fear an all-
powerful Germany here," said Havel's quiet-spoken, fair-haired press
secretary, Daniella Retkova. "East Germany, perhaps, for its right-
wing, racist elements we saw on television last night, but basically we
look to all of Europe—membership in the Common Market eventually, the Council of Europe perhaps earlier." Retkova noted that
Havel was planning state visits to most other EC capitals, and was
getting to know EC leaders better, emphasizing "we don't want to be
annexed again. Our goal is become part of the European Community, full members."

Later that day, on the other side of the river, I enter a grim,
Stalin-era office building, which was, until recently, the headquarters
of the state planning agency. I ask for Vladimir Dloughy, the thirty-
six-year-old minister of the economy. I notice that the long, dimly lit
corridors and the offices are empty. No one is stirring, except an
elderly guard, looking sad, bored, and tired. He waves me through,
and I am taken by a young secretary to the top floor. "This office, in
which we are sitting," Dloughy says, waving his arm in a circle, "is
where, since 1949, everything of importance to the economy was
settled, but that is finished, finished for good."

We are sipping sweet Turkish-style coffee. "I do not want to
control. I have no control, and worse, we are in a recession this year,

and it will be worse next year, in 1991, and maybe in 1992 we will see some improvement," he says, grimly. "But we do, we really do want foreign investment—not just yet, and not only German, obviously, but French, German, Italian, and American . . . no one will have a monopoly here." But we agree that the West Europeans are the best placed, despite the steady flow of American tourists and businessmen looking for opportunities.

RECALLING MOSCOW
AND EAST EUROPE IN THE 1970s

My thoughts went back to my stints as correspondent in Moscow during the Brezhnev period and then roving for *Business Week* throughout East Europe between 1974 and 1976. During that exciting era, too, American businessmen, lawyers, consultants, conference organizers were pouring in, signing preliminary deals, letters of intent, establishing joint ventures, and getting plenty of media attention. Americans, enthusiastic about Soviet leader Leonid Brezhnev's call for "detente" with the West, extolled the vast potential markets for consumers and the developing low-cost manufacturing bases in the East Bloc, while also warning that formidable obstacles remained.

Indeed there were. And yet, in the end, the Europeans found the solutions and won the markets and considerable political influence and prestige. It was not Americans, but West German, French, and Italian companies and banks that wound up with the biggest contracts during that period—and the trade.

One of the most controversial, lucrative contracts was the building of the multibillion-dollar Siberian gas pipeline stretching from the heart of the Soviet Union to Western Europe—which the Reagan administration had so fervently tried to block. Understandably, until the early 1980s, the American opposition angered the Europeans, but it also encouraged them not to give in. Mrs. Thatcher was in complete agreement with her EC partners in opposing Washington's hardline approach, in part because British engineering and construction companies were among the important beneficiaries of Soviet contracts for the pipeline, along with German and French steel and equipment manufacturers, and in some cases as licensees of American companies. She had displayed similar support for her European partners during U.S. attacks on Airbus, and Europe won.

Consider the following figures prepared by the OECD and released in its 1991 year-end report, covering trade with the Soviet Union and Eastern Europe: Total U.S. exports had fallen sharply from the 1986–89 period of an annual average $3.3 billion to $1.9 billion in the second half of 1989, while imports fell from $2 billion to $1 billion. Germany remained by far the largest trader with the Soviets and East Europe, although its total also declined: Germany's total exports fell from $10.8 billion in 1986–89 to $6.9 billion at the end of 1989, while imports fell from $9.1 billion to $5.4 billion. The Community's total trade with the region, while it also declined, far outweighed that of the United States—exports fell from $23.6 billion to $14.9 billion, while imports fell from $28.4 billion in the 1986–89 period to $16 billion at the end of 1989.[11]

The OECD study also showed that Italy was doing nearly twice as much trade with the formerly Communist countries as the United States, while Austria and Britain were close to the U.S. total.

Was the United States about to be outsmarted, outmaneuvered in Eastern Europe and the Soviet Union again?

After you have taken account of the prevailing caution and fears in the United States about the fragility of democratic reforms, the problems of the nonconvertibility of their currencies, lack of qualified, profit-motivated managers, and so on, listen to a very worried Democratic Senator Joe Biden from Delaware, chairman of the Senate Foreign Relations European Subcommittee. It was March 28, 1990, and Biden was warning that West European and to a lesser degree, Japanese competitors "are racing to establish strong footings in Eastern Europe. . . . As long as the governments of Europe and Japan are backing their companies with financing, guarantees, insurance, etc., our firms, who are asked to go it alone, will not be able to compete."

Biden had a point and was right to worry about Europe's flexible approach to transferring sensitive technologies, providing generous government-backed and subsidized financing, to former Communist regimes throughout Eastern Europe. If the Bush administration did not respond with active help for its businessmen, Biden predicted, "the United States could well be left out."

It may well be too late. Just over a year later, May 14, 1991, Stephen Cooney, director of international investment for the National Association of Manufacturers, told newsmen in Washington that the European Community had a strong export-assistance program for its businessmen, whereas "we don't . . . the EC is miles ahead of the United States in commercial relations with the Soviet Union and Eastern Europe." Many officials within and outside the administration agreed, and examples were sprouting everywhere.

Item: West Germany, with Bonn's support, began retraining one thousand Russian-language instructors to strengthen the teaching of German at Goethe Institutes in Moscow, Warsaw, Prague, and Sofia, as part of a determined effort to promote the German language in the area, where it is already strong. As part of an effort to become the region's second foreign language after English, Elisabeth Guigou, France's hard-driving minister for European Affairs, who succeeded Mrs. Cresson in that post, said that tens of thousands of people are studying French at thirty Alliance Française centers throughout Eastern Europe. In addition, eleven French cultural centers, many expanded or opened since April 1990, are now operating in Romania, Czechoslovakia, Hungary, Poland, Bulgaria, and the Soviet Union.

Item: In East Germany, mergers, or those planned, between East and West German companies had grown so far and fast that Sir Leon Brittan, the EC commissioner in charge of competition policy, bluntly warned that they were creating monopolies that could squeeze out foreign rivals. He was clearly referring to mainly U.S. and Japanese companies and banks.

Item: Italy's Fiat, which has been producing cars in the Soviet Union since the 1960s, and already accounted for about half of all the two million foreign cars produced in Eastern Europe, signed another major car-manufacturing agreement with the Soviets in early 1990. The agreement contained an unusual provision: all transactions in the joint ventures would be handled in ECUs, the first important extension of the EC's future currency into the area and a major coup for the EC.

Item: The European Bank for Reconstruction and Development, with forty countries and two EC institutions as members and initiated by Mitterrand, was the first regional bank established without predominant U.S. leadership. The U.S. shareholding was a modest 10 percent. That was the single largest share, but the combined holdings of the EC nations, the EC Commission, and the Luxembourg-based Bank for European Investment provides them the majority. And the Europeans will run the bank, known as the EBRD, under the direction of its high-strung, haughty, prolific writer and president, Jacques Attali, who since 1981 had served as one of Mitterrand's closest advisers. English this time will be only one of the official foreign languages, along with French, German, and Russian.

The list goes on.

The evidence seemed conclusive. Germany, followed by France, Italy, and Britain, backed by their governments, EC institutions, and predominantly European banks, would come out ahead of the United States in trading with Eastern Europe and the Soviet Union. Hungary was perhaps the only exception. Cultural affinities and history had a lot to do with West European predominance. So did the reluctance of many U.S. businessmen to plunge into areas where privatization of the economy had only begun. When asked by *Fortune* magazine what worried them most in Eastern Europe, senior U.S. executives repeatedly said "backlash": one-fourth of those interviewed warned that if the reformers in Eastern Europe moved too quickly hard-line Communists would return to power.[12] "There has been too much change too soon," an executive said.

If the Europeans were enthusiastically, actively moving eastward amid strong prospects for succeeding, they were not ignoring the West, meaning the United States and Latin America. Indeed, the New Europe was also moving across the Atlantic in a new bid for growth and influence in the New World.

Leaping Across the Atlantic: Reversing the American Challenge

I want to be the president who stands up and fights for
American companies, American products, and American
workers.

—GOVERNOR MICHAEL DUKAKIS

That was the strident populist message Democratic presidential candidate Dukakis tried to convey to labor groups during the final weeks
of the 1988 national campaign—in effect, calling for opposition to
what had become a major surge of foreign investment in the United
States. Stung by a counterattack from Republican vice presidential
candidate Dan Quayle, who said he welcomed foreign investments,
Dukakis stood before a crowd of workers at a components plant
owned by the Moog Automotive Company in Wellston, Missouri, and
congratulated them for having emerged as one of the few American
"survivors" in the battle between U.S., Japanese, and European automobile companies.

What Dukakis did not know on that early October day, and
learned to his embarrassed astonishment only later, was that the
family-owned firm had been sold eleven years earlier to IFINT, a
Luxembourg holding company controlled by one of the most power-

ful dynasties in Western Europe—the Agnelli family of Italy.

Moog, a $425-million-a-year company, was by no means the most important European investment in the United States, nor was it the most recent. But the Dukakis gaffe illustrated how fiercely politicized the issue had become, amid many predictions that The Big American Buyout would become the predominant political issue of the 1990s, possibly resurfacing in the U.S. presidential campaign in 1992. The warnings coincided with the publication of books and articles, which stirred the debate and helped mount pressures in the U.S. Congress, determined to force the Bush administration to reduce, control, or, at least, rigorously monitor the flow of foreign investments, and to restrict the political lobbying by foreign companies in the United States.

EUROPE BECOMES THE TARGET

Japan was the most conspicuous target, frequently cited as the most dangerous and undesirable among the foreigners buying into America. A confidential poll commissioned for leading Japanese companies and published in February 1989 showed that more than two-thirds of Americans felt Washington should actively discourage any further Japanese investment in the United States; 44 percent of the Americans interviewed said they were unwilling to work for a Japanese company, and a clear majority conceded "a degree of cultural bias" when judging the Japanese. The U.S. Conference Board, in a similar study a year later, concluded that only 55 percent of American executives were "comfortable" with Japanese investments, but the percentage jumped to 88 percent when they were asked about British investments and to 77 percent when asked how comfortable they were about investments from West Germany and the Netherlands.

There are many cultural affinities between Europe and America, as the studies showed, but the Europeans, flush with cash, had gradually become more confident and aggressive. And thus, as transatlantic tensions grew over trade-related issues, and later over the Gulf War and its aftermath, Europe attracted Washington's fire.

At the height of an intense transatlantic dispute over access to U.S. and EC-sponsored research programs in the field of semi-conductors during the spring of 1989, a Dutchman—Gerrit Jeelof, chairman of Philips's U.S. subsidiary, North American Philips—complained during a conference at the Fletcher School of Law and Diplomacy in Medford, Massachusetts, that he and many of his European colleagues were "offended" by the way in which they were being treated in the United States.

"Foreigners keep out—that is what we hear now," he grumbled, while another senior European executive warned that "America better be careful—we may retaliate, and let's face it, U.S. interests are vulnerable in Europe." Because of registration and other surveillance procedures required by the U.S. government of foreign firms engaged in high technology or defense-related work, an attitude had emerged which Jeelof said amounted to being treated as "second-class, corporate citizens, when, in fact, we do $5 billion in sales, employ a lot of people, do a lot of research, and are, in fact, good corporate citizens in the United States just as IBM is in Europe." He and other European executives and government officials have regularly cited Buy American legislation, which discriminates against non-U.S. companies in supplying federal, state, and local government agencies with everything from structural steel and buses to school materials, while subsidiaries of U.S. companies operating in Europe enjoy relatively easy access to similar EC markets.

I will not repeat here the well-researched examples, ample statistics, and analysis contained in recent books on the subject of foreign investments in the United States.[1] They depict how and why foreign investments are changing the American economy, and they eloquently, alarmingly, assess the pros and cons for the U.S. policymakers of restricting the growing flow of capital, technology, and human resources from Japan and Western Europe. Most of the authors recommend requiring far more detailed reporting from investors on their backgrounds, ownership, and assets and resources, coupled with restrictions and permanent review procedures—under the rigorous control of the U.S. government.

Less understood are the reasons for Europe, Inc.'s new drive into both North America and Latin America, where EC countries have become the region's second-largest trading partner. As direct investments have risen to a record $32 billion, they now equal more than a third of the U.S. total. The inroads in the Americas have been characterized by success stories, some embarrassing failures, and political controversy. Behind the new strategy are a new breed of youthful, hard-driving European executives bent on becoming global players, including even some East Germans who in early 1990 acquired a small American company near New York City—the first complete takeover in the United States organized by a formerly Communist regime.

Some of the tense transatlantic controversies, such as access to government-funded research programs have been resolved or were being negotiated as tensions eased somewhat in 1990 and early 1991. But fundamental differences and political pressures remained on both sides of the Atlantic. Whenever one issue was resolved, another exploded, fueled by new ammunition, not always provided by the American side.

EUROPE ALSO COMPLAINS

For example, on April 18, 1991, the EC Commission delegation in Washington released its sixth annual report on U.S. trade barriers and what it termed "unfair practices that impede European companies doing business in the United States." The eighty-seven-page report, thirty pages longer than the 1990 report, cited dozens of examples, such as U.S. trade legislation, tariffs, customs and tax barriers, Buy American provisions in public-procurement regulations, alleged misuse of national-security restrictions, and long-disputed extraterritorial provisions in U.S. laws, extending American laws to those outside American jurisdiction. This issue first surfaced dramatically in the embittered dispute between the Reagan administration and Britain, France, and West Germany over the building of the Siberian gas pipeline during the early 1980s. The EC's most recent accusations were partly responding to the U.S. government's National Trade Estimate Report on Foreign Trade Barriers published March 30, 1990, which, in a similar spirit, singled out a wide range of barriers to American exports in the EC, Japan, and other areas.

Both sides argued that the barriers cited were dangerous and violated rules of the multilateral trading system and urged they be abolished. It was perhaps only a coincidence, but the following did not help: a week before the EC Commission's 1990 report was released, the U.S. Justice Department in Washington announced that it was considering extending its antitrust laws to cover American subsidiaries of foreign companies that were found to be engaged in price fixing, the carving up of markets, and other practices considered anticompetitive in their home markets. What this meant was that Washington could file antitrust suits against these foreign-owned companies for damage that their collusion might cause to American companies operating outside the United States.

British, EC, and Japanese officials in Washington expressed a mixture of surprise, shock, and anger. A senior British diplomat in Washington, summing up the reaction of many colleagues in the capital, bluntly warned that the move would mean "trouble." Washington, however, appeared determined. "The Justice Department will not tolerate violations of the U.S. antitrust laws where we have jurisdiction, which impair export opportunities for U.S. business," a senior antitrust official told the *New York Times*.

RANKING FOREIGN INVESTMENTS

Such skirmishing neither dampened nor slowed the determination of Europeans, among many others, to place their money in America.

The overwhelmingly largest, outside investors in the United States have been West Europeans and Japanese, who collectively drove total foreign investments held in the United States to well over a record $2.5 trillion in 1991, up from a modest $107 billion in 1970. It is important to remember when looking at investments that they include all forms—portfolio investments in securities, bonds, and the like, as well as ownership of property, real estate, and plants, including farmland, skyscraper buildings, and luxury apartments. The largest share, equal to about two-thirds of the total, represented portfolio investments. And in this overwhelmingly largest slice of the foreign-investment pie, according to most experts, the Japanese have been the predominant force.

The recent political controversy, however, has focused on foreign direct investments in plant and property, which affect jobs and people's daily lives. Here Western Europe, led by EC member countries, has been the predominant force. Of the $401 billion invested by foreigners in American plants, buildings, research centers, joint ventures, farms, service organizations, such as advertising agencies and distribution firms in which foreigners had a stake of 10 percent or more, Britain alone accounted for 30 percent of the total, equal to $122 billion, nearly double the amount of Japan's direct investments, according to 1990 U.S. Commerce Department figures. And these figures were based on book value at the time of purchase, thus greatly understating current values.

Lawmakers in Congress, seeking a crackdown on foreign investments, have criticized the Commerce Department for neglecting several billions of dollars in hidden or miscalculated foreign assets. Democratic Congressman John Bryant of Texas in a speech April 4, 1990, cited estimates placing the total of foreign direct investments at around $3 trillion, although his aides conceded this, too, was but an estimate.

According to the same Commerce Department figures, the Netherlands, among the Europeans, was in second place, well behind Britain, with $55.7 billion, followed by Canada with $29.7 billion, West Germany with $26.9 billion, and France with $17.1 billion. But all investments were growing, particularly those of France, in a spate of new takeovers in 1989 and 1990, including those by France's largest publisher, Hachette, chemical conglomerate Rhône-Poulenc, Aérospatiale, Alcatel Alsthom, Thomson, Usinor-Sacilor, Schneider, and others to which we shall return.

AMERICANS ALSO HELP THE EUROPEANS

An important reason for the westward push was that, despite the rhetoric about protectionism and their determination to be present in the U.S. market, European business leaders were being actively supported by the European Community's political machinery, EC member governments, and, increasingly, by the Commission's expanding Washington office, which in January 1990 was taken over by Andries van Agt, a forceful, outspoken former Dutch prime minister. Following in the nimble diplomatic and lobbying footsteps of Britain's Sir Roy Denman, the lanky, humorous former top EC Commission trade negotiator, was not easy. But both envoys for the EC Commission fervently argued the Community's case, not only in the corridors of Washington, but during extensive traveling in America.

Meantime, in New York, senior American bankers with close European connections, and ostensibly "outsiders," were working for Europe on the "inside" because of their talents, backgrounds, and interests. They included Lazard's Rohatyn and Robert Hormats, formerly assistant secretary of state for economic and business affairs, who had become vice chairman of Goldman Sachs International, the New York investment firm. They, among others, have friends high up in European centers of economic and political power and they regularly participate in international gatherings organized by such bodies as the Aspen Institute, the Geneva-based World Economic Forum, and the Council on Foreign Relations. They are not only bankers, but lawyers and consultants, often based in New York or Washington, and they shuttle frequently, helping their clients find detailed data, financing, access to influential policy-makers, and so on.

"I am as at home in Washington now as in Brussels, helping our European clients in America, and vice versa," said Robert Lighthizer, a former U.S. deputy trade representative and partner of Skadden, Arps, Slate, Meagher & Flom, the large New York-based law firm, which in the spring of 1990 joined the list of more than a dozen U.S. law firms that had already established Brussels offices.

For most of the intermediaries, dealing with Europeans is not much different from handling Americans. "We deal with Europeans like any other investor; they are generally treated like a domestic investment, but it is also true that there are other sensitivities . . . foreign investment in America will be a highly critical issue for the 1990s, particularly as the [Bush] administration focuses on the antitrust aspects of foreign investments," said Hormats in his New York City Broad Street office. Among other foreign investments handled by Goldman Sachs was the $3.1 billion acquisition in 1987 of Chesebrough-Pond's, the large U.S. cosmetics company, by Unilever, the Anglo-Dutch food and consumer-products company, which *Business Week* ranked as among the ten most successful deals of the decade.[2] Goldman Sachs and Lazard were ranked by Wall Street analysts as the two biggest advisers on inter-European mergers in 1990, out of a total of twenty investment bankers and other dealmakers operating in Europe.

Another driving force, little known to most Americans, are representatives of about forty-five states, cities, and ports, most of whom compete fiercely against each other around the world. They lobby hard for EC investments on behalf of their regions from permanent European offices in such centers as Brussels, London, and Frankfurt.

California, for example, which traditionally has looked to Asia for international business, in 1989 opened its second European office in Frankfurt after opening a London operation several years earlier. "We only gazing to the Pacific? . . . Who gave you that idea?" commented a half-joking state official. "California now considers itself in the middle—between the Pacific and the Atlantic . . . that is why we are moving closer to Europe," he said emphatically. The official, James Philips, was speaking during a crowded reception at the annual

World Economic Forum in the posh Swiss ski resort town of Davos, where high-powered delegations from the states and Canadian provinces traditionally came to woo potential investors, along with delegations from China, the Soviet Union, and Turkey, among others.

"We've got to hustle," said Denis Rufin, in Brussels where he heads the office of the state of Virginia, opened in 1955, noting that the number of foreign companies operating in his state had risen from 24 in 1968 to 315, employing some 57,000 Virginians. And since the 1992 program was announced, the numbers of state delegations visiting Europe, usually with the governors in charge, has soared. "Nineteen-ninety-two, and what is happening here in Brussels as a result, has provided a lot of new interest and impetus," Rufin added.[3]

REMEMBERING THE BERLIN-TOKYO AXIS

Back in America, the highly sensitive security dimension of foreign investments invariably raises the specter of the beginning of World War II. Fears of possible actions through such Nazi-controlled industrial giants as chemicals manufacturer I. G. Farben, which claimed nearly a third of the U.S. market for synthetic dyestuffs, prompted an immediate seizure of its assets, and those of other German companies and banks. The German-American Bund, described in Chapter 2, also was disbanded in this period, and some of its leaders arrested, as the Roosevelt administration seriously began to fear the Nazis' threats to act against American business interests around the world, including in South America.

Today's apprehensions about a revived German-Japanese military-industrial complex have always simmered, usually just below the surface. This was reflected in the reaction in the United States to the announcement by Daimler and Mitsubishi in March 1990 that they intended to cooperate in high-technology areas, including aerospace. Many articles in America, and cartoons, recalled that during World War II their predecessor companies manufactured the formidable Messerschmitt and Zero fighter planes, and that each company—in its contemporary form—has remained its country's largest manufacturer of military aircraft and other forms of sophisticated weapons, and a challenge to American economic power.

Consider, too, the first heated discussions between Bonn and

Washington in 1988 over the participation by German chemical companies in helping Libya build a plant capable of making poison gas, which prompted the poignant phrase by William Safire: "Auschwitz in the Sand." David Marsh, the *Financial Times* Bonn correspondent, recounted in his thorough, readable book on Germany how Chancellor Kohl, who began his career in the chemical industry, told him during an interview that American complaints about the plant reflected a lot of U.S. irritation over the worldwide power of German chemical companies.[4]

Kohl had a point. By 1990, the former divisions of I. G. Farben—broken up in the postwar era into BASF, Bayer, and Hoechst and totally de-Nazified—had completed highly successful investments in the United States. Hoechst, for example, in early 1987 created irritation and apprehension in American business circles with its $2.8 billion acquisition of Celanese, the large American fibers firm. That bid was held up for several weeks pending an antitrust investigation. Industry insiders and Hoechst firmly believed the routine investigation was meant to obstruct the takeover, on the grounds that German economic power was again thrusting itself into the heart of corporate America. German executives and diplomats based in the United States were furious, but, as the deal went forward toward approval, they kept quiet in their public statements.

Neither of these incidents, nor others, stopped or slowed the flow of European investments. Siemens, the Munich-based electronics giant, still smarted over threats against its U.S. business made by the Reagan administration because of the CGCT controversy in France, but brushed off the threats. Siemens, as we saw in Chapter 1, was competing against AT&T for control of the French telecommunications company, but lost out to Ericsson. The Reagan administration threatened the German company because Washington was convinced the Kohl government was using unfair inducements in Paris. "It was an incident now almost forgotten . . . we are doing extremely well in the United States," a Siemens spokesman told me in Munich three years later, emphasizing that the company planned to double its percentage of total sales in the United States from the current level of 10 percent.

Business Week reported in late 1990 that of the eleven largest foreign employers in the United States the first three were West European (respectively, Germany's Tengelmann, Britain's Hanson, and Switzerland's Nestlé), employing a total of 172,000 people; the fourth was Japan's Honda, employing just over 46,000 Americans; but the next five were, again, all West European, including Siemens, with a combined total work force of about 140,000 people.[5]

ARE FOREIGNERS DANGEROUS?

In their comprehensive assessment, economics professors Edward Graham and Paul Krugman concluded that the U.S. government should have "little problem in identifying potential fifth columns during time of actual war or circumstances leading to war, even without the imposition of new registration and reporting requirements for all foreign direct investors."[6] They rightly noted that a foreign attempt to buy out Boeing, for example, would be blocked immediately, as would any U.S. attempt to acquire a controlling share in any of the Airbus shareholders. Foreigners are prohibited from owning radio and television stations and more than 25 percent of any American airline; similar rules apply to non-Europeans in virtually every Community country.

In the past decade, only one foreign investment has been rejected outright by Washington on security grounds—the proposed acquisition in 1988 of Memco Manufacturing, a supplier of aircraft components to Boeing, by the China National Aero-Technology Import and Export Corporation, a Beijing-based trading organization. But by mid-1991, the Bush administration began displaying new flexibility regarding foreign investments in previously off-limits sectors, such as ailing domestic airlines.

As Graham and Krugman argue sensibly, the dangers of growing foreign investment in America has been greatly exaggerated, and looking at the issue purely from an economic perspective, the total amounts are well below those of U.S. investments abroad. They note that foreign-owned firms control between 3 percent and 4 percent of the American economy, and between 7 percent and 10 percent of the banking sector. But, as Krugman predicted, the issue will remain politically explosive: "This question will continue to be a major political issue in the 1990s, because we still don't have a clear idea of how important the foreigners are. What is clear is that the role of foreign-owned firms in the U.S. economy increased sharply in the 1980s, and will continue to rise, causing more controversy."[7]

The White House, under Bush and Reagan, has opposed cracking down on foreigners, arguing it would conflict directly with the administration's vigorous attempt to defend the idea of open markets in the world economy. Yet leading lawmakers, notably, Congressman John Bryant, have argued repeatedly that the United States is the only country in the West that does not carefully track foreign investments in its domestic economy. Bryant, a four-term Democratic congressman from Dallas, Texas, has repeatedly introduced an amendment to a bill bearing his name which, he said, "only asks major foreign investors to sign in as they walk through our open door. . . . America has been selling off its productive assets—selling the family jewels for a night on the town." The Bryant proposal would simply require detailed reporting on foreign investments, their origin, purpose, and so on.

Clyde Farnsworth, a veteran foreign correspondent, who has followed the issue closely for the *New York Times* in Washington, believes that the administration will continue a cautious, open approach to foreign investments, but that some of the twenty-four previously pending bills requiring expanded reporting by foreigners stood a better than even chance of being passed by both the House and the Senate in the 1991 congressional session.[8]

REVERSING THE AMERICAN CHALLENGE

The image of an America besieged recalls vividly the fears about American multinationals in Europe, captured succinctly in the late 1960s in the best-selling book *The American Challenge* by Jean-Jacques Servan Schreiber. He began with gloomy, alarmist predictions that within fifteen years the world's third-largest economic power after the United States and the Soviet Union would not be Europe, but American industry in Europe. The amount of U.S. capital invested in EC fixed assets appeared huge at the time the book appeared in 1968—about $14 billion, according to U.S. estimates cited in the book, a modest 10 percent of today's level, unadjusted for inflation and exchange-rate differentials over the years. American companies, Servan Schreiber argued, "continue to carve up Europe at their pleasure," but he concluded, "If tragedy is upon us, the final act has not yet been written."[9]

Indeed, as American direct investments have continued to rise in the twelve countries of the EC—approaching a record $140 billion in

1990—the fears about an American buyout in Western Europe have virtually disappeared. The early 1960s, when newcomer Paris correspondents like me could win praise from New York editors for using a snappy question to lead a long feature article on fast food coming to France—Hamburgers in Paris?—were gone forever. What has occurred in Europe since *The American Challenge* appeared was a similar siege—in reverse. European business was modernizing, adopting American management methods. Europeans were going global and, surprisingly, this was occurring not only in the high-tech sectors, such as aerospace, automobiles, electronics, telecommunications, and nuclear energy, but in sectors widely assumed to be chronically ill, such as steel.

UP FROM LONGWY

Item: On March 14, 1990, Usinor-Sacilor, the state-owned French steelmaker and the largest in Western Europe, announced plans to acquire J&L Specialty Products Corporation, the second-largest producer of stainless-steel sheets in the United States.

This little-known—and still nationalized—French steel group has emerged as the world's second-largest steel producer, behind Nippon Steel of Japan. The day the J&L agreement was announced, Francis Mer, the handsome, chisel-faced chairman, a mining engineer by training, who directed years of painful, violent restructuring of France's ailing steel industry, said the move was aimed at reinforcing the group's worldwide position. "The American market is the first in the world . . . and with the dollar worth less than last year, better to make an acquisition this year," Mer said. Although few outsiders noticed, Mer had already acquired, or bought important numbers of shares in, about a dozen other smaller steel companies in Europe and in the United States, including Saarstahl Voelkingen, which made Usinor the second-ranking steelmaker in Germany.

I recalled a tense interview with Mer more than three years earlier in his spacious office at La Défense's office-building complex on the outskirts of Paris. "Longwy may be something of a symbol," he said, "but it is only one of my many concerns as we attempt to close the gap with our West European competitors, many of whom are already profitable."[10]

The "Longwy" Mer mentioned was the symbol of what at the time was tragically wrong in northern Europe's outdated steel-producing regions, victims of worldwide competition, collapsed steel prices, and poor geographical location. Usinor and Sacilor, which were to be merged under Mer's chairmanship, had not earned a profit in twelve years.

A grimy town of ninety thousand in northeastern France on the borders of Belgium and Luxembourg, Longwy was the site of violent clashes between riot police and workers throughout the early 1980s. As I headed for the labor-union offices, my ears ringing from the clanging of the mills and whistling of the trains in the yards, I sensed the gray, overcast, polluted air pressing in on the depressed area, and recalled a comment by a plant executive, who conceded grimly that the latest planned cuts in the work force amounted to "a death sentence" for the plants and blast furnaces that had dominated Longwy's life and the surrounding valley for a century.

The unions were preparing for a last-ditch stand at a protest rally scheduled for the following day in Metz, the region's capital city. "We will fight management on the streets of Metz, and we are not afraid of repression," said Fernand Tiberi, an embittered official of the Communist-dominated CGT union, whose father migrated from Italy to work in the area several decades earlier. "I will be there, ready to meet with them, but the CGT is wrong to think we can build a protected wall around Longwy steel," countered Jean Jacquet, president of the local Sacilor subsidiary. "All we can talk about is timing."

The next day, amid tight police security, several thousand steelworkers marched calmly in the streets of Metz, the capital of the Moselle region, which first prospered in the ninth century under Charlemagne's rule.

EUROPE'S STEEL BECOMES PROFITABLE

Meantime, the "Mer Plan" to restructure the industry and restore profits went forward, including an additional fourteen thousand layoffs and further plant shutdowns in Longwy. The picture was the same throughout the rest of Europe.

Between 1980 and 1988, ailing EC steelmakers eliminated 261,-000 jobs and 30 million tons in production capacity. Governments and Brussels spent about $50 billion in subsidies and low-interest loans to ease the impact on workers and to provide companies like

Usinor-Sacilor and Germany's Thyssen group a sound financial base, much of it under plans devised by Davignon, then the Commission's industry commissioner. By 1990, EC steel output had reached nearly 140 million tons, making the Community the world's second-largest steel producer after the Soviet Union. Thyssen, Germany's largest producer, reported a pretax profit gain of 50 percent, the best year in its history. Usinor-Sacilor reported its first profit in fourteen years in 1988. Meantime, British Steel, also profitable and privatized, disclosed that it, too, was seeking an acquisition in the United States.

Steel, while a striking example, was by no means the only European industry buying into America. Advertising. Aerospace. Chemicals. Pharmaceuticals. Cosmetics. Electronics. Food. Beverages. Publishing. Television. Tires. Electric equipment. The list goes on. On just one day—April 25, 1990—Beffa of Saint-Gobain, a former colleague and friend of Mer's, announced the French glassmaker had agreed to acquire the Norton Company, a materials maker based in Worcester, Massachusetts for about $1.9 billion. Meantime, in Washington the Justice Department approved a French tiremaker's acquisition of Uniroyal Goodrich Tire, making Michelin the world's largest tire company, with more than 20 percent of the world market, compared to roughly 17 percent each for Goodyear Tire & Rubber of the United States and Bridgestone of Japan. In Turin, Giovanni Agnelli was beginning to map what would soon become a major tie-up with Ford in the United States.

Why were Europe's revitalized industries pouring profits into modernizing plant and equipment, research and development, and, of course, acquisitions? Basically, they were propelled by the relatively low dollar, the stable political scene in America, and their own pressing needs to expand internationally—much of the initial drive inspired by the 1992 plan.

European corporate treasuries, as many analysts noted, were bulging with cash. Profits were growing at twice the rate of wages, as it became apparent that many of the analysts had drastically underestimated European industry and its managers' acumen, who were being encouraged by Europe's accelerating movement toward economic, monetary, and political union. The upbeat environment that characterized the late 1980s was beginning to dissipate in 1991 as the U.S. slowdown continued, but new European strategies quickly surfaced. For example, on January 9, 1991, France's pharmaceutical maker Sanofi and Kodak's Sterling Drug subsidiary announced plans to merge their worldwide pharmaceutical interests—in a cash-free joint venture. Other players, also worried by their internal pressures and the American recession but already established in America, remained determined to hang on whatever happened—to the American economy or the Middle East.

Innovative approaches to the United States also surfaced, in some cases blending art and business. France's largest oil company, Elf Aquitaine, which was planning to build on previous acquisitions in the United States by listing its stock on the New York Stock Exchange, sponsored a major art exhibit to coincide with the listing. The exhibit of the works of neo-Impressionist French painter, Georges Seurat, opened at the Metropolitan Museum of Art in the summer and would run through early 1992. Similarly, several years earlier, Olivetti had sponsored an exhibit of art treasures from Venice, which De Benedetti told me was an excellent way of raising his company's—and Europe's—image in American eyes.

THE UNION JACK FLIES OVER MADISON AVENUE

Britain's Martin Sorrell was once described by the legendary figure of American advertising, David Ogilvy, then seventy-seven, as an "odious little shit." Sorrell, then forty-four and head of a London-based marketing conglomerate known as WPP Group PLC, was in the final stages of acquiring the Ogilvy Group for around $864 million, in what turned out to be the biggest unsolicited takeover in the history of Madison Avenue. It was the spring of 1989 and WPP was well on the way to becoming the world's largest advertising and public-relations group. Two years earlier, Sorrell had acquired J. Walter Thompson for $566 million, a firm established more than a century before, followed by WPP's purchase of Hill and Knowlton, the world's largest public-relations and lobbying company, also based in New York.

But Madison Avenue didn't take kindly to Sorrell, who for all his glittering success and financial brilliance was widely perceived as "an odd duck," according to veteran *New York Times* advertising columnist Randall Rothenberg.[11]

Advertising buffs in London relish telling the story of how Sorrell, walking down Regent Street on a fine day in 1976, saw the name Saatchi & Saatchi on a building and thought it was a Japanese company. Through friends, Sorrell, who had already graduated from Cambridge University, and was armed with an MBA from the Harvard Business School and several years of consulting experience, found out that the Saatchi brothers, who ran the agency bearing their name, were British, and in deep trouble. He accepted their offer to join the ailing firm and from 1977 until he formed WPP in 1986 Sorrell helped run the world's number-one agency and gradually turned it around.

Rothenberg and many other sources, including London bankers, have always said that the short, stocky, and tense Sorrell was the linchpin in Saatchi's spectacular success, reflected in its glamour stock status on the London Stock Exchange and by a string of successful acquisitions in 1986: Ted Bates Worldwide, Dancer Fitzgerald Simple, Backer & Spielvogel—all household names in the advertising world of Madison Avenue, over which, as *Time* magazine concluded, the Union Jack was now flying triumphantly.

WPP's list of clients included over two hundred ranked on *Fortune* magazine's list of the world's top five hundred corporations. Many operated in Western and Eastern Europe, and to my surprise the first time I met Sorrell in London—thirteen days after the collapse of the Berlin Wall—he had already been thinking hard about the New Europe, including its eastern dimension.[12] His answers to detailed questions reflected caution, pragmatism, and enthusiasm about Europe's prospects, but what came through above all were his talents as financial wizard; he was a tight-fisted manager. It was easy to see why the cozy New York world of advertising felt uneasy with him and why some, like Ogilvy, accused him of not understanding how it worked and resented his intrusion.

The flamboyant British-born Ogilvy remained chairman of the agency's board, but clearly this was not his cup of business tea, and the outspoken Ogilvy said so publicly before retiring to his château in the Loire region of France. What happened? Had Ogilvy and Mather, and the legends of its founder, who had invented "The Man in the Hathaway Shirt" advertisements, suddenly gone "European"?

Graham Phillips, another British-born executive at the agency who took over as chairman and chief executive, insisted that nothing much has changed, brushing off the image of the Union Jack flying over Madison Avenue. "We're now more productive," said Phillips, sitting on a stylish sofa in his spacious office in a restored early twentieth-century skyscraper on New York's West Side, in the spring of 1990. A year later, WPP was struggling against falling ad revenues in recession-hit America. Its stock had plummeted amid fears that it would have trouble servicing its debt and possibly be forced to sell some of its acquisitions. Wall Street analysts concluded that Sorrell was now paying heavily for the high price paid for Ogilvy, just as the Saatchis—who by now had gone into semiretirement—overpaid in their takeover of Ted Bates.

EUROPEANS ALSO MAKE MISTAKES

Simply moving into the United States, particularly through a corporate takeover, is not enough to ensure success, as Sorrell and others learned. Some European companies have failed badly to understand American culture, the American mind, the market, consumer habits, and traditions. These Europeans have proven as inept as some Japanese firms, which are even more removed from American culture, traditions, and psychology. Most Europeans, however, have learned their lessons; many, who rely on American managers, do better, just as American multinationals found they were accepted more easily in Western Europe once they put European executives in charge of their operations.

Some of the experiences of the Europeans in America are hardly paragons. Consider the publishing business. Germany's Bertelsmann, the world's largest publishing group, was among the first to buy into American media and entertainment companies In 1986, Bertelsmann spent about $808 million to acquire Doubleday, the U.S. publishing house, and RCA records. But in 1989 its U.S. book clubs began posting growing losses and several top managers quit in frustration, citing "rigid" German management styles imposed from above. Its executives conceded that they did not fully understand the American market—for book clubs or records. A major reorganization was launched in 1990, partly aimed at finding American managers to run the company's divisions.[13]

Similarly, Bertelsmann's great rival, France's Hachette publishing group, announced in May 1990 plans to sell *Woman's Day*, which has one of the largest circulations in the country and is one of thirteen publications owned by Diamandis Communications, which had been acquired by Hachette for $712 million in 1988.

Within a year, Peter Diamandis, the company founder, and several senior executives who had stayed on resigned, protesting Hachette's strategy and decisions. To shore up the group's lackluster performance, Daniel Filipacchi, Hachette's chairman, took over the U.S. group. An exasperated French Hachette executive told me: "We have made mistakes, understanding the market . . . and these are difficult times in American publishing, so we felt we had to have our own people in charge, to provide the direction."

EVEN LAWYERS HIT SNAGS

And yet even some of the most "Americanized," erudite Europeans admit that American corporate culture can present a formidable barrier and that misunderstandings abound in the two cultures. These exist, they say, despite the removal of transatlantic barriers to trade, freer movement of people, and the rapid buildup of networks in such sectors as television, where American impact has been strong, as we shall see in Chapter 6.

Meet Alexander Riesenkampff, a successful American-trained West German antitrust lawyer from Frankfurt. Blue-eyed and mustached, with an erect, aristocratic bearing and a friendly, forceful voice, he is a lover of art, music, and French cuisine, who vacations in New England. He has come closer to understanding America and its corporate culture—than many other Europeans I have come to know in several decades of business reporting. Born in Riga, which eighteen years earlier had become the capital of independent Latvia, he studied law and economics at the universities of Munich, Bonn, and Cologne. In his early twenties he began his studies in the United States, earning graduate degrees in business administration at Columbia University and in law at the University of Pennsylvania, where, upon graduation, he was admitted to the bar.

Riesenkampff (which means gigantic battle in German) has served as a member of Frankfurt's city government, belonging to the prestigious clubs of the country's prosperous, powerful financial capital, where he hobnobs with many of his American clients. And yet, he says, "I have known the U.S. for thirty years, and I'm still not sure I, and more important, influential parts of German industry, understand America."[14]

He compared the puzzling role of lawyers in business. "Americans don't go to the bathroom without consulting their lawyers, whereas Germans tend to look at lawyers as trouble-shooters, to be called in only when they get into difficulty, and this, in turn, leads to trouble," says Riesenkampff. He adds that his usual practice is to steer his German clients seeking American investments to associated U.S. firms, but he keeps up with them through the firm's Philadelphia office. Causing confusion and difficulties in transactions, says Riesenkampff, are American habits—calling each other by first names, which deceivingly creates the impression of familiarity. "Concepts, or the roles of similar-sounding jobs, like notaries, are totally different in the two cultures—complicating our dealings with each other," he adds.

THE BAVARIAN CONNECTION

Some Germans have proven uncanny in bridging the transatlantic cultural gaps, the undisputed master having been Bavaria's gregarious Franz-Josef Strauss, who died in 1988. His clout was unusual, stemming from his position as the Bavarian state's highly popular prime minister, and from having served since its founding as the chairman of the supervisory board of Airbus Industrie.

Interviewing Airbus executives in Toulouse a year before his death, I asked whether Strauss ever helped clinch any important deals in the United States, a particularly difficult market for Airbus at the time. "He certainly does not carry an order book around," an executive said, laughing, "but let me tell you how Strauss helped on Northwest Airlines." The U.S. airline, several months earlier, had announced it was ordering ten A320s and taking options on an additional ninety, which was considered a major marketing coup, representing the largest U.S. contract in Airbus's history and a major blow to both Boeing and McDonnell Douglas. More advanced European technology in the new plane was widely cited as the main reason for the $3.2-billion order.

But well before the deal was signed, Strauss had begun working behind the scenes on the German-admiring American chairman of Northwest Airlines, Steven Rothmeier, who had repeatedly turned down Airbus planes in favor of Boeing. Convinced that the venture—and its Germanophile chairman—merited his personal attention, Strauss invited Rothmeier to Bavaria for hunting and relaxation. Airbus's chairman, Jean Pierson, said, "You have to realize that Mr.

Rothmeier has a very German background, and even lives in a Bavarian castle, and so, when appropriate, I do not hesitate to call on Mr. Strauss to help us lobby." What did they talk about? "Never business—only hunting, America and Bavaria—the mix was perfect," insisted a company insider afterward. "There is something about Bavaria that appeals to Americans," he added. "Perhaps it is the charm of Munich, the castles, the mountainous scenery, postwar memories, I don't know, and it helped, but, of course, no one has yet come up with a replacement for Strauss."

EAST GERMANY MAKES A MOVE

But how do you bridge the gap between East Germany and America? A leading Bavarian bank hit upon a successful formula for an unusual feat—engineering the first takeover of an American company by an East German firm several months after the destruction of the Berlin Wall. Founded in 1835 by Bavaria's King Ludwig I, the Bayerische Hypoteken und Wechsel Bank of Munich, through its New York branch, helped organize and finance the transaction. "We are proud to have been instrumental in bringing about this investment by a GDR company," Hans-Hubert Friedl, the bank's managing director in charge of international operations, a 1982 graduate of Harvard University's Business School, told a news conference in New York on January 10, 1990.

The acquiring company was Polygraph Export-Import of East Berlin, the foreign trading subsidiary of East Germany's printing-machinery industry, with annual sales of $600 million. Its president, Thomas Schneider, predicted the acquisition would be followed by similar moves in America by other East German companies. That would have been unthinkable before the collapse of the formerly Communist East German regime. "Clearly, events in East Germany changed things," said Robert McKinney, the American vice president of marketing of the newly acquired company, whose name was changed by the new management from Royal Zenith to Planeta North America, Inc.; Planeta is the name of the *Kombinat*'s main plant, located in Radebuel, a small town south of Dresden. Since 1968, Royal Zenith had been acting as its exclusive distributor in the United States and was a vital outlet, representing 20 percent of total East German sales of printing machinery.[15]

Relaxing at the U.S. headquarters, in an industrial park located on a hill overlooking a residential area of Great Neck, Long Island, McKinney recalled how the FBI kept visitors from Polygraph under constant surveillance while in the United States and how previously some potential U.S. customers simply refused to buy the East German equipment because, McKinney noted, "they kept telling us—no . . . it's Communist." Similarly, deliberately cumbersome red tape and procedures on both sides complicated trips by Zenith executives and their customers to East Germany. "Everything has now changed and they are—well, just German," he added.

But like so many U.S. firms acquired by foreigners, Planeta's U.S. headquarters shows no visible signs of anything particularly foreign— the plant site, the offices, the pleasant New York-accented reception- ist, the bright-colored landscape paintings on the walls are as Ameri- can as apple pie.

How about language? "I can understand some German, enough to get by, but it doesn't really matter, because there are more impor- tant elements in our strategy," McKinney said. Indeed, the East Ger- mans plan to use their U.S. base for boosting their sales in North America and training their personnel in sales and marketing, an area in which East Europeans are desperately underdeveloped. To make sure East Berlin is kept in the picture and to guide Planeta teams coming from Germany, Frank Seiffert, an East German executive, moved to the Long Island area with his wife, to liaison, with the title of vice president.

As I was being driven to the Great Neck railroad station by Henry Robinson, the company's driver and handyman for twenty-six years, I asked what it was like working for a company that only months before had been dominated by one of the most ruthless, undemo- cratic regimes in all of Eastern Europe. "Heck, I just don't see any difference. . . . I still pick these fellas up at Kennedy [airport], they all speak good enough English, act friendly. With them, I got no problems." Germany, it seems, was finding the right approach to America.

HOW THE FRENCH CAUGHT ON IN PRINCETON

What happens when a very traditional, and state-owned, French com- pany moves in?

Peter Neff is a U.S. Navy veteran, a 1969 chemistry graduate of Rutgers University in New Brunswick, New Jersey, who with his wife and their three children now lives in Skillman, New Jersey. For fourteen years, Neff was president of St. Joe Minerals Corporation, a leading U.S. chemicals manufacturer. Chemicals and New Jersey had been an integral part of his life. He thus seemed like the ideal candidate to head the American operations of a European company he barely knew—Rhône-Poulenc, France's largest chemical company, which is state-controlled. The job being proposed was the presidency of the company's then-fledgling U.S. operations. Bothering Neff, as he considered the offer, was his lack of French and the problem of fitting into French corporate culture.

But back in Paris, hard-driving Jean-René Fourtou, who took over as chairman of the company in 1986, was not worried. His priority was making Rhône-Poulenc one of the top five chemical companies in the world. In 1990, it ranked ninth. The American market was the key. And Neff was an ideal choice.

"I thought my lack of French would matter, but it didn't, because the goal was survival, with the United States at the center of the strategy, and so I accepted the presidency," explained Neff at Rhône-Poulenc's U.S. headquarters, located in a sprawling modern headquarters complex just off Route 1 near Princeton, New Jersey. When we met, Neff was directing the digestion of the French company's nineteenth—and so far its largest—U.S. acquisition: the Rorer Corporation, the diversified American drug manufacturer of Maalox, which Rhône-Poulenc had purchased for $3.1 billion. It provided what Neff described as "critical mass" in the highly competitive American market, generating about 25 percent of the group's total sales. "But our problems of integrating the new corporate cultures would continue," he said.[16] Integrating into what?

1992 PROVIDED A LOT OF PUSH

Keep in mind that Rhône-Poulenc was only one among several hundred EC-based companies expanding into the United States as part of their worldwide strategy to compete with Japanese and American industries, drawn, pushed, and helped by what had been happening back home. Having participated in many EC-sponsored and -subsidized research programs, and determined to benefit from the deregulated, more open European Community Market in 1993, Rhône-Poulenc, like most of its U.S. and Japanese competitors operating in Europe, was building a global base for further expansion.

"For us, 1992 was an opportunity and we seized on it, as part of the liberalization and deregulation going on in Europe. . . . Our new moves in America were an extension of this movement," Fourtou told me a year after taking over as chairman. At the time some of his critics openly questioned whether his previous twenty-three years of experience as a management consultant qualified him for running the company, yet within two years he had made a total of thirty-five acquisitions after having dropped just over twenty businesses. He was not yet fifty years old. It was quite a change from the Rhône-Poulenc I knew in the early days of my reporting career in France.

When I first began reporting on France's largest maker of chemicals and pharmaceuticals in the early 1960s, Rhône-Poulenc was respectfully called *la belle dame* of the nation's industrial establishment—and prided itself on being the most secretive. I once asked a shareholder at an annual meeting whether he knew who controlled the corporation. He admitted that he had never heard of the Gillet family, which since 1838 had owned Rhône-Poulenc and had built it into the nation's biggest—and probably its most hidebound—company. In January 1964, the company broke tradition on two counts: it moved its Paris headquarters to a building on fashionable Avenue Montaigne, and it named a former central banker and distinguished finance minister as president: Wilfrid Baumgartner.

Baumgartner, still smarting for having been eased out as General de Gaulle's finance minister, had no experience running a company, much less a complex consisting of a holding company that in 1963 had become the first French company to pass the $1 billion mark in sales. But he and the Gillet family knew the company needed money to survive in what already loomed as a highly competitive environment. Baumgartner, who enjoyed meeting foreign business leaders and bankers, also had a flair for projecting his image, and told me in our many talks well after his retirement that it was silly for French industrialists to cultivate *mystique.* In fact, he loved publicity.

In the springtime of 1964, I had persuaded Baumgartner to become the subject of a cover story in *Business Week,* one of the first such stories on any major French company. We entered a top-floor office in order to get to the roof for the picture taking, because New York editors insisted that we get the Eiffel Tower in the background, to identify the company with the city. As we filed into an office, the secretaries were startled by this white-haired, distinguished, elegantly dressed gentleman trying to climb through a window, followed by an American reporter and a photographer. "Excuse me for having disturbed you," he told the wide-eyed ladies, who clearly had not recognized him. "I am Baumgartner, your new president," and then stepped through the open window.

Twenty-six years later, in 1990, on a Chicago–New York flight, I found myself sitting next to a thirty-eight-year-old Rhône-Poulenc executive, as American as they come, who did not realize he was being interviewed. What was it like working for a French company? "Not easy," he replied, "particularly with the neighbors always harping at the fact that I work for the foreigners . . . but when I mention the name, those who ask the questions calm down a bit, because, well, we all consider the Japanese the enemy . . . we consider the French tied into our side, and that helps, but there is no doubting I am working for a French company." What was the biggest plus factor? "Getting international experience—it's great, the traveling to France, my wife is learning the language . . . it is something of a cultural revolution in our family, and I'm not at all sure I could be doing this with an American company."

Blending the two cultures within Rhône-Poulenc has not proven easy, even though short courses in French language and culture are offered free to all employees, along with regular exchanges of technicians and managers. About three hundred of the company's eight thousand U.S. employees now can "handle" French. Company insiders quickly point out that mentalities differ sharply. "The French love to study things to death, and they have trouble making decisions, perhaps because so many of them in industry are engineers by training," an American executive said. "We are more flexible, more open, ready to move based on feel, the idea that we can say: 'Go for it!' which still poses problems for the French." Just being a foreign company can also pose obstacles when recruiting graduate engineers and potential managers on campuses of American universities, a problem shared by many other Western European companies and even more by Japanese companies operating in the United States.

Rhône-Poulenc executives say they regularly swap experiences with executives in other foreign companies in the area, such as BASF, Bayer, Hoechst, Switzerland's Hoffmann–LaRoche, and Sandoz, all multinational pharmaceutical companies. "Comparing notes helps, because we tend to have similar problems," said Neff, adding, however, that, according to his estimates, only 30 percent of the chief executives of the major European chemical companies in the New York–New Jersey area were American. Convinced that imported Europeans are more prone to make mistakes, Philippe Desmarescaux, Rhône-Poulenc's board member responsible for the United States, said that if they are to continue succeeding the French will have to become "more American." As a first step, in April 1990, two of Rhône-Poulenc's strategic business units were moved to Princeton, from Paris, with worldwide authority, independent of Paris, the first move of its kind in the company's history. The obligatory language in some staff meetings became English, to the annoyance of French employees.

JOINING AMERICA AND JAPAN

While individual European companies and banks investing in the United States—taken together—add up to enhanced Western European economic power, there are only a few examples of EC-based companies teaming up with their American and Japanese competitors to produce a single, industrially significant product for the world market.

One example is a most unusual aircraft-engine consortium, located in a converted red-brick schoolhouse in East Hartford, Connecticut. At the time of my visit in the spring of 1990 it was already being studied as a model for future collaborative efforts—between the United States, Japan, and Western Europe. "When we started out, we had seven different reasons for cooperating," said Nicolas Tomassetti, president of the consortium, which comprised the following groups: Britain's Rolls-Royce, West Germany's MTU, Italy's Fiat; three Japanese companies, Fuji, Kawasaki, and Mitsubishi; and the American coordinator and project leader, United Technologies' Pratt & Whitney aircraft-engine division. "We could be the model of the future," said Tomassetti, who has spent his entire career at Pratt, spanning several decades.[17]

The East Hartford project was started in Britain in 1984 to build a new engine, the V2500, for the Airbus A-320, but because of technical problems that Rolls-Royce was unable to resolve the project was moved to the United States with Pratt in charge. The consortium now also builds the engines for the "stretched" version of that plane, the A-321, as well as for the McDonnell MD-90 and Boeing's B-737 family of passenger planes. The group assembles and coordinates engineering; components, however, are made by the partners and shipped to assembly facilities in East Hartford and Britain and then marketed by a single management group, similar to Airbus's operation in Toulouse. "It is a complex, cumbersome operation," Tomassetti said, "but it works."

Scattered in several sites in East Hartford are an international team of 160 people—including 37 British engineers, 11 Japanese, nine Germans, and two Italians, on loan from the seven shareholder companies, and, says Tomassetti, "the cultures mix, we work as a team . . . everybody does their part." There was only one reported casualty—a divorce, involving a British couple. "She was the problem," said Alan Brothers, the consortium's British press officer, "she never had wanted to leave Britain."

The venture in East Hartford was being viewed as a possible model for larger collaborative effort in other high-technology areas. Several of the partners had already signed agreements committing them to future cooperation. Daimler, which controls MTU, and United Technologies announced an alliance on March 27, 1990; a few weeks later, Daimler's MBB announced that it was forming a new joint venture with Aerospatiale of France, which already controlled 30 percent of the world market for helicopters. That followed the even more startling announcement that Daimler was joining forces with Japan's Mitsubishi, and possibly, for starters, might build an automobile plant in the Soviet Union. French and British companies immediately expressed interest in joining these ventures, which were expected to cover sectors ranging from automobile components to helicopters and other new-generation aircraft, including possibly the new supersonic aircraft already being studied by Britain and France.

"Europe can only gain from these ventures, because they provide the opportunity to tap new management methods and technology needed badly for the future," a German executive said. "Americanizing or Europeanizing per se is only an aspect of the strategy."

EXPANDING SOUTH OF THE BORDER

The scene was the annual meeting of the Inter-American Development Bank being held in Montreal April 1, 1990. Many delegates had agreed that debt reduction for Latin America had probably been overemphasized by policy-makers administering the debt plan of the U.S. Treasury secretary, Nicholas Brady. William Rhodes, a Citibank executive, said that the plan had gone "much slower than one would have hoped," while a West German Dresdner Bank executive emphasized that corrupt, inefficient bureaucracies and practices in Latin America would require what he termed "a complete break" with the past before private investments from Europe would go forward.[18] The warnings reflected the power and interests of the two predominant powers; everyone knew about the United States, but few delegates had realized the growing importance in Latin America of the European Community and several of its key members.

Consider the following:

- On January 1, 1990, the share of Latin America's debt held by West European banks had climbed to 38.6 percent, which was substantially more than the North American share of 30.8 percent and the 20 percent held by Japanese banks.
- Although Latin America's share of the Community's external trade had fallen from 8.2 percent in 1985 to 4.5 percent in 1989, the EC has remained Latin America's second-largest trading partner.
- The total value of trade between the EC and Latin America had risen to an estimated $50 billion in 1990, compared to an estimated nearly $100 billion with the United States; Germany, France, Italy, and Britain were the European leaders.
- EC members' total direct investments throughout Latin America had reached more than a record $32 billion in 1990, compared to $80 billion by the United States, and they resumed their rise in 1991.

The historical ties of EC member countries to Latin America go back to the fifteenth century, when explorers and military leaders from Spain, Portugal, and then Britain, France, and the Netherlands imposed their colonial rule, religion, civilization, and languages. The prospective celebrations of the five hundredth anniversary of Christopher Columbus's first voyage to the New World in 1492 have touched off emotional debate, religious battles, demonstrations, and publication of new books in Latin America and Europe. Many focused on charges that the arrival of the Europeans brought, among other things, ecological disaster, servitude, exploitation, disease, and the ultimate extinction of Indian cultures.

But successive waves of nineteenth- and 20th-century immigration and trade from Western Europe established new ties with the New World, as cities like Buenos Aires, Rio de Janeiro, and Santiago, swelled by several millions of European newcomers, became heavily influenced by local British, Italian, and German cultures.

At the urging of Latin American governments, starting around the mid-1970s, the European Community began establishing modest aid programs for the region, seeking a "third way" to offset American predominance in the region. Shortly after the Socialists took power in 1981, Claude Cheysson, Mitterrand's foreign minister, invoked the term in promising French-led European military aid to Nicaragua, and immediately infuriated Washington and irritated Moscow. But the legacy lingered; whenever the incident was cited in conversations, Cheysson was praised by Mexicans and Central American leaders as "one European who understood" the region's frustrating predicament, caught between the United States and the Soviet Union as its prime supplier of economic assistance and arms.

More than a decade later, reaffirming their ties, EC foreign ministers and their counterparts from Argentina, Bolivia, Brazil, Chile, Ecuador, Mexico, Paraguay, Uruguay, and Venezuela signed a declaration in Rome in late December 1990. It committed the Community to deeper cooperation in science and technology, trade and economic development, amid appeals by the Latin Americans that Europeans should not forget their desperate needs.

One EC member, because of its historical, linguistic, cultural, and political ties, believes it has a privileged position and could serve as Europe's voice and leader in the region—Spain.

A SPANISH TELECOM COMPANY LEADS

When I first met Luis Solana, he was fifty-two and completing his sixth year as chairman of Telefónica de España, Spain's main telecommunications company, which is 30 percent government owned.

A Socialist, close friend of Prime Minister González, a lawyer by training, and an enthusiastic member of the European Roundtable, he met with me at Telefónica's neo-baroque headquarters building in the heart of Madrid's business district, in offices that strangely reminded me of New York City. "You are right—this building, Europe's first skyscraper, was designed by ITT when they owned it and us . . . before Franco partly nationalized it in the 1930s," Solana said with a chuckle, gesturing in the boardroom to a full-length portrait of Alfonso XIII, grandfather of the present King Juan Carlos I. "We are refurbishing the building to look like it was then, when he [the monarch] was in charge, and it is something of a replica of an ITT building in New York," Solana said.[19]

ITT executives in New York later confirmed that the building had indeed been designed by the company architect, Louis S. Weeks. "And like ITT," Solana added, "we are deeply interested in Latin America."

Solana's outspoken conviction, shared by González, as well as by most Spanish business leaders and bankers, was that Spain, buttressed by its EC membership and the Community's institutions and funds, could provide new leadership for developing the region—and making money—while providing an alternative to the overwhelming American predominance in most Latin American countries. "We cannot afford U.S.–style deregulation of our telecommunications industry here in Spain, but we must modernize and expand—at home and abroad—which means buying and being European above all," Solana said, adding quickly, "Latin America is our logical growth area outside Spain . . . we speak the same language, share a similar cultural heritage, and we understand the Latin Americans better than, say, you Americans, or the Swedes, or the French."

At the time of our talk in December 1988, several weeks prior to resigning, Solana was concentrating much of his effort on purchasing a 40 percent shareholding in Entel, Argentina's state-owned phone company. He also expressed interest in buying a roughly similar share of Cia. de Teléfonos de Chile, or CTC, that country's main telecommunications company. It was one of those ironies of history that ITT had obtained control of CTC in 1927 and that by 1970 it had become the American conglomerate's largest telephone property in Latin America, prior to being "taken over" by the left-wing government of Salvador Allende, yet, as Rand Arakskog, ITT's chairman, noted, was never formally expropriated.[20] Didn't the ruling military regime in Santiago, which overthrew Allende, bother him, a dedicated Socialist? "Pinochet does not bother me, because what interests us is taking advantage of the wave of privatization in Chile, Argentina, Mexico, and elsewhere in Latin America," Solana said.

Within a year, Solana had been replaced, but his policies were being continued by Candido Velázquez-Gaztelu, also a Socialist and fifty-two when he took over. He had previously headed Spain's tobacco monopoly and worked for Coca-Cola, and told everyone he met that his main goal was to earn profits[21]—and to continue expanding, including in Argentina, where the telephone system was so dilapidated that residents of Buenos Aires are fond of complaining that when it rains the city's entire system goes down for hours.

ARGENTINA PRIVATIZES AND EUROPE MOVES

Inspired partly by the EC drive to deregulate, privatize, and generally improve its state-controlled telecommunications, transportation, energy, and other public-service sectors, Argentina's President Carlos Menem and members of his government have never hidden their interest in attracting Europeans to their own privatization program, and, they repeatedly emphasized, Spain had no monopoly as far as Argentina was concerned.

For example, in charge of privatizing Entel, Argentina's unprofitable telecommunications company, was dynamic, brown-eyed former congresswoman—María Julia Alsogaray, whom I met for the first time as she was leading a business delegation to the annual World Economic Forum in Davos in February 1990. "Spain is only one of the countries we are looking to as we privatize and, most important, modernize our telephone system, which we know is in desperate shape," she said. "Basically, we are looking for as many Europeans as possible to come and participate."

Argentine businessmen accompanying her to Davos, talking up opportunities for investment at every cocktail party and dinner, were even more eager to attract Europeans. "We look to all of Europe, and wish they could be more together, more present in Argentina and not so obsessed with Eastern Europe," a Buenos Aires banker commented over drinks at the Derby Hotel, where we were staying. "After all, we have many tens of thousands of Italians and Germans living in our capital, which we like to think of as the most European city in Latin America. . . . It is a terrific opportunity for Europe. Why don't more of them come down and exploit it, say the way the French are moving into the United States?"

It was a classic pitch made in many other capitals around the world, of course. Yet, in early November 1990, three European telecommunications companies, including Telefónica, signed agreements to take control of the country's telephone network; the others included Stet Società Finanziaria Telefonica, Italy's state telecommunications holding company, and France's Cables & Radio, a subsidiary of state-controlled France Télécom. Their bankers, led by Citicorp and J. P. Morgan of New York, swapped more than $2.3 billion of Argentine debt for equity in two new holding companies, which would own two companies—one covering southern Argentina, the other the northern half.

Elsewhere in Latin America, the Europeans were also on the move. Several months before completing the Entel deal, Telefónica announced that it would buy from Bond Corporation International its controlling interest in Chile's CTC, which Solana had been seeking. France's aerospace company Dassault, which had supplied Mirage fighters to seven Latin American countries, including Chile, was seeking to expand sales of advanced military and civilian planes there, following plans by the West to lift the embargo on sales of such equipment, after the decision by the Pinochet regime, which had seized power in 1973, to establish a democratically elected government. That move followed the announcement by Scandinavian Airlines that it would acquire a 30 percent shareholding in LanChile, the national airline, and would increase its stake to 35 percent following a new issue of shares.

These moves, among others, followed by a year the EC Commission's plan for expanding Europe's trade relations with Latin America, aimed at bolstering democracy in the region; we shall return to this in Chapter 9.

Appealing to the EC to be more active, Jacques de Larosière, governor of the Bank of France, noted that "Latin American countries are now looking to the European for [organizational] inspiration." He cited the Southern Cone Common Market, including Brazil, Argentina, Uruguay, and Paraguay, and a Central American regional financing scheme being established, which resembles the European Payments Union set up in postwar Europe. "Latin America increasingly shares a common vision of the economy and politics in the area with Europe," said Larosière.[22]

CONCLUDING

- Despite such upbeat exhortations, the United States, not Latin America, according to most observers, would continue drawing the largest share of European investments in the Western Hemisphere, certainly until the end of the century.
- Meantime, Western Europe, for all its new determination, would never, in the foreseeable future, replace the United States as the predominant economic and political force in Latin America, including Mexico and Argentina.
- Nevertheless, the leap across the Atlantic discussed in this chapter reflects Western Europe's collective determination to be a far more active player in North and South America, primarily through investments and trade cooperation under EC Commission auspices.
- U.S. policy-makers would continue facing the paradox of a European Community seeking more autonomy, through its 1992 program and movement toward political union, while playing a far greater role in the economic life of the United States, both as a trade partner and, increasingly, a challenger.
- Finally, "the magnet effect" of Europe-1992, as it was coming to be widely called, was catching on in Latin America, both for expanding trade and investment ties, and as a model for linking its disparate nations. Reacting to what was happening in Europe, President Bush in 1991 obtained congressional approval to pursue his plan for creating a vast $6 trillion, barrier-free economic and trade zone stretching from Alaska to the southernmost tip of Latin America, which would easily eclipse the European Community and Japan in terms of population and economic power.

It is, therefore, time to look harder, and deeper, at what the Community's unity formula is really all about, and what and who are behind it.

Inside the New Europe:
Integrating Through Networks

What is the biggest obstacle to a European *Dallas*? I
would say cultures and, specifically, languages. The
Germans do not learn French and the French do not
learn German and neither learns Dutch. Everybody
learns American.

—GASTON THORN

It was a balmy day in Luxembourg in late July 1989, and Thorn, the
feisty former EC Commission president and prime minister of his tiny
country, was grappling with the heated controversy then raging in
every European capital and Washington over the following question:
by what right did the EC establish a quota limiting the number of
American films shown on European television? The target most frequently cited—immensely popular with Europeans of all ages—was
Dallas, the U.S.-made television series. Just as the Community was
tightening imports of electronic goods and automobiles from Japan,
a French-led drive to reduce the flow of U.S. programs was underway,
aimed at forcing EC member governments to guarantee that, wherever "practicable," and "by appropriate means," a majority of television programs shown would be of European origin.

The odds were overwhelmingly against such a protectionist policy

171

succeeding, if for no other reason than the one indicated by Thorn—
the popularity of American TV glamour, style, excitement, sex, and
adventure with which many Europeans identified easily; not to mention the low costs to European stations of buying American films. In
1991, a European TV station could buy a U.S. television film already
shown in America for about $70,000; an original production of com-
parable length for a European film costs up to $1 million or more.
Since the early 1980s, with the dizzying pace of commercial television
expansion in Europe, triggered by deregulation and the explosion of
satellite and cable transmission, the demand for filling the huge
demand for programs had risen fivefold, with no signs of slowing
down.

And yet Europe, strapped for funding, programs, and talent, has
found itself racing and struggling to fill the gap with its own programs and technology for this would become the world's single largest market—some 500 million people and a combined GNP of more
than $8 trillion. An entirely new form of integration is being molded
in this vast European area, and new concepts were being defined to
reflect what is happening, including a label—networking.

THE CONCEPT

Television's growth in Europe is only one striking example of the
concept of linking and integrating European states and regions in
Western and Eastern Europe. Modern methods of transacting business, educating, and traveling are other means being used to integrate Europe and their activities are also being extended into virtually
every sector of economic life: publishing; telecommunications; road,
rail, and air transport; retail banking; stock exchanges; languages;
education and training at all levels; as well as advertising and marketing.

Providing political momentum and a minority share of the financing is the European Community. The predominant support for
the design, construction, and promotion of the interconnecting systems are multinational European corporations and banks, whose
executives, convinced that a new era is dawning, have begun to exploit an underlying concept—that of "Euroconsumer." Oversimpli-
fied, this involves identifying—and catering to—new categories of
consumers in this vast nineteen-nation zone—dubbed by EC officials

"the European Economic Area"—whose tastes, habits, material requirements, and aspirations are similar and, in many cases, converging.

A single event dramatically illustrates the trend. On the evening of October 30, 1990, some forty meters below the bed of the English Channel, French workers cheered as a thin steel probe from the English side pierced the wall of chalk marl facing them. A five-centimeter opening created by the probe abruptly ended Britain's status as an island—for the first time since the Ice Age ended, eight thousand years earlier, and the waters covered the land bridge joining Britain and Continental Europe.

From that moment on, it became clear that the tunnel being built would probably meet its deadline to be in operation by the summer of 1993. But, the event irrevocably tied Britain more firmly than ever before into what was happening in the rest of the Community. "What does all this 1992 Brussels, EC-planning mean to me? Not much," commented Philipe Thomas, a London taxi driver, who had never traveled outside of Britain, and was proud of it. "But the Eurotunnel . . . that's something else, because it will mean one thing—we'll be part of Europe, being integrated, just like the invasion over here by foreign television."

TELEVISION GETS THE ATTENTION

President Mitterrand is fond of noting, whenever the subject of European television is raised, that while Europe consumes about 125,000 hours of television programs annually, it produces only 25,000. He warns the situation will most certainly worsen as demand skyrockets to around 300,000 hours by the early 1990s. In other words, more than 70 percent of all popular films shown on European television would continue pouring in from the United States and, increasingly, from Latin America and Japan—but more than two-thirds from the United States. Unless, of course, the Europeans are quickly able to match the American output.

Mitterrand is the most outspoken of Europe's leaders deeply concerned about seeing his citizens, old and young alike, glued to their TV sets watching dubbed versions of *Eight Is Enough, Charlie's Angels, Star Trek, M*A*S*H, Miami Vice,* and for news, Cable News Network, the Atlanta-based television channel. Since the late 1980s, but particularly during the Gulf War, CNN has become a prime source of news for growing numbers of Europeans, including all European-based media, EC heads of state and their governments.

But, realistically speaking, could a share of this vast, new entertainment and news market be somehow guaranteed for Europeans?

The television program quota concept originally contained a figure—60 percent—proposed by France. But the idea of citing a percentage was defeated by a combination of British, German, and Dutch insistence that this would set yet another ugly example of Fortress Europe. Nevertheless, the basic idea behind the quota was adopted, because EC governments were interested in helping build a fledgling industry. Edith Cresson, France's outspoken prime minister, when minister for European affairs, described the directive for which she voted—and still supports—as "but an aim." The United States, however, continued to attack the quota as just another device to create what Delors dubbed "a European audiovisual area," and Bush administration officials depicted as "pure European protectionism."

In the interests of European competitiveness and of preserving Europe's cultural identity, Delors, reflecting Mitterrand's view and Cresson's, warned repeatedly, "The Community does not intend to allow the Japanese to monopolize audiovisual technology or the Americans to monopolize programs."[1] Washington saw this as a confirmation of their fears.

Delors's warning, backed wholeheartedly by European electronics companies and media leaders, and many European politicians, helped galvanize public opinion in favor of European producers' developing their homegrown programs, with their own themes, characters, settings, and financing. Thorn, like many Europeans interviewed on the subject, fudged. "Yes, it [the quota proposal] is a terribly protectionist reflex," he conceded during our talk in Luxembourg. "But there is a lot more to it than that."[2]

Thorn quickly, enthusiastically turned to the need for the Community to develop its own capacity in the fast-growing audiovisual field, as Delors had urged, reflecting the views and policies of his Luxembourg-based employer. Since stepping down as EC Commission president in 1985, Thorn had become vice chairman of one of Europe's largest multilingual television, radio, and film conglomerates, Compagnie Luxembourgoise de Télévision. Headquartered in a castlelike stone building located in a Luxembourg city park, CLT had stakes in film-production companies; in satellite and cable TV stations in Britain, France, and Germany; and in ASTRA, Europe's first private satellite operator. ASTRA by the spring of 1990 was beaming a wide range of programs, mainly in English and German. "It is also true that European production should be encouraged," Thorn insisted. But how?

NETWORKING THROUGH COPRODUCTIONS

Partly in anticipation of governmental and media-company support for European programs, coproductions began to proliferate. A survey of 50 recent coproductions in 1989, representing 275 hours, showed that 40 percent, the largest proportion, were intra-European. Some of these were being financed by modest but growing budgets of the EC Commission; by 1990, the levels of EC spending had reached roughly $275 million annually, while equally large amounts were being spent by state-controlled and some private television networks, often working together. And in late 1989, twenty-six countries from Western and Eastern Europe, plus the Soviet Union, Turkey, Yugoslavia, and the EC Commission established Eureka Audiovisual, a Brussels-based organization committed to reinforcing Europe's capacity to create and produce films; to distribute European programs worldwide; and to promote development of European technologies for film production. The Strasbourg-based Council of Europe also finances European coproductions through its affiliate Eurimages.

An example of a highly successful multinational venture was *Eurocops*, a series of six crime stories, each produced by a team in six different European countries—Germany, Italy, France, Spain, Austria, and Switzerland—which became an instant hit in virtually every country. The series, which depicted familiar police forces tracking gangsters and smugglers in familiar settings in East and West Europe had become so popular in 1990 that one of the one-hour episodes, shot by ZDF, the West German network, beat *Miami Vice*, the U.S. detective series, in local ratings. The *Financial Times's* television critic, Raymond Snoddy, praised the series as "a milestone of a kind," and reported that even in Britain the series drew an audience of about two million people, which he rated "good . . . viewers were apparently not put off by subtitles." The program, he said, had "a distinctive character" and avoided coming out as "Euro-pudding," a reference to the virtually impossible task of merging European characters and settings into some form of "European" mold.[3]

In France, European teams working under the direction of TF 1, the nation's leading state-owned television network, coproduced *Riviera*, a 260-part soap-opera series. It was aimed at screens in Italy, Britain, Germany, Spain, and France, but resembled many other lackluster American programs of the same genre, and thus was widely panned.

During the Gulf War, complaining about the lack of "a European voice" in television coverage, compared to CNN, a grouping of twelve state-controlled stations began to discuss plans for a rival European network. By the summer of 1991, the group was seeking $81 million in seed money from governments and the European Commission to launch what would be a twenty-four-hour channel, beaming news programs from a satellite in English, French, German, Spanish, and Italian, thus eliminating the need for dubbing or subtitles. Its name: "Euronews." Its reach: An estimated thirty million viewers from Britain to Turkey and Scandinavia to North Africa, possibly in late 1992.

Meantime, the BBC in Britain, Canal Plus, France's pay television station, and Bertelsmann in Germany were all establishing European-wide news and entertainment programs aimed at offsetting what even German media planners were now describing as "American cultural imperialism."

In other cases, European producers were teaming up with Hollywood, relying on American actors and actresses and on financial support from large U.S. film groups. "Time-Warner, among others, has been coming through here, seeking to make deals for production, and we are only one among many potential partners in this field," Thorn explained. "Wherever possible and where appropriate, we will support European productions—for Europeans."

WHAT HAPPENED TO AMERICAN CULTURE?

There was a catch, however, for as Thorn noted, English is Europe's common-denominator foreign language. No "Eurolanguage" has yet been discovered. Indeed, the working language for the *Riviera* series was English. The paradox is that, while English has remained Europe's second language, American cultural influence, as a model for youth, has waned considerably throughout Europe, become distant, in many cases irrelevant, and sometimes worthy of criticism and open attack, particularly when handy, classic American symbols disturb the European status quo and long-established interests.

An unpleasant example of recurring anti-Americanism made headlines throughout Europe on a spring day in 1989 when a handful of left-wing protesters hurled eggs, flour, and tomato sauce at the Walt Disney Company chairman Michael Eisner in Paris. Eisner and a handful of Disney executives were visiting Europe, promoting investor interest in the vast $4.2 billion Euro Disneyland theme park being built east of the capital, which is due to be opened in the spring of 1992. Investors oversubscribed the stock listing on exchanges throughout Europe, but not the protesters, who viewed the operation as a "sellout to American imperialist interests."

As Eisner, an American, commented later, "They [the protesters] knew there were going to be cameras available" to dramatize their message: American culture was destroying European values. He was correct in identifying the protest as a highly politicized left-wing attempt to embarrass Mitterrand's Socialist government. And, as everyone agreed, the protest would never halt the building of Disney's spectacular, U.S.-inspired entertainment facilities at the farmland site, or of the hotels, office buildings, campgrounds, and golf courses, which were also being built, and creating jobs in the region. Disney executives stuck to their estimates that eleven million visitors were expected annually once the theme park opened, the first of its kind outside the United States and Japan. Nevertheless, the protests dramatically reflected an underlying anti-American mood and sentiment shared by many in the New Europe.

AMERICA LOSING OUT

Consider a few other examples, not directly related:

- One year before the Disneyland incident, the Atlantic Institute, a private Paris-based foreign-policy think tank, which had pioneered the idea of coordination and cooperation within the Western alliance, closed its doors for lack of funds. In 1984, terrorists had bombed the institute's headquarters, apparently believing it had direct NATO connections. The institute continued to function until the end, but gradually lost funding from companies and private contributions, as Continental European and British institutes and think tanks, some backed by national governments, flourished. The institute had indeed been strongly marked by its U.S. ties and funding; the last director general, Andrew Pierre, like his predecessors, was American and formerly of the Council on Foreign Relations in New York, which began its own study of European developments.

■ J. William Fulbright, the former senator from Arkansas who introduced the Fulbright Program for educational exchange four decades earlier, told my colleague Barry James early in 1990 that he was deeply worried about declining standards of American education and Europe's reaction. "The West Europeans are beginning to show considerable superiority to us, not to speak of the Japanese," he said. James asked the eighty-five-year-old statesman about the steep decline of American studies in Britain and possibly elsewhere. "That's because the United States is beginning to look irrelevant to a lot of people," Fulbright explained.[4] Many random conversations with young students and workers in my travels throughout Europe confirmed Fulbright's conclusion—America is still admired but no longer considered relevant to Europe's future.

■ Meantime, U.S.-government-funded cultural, information, and travel programs and consulates in Western Europe had been scaled back, starting in 1983. Funds, facilities, and staff were being shifted to Eastern Europe and Central America, which senior U.S. cultural officers said reflected "newer, higher priorities as they were perceived in Washington." Robert Lapiner, formerly the European director of the Council on International Educational Exchange, told me in June 1990, as he left for a deanship at UCLA in Los Angeles: "In the political and cultural spheres, the U.S. has turned away dramatically from Europe. Gone are the American cultural centers and libraries in provincial cities across Italy and France. The U.S. is the only country of note, for example, not to have a governmentally supported center in Paris; Belgium, Sweden, Poland, the Netherlands do. USIA is cutting staff, and has no real program money available anymore, and the Fulbright program no longer offers scholarships to students in any appreciable number."

PLASTIC CARDS, PHONES, AND SATELLITES

The precursors of what was coming in the 1990s could be seen sprouting throughout Western Europe.

Item: I have just walked by the London police barricade near 10 Downing Street on my way to an appointment at the House of Lords. I spot a familiar red phone booth on the street, and, to my surprise, it bears a message from Visa, the network to which my Paris bank belongs: I can use my card to place calls. After picking up the receiver, inserting my card, and talking with a colleague in our London office, I am later billed in francs. It is late 1990, as Visa, Eurocard, American Express, and other credit-and-debit card systems are proliferating, already accounting for 11 percent of all retail transactions in Britain.

Item: The *Financial Times* publishes a survey showing that more than fifty satellite television services will be operating over Western Europe by 1991.[5] Some surprising applications: more than 200,000 Japanese businessmen, diplomats, tourists, and their families, scattered throughout EC countries, already watch several hours of news from home every day—beamed from Tokyo. Turkish workers in Germany can keep up their culture through regular weekly educational programs, also transmitted via satellite. Rupert Murdoch's Sky Channel, notably its news programs, is beamed via satellite throughout Europe, the first of the channels already competing head on with CNN.

Item: I begin to notice in my travels that more and more people are using hand-carried, wireless telephones—in cars and planes in particular. Throughout the Nordic countries of Finland, Norway, and Sweden, national borders pose no problems, because the telecommunications support systems are already standardized. The trend is spreading throughout the Community, as the EC Commission and other bodies set new, harmonized standards for cross-border dialing; industrial consortiums are established to supply what is billed as the single most-profitable market in telecommunications for the 1990s.

Item: May 18, 1990, on a deserted stretch of newly built track, near Vendôme in France's Loire Valley, a sleek, snout-nosed blue-and-white locomotive pulling several cars swiftly picked up speed. Within minutes, hurtling down the track, stirring up clouds of dust, the latest prototype of France's Train à Grande Vitesse, the TGV, was living up to its reputation as the world's fastest train. Clocked at 515.3

kilometers per hour, the TGV thus broke its own previous record of 482.4 kilometers per hour set December 5, 1989. That was still ahead of West Germany's fastest train, the ICE, clocked at 406.9 kilometers per hour in 1988.

RAILROADS SET AN EXAMPLE

These aerodynamic, futuristic-looking trains recall how the steam engine helped open America's Far West frontiers in the nineteenth and early twentieth centuries. Of course, Western Europe lacks a U.S.–style frontier, but contemporary European railroad builders were providing their own, spectacular examples of success—drawing the New Europe's people and regions closer together, in anticipation of the borderless Community of the 1990s. Consider the case of Coquelles, a village near Calais, on the Normandy coast of France. Its days as a restful town near La Manche (the sleeve), as the Channel is called, are numbered. When the fifty-kilometer Eurotunnel is completed, one of two giant freight and passenger terminals will be operating there, destined to be as large as Europe's major airports, and shuttle trains will be whisking people and cargo away at the rate of one every quarter of an hour. They will make the crossing in 35 minutes—carrying nearly 45 million passengers each year.

Here was a mammoth construction project, whose costs by 1991 had escalated to $15 billion since digging began in late 1987, the largest privately financed project in the history of civil engineering; only the Seikan Tunnel in Japan is longer. Its impact extends well beyond its immediate surroundings, where the price of real estate, up and down the Normandy coast, has soared—anticipating the boom expected to accompany the opening. Similar expansion has gradually spread across the Channel, starting near the port town of Folkestone. This is where the British shuttle facility will be, the rail line spreading northward through Kent to central London. Although Britain had to struggle to match France for modern connecting road and rail links, a striking example of a "Euroregion" is emerging on both sides of the once-formidable watery obstacle. Both Kent, on the English side, and Nor-Pas-de-Calais, on the French side, or being integrated and reviving economically; travelers and homeowners already cross over seeking bargains as if the barriers never existed.

Consider Dunkirk, hard hit by unemployment caused by decline of the once-prosperous steel and textile industries. Local planners proudly tell visitors that the combination of the Eurotunnel and the Single Market will enable the region to become one of the largest ports in northern Europe, rivaling Antwerp in Belgium and Rotterdam in nearby Holland. "We will be on a new westward-leaning axis, running from London through our region, with Lille at the center, to southern Europe," said Rémy Chassaignon, director of international development for the Nord-Pas-de-Calais region, "meaning a new lease on life for us, and for foreigners opportunities for investment."[6]

Lille, the largest city in the region, which has already attracted new investments, has been touting the fact that it, too, will be within fifty minutes of Paris. That, I noted, was almost the time it took me to reach my office in suburban Neuilly via the Paris subway from home in the city's 14th arrondissement.

In Edinburgh, Scotland, Cameron Buchanan runs a century-old family wool merchant firm, and has been an active supporter of Britain's integration into the European Community since his hectic days as a student at the Paris Sorbonne in 1968. Fluent in four European languages, including French, Buchanan is among Scottish leaders pressing the government in London hard to link Scotland with the rest of Europe via the new high-speed rail network being built. "The TGV is our opportunity, to develop, to become part of Europe, in an integrated, real sense—via London," he said. "But the investments required to build the links are also indispensable."[7]

A RAIL BOOM SHAPES UP

Everywhere I went, bearing out Buchanan's analysis, there was visionary talk of a renaissance for railroads. For the first time since the late nineteenth century, Europe was embarking on a railroad-building boom and creating a vision that captured the imagination—that of a European high-speed network, knitting thirty thousand kilometers of new, or upgraded, rail lines together into nine separate corridors from Scotland southward, then fanning in all directions throughout the Continent. According to a joint report from the heads of government-controlled railroads in the twelve EC member countries and those in Switzerland and Austria, the new rail network represented a solution not only to passenger comfort, but to worsening air and road congestion, while providing energy-efficient, relatively clean and low-cost transport for millions of travelers.[8]

If built as planned, the new TGV, the ICE, or other high-speed trains will whisk passengers from Brussels to Madrid in 8 hours, instead of 16 1/2 hours as currently; from Paris to Rome in 7 hours, instead of nearly 13 hours; from London to Berlin—via the Eurotunnel—in 8 1/2 hours, instead of 16 1/2 hours.

Assuming the mind-boggling obstacles are overcome—financial, political, cultural, technological, environmental—and that the planned network manages to function by the year 2010, the railroad presidents concluded, Europe could have "the most economical and sophisticated surface transport system in the world," a conclusion endorsed later by the EC Commission. The cost was conservatively estimated at about $100 billion over twenty-five years, which the railroaders' report argued could be financed by a combination of private and public funds, including EC financial institutions, such as the European Investment Bank. The newly formed European Bank for Reconstruction and Development, the EBRD, was already examining possible financing for railroad modernization in Eastern Europe and the Soviet Union.

And although the plans seemed futuristic, Morocco, in the spring of 1990, revived studies and talks with its European neighbors of building a deep tunnel, or a bridge, between Gibraltar and Morocco, which would link North Africa with southern Spain. In Italy, feasibility studies began on building a bridge across the Strait of Messina, linking the mainland with Sicily. And Sweden had revived long-dormant studies that would lead a road-rail link to Denmark, and with it, the rest of the European Community, coinciding with Stockholm's plan to join the EC by the mid-1990s.

A TGV FOR EVERYBODY?

When it came to who would build what, there was little doubt that in the very high-tech end of the railroad business France had the edge. True, there was a formidable potential competitor in the form of Germany's ICE and the Transrapid, a high-speed magnetic levitation train, which used magnets to propel it at up to 435 kilometers per hour. But, as experts, including Germany's, conceded, the system cost twice as much as the TGV to build. Fiat, the Swedish-Swiss group

Asea-Brown Boveri (ABB), and Japan's Mitsubishi also offered highly advanced, operating rail systems.

But by early 1991 France's GEC Alsthom, builder of the TGV, already had orders from several EC countries, and had acquired the rail-equipment business of Fiat, a first step in Italian-French cooperation to develop a modern north-south rail axis via the Alps. The move also accelerated progress toward a long-cherished twin goal of European railroaders: winning passenger and freight traffic from the Community's airlines, and second, exporting their trains. New high-speed rail networks were also being planned in Canada, the United States, Brazil, Eastern Europe, the Soviet Union, South Korea, Taiwan, and Australia, representing more than $50 billion in construction costs.

Can the new passenger trains compete against the airplane?

Railroad buffs cite what happened in 1981 as the first TGVs began rolling between Paris and Lyon—a 512-kilometer trip that used to take just over six hours on the regular intercity express train. The sleek orange-and-white trains carried passengers between the two cities at speeds of up to 270 kilometers per hour. Société Nationale des Chemins de Fer Francais, the SNCF, France's national railroad, gradually decimated Air Inter, the state-owned domestic airline, carrying ten times as many passengers as the planes, equal to an estimated 90 percent of the traffic between France's largest and second-ranking cities. By the autumn of 1989, a Paris–Le Mans, Brittany line opened that reached southward to Bordeaux. Another line would, in the 1990s, reach Madrid and Lisbon; shortly after starting up, the first-class-only trains on the new route were jammed.

Meantime, another new line thrusting southward from Lyon to Marseilles was being built. And to the north building was starting for the Paris-Brussels-London route—via the Eurotunnel—which included branches that would be extended to Amsterdam and eastward to Cologne in 1993. EC transportation planners were delighted, but the new trains also stirred up opposition. Environmentalists vehemently attacked the trains in Britain, Belgium, Germany, Switzerland, and even, finally, in France. The SNCF, determined to cut the Paris-Marseilles trip to three hours from four hours and forty minutes, began laying plans in early 1990 to cut through the scenic Provence country, made famous by Cézanne's paintings, touching off hostile demonstrations throughout the region.

"Our attitude is the same as that of those opposing the TGV

coming through Kent," said Francis Wishart, a British painter who lives and works in a farmhouse in the region and has been organizing many of the demonstrations and petitions. "The train is an ecological catastrophe, which would make life unlivable here," he told Robin Smyth of the London *Observer*.[9] The SNCF, however, determined to continue expanding, planned spending $33 billion throughout the 1990s to expand the TGV network in France by another 3,500 kilometers.

Railroads were also beginning to find technical solutions to their traditionally incompatible rail gauges, electrical power, and switching systems, in most cases designed as defensive measures in the event of war. "Many of us still recall the Wehrmacht rolling through Europe on trains," commented a Belgian official. Percy Barnevik, the goateed, bespectacled Swedish engineer, president of ABB, told me during an interview at the company's Zürich headquarters how his engineers had developed microcomputers enabling a railroad to run different, incompatible electric locomotives on the same line. "Railroad technologies are being developed that make competing systems compatible for the same system," he said, "but that is certainly not the only problem. . . . There are twenty-four [locomotive manufacturers] in Western Europe and thirteen in Eastern Europe, compared to two in the United States and three in Japan. Most people, including myself, are 100 percent convinced there will be a shakeout."[10]

As Barnevik indicated, Europe still had a long way to go in integrating its transportation networks. A comprehensive report published by the European Roundtable in June 1991 cited a wide range of shortcomings: the incompatibility between freight and passenger rail transport systems; the lack of standardization of containers, as well as the environmental problems posed by TGV-type trains as we have already seen. The Roundtable called for establishment of a European research center to focus on Europe's future infrastructure needs, including modern highways connecting with Eastern Europe.

AIRLINES ALSO TAKE TO NETWORKING

Meantime, West European airlines were being forced gradually to liberalize long-established monopolistic practices in response to strong EC Commission pressures aimed at creating more competition and lower fares. But the airlines, all state-controlled, and fearful

that Air Inter's unsuccessful battle against the TGV would be repeated elsewhere, began their own brand of networking. The most
visible step was what the airlines described as "restructuring." Skeptical consumer groups attacked this as "cartel building." But the EC
Commission, under the driving determination of Sir Leon Brittan, in
early 1990 began to allege violations of EC antitrust regulations,
which most of the airlines and their associations vowed to fight. The
airlines countered by charging, among other things, that Brussels
would wind up "overregulating" the European airline industry.

Most European carriers were merging operations with other,
often competing airlines, and in some cases acquiring smaller airlines. Some examples: British Airways, KLM Royal Dutch Airlines and
Air France had, by early 1991, worked out arrangements for each to
obtain a minority shareholding in Belgium's Sabena World Airlines.
Their goal was to link their routes, and to build Brussels into a major
hub, with new or expanded service to seventy-five European cities in
1995. That is known as the U.S.-inspired "hub-and-spoke" system of
operating airlines. As the airlines sought to build links, several European airline chairmen I met in the course of writing this book would
begin their interviews by vowing Europe would never implement a
U.S.-style, "open-skies" deregulatory program. Why? Because that
would only "open" Europe to fierce, unfair competition from the
United States and carriers throughout Asia.

For example, Bernard Attali, the brilliant, affable chairman of Air
France, and the twin brother of Jacques, who, as we noted earlier,
became chairman of the EBRD bank after leaving the Elysée, told
shareholders in 1990 that he considered his airline "at war." Against
whom? "The United States, Japan, everyone," he said, citing American Airlines and Japan Air Lines. "We, too, have a global outlook,"
noting that Air France had several months earlier acquired the previously private UTA French airline as well as Air Inter. "You keep
talking about the American experience," Attali said to me on several
occasions during our talks. "But look at what is happening to your
airlines. . . . They are in deep financial trouble, and American air fares
have risen dramatically." It was difficult to argue.

The EC Commission began a modest effort to push liberalization
with new regulations, which came into effect January 1, 1988, giving
airlines more power to cut fares and open new routes. A year later,
the package was expanded to include such innovations as permitting
airlines to operate on domestic routes outside of their country of

origin as a continuation of international flights. This rule also applied to the smaller carriers, and the EC Commission quickly made sure that the new rules—and above all, the Rome Treaty's antimonopoly provisions—were being reinforced. The Commission, for example, challenged both the Sabena and Air France moves as violating the antitrust provisions of the Rome Treaty in what became a protracted political and legal battle between the airlines and the Commission.

Meantime, smaller, regional airlines began sprouting. For example, British Midland, and Air Europe, both independent British airlines, were among the first to take advantage of the deregulated environment, operating low-cost flights from London to points throughout Europe. EC authorities began forcing large national carriers to divest themselves of holdings in regional carriers to spur competition. New European regional passenger planes were being built, or planned, as new routes loomed, along with export markets.

Did any of this matter for the average air traveler in Europe?

Some fares came down slightly in response to EC Commission pressures, and some services improved, but not by much. In fact, West European domestic fares remained among the world's highest, and substantial increases in U.S. air fares in 1990 were repeatedly cited by European airlines to justify their policies. However, the Brussels-based European Bureau of Consumers Associations, representing consumer groups in the twelve EC member countries, repeatedly attacked the Commission for its weak, slow progress and warned that approval of the U.S.-inspired "hub-and-spoke" concept would lead to dominance by major airlines of airports, relegating the smaller carriers to the dependent role of simply feeding the larger airlines.

EUROPE'S WORSENING CONGESTION

Virtually every government-owned European airline defends high fares within the Community, usually citing a litany of problems familiar to anyone who travels in Europe: congestion, overcrowded airports, long delays in takeoff and landing, rerouting, and air-controller strikes—ironically protesting tiring, dangerous working conditions. Airlines argued that their costs were kept unnecessarily high because of operating in an inefficient environment, citing air-control systems. There were forty-two centers operating in Western Europe, compared to twenty in the United States. In an interview,

Heinz Ruhnau, chairman of Lufthansa, complained, "Our systems are so ridiculously designed that one system cannot talk to another in many areas . . . we have to use the old-fashioned telephone to communicate."[11]

Meantime, positioning themselves for the looming competition with high-speed trains, airlines have been pursuing their own expansion plans, often in cooperation with airports, which some visionary airline officials believe should be linked to the new high-speed rail networks taking shape throughout Europe. "Flying over short distances will be superfluous," Ruhnau told me in his office at the heavily congested Frankfurt airport. "The threshold for flights will go up to 500 kilometers from the current 300–350 kilometers. . . . What this means is that you will need a railway station at every airport." Some cities, like Zürich, have already set the example by having regular trains pass through the city's Kloten airport; combined TGV-airport stations, or trunks, were to be in place by mid-1990 at the Satolas airport near Lyon, Charles de Gaulle airport near Paris, and Zaventem, Brussels' airport. The transportation networking was progressing, but Europe was still a long way from its cherished goal of establishing unhindered movement of goods, persons, services, and capital within its borders.

BUILDING ON THE EMS

From the mid-1980s onward, substantial progress had been made in merging the Community's banking and financial networks and removing exchange controls. Yet, the Common Market still lacked a single currency, its own version of the dollar and the yen. Widely divergent, highly complex and restrictive banking and insurance regulations remained in effect throughout EC member countries. There still was no single, pan-European stock market. Divergent fiscal, tax, and monetary policies were still pursued in member countries, each with its own, different central banking system and policies. Portugal, Greece, and Britain, as late as mid-1990, were still outside, but moving toward joining, the so-called the exchange-rate mechanism, the ERM. This mechanism, by which members are obliged to intervene in the markets to keep their currencies in close alignment, has become the most tangible operational component of the European Monetary System, the EMS.

What is its purpose? The EMS, adopted in 1978 by the heads of state and government of the then nine EC members, was Europe's first major step toward monetary integration. The visionary architects were Valéry Giscard d'Estaing and Germany's Helmut Schmidt, both former finance ministers, who at the time were not only friends but respectively, president of France and chancellor of West Germany. Both were fervently convinced that the Community's loss of economic momentum and growing unemployment would continue dangerously unless the idea of monetary integration was revived. It had been first suggested in 1969, and revived again in 1971, amid growing conviction that Europe needed to respond to the disappearance of the U.S.-led Bretton Woods system of coordinated monetary cooperation established by the West's trading partners during postwar reconstruction.

The operational goals of the EMS were threefold: first, to create a zone of greater monetary stability at a time when European currencies were being buffeted by high, divergent, and virtually uncontrollable currency and inflation fluctuations. Second, to create an institutional framework for closer cooperation between EC finance ministries and EC central banks at a time when convergence of monetary policies still remained but a visionary goal. Finally, the new system was to lay the groundwork for something that seemed even more futuristic at the time—economic and monetary union.

A giant step was unexpectedly taken by all the EC governments— minus Britain—to move toward that goal, known as EMU, at a special summit meeting in Rome on October 28, 1990. Not only did the eleven EC governments agree to begin a process of transferring monetary powers to an independent monetary authority, resembling a mixture of the U.S. and German federal reserve central banking systems, starting January 1, 1994. But they committed themselves to converting the already-existing European Currency Unit, the ECU, into what would become the Community's single currency by irrevocably linking their exchange rates. Delors, the main architect of this plan, predicted that this linking—the ultimate, operational goal of EMU—would be reached by the end of 1999. The strategic goal of EMU is providing Europe with a counterweight to the dollar and the yen.

TRYING TO SPEND THE ECU

I always remember the first time I saw—and physically held—an ECU coin.

Resembling U.S. silver dollars, the first ECU coins were minted in Belgium, the first country to have also opened ECU-denominated accounts for EC institutions, such as the European Investment Bank. Sporting the bearded face of the Holy Roman Emperor Charles V, my coin was attached to the annual greeting card mailed by Germany's Commerzbank at Christmastime 1987. The large Frankfurt-based bank was using the coin to tell the world of its involvement and support for uses for the ECU that had been developed by companies and banks. These included settling intracompany accounts, raising funds in capital markets, bidding on export contracts, and covering foreign-exchange transactions.

Trying to spend the ECU was something else again. A symbolic, collector's item, it wasn't accepted, even in Belgian shops or restaurants.

But it was traded. By 1990, the ECU ranked fifth in international bond issues, accounting for 6 percent of the worldwide market. And its use was spreading. In 1990, some traveler's checks and credit cards were being denominated in ECUs. The French Relais & Châteaux luxury hotel chain adopted an ECU-denominated voucher for use by customers as gifts and promotion. To the chain's happy surprise, thirty million ECU worth were snapped up in the first two months. Salary checks of EC Commission employees are denominated in ECUs, and the annual EC-sponsored tennis championship prizes are worth 200,000—ECUs.

In a major coup for ECU backers and to the annoyance of the United States, the EBRD, the London-based development Bank for Eastern Europe, agreed to grant loans in ECUs and not necessarily in dollars. Fiat of Italy, among others establishing joint ventures in East Europe and the Soviet Union, also denominated their operations in ECUs. Giovanni Agnelli, Fiat's chairman and a vice president of the Association for the Monetary Union of Europe, a group of leading European businessmen promoting EMU, told a conference in Brussels that "the ECU can tear down one more wall in Eastern Europe: the wall of inconvertibility of the rouble, the zloty, the florin, which still divides these economies from each other and from us. . . . In our venture [to build a car plant], the ECU-based system isolates it from the price distortions of the planned economy and helps our Soviet partners to reason in terms of market prices."[12]

In other words, the ECU is fulfilling the role of a unit of account, a denominator, arranged in a basket of EC member-state currencies linked in the EMS and weighted according to their GNP levels. The German mark, the EC's dominant economy, accounts for just over 30 percent, the French franc 19 percent, the British pound 13 percent, the Italian lira 10 percent, the Dutch guilder 9.4 percent; the Portuguese escudo and the Greek drachma were at the lowest end of the range of currencies—each accounting for less than 1 percent.

Although Europe's monetary system remained a hybrid, it provided the Community the means to stabilize its widely differing currencies. Thus, when a currency within the system diverges from its fixed parity, central banks intervene by adjusting their national currencies to fixed threshold levels. This then was the ERM, the exchange rate mechanism, which Britain had long shunned. It has led to greater stability between participating currencies by reducing exchange-rate volatility, enhanced by ever-greater coordination of monetary policies by the EC finance ministers and their central banks. Finally, the ECU has fulfilled what central bankers regard as its most important role—serving as a reserve asset and a means of settlement for central banks within the EMS-ERM network. The official value of the ECU is set every day in Brussels by the EC Commission, once the member-country central banks transmit their currencies' dollar exchange rates, which are then calculated into ECU based on their relative weights in the basket.

THE DELORS PLAN

Transforming the ECU into the Community's one and only single currency would require what Delors repeatedly described as a "quantum leap," a move that, while opposed by Margaret Thatcher and John Major, had support in the British business and banking community and throughout Europe's banking world. Giscard d'Estaing, who remains a strong advocate of EMU as an influential member of the European Parliament, repeatedly urged, as he put it, "that the time has come for Europe to act with one currency, for the ECU to come into its own, with its personality, its own weight worldwide." The basic outline for the plan is contained in the Delors Plan, which was adopted unanimously by a blue-ribbon committee of seventeen leading central bankers and financial experts, chaired by Delors. Among the signers was Robert Leigh-Pemberton, governor of the Bank of England.

The proposed plan, which was being negotiated at one of the two parallel intergovernmental conferences that began in Brussels in early 1991, to which we shall return in Chapter 8, is divided into the following, closely-tied, three phases:

- Phase I, which was completed in 1990, established loose, voluntary methods for achieving convergence of economic policies among EC member countries, and the removal of exchange and capital controls. This phase also prescribes incorporation of all the EC currencies in the ERM, which Britain finally joined in the late summer of 1990. Only the Greek and Portuguese currencies, because of their weak economies, stayed outside the ERM. Mrs. Thatcher brought the pound in, following intensive lobbying from within her cabinet, and by British business leaders and bankers, who feared London would lose its attraction as the EC's main financial center.

- Phase II, scheduled to begin in January 1, 1994, represents a far more radical and complex step, because it will mean establishing a new, powerful federal body: the European System of Central Banks, which became immediately known as the Eurofed. Similar to the American and German independently run federal reserve systems, the Eurofed's governing council will comprise the heads of the twelve central banks, whose main responsibility is coordinating and, ultimately, shaping monetary policies for the Community, independently of national and EC controls or influence. Implementation will be by a management committee appointed by a committee of directors, which will report to the European Council, and other governmental bodies. The Eurofed's formal powers will not be transferred until January 1, 1996.

- Finally, in Phase III, possibly beginning in 1997, according to Brussels sources, all EC-member exchange rates will be fixed irrevocably, thus permitting establishment of a single European currency, and coinciding with the totally free movement of capital, and the placing of full authority over the Community's monetary policy in the hands of the Eurofed. Several variants were proposed during the intergovernmental conference during 1991, including a plan for creating a thirteenth currency, dubbed by the British a "hard" or "parallel" ECU, which could also serve as a future common currency. Delors, however, backed by Kohl, Mitterrand, and Andreotti, considered the proposal as unsuited for EMU's ultimate goals, and a compromise was sought to accommodate British reservations. This involves agreement to adopt the single EC currency only if there is unanimous agreement among all EC member states participating in this final phase.

INTEGRATING STOCK EXCHANGES

Meantime in a related development, Common Market stock exchanges were discussing and planning ways of developing a Community-wide market in securities. Exchanges in Britain, Germany, France, and Italy had already modernized their procedures for trading, and the EC Commission had implemented directives to liberalize access to trading throughout the Community. A concerted effort to tighten insider trading rules and to crack down on laundering of funds from illegal drug dealing was also going forward.

But the vested interests of the most important exchanges, notably London, Frankfurt, Paris, Milan, and Amsterdam, and differences between members' regulations and tax systems slowed progress on integrating exchanges. The prospects of an economic slowdown, following the U.S. recession in 1991, also dampened the outlook. Nevertheless, brokers, bankers, and exchange officials are convinced that standardized, integrated markets are necessary, both for creating greater liquidity and for providing links to Eastern Europe, and they are confident that sometime during the 1990s a pan-European market will be established.

HUNGARY BEGINS

Pointing the way was Hungary, which since 1983 had operated a fledgling bond market in Budapest. "It's still very small compared to what you have in the West," Zsigmond Jarai, deputy managing director of the Budapest Bank told me when I first visited the exchange in late 1988. Downstairs, amid the buzz of computers, several dozen Hungarians, including young people, were studying, discussing, and placing orders for bonds issued by 320 state-owned Hungarian companies. In the middle of our talk, Jarai, who also was the chairman of the group establishing Hungary's first stock exchange, took a phone call. He spoke German, and said to me later: "Since you heard, let me tell you who it was—one of our German advisers, a leading banker . . . but we also are building ties with German exchanges, and bankers in Vienna, as well as the World Bank."

Two years later, marking the beginning of Hungary's privatization program, which aimed to return four hundred state-controlled companies to private ownership over five years, the stock exchange was open for business.

The date: June 21, 1990. In crowded first-floor offices of the International Trade Center in downtown Budapest, Hungary launched its first privatization through a public offering. Ibusz, the state-owned travel company, was listed not only on the new Budapest exchange but on the Vienna stock exchange. Hungarian bankers said their goal was to extend the offerings of privatized companies to other EC exchanges, and that several dozen shares would be listed by the end of 1991. Hungary also was studying possible links to Poland's fledgling stock exchange which began operating in Warsaw in April 1991 for the first time since the day Hitler invaded Gdansk in 1939. Polish officials said that the new exchange would conform to EC standards, and was drawing heavily on the experience of the Lyon stock exchange, France's second-largest market.

"It is part of our determined effort to become part of the Common Market's financial and banking system, which is where we belong," a senior Hungarian banker said. "The United States did it. Why not us?"

THE ORIGINS OF "DIXIE"

This is not the place to retrace the colorful, complex banking history of the United States. Some comparisons are, however, worth noting between the Community's efforts to integrate its banking and monetary systems and those of the United States well over a century earlier.

For example, during the American Civil War, more than five hundred American state-controlled banks were issuing demand notes, printed by private engravers, and, according to one American history buff, Jeffrey McCord, they were "designed according to the whim of each bank's management . . . but distance from the location of the bank affected their value, with notes issued in the West automatically discounted in the East."[13] By 1860, with war between the states brewing, McCord stated, more than nine thousand paper bills of all kinds were in circulation, a chaotic monetary scene that more than rivaled Europe's disparate monetary systems circa 1991.

Among these bills was a $10 note issued by the Citizens Bank of New Orleans. Printed on one side was "ten," and, on the other, "dix," the French word for ten, in keeping with the French cultural influences in Louisiana. Gradually, as the notes became favorites of gamblers working the Mississippi riverboats, their popularity spread throughout the entire South, taking on the name "dixies." And thus, through this association, the South became known as Dixie, or Dixieland, according to George Ridge, a colleague and professor of journalism at the University of Arizona, who first called the story to my attention.

Only following the Civil War in 1865 did a single monetary system emerge—in Louisiana and elsewhere in America—clearing the way for the introduction of the country's first, single national currency—"greenbacks"—along with uniform banking regulations. Even taking into account these reforms, it would take several decades of severe financial crises, banking scandals, and, above all, pressures for reform by Congress, before the United States established its Federal Reserve System, in 1913.

American Ambassador Niles in Brussels is fond of recalling for his European friends that, as he puts it, "our financial system is not 100 percent-centralized. Interstate banking, for example, has remained a no-no and insurance has remained a state prerogative down to this day."[14]

Item: Shortly after arriving in the United States, recalling my talk with Niles, I tried cashing a check in a New York City bank drawn on my account in Washington, D.C. Eventually it would have been cashed, of course, but only after clearing several days later. I gave up and used a check drawn on the paper's New York account, which was cashed immediately.

OVERCOMING LANGUAGE BARRIERS

There is far more to unifying, harmonizing, and integrating than a single currency system. Consider, for example, the question of languages.

Sometimes even Americans forget that we have another major, long-established advantage over Europe—the English language. True, in many U.S. cities, such as my hometown, Yonkers, New York, Spanish is essential for communicating in formerly middle-class neighborhoods. Across the nation, foreign languages, such as Chinese, Vietnamese, Cypriot, Slavic dialects, Russian, and German are again flourishing as new immigrants arrive. But almost everyone learns to speak, read, and write the nation's predominating language for U.S. government, schools, businesses—English.

By comparison, despite many efforts to promote the teaching of foreign languages, Europe's ancient cultural and linguistic barriers have remained in place—proudly supported by heads of state and government, who always insist on speaking their countries' languages in public. Bridging these barriers, in the view of EC planners, represented a goal more difficult to attain than creating technological and industrial networking through railways, EMU, single bank notes, and common television systems. Why? Because of the virtual impossibility of merging, or harmonizing, the European Community's nine official languages: English, French, German, Italian, Spanish, Portuguese, Danish, Dutch, and Greek.

In addition, Western Europe boasts nearly sixty minor languages and one hundred dialects still spoken by an estimated thirty million people in virtually every EC country, such as Alsatian, Flemish, Gaelic, Cornish, Breton, Corsican, Sardinian, Occitan, Catalan, and Basque to name but a few. Many are being actively revived, including in universities located in regional capitals, such as Corté in central Corsica where the university is promoting the study of Corsican and other Mediterranean island cultures.

ENGLISH REMAINS ON TOP

Partly because of necessity, convenience, and the heavy, continuing American cultural influence in the world, English is the Community's predominant foreign language, as even casual visitors to most major

European cities discover by just wandering into heavily frequented streets or shops. According to recent EC Commission studies, 51 percent of EC residents speak English; French is in second position (42 percent), followed by German (33 percent), Italian (21 percent), Spanish (18 percent), and Dutch (7 percent).

But these figures hide the reality bothering EC planners—native English speakers are notoriously weak in learning foreign languages, and Latin-culture countries are almost as weak. According to EC surveys, 66 percent of citizens in EC member countries spoke no foreign language whatever; 25 percent spoke one foreign language, and only 10 percent spoke two or more. Let us examine the countries more closely, starting with Ireland. An estimated 80 percent of the Irish spoke no foreign language; only 17 percent spoke one, excluding Gaelic, and only 3 percent can handle two foreign languages— the worst record in the Community.

The runner-ups fared little better. In Italy, 76 percent of the population spoke no foreign language; 19 percent one and 6 percent two or more. Portugal's performance was virtually identical. In Britain, 74 percent of the citizens spoke only English; 20 percent spoke one foreign language and 6 percent two or more. In France, 67 percent of those surveyed spoke no foreign language, 26 percent one, and 7 percent two or more. Greece's score was virtually identical. In West Germany, 60 percent of those surveyed said they could speak no foreign language, while 33 percent said they could handle one, and 7 percent could speak two or more. From there on, foreign-language-speaking capacity begins to improve, and, not surprisingly, the best are the EC's smallest and northernmost countries, which traditionally have been Europe's most active traders.

In Denmark, only 40 percent of its inhabitants speak no foreign language; 30 percent speak one and 31 percent speak two or more, the highest score in that category. In French-speaking Belgium, 36 percent speak only one language; 23 percent one foreign language, and 22 percent two or more. In the Netherlands, only 28 percent speak no foreign language; 29 percent speak one, and 44 percent can speak two or more foreign languages. Finally, the best performer was tiny Luxembourg, where only 1 percent could speak no foreign language; 10 percent could speak one and 89 percent two or more foreign languages. The pattern shows up starkly among the Community's top leaders. Neither John Major, Helmut Kohl, nor Francois Mitterrand speaks any foreign language well enough to use it during their business conversations—the way Giscard d'Estaing and Schmidt use English as their common foreign language.

The older generation of European leaders takes this handicap in stride. Following the 1981 elections in France, I asked the new Socialist prime minister, Pierre Mauroy, how he and Mitterrand would communicate with President Ronald Reagan. "I suppose we shall manage through interpreters," he replied, "because for our generation the foreign languages learned were Greek and Latin." Not long afterward, Claude Cheysson, Mitterrand's new foreign minister, used his excellent English to respond to questions by American television reporters in London. But when Cheysson flashed on that evening's state-owned French television network—his voice dubbed into French—Mitterrand, irritated, ordered that henceforth all members of his government would speak French in public—regardless of their proficiency in other languages.

It should come as no surprise, therefore, that for reasons of national pride and prestige the Community decided to operate in no fewer than nine official languages cited above. However, within many EC institutions the working languages are English, French, and German, but English predominates.

SWITZERLAND PROVIDES A MODEL

What has become clear is that English, while growing in importance, will by no means replace other Community languages, and second, Europe will never invent a totally new, common language, such as a Euro-Esperanto, to cover the entire Community, as some visionary linguists suggested. Only one solution made sense: learning more EC languages. And there was a model: Switzerland, where the vast majority of citizens speak one of their own official languages— French, German, Italian, or Romansh—as well as English and usually another European language. "Switzerland works not only linguistically, but the fact that they have resolved that problem reinforces their power. . . . We want to accomplish the same thing at the Community level," commented an EC official.

That message, starting around 1987, penetrated to even the remotest corners of the Community. I recall a talk with the mayor of the tiny Greek island of Kos, six kilometers from the Turkish coast, the easternmost point of the Community. The economic life of Kos, similar to that in many other nearby regions, was being totally transformed by tourism. "We are so far in the east people think we belong to Turkey, but we are members of the European Community, and we are now getting twenty flights a week, including the jumbos, meaning 350,000 people every year," said Kostas Kaiserlis, the forty-two-year-old mayor, who also runs the town's pharmacy."[15]

"This means our children are all learning Community languages—that's new for us here, and revolutionary." EC funds have been earmarked for rebuilding Kos's hotels and roads which has proven a major factor in stopping migration westward to the Greek mainland, Europe, and the United States. "Young people, taking advantage of what the EC offers, including language training, is keeping them. . . . they now do well here," said the mayor." What languages were Kos youth learning? The majority study English, with German in second, fast-growing place, followed by French, said Kaiserlis.

In dozens of similar conversations with students, young professionals, and graduate students, particularly those under twenty-five, I was struck by their enthusiastic determination not only to learn European languages but to travel and, increasingly, to study at educational institutions elsewhere in the Community. To be sure, programs designed to facilitate study in the United States, starting with the Fulbright scholarship program in the 1950s, have remained highly popular; about 350,000 foreign students, mainly from Europe, study in the United States each year, compared to 55,000 Americans who study abroad, mainly in Western Europe. This is a relatively small number, considering that national enrollment in U.S. colleges and universities totals about 12 million students.

Since the 1992 program began picking up steam, enthusiasm—and determination to become prepared linguistically—has soared among youth. A survey by a French magazine of two thousand high school students showed that a clear majority rated the Single Market "a good thing," with about 10 percent fearful of unemployment and other "dislocations." The most enthusiastic supporters were youth in Ireland, Italy, Portugal, Britain, and Spain. The surprise was contained in the following response: three out of four young people contacted said they not only expected to work in another EC country at some point in their careers, for at least several years, but felt unprepared.

STUDYING ON THE EC

Scholarships and exchange programs are helping to alleviate some of the pressures; many of them were operating under such names as ARION, COMETT, ERASMUS, EEROTECHNET, EURYDICE, TEMPU, and ECTS. All these labels represent some of the most important of the programs being established under EC auspices and funding, which in 1990 helped about 50,000 students in member countries to study or work in other EC countries. This was but a very modest start, considering that some 6.5 million students are enrolled in universities and other institutions of higher education throughout EC member countries. But the programs are being expanded, or new ones established, such as LINGUA, which, for the first time and with more than $200 million funding, will make teaching of at least one foreign EC language compulsory in every country of the Community in the 1990s.

Consider ERASMUS, easily one of the most sought-after programs. The label is shorthand for European Community Action Scheme for the Mobility of University Students, suggesting the visionary concepts of the Dutch Renaissance scholar, Desiderius Erasmus, who taught throughout Europe and felt that studying abroad was essential for one's intellectual development.

Launched in 1987, the program offers scholarships of up to $6,500 to cover the costs of travel and language training in fifteen hundred universities and institutions that have agreed to participate. In the first year of operation, some twelve thousand students were enrolled in what Vasso Papandreou, the EC Commissioner for social and educational affairs, a Greek Socialist and former minister, described as "the most important vector of inter-university cooperation and student mobility in Europe." More than triple that number applied, however, and the funds available to students are very meager; many participating students, annoyed and frustrated, told me they were disappointed the Community couldn't do more, even though their numbers were expected to reach 73,000 students in 1991.

Martha Torre, a twenty-four-year-old student from Oviedo in northern Spain, studying for her doctorate in law at Paris II University, told me she was being paid about 1,500 francs per month, ($300) plus the price of a bus ticket home (700 francs). "It isn't very much, and I barely manage," she said. But, she added, the main advantage of ERASMUS was that it provided direct access to the foreign university. "It is a network, avoiding the bureaucracies and the embassies . . . that is magnificent!"

BUSINESS SCHOOLS EUROPEANIZE TIES

Other institutions of higher learning are already far ahead of the universities. Leading graduate business schools in the major West European countries, for example, were making at least one other EC language obligatory for graduation.

Among the pioneers is INSEAD, at Fontainebleau. When INSEAD opened its doors to sixty-five students in 1959, it was widely hailed for wanting to break down national barriers by training global minded managers, primarily for American and French multinational companies, banks, and consulting firms. Anticipating their future needs, the founders made English, French, and German the working languages of the school. Similar approaches have been established at its main rivals, such as the London Business School, at the International Institute for Management Development in Lausanne, Switzerland, and at prestigious national schools, such as France's HEC and Lyon's ESC Graduate School of Business. But, as George Bain, a Canadian, and head of the London school, put it: "Languages are only one part of it—what we are offering is a European MBA, unique by American standards, and that means a complete program for our future business leaders, by avoiding copying American methods, and doing things our way."[16]

Bain and his colleagues at other leading European business schools now comprise a loose network, regularly exchanging views, while developing and sharing strategies to cope with their alarming problems—the boom in demand for MBA programs, the shortage of qualified professors, the rising demands by companies for executive training programs, which are being caused by the dizzying growth in complexity of doing business in the New Europe. Although American business schools continue turning out seventy-five thousand MBAs per year, compared to about ten thousand in Europe, the European schools have proven themselves far less "provincial" than American schools, Bain said, in his cozy, well-appointed office overlooking the LBS's sprawling campus on Regents Park.

"What does it mean to be international in our terms? It means foreign nationalities in the school, students and faculty, compulsory language courses, and international materials—not just U.S., Harvard case materials," he said. "Americans, and I include Canadians, rarely look at non-American materials . . . we have to look across the Atlantic. Average Americans in this context are very insular," Bain added.

Meantime, as formerly Communist regimes privatized their economies and attempted market-oriented reforms, their planners quickly realized they lacked trained managers. And, just as quickly, they began asking European and American business schools for help. The Europeans, because of geographical proximity and historical ties, were among the first to respond. Consequently, Europe's management networks have been gradually, cautiously extended to universities, professional schools, and management institutes in Budapest, Prague, Warsaw, Kiev, and Leningrad. Lacking, most of all, were professors and administrators to staff their fledgling programs. As a result, European and American business schools have offered scholarships to East European and Soviet professors and organized training seminars, notably in areas considered taboo for many years by Communist regimes, notably marketing.

MARKETING IS "IN"

Indeed, marketing in the New Europe has become one of the hottest subjects among academics and professionals on both sides of what was once known as the Iron Curtain. Among the first to take the initiative have been West German executives from the world of publishing and television, seeking access to East German radio and television stations. Their goal is to acquire broadcasting and publishing outlets in East Germany, while offering commercial advertising in the West to also reach German-speaking consumers in Hungary, Czechoslovakia, Poland, and western regions of the Soviet Union. From newly opened branch offices in Berlin, Budapest, and Prague, educators, consultants, multinational advertising agencies, banks, and insurance companies stepped up their search for someone known as the "Euroconsumer."

Here is a notion that has been widely cited, discussed, and debated as trade barriers have begun to disappear in East and West Europe, yet it lacks not only meaningful definition, but contrasts sharply with the reality of the Community's divergent, deeply ingrained national habits, traditions, and languages. Paradoxically, it also helps explain the success of German unification, for as Willy Brandt said at the time the Wall was opened: "We are now in a situation where that which belongs together will grow together." In other words, East and West Germany, now reunited as an enlarged EC member, might not, necessarily, provide an example for the rest of the Community, even though they shared a common heritage, traditions, and language.

The implications of the German example for the world of marketing remained a subject of intense debate, dramatically expressed in a full-page English-language newspaper advertisement run January 31, 1989, by a leading London agency, Colman RSCG: "Will 1992 Create a New Breed of European Consumer?" The ad showed a woman's face with its features labeled: German hair, Spanish eyes, Roman nose, Latin tan, and English stiff upper lip; it concluded that "talking to a Frenchman in French or a German in German is still many people's idea of pan-European advertising."

The message was simple: Those destined to succeed in the marketing-advertising world of the New Europe, the agency emphasized, will be those who address consumers sharing similar lifestyles. This means exploiting the idea that a mobile, gregarious executive living in Paris, for example, has a lot more in common with his or her counterpart in Milan, London, Berlin, or Budapest than with a fellow citizen in rural or lower-middle-class France. While that was not a revolutionary notion, it pinpointed the paradoxical, complicated task of establishing network standards, norms, in the fast-changing world of lifestyles, clothing, services, food, and beverages.

BUILDING EUROBRANDS

Martin Sorrell told me that, as we entered the 1990s, consumers in the New Europe were becoming more divergent, rather than similar. "We have to come to the general conclusion that global branding, as a blanket concept, is rather naïve, except in very specific circumstances, such as detergents," he said.[17] I put the same question about whether the Euroconsumer is a myth, to Floris Maljers, the balding, quiet-spoken chairman of food giant Unilever's, who is based in Rotterdam, and a client of the agencies in the Sorrell group. "There isn't much difference between washing a T-shirt in Copenhagen and one in Naples," he commented, adding that the company had already concentrated production of detergents in three plants. "If we had not been thinking about Europe, we would have wound up with ten or perhaps twelve units."[18]

Sorrell and Maljers are among those business leaders building networks to shape and influence the consumer habits of the New Europe. Like many of their competitors they are building "Euro-brands" wherever possible, while shaping images to appeal to local or regional tastes. This meant developing "Euro-ads," for example, which were commercial films and advertisements whose message and execution were identical—except for language and sometimes music.

Thus, Captain Bird's Eye's frozen fish sticks (made by Unilever) is portrayed in ads as adventurous, vigorous, and romantic, designed to make the fish sticks appeal to consumers throughout Europe. The television commercials used in Germany, however, were shown accompanied by the music of a marching band, whereas in Italy the Captain Bird's Eye theme song was sung by children.

American influence remained strong. The latest craze throughout late 1990 and early 1991 has been advertising products with purely American themes, images, and settings. They reflected Gaston Thorn's earlier comment about the *Dallas* television series, namely, that Europeans can easily identify with blue jeans, pickup trucks, and laughing young people more easily sometimes than with their own national cultures.

Other forms of U.S.-inspired networking also have been shaping the process: the spread of convenience foods and technology, such as microwave ovens, U.S.-style supermarkets, greater use of commercial television on privatized television networks. Insurance companies, such as Germany's Allianz, are also marketing casualty policies in both East and West Europe as if it were one, single market. And the EC Commission and the European Court have been doing their part—removing, where possible, thousands of nontariff barriers, as part of the 1992 program. In other words, there is a lot more involved than marketing.

The Court has been particularly active, having struck down national rules restricting imported ingredients used in products ranging from Italian pasta to German beer and sausage. The removal of the barriers to trade in such seemingly mundane items is aimed at reducing costs in the food industry by between $575 million and $1.1 billion annually.

In an effort to circumvent the fiercely defended import barriers, large U.S. and European multinationals, like Unilever, Nestlé, and

France's BSN group have been taking advantage of a deregulated financial environment to acquire smaller food companies whenever an opportunity presented itself. BSN's acquisition of RJR Nabisco's European cookie and cracker business for $2.5 billion in June 1989 is but one of the largest and most spectacular examples.

BUT EUROPE COSTS MORE

The BSN acquisition not only transformed the company into Europe's third-largest food company, but further enhanced the popularity of its canny, good-humored, and visionary chairman, Antoine Riboud. But Wall Street analysts, who praised Riboud's audacity in clinching the deal in the face of intense competition, also suggested he may have paid several million dollars more than the five units were worth.

Thus the BSN-RJR acquisition provided yet another grim reminder of how far Europe still has to go to match the United States in lowering the costs of doing business—and living.

Looking back over the rapid proliferation of networking discussed in this chapter—the buildup of Europe-wide television, railroads, airlines, a single monetary system, the intensification of language training and marketing techniques—a disquieting conclusion emerges; the costs of everyday living, traveling, and doing business in most EC countries has remained considerably higher than in the United States. And these higher costs have only been inching downward, despite relatively low inflation rates in virtually every EC country.

EC consumer groups have estimated that the average weekly grocery bill for an average family of four is about $25 higher than a comparable family's in the United States. A business phone call in the summer of 1991 from Milan to New York cost about $5 a minute, twice as much as a call in the opposite direction. The price of regular airline tickets on many of Europe's most heavily frequented routes is still far higher than on comparable routes in the United States. There is no shortage of examples.

Indeed, something is not working as it should, and there is a reason: deeply entrenched interests and forces, many openly protectionist and obstructionist, are at work. Let us examine who and what they are.

The Anti-Europeans:
Coping with a Fortress, Black Spots
and Pretexts

The Japanese Are Killers—How the Nipponese Have
Patiently and Pitilessly Organized the Encirclement and
the Smothering of the French and European Economies.

—LE NOUVEL ECONOMISTE

That headline in one of France's leading weekly business magazines
early in 1990 captured the underlying mood of near hysteria in Paris
and several other Western European capitals, fearful that a rapidly
growing wave of Japanese investment in the Community was achieving its goal: weakening and eventually eliminating the EC as a major
global competitor. "This is World War III . . . and it is economic," the
French report warned, concluding that the accelerating expansion of
Japanese industry and banks into the EC was but one step in Japan's
plan to "conquer" all Western industrial economies, demanding
fierce resistance.

West Germany's *Der Spiegel*, in a similarly oriented, two-part series, branded the new tide of anti-Japan sentiment as "Nippo-
phobia," warning that the "Japanese attack" on Europe was only

beginning. "They want to rule the scene alone," concluded *Der Spie-gel.*[1]

JAPAN TARGETS EUROPE

The anti-Japanese wave resembled what had occurred in the United States less than a decade earlier, as Asia's mightiest economic power began driving for market expansion and power in the European Community, which Japan now regarded as the world's most attractive market after the United States.

The strategy is part of Japan's more specific intention to challenge Europe's growing efforts to develop advanced technologies in fields such as automobiles, high definition television, electronic components, and computers. "The Europeans were perhaps right in fearing us when we began to square off in the late 1980s," a senior MITI official told me in Tokyo, "and although they would never match us for innovation and the like, we had only one choice—invest, move in, become part of Europe, from within, meaning, of course, the EC and now Eastern European countries, meaning Hungary and East Germany. . . . The Europeans were awakening and we had to be ready, if necessary, to join them."[2]

I recall during other interviews in early November 1989 in Tokyo how Japanese officials, bankers, and executives appeared shocked and angered with the wave of articles and declarations about their "invasion" of Europe.

At the end of May 1991, Japan's foreign ministry summoned the French ambassador in Tokyo to protest remarks made several days earlier by incoming prime minister Edith Cresson, who had accused Japan of being an unfair trader, having already destroyed the American car industry. Several days later, a ministry spokesman back-tracked, explaining that his government's first reaction should not be construed as being hostile, and that France and Japan should cooperate. It was difficult to understand how genuine Japan's reactions were, but clearly they are less restrained when their interests are threatened, reflecting a new, tougher mood when dealing with European leaders and the media. Commenting on Edith Cresson's attacks on Japanese trading practices in late June 1991, the *Mianichi,* a leading Japanese daily newspaper described her as "an inedible salad."

For example, the executive of a leading computer manufacturer told me during my Tokyo visit he was on the verge of canceling the company's advertising with *Der Spiegel,* protesting its series. "We are retaliating on the basis of what our German director is recommending . . . but we're not sure, here in Tokyo, whether it is worth it," he said, shaking his head, "and we will pursue our interests in Europe in any case."

Thus, driven by anger and alarm over rising EC protectionism, mixed with doses of anxiety and paranoia, Japanese companies, banks, and the government accelerated their spectacular push—acquiring companies, banks, buildings, real estate, art treasures, castles, country clubs, vineyards, hairdressers, and graduates of Europe's leading business schools, while building new factories, golf courses, and schools and sponsoring Japanese-language television programs and newspapers. By the beginning of 1991, there were more than 1,000 Japanese plants, banks, financial and consulting groups operating throughout EC member countries; a growing resident Japanese community of over 75,000 men, women, and children; and the fastest rate of growth for direct investments for any area outside Japan.

A study published in March 1991 by the Japan External Trade Organization, a branch of MITI, showed that the trend was accelerating. Reflecting the results of a survey of 678 Japanese companies conducted between September 1990 and January 1991, the study showed that not only were their investments continuing to rise, but the Japanese companies were unifying their European production and marketing operations and setting up European-based centers for design and research—a direct response to allegations that Japanese industry was only using Europe for "screwdriver" plants, meaning to assemble products only. The JETRO study also showed that Britain remained the most popular location for Japanese investments, followed in importance by France, Germany, Spain, Italy, and the Netherlands, respectively.

"Nothing was off limits," commented a senior EC official, "except perhaps the Eiffel Tower and the Brandenburg Gate."

When, suddenly, on July 18, 1990, it was disclosed in London that Fujitsu, Japan's leading computer maker, was negotiating for control of ICL, Britain's only manufacturer of mainframe computers and a major supplier to the government, a shocked British executive described it as "a national tragedy." American analysts saw it as the first step by Japan to challenge IBM in Europe—with European help. Less than a year later, in the summer of 1991, Fujitsu had completed purchasing an eighty-percent shareholding in ICL, and in a related move shortly afterward, control of the computer division of Nokia, Finland's largest company. Elsewhere in the European Community, other Japanese companies, such as NEC, Fuji Electric, Mitsubishi, Hitachi, and Canon, had acquired stakes in or were establishing their own joint ventures with other EC-based electronics companies, such as Italy's Olivetti, Germany's Siemens, and France's Bull.

It was difficult keeping track of all the studies as Japanese companies continued arriving, and puzzling everyone. What was motivating the Japanese? How should European companies, their governments, and EC institutions respond to what was clearly a dilemma: how could Europe continue battling Japan as Mrs. Cresson of France, among others, was urging, while claiming to be an open, liberal, non-protectionist trading zone? Here was yet another example of Japan's moving into an area where it already had built markets, puzzling many analysts. What was motivating the Japanese?

EUROPE BOTH HELPS AND FIGHTS BACK

The Japanese have drawn Europe's grudging admiration, as well as encouragement in the form of generous subsidies and tax advantages from EC member governments and regions delighted to be welcoming a potential source of new jobs and prosperity. Japan is, in reality, both an enemy and a friendly investor, both helping and battling Europe. No government or outside authority forced ICL to accept Fujitsu's offer. Mrs. Thatcher fought long and hard throughout the early 1980s to entice Nissan to build its second-largest automobile plant outside of Japan in northeast England—as she said, to set an example of how a modern car industry should flourish in Britain. Although restricted to around 12 percent of the combined EC market by national import quotas, mainly in France, Italy, and Spain, Japanese car makers were convinced the EC market still represented enormous potential, hopeful they would reach 20 percent of the market before the year 2000. Car ownership in the EC, according to Japanese estimates, averaged about 380 per 1,000 persons, compared with about 600 in the United States, and represented the second-largest single car market in the world.

But a market for whom? "We must construct Europe for the

benefit of the Europeans, not the Japanese," thundered Jacques Calvet, the volatile chairman of France's large family-controlled Peugeot automobile group. His fear, expressed as an articulate spokesman for protection in the automobile industry, was that Nissan, Toyota, and other Japanese cars would roll out of their modern, automated EC-based plants, absorbing as much as 60 percent of the market's growth, leaving precious little for the six main European producers, which besides Peugeot include France's state-owned Renault, Germany's Volkswagen and Daimler-Benz groups, plus GM and Ford. "Look at what happened to the car industry in America, let alone other industries," Calvet said. "This is a terrifying threat."[3] Two years later, in early June 1991, he warned that new agreements between European car manufacturers and the Japanese would be "suicidal."

Agreeing was Cesare Romiti, Fiat's tough chief executive, who reminded audiences that the EC car industry directly employed 1.7 million people, more than double that number if suppliers and service companies were counted. "I believe that it would really be an unforgivable sign of folly and thoughtlessness if we Europeans were to lose control of it," he warned, urging the establishment of a "harmonized" quota on Japanese car imports as part of a "transition" period that would keep Japanese producers at bay between five and ten years, providing EC car producers the time to reorganize and invest, while obtaining far greater access to Japanese car markets.[4] The EC Commission throughout 1991 has been negotiating an agreement with Japan along roughly those lines.

The truth is that, despite admirable design, engine power, and high profits, the Europeans still have a long way to go in matching Japanese performance at the factory level.

Ford, for example, estimates its European plants are 50 percent less productive than similar factories in Japan; absenteeism at the Nissan plant in Britain runs only at about 2.5 percent, compared to 10 percent in most French, Italian, and German plants, and close to 30 percent at some of Sweden's highly automated car plants.

Here is yet another paradox: Japan is up against many of the same protectionist barriers being challenged by U.S. trade negotiators and in Brussels by EC Competition Commissioner Brittan. Edith Cresson, while minister of European Affairs, ever defensive and aggressive, enjoyed telling visitors that in her view the concept of Fortress Europe was dreamed up—diabolically—by the Japanese and planted in the minds of Americans, who then used it to attack EC protectionist practices—for the benefit of Japan.

Cresson, who certainly hadn't changed her mind as prime minister, may have had a point, but as she knows only too well there are no simple or easy answers—or relief—because barriers and obstacles have been built and are being maintained by powerful private business groups, governmental bureaucracies, and individuals, determined to block, or at least slow the process toward a more efficient, competitive Europe. Pillars of resistance are everywhere in business and government—in flagship EC airlines, electronics, telecommunications groups, banks, and financial institutions, and among government ministries throughout the Community, most notably in foreign and finance ministries and often at lower, or middle, echelons.

During the mid-December 1990 Rome EC summit meeting, a group of journalists were sharing a nightcap with Delors, who, unexpectedly, began musing aloud about "those" who would obstruct progress toward EMU, but he declined to say who he had in mind. The next day, this time on the record, he told us that he feared not only Major and Britain's opposition, but that of the influential finance ministers of Germany, the Netherlands, Spain, and, not least, his own country, "as if they had never heard about the Delors Plan before." Clearly, there was new wavering on EMU, particularly in Bonn and London, as negotiations began, both delighting and puzzling the Japanese trying to assess what such apparent indecision meant for their long-range trade strategy.

In the Japanese capital, the abrupt resignation of Cresson as European Affairs minister in early October 1990, to immediately become president of a private French company, was interpreted as a victory. But in her first appearance as Cresson's successor on October 9 in Luxembourg, fair-haired, Elisabeth Guigou bluntly quashed that perception, announcing that France would not accept the Commission's position on liberalizing car imports from Japan. Consequently, and with a mixture of barely concealed annoyance and frustration, Japanese government officials, planners, and executives fought back, resisting major trade concessions in regular trade-liberalization negotiations held in Brussels and Tokyo, while Japanese industry continued investing heavily in plants throughout the Community to circumvent future EC barriers to Japanese imports.

And to the puzzlement of many Europeans, despite the EC's

chronic, $20 billion-a-year trade deficit with Japan, Tokyo planners made it clear they had no intentions of slowing the spending spree. Their executives, whenever I met them, exuded patience, often mixed with frustration and a touch of disdain for European business leaders in general. But they always appeared determined to succeed and ready to overcome obstacles when faced with Europe's most deeply entrenched habits and mentalities. This prompted some Japanese officials, who knew Europe well to conclude in private conversations that Europe did not "understand" Japanese methods and never would.

SAVING A PLANT IN MONTLUÇON

Consider the case of Sumitomo in Montluçon, France. When I first visited the former Dunlop tire factory near that dreary industrial town in the center of France in the spring of 1987, Marcel Mathieu, a thirty-year company veteran, gestured to the green lawn, freshly planted flowers, and his blue blouse. Inside the plant, against the backdrop of hissing and clanging and the stench of rubber, he pointed to Japanese machinery being adjusted by French workers, all wearing identical garb.

"All that you see, such as our blouses, are reforms started by Sumitomo, as part of their drive to modernize these operations . . . they saved us from going under." Even the most militant trade-union leaders at the plant, including Communists, agreed that progress had been made since Sumitomo Rubber Industries acquired the ailing Montluçon operations from Dunlop Holdings of Britain three years earlier, along with its other West European plants. At the time of the takeover they were dirty, poorly managed, overmanned, and on the verge of bankruptcy.

What had occurred at Montluçon was more than just another story of a Japanese acquisition in the Common Market. It was a very rare example of a large Japanese company's acquiring existing and troubled plants in several Western countries and then subjecting them to a complete overhaul. Usually, Japanese companies buy or build new plants, positioning themselves in advanced, or mature, industries. Sumitomo began by cleaning the Dunlop plants, laying off several thousand workers, reorganizing, investing, and training French workers in Japan. The psychological obstacles in motivating middle-level managers, proved the most difficult to overcome. They surfaced shortly after the first Japanese executives arrived in early 1984.

Former Dunlop managers winced as they recalled how a senior Sumitomo executive, shortly after arriving from Tokyo, told them they should be prepared to sweep the floors in plants if no one else was available, and that they should remain on the shop floor with workers, not returning to their offices until 5 P.M. "That was pure shock therapy—difficult, if not impossible, to accept, even today," commented a French manager. Japanese executives at the site told me of their headaches. "Changing mentalities and instilling a sense of teamwork has been the most difficult task here," said Akio Oyamada, one of thirty-five Sumitomo executives who had been assigned to supervise the overhauling in France, West Germany, and Britain. His colleagues later told me his efforts provided Japan valuable lessons that would be applied to old, inefficient, rundown plants they acquired in Eastern Europe during the early 1990s.

French workers were by far the easiest employees to train, including by stints in Japan, usually of several weeks' duration. "We were among the first to fight for saving this plant and went along with what the Japanese wanted and brought, including training," said Norbert Palisson, secretary general of the Communist-led General Confederation of Labor. "They treated us well." But, he warned, the CGT and other unions would also fight for higher salaries and benefits and against any attempt to reduce the influence of the union and the Communists, who also controlled the municipal government.

Indeed, Sumitomo realized in Montluçon that it faced a more fundamental problem that extended throughout Western Europe— private and public-sector companies that had enjoyed cozy, protected markets, or monopolies, which resisted change. Many were small and medium-sized businesses that had been accustomed to operating within only their own country, and were unprepared for outside competition. In my conversations with Japanese planners in Tokyo in November 1989, and later in Europe, I found they had no illusions.

"We have studied Europe and compared it to the United States. . . . Frankly, we are more worried about the Common Market, because Europeans are more vulnerable, have more to lose, are weaker than the U.S. and thus are more protected, determined to defend their interests," said my MITI source. We knew each other from his days in Paris and London, where he had served as a junior trade official.

Now, nearing forty, and holding a very senior job in Tokyo, he spoke on condition that he not be identified. "At the same time, the Europeans have learned many tricks from the Americans, aimed at trying to weaken us by protectionism, and that is what we find . . . except in Britain," he said, controlling his annoyance. "But we do intend to make our weight felt, to work from within. . . . We know where the enemies are, the pockets of resistance. . . . It is they, the Europeans, mainly the French and the Italians, who are the true anti-Europeans, not us."

EC BUSINESS PROTECTIONISM

My MITI source, who had not changed his mind in 1991, was referring to the many groups scattered throughout the Common Market that had vested interests in slowing the Community's effort to unify politically and economically. They preferred instead, if necessary, to see a Europe weak and divided, but above all not threatened from the outside. These groups repeatedly used epithets such as "Japanese menace" or "the common enemy" as a pretext for keeping or reinforcing government protection, particularly in France, Italy, Spain, Greece, and Portugal, and to a lesser degree in Germany and Britain. Even Delors on several occasions, warned that "We will not be a fortress, but Europe will not be a sieve, either," a reference to Japanese, U.S., and South Korean multinationals. Delors vehemently opposed protectionism in public, but behind the scenes demonstrated "flexibility," as Brussels insiders were fond of saying, whenever French interests were under attack by EC competition authorities.

West Germany industrialists, bankers, and political leaders, for all their talk of Germany's "free, open, liberal" economy, fully deserve criticism and allegations of some protectionist tendencies, and, particularly, resistance to ownership of their manufacturing and banking assets by non-Germans. The powerful Frankfurt and Munich banks have made sure that German companies remain under German control. Bankers and financiers could cite only several hostile takeover attempts in Germany's postwar history, noting that "friendly" banks and companies control just over 55 percent of the shares of the country's listed companies.

A notable exception to the rule jolted Germany in May 1991 as Italy's patrician industrialist Leopoldo Pirelli, who controls the large tire manufacturing company bearing his name, acquired a major share of Continental, a large, Hannover-based competitor. Although at first it appeared that Conti would fight and win, the two firms gradually began to talk of "cooperation," under pressure from influential German bankers. "U.S.-style raiding here is simply unthinkable," said Riesenkampf, the Frankfurt lawyer.

Another example of Germany's keeping its guard up—while modestly deregulating—is the traditionally hidebound, bureaucratic West German Bundespost, the country's postal and telecommunications monopoly. Only in 1989 did it, and its French counterpart, France Télécom, begin responding to EC and U.S. pressures to privatize and deregulate its operations, and to somewhat reduce rates being kept artificially high. This was reflected in the relatively higher rates of transatlantic phone calls originating in the Community. What were the postal authorities resisting and why, particularly in supposedly superefficient Germany?

Tyll Necker, president of the powerful Federation of German Industries, the BDI, representing about eighty thousand German companies, and longtime supporter of European integration, told me that three groups opposed rapid deregulatory change: German labor unions, which feared job cuts; regional politicians, who feared that telecommunications and postal services would be reduced or cut in remote areas; and, finally, small and medium-sized companies, which were longtime suppliers to the Bundespost, but totally unprepared for new competition, much less exporting." These were companies with no sales force, relying on one customer, who were now afraid they would go out of business," said Necker, adding that "telecommunications have been a state-run business for a long time here in Germany and elsewhere in Europe. Innovation is fairly slow. Political influences are heavily felt. The resistance is slowing, of course, but it is still here. That is reality."[5]

Necker, who in 1973 founded his own small software and business-consulting firm in the small town of Bad Oldesloe, near Hamburg, knew what he was talking about, and his opinions are borne out by many studies. Survey after survey showed that the Community's 13.4 million small and medium-sized companies were among the most vulnerable to reforms and would resist change. Many lacked a strategy. In France, out of five hundred such companies surveyed in early 1990, only 20 percent had any plans to cooperate with another EC-based firm; 70 percent had virtually no idea of the European potential for their exports. On a more positive note, 51 percent of the companies surveyed said they were studying foreign languages, but 86 percent had no idea that EC-financed research funds were generally available. About 82 percent said they were unaware of pending changes in EC customs regulations.[6]

GOVERNMENT FOOT-DRAGGING

Much of the resistance to change also comes from member states themselves. Long-entrenched government support of the European economies bears much of the blame for Europe's relative inefficiency and weakness, and it has taken many forms: generous EC and national subsidies, import duties and quotas, local-content rules, export restraint agreements, national favoritism on taxation and bidding for contracts, and the outright ignoring, or shelving, of liberalization measures enacted by European institutions as part of the 1992 program. Bureaucracies bear much of the blame, many of them overstaffed and determined to protect their interests, and, in many cases, to block inroads being made on long-established and influential state-controlled interests, lobbying hard for their interests in Brussels.

Brittan and his colleagues in the Commission competition directorate have pursued a vigorous campaign to slow subsidies and to force state-owned industries to file financial reports to the Commission. But in many cases Brittan has been forced to accept compromises forced through by fellow commissioners and, in some cases, supported by Delors. For example, in early 1990, the Commission greatly watered down its approach to France's state-owned auto maker Renault when Paris refused to take back payments made to the company in previous years. Critics noted that in both France and Italy state-owned businesses account for about one-third of the GNP in each country, and close to 10 percent in Spain, all backed by influential government and business lobbies in Brussels, Paris, and Rome.

Then there are frequent examples of obstructionism by customs officials at borders. In November 1990, based on complaints filed with the European Parliament, the Commission reported, for example, how a Danish student was forced to send her luggage home after arriving in Italy for a university course because she could not afford to pay the value-added tax on her possessions demanded unlawfully by customs officers. And "harassing and vexatious" border formalities were applied to a Belgian resident, who was forced to send her husband's coffin to a French consulate before she could bury him in his native France.

Are these isolated examples of what a British EC official described as "bloody-mindedness"? Or could anti-Europeans, at all levels, halt or slow the progress being made? As the Community entered the final stretch in the run-up to midnight December 31, 1991, it was already clear that the Commission would have great difficulty enforcing implementation of some key measures contained in the original Cockfield Plan. Some of the original proposals have already been shelved, or are dying, such as the Commission's proposal for a 15 percent withholding on interest to be applied throughout the EC. Britain and Luxembourg, backed by their private and state-controlled banks, maintained total opposition to the plan, which required unanimous agreement for implementation. Meantime, efforts to bring national value-added tax and excise tax rates closer together have been postponed until 1997. Border controls have not yet been eliminated in many areas; British security officials, in particular, argue that they are indispensable for controlling terrorists, illegal immigrants, and drug traffickers.

By mid-1991, this is where implementation of the 1992 plan stood: just over two-thirds of the 282 measures outlined in the 1992 program had been proposed to the Council of Ministers by the Commission. And the Council had implemented nearly 200 of the directives, but national parliaments had adopted only 65 percent of the laws needed to implement the directives.

The Commission, acting through the European Court of Justice, responded to complaints by instituting "infringement proceedings" against offending governments. But often governments pleaded for more time, citing the press of other business. "It is a slow, difficult process, considering that governments have eighteen months to implement, and we have only fifteen full-time staff people for the moment," complained an exasperated Commission official.

Some countries performed better than others in implementing the program, and there were surprises in some of the rankings published by the Commission and private research groups. On a scale of one to ten on commitment to the EC's Single Market program member governments score as follows: The worst offenders, according to the survey and other observers, were Italy, Portugal, Greece, Belgium, and Spain. The best performers were, surprisingly, Britain and Denmark, followed by West Germany, France, and Ireland. In the middle were the Netherlands and Luxembourg. "Say what you will about British reservations regarding Europe, they have been the best in implementing the 1992 program, and the Italians, despite their expressions of enthusiasm for Europe, have been the worst," commented a senior Commission source. Beffa of France's Saint-Gobain complained that some of the 1992 Program texts are "excessively rigid."

GERMAN BEER TRIUMPHS

In specific cases, however, even implementation of market-opening measures meant very little, if anything. Consider the case of German beer, the nation's most popular alcoholic beverage: Germans quaff, on average, 144 liters annually, the highest average in the West, trailed by Denmark (126 liters), Belgium (119 liters), Austria (117 liters), and Britain (110 liters). But for nearly four centuries, German beer has also been protected by a famous law known as the Reinheitsgebot. This is a so-called "purity" law, promulgated by Duke William of Bavaria in 1516. The law had been faithfully upheld by several hundred powerful brewers, who also owned the bars, taverns, and inns serving their beers, often within a fifty-kilometer radius of their breweries. The law's purpose is to strictly limit the content of beer in Germany to water, hops, malted barley, and yeast. Strictly outlawed, in the interests of "purity," were additives such as sugar, wheat, rice, or unmalted barley.

Beer brewers throughout Europe anxious to sell their beer in Germany—notably the Danes, Belgians, and Dutch—and in the United States repeatedly attacked the law as outrageously protectionist, noting that imported beer still accounts for less than 2 percent of the huge market, worth an estimated $12 billion a year.

Finally, in 1987, responding to widespread complaints that the ancient law conflicted with EC directives "harmonizing" trade in food and beverages, the European Court of Justice ruled that it was illegal under the Rome Treaty, thus—theoretically—clearing the way for foreign brewers to sell in Germany. But, faced with hostile advertising campaigns against "impure" foreign beer, financed by the German breweries, and by their threatening pressures on importers, the liberalization wave was halted. The head of a small beer-importing company near Stuttgart complained: "Germans, after all, are the biggest beer consumers in Europe, but who wants to, who can afford to, go through that much trouble?"

Today, foreign beers can be bought, mainly in Germany's luxury hotels, restaurants, and specialty food shops and some taverns, but the market is still dominated—and fragmented—by some thirteen hundred breweries in East and West Germany, selling under several thousand different labels. Some foreign brewers began shifting their marketing to light and nonalcoholic beers, but they, too, will be subject to some form of "purity" certification.

"Look, this is just the way we are—we like our beer the way it is, the way the French love their wine they way it is," commented Ulrich Wickert, the evening anchorman for West Germany's ARD television network and author of a highly perceptive book on France published in 1990. "You are not going to change Germany, its tastes, or France for that matter, with a law from Brussels."

FRAUD ON EC FARMS

But there were far more troubling obstacles to creating open, efficient markets. Well-documented cases of fraud, waste, and inefficiency have become deeply ingrained in the daily workings of the EC Commission and, most conspicuously, in its handling of farm subsidies. Despite cost-cutting reforms, farm-support programs since the mid-1970s have continued to absorb about 65 percent of the EC's annual budget, which in 1991 totaled nearly $70 billion. The evidence began to appear, thanks to the EC's Court of Auditors, the Community's financial watchdog agency. Its investigators accused member states, and the Commission, of widespread waste, mismanagement, and cases of criminal fraud in the farm-export program. The Court, which incidentally has no enforcement powers, released a detailed, explosive report in mid-1990, following two years of investigation. In dry, bureaucratic style, it described cases of rigged bidding on lucrative contracts by traders; fraudulent labeling of farm products benefiting from heavy subsidies; and outright failure of EC member-country customs officials to verify goods crossing borders, because of vague, poorly defined lines of responsibility.

The Thatcher government immediately pointed to the report as proof of the need for tighter political controls over the Commission. Sir John Hoskyns, formerly her adviser and head of Britain's Institute of Directors, described the situation as "a complete fiasco."

No official cost figures were produced, but the European Parliament has estimated that "financial irregularities" in EC-funded agriculture programs alone were costing the Community about $4 billion each year. Senior EC officials, declining to be identified, have described the practices as occurring in "a shadow zone," representing "a new form of criminality," most likely with ties to Italian criminal organizations, notably the Mafia, and terrorist groups, notably the Irish Republican Army (the IRA).

Delors, in several follow-up speeches, warned that "the credibility of the Community is at stake," and strongly urged national governments to crack down on the fraud, but quickly emphasized that the EC Commission lacked power to prosecute offenders. He has repeatedly urged that the Commission be given special enforcement powers. The president of the Luxembourg-based Court of Auditors, Marcel Mart, partly agreed with Delors's assessment shortly after the report was issued, complaining that practically all EC revenues, particularly for agriculture, are collected by national governmental bodies, not EC institutions. The Court would like to see its powers increased, but only the Netherlands has backed that idea. EC officials believe it will be several years before any further major reforms will be undertaken.

And what many regarded as wasteful—but legal—spending also continued. Detailed studies by the OECD and the EC showed that through 1990 individual member-government subsidies had risen to more than $100 billion annually, equal to 3 percent of the Community's GNP. Nearly a fourth of the total went to state-owned railways, all of which were operating in the red throughout the Community. Textile and coal industries were also benefiting, along with state-owned aerospace and defense industries, as we saw in Chapter 4, and the latter have been under heavy attack by the Bush Administration.

Those targeted for streamlining hardly favored reform and vigorously fought back to protect their privileges, often through demonstrations in the streets of their capitals. Among them were Bavarian and French farmers in, respectively, downtown Bonn and Paris; Lorraine miners and steelworkers in Metz; civil servants, air controllers, airline ground personnel, railroad and postal workers, teachers and nurses in Rome, Madrid, Paris, and Brussels. Often, these were sporadic demonstrations lasting only a few days, but they succeeded in causing infuriating delays and discomfort to the public, while sending a clear signal to European political leaders: established government-supported privileges were not to be tampered with, particularly by Brussels. "Brittan behaves like a sheriff going after outlaws in the Wild West," complained Milan's conservative daily *Corriere della Sera,* commenting on the commissioner's determination to force reductions in what he termed "distorting" government assistance and financing to state-controlled industries.

FARMERS BATTLE THE HARDEST

The EC's estimated eleven million farmers, many working only part time, were among the first to take to the streets of Europe in protest against reforms. Although the number of farms in the Community had fallen 35 percent from 1970 levels to six million, farmers through their powerful lobbying organizations in Brussels succeeded in resisting major reductions in their long-established support programs. Established as a trade-off between de Gaulle and Adenauer, who favored, respectively, French farmers and German industry, the EC's Common Agricultural Policy, the CAP, became the major, dominating issue during the multilateral trade negotiations known as the Uruguay Round, organized under auspices of GATT, the Geneva-based General Agreement on Tariffs and Trade. And the Community, defending the CAP, virtually wrecked the talks.

In early December 1990, as some 2,000 delegates from 107 nations gathered in Brussels for what was supposed to be the final round in the GATT talks, more than 30,000 angry farmers rampaged through the city, braving tear gas and rows of police, bitterly warning of a sellout. Reducing farm subsidies was, however, regarded by GATT negotiators as crucial for safeguarding the multilateral trading system built up after World War II. Inside the conference room, EC negotiators were single-mindedly opposed to compromising. But there were broader stakes in a successful outcome.

Substantially reducing the farm subsidies in the Community, and in other farming countries, including the United States, would, according to the International Monetary Fund in Washington, increase the foreign-exchange earnings of Third World farm exporting countries by $50 billion. But the Community has repeatedly resisted attempts to phase out CAP subsidies beyond a modest amount—30 percent, covering the years 1986–96, which the United States judged totally inadequate. In Brussels, as the marathon GATT talks adjourned in deadlock, fears were widely expressed that a failure to resolve the U.S.-EC dispute would trigger waves of protectionism among the world's trading nations.

Powerful farm lobbies, whose members benefited the most from the EC programs, were relieved, as was Delors, who took a hard protectionist line, pledging that the Community would continue maintaining what he termed "a sound balance between rural and urban development." And, he snapped at the 1990 Rome summit meeting, "it is not up to the United States to tell us how to organize our agricultural policy."

But, in reality, as some independent American farm economists have noted, both in the United States and in the Community the subsidies have made the rich richer, while ignoring needy, traditional farmers. As a result, concluded C. Ford Runge, who has followed the EC closely from the University of Minnesota, "Europe's farm sector [has come] to look more and more like the most oversupported, overcapitalized parts of U.S. agriculture. In the name of preserving European rural life, the CAP has led to the Americanization of European agriculture."[7]

What this means, more specifically, says Runge, is that the top 18 percent of American farmers receive about 90 percent of government-financed direct payments; a similar situation exists in the Community, he said, citing German estimates showing that 60 percent of all CAP payments go to 20 percent of West Germany's richest farmers. What is needed, he argues, is "more equitable distribution of benefits." But this approach, as we shall see, is easier proclaimed than done and it applies not only to agriculture. Poorer regions in Europe have been seeking substantial new funding from the EC and their governments to build new roads, rail lines, factories, and schools to avoid being left behind by the development of richer regions.

A major vehicle for development of poorer regions is the Community's European Regional Development Fund, which has absorbed roughly a quarter of the EC's total budget. Funds available have been doubled to nearly $70 billion over four years, starting in 1990. Its goal: reducing economic and social disparities between the richer and poorer regions of the Community. The rising EC funding has been matched many times over by EC member governments, each of which aggressively seeks investments for these and other, more-developed regions, virtually always with generous tax advantages, subsidies, and other forms of help from local, regional, and central government authorities.

THOSE UNTOUCHED

Many Europeans, notably the poor, feel untouched by all the excitement over GATT, CAP, the 1992 program, deregulation, the Japanese, regional funds, and the like.

Take, for instance, the Simon family. Paul Simon, the father, is a modest farmer who owns a small herd of a dozen cows and works twenty-three acres of hilly, sparse land near Sainte Livrade, a small village in the hilly Lot and Garonne department of France, ninety kilometers southeast of Bordeaux. He is typical of many millions of poor farmers, artisans, average workers, and shopkeepers, who simply have no stake in the New Europe, 1992-style integration, or, for that matter, in much of what we are dealing with in this book. Many of these European citizens have no lobbies representing them. They rarely travel, do not use credit or debit cards to pay their bills, and have little contact with foreigners, usually speaking only one language, their own. Many live in remote areas, where the high-speed trains are not scheduled to pass, where new highways and regional airports will not penetrate soon, if ever.

"As you can see, I am not one of the big, powerful farmers or businessmen well represented in Brussels. I am stuck, and the farmers around here eventually will disappear," said Simon, who had just turned fifty when we first met in 1989. As a child, he came to the region from Brittany, and raised two children on the land with his wife of twenty-five years, Mauricette, a slight, retiring woman, who helps him milk the herd every morning. They usually rise at 6:30 A.M., work steadily until 8 P.M., and then watch television before retiring. They have never taken a vacation.

"What troubles me is that my children don't want this life and will join those who have left farming—we're now only 8 percent of the population, whereas we used to be 15 percent, and our numbers continue going down," Simon told me, dejected. "Not even the girls from the countryside want to marry farmers anymore—except the big rich ones and there are very few of that kind around here."

Then there are Europe's unemployed. As the Community entered 1991, the jobless rate remained disturbingly high—8.7 percent, representing about 13 million people. The OECD and other forecasting groups predicted the level would rise again in 1992 to around 9.2 percent as business and industry throughout Europe cut back on payrolls in order to reduce costs further. Europe's record has been far worse than those of the United States and Japan, whose unemployment levels are expected to remain steady, but at lower levels—6.7 percent in the United States in 1992 and 2.3 percent in Japan, according to the OECD's year-end report. But these statistics hardly tell the story.

The face of Europe's jobless was in the bored, blank, often depressed expressions in the faces of young men and women seen in the streets, railroad, bus and subway stations of the Community's cities, often asking for handouts after explaining their plight. These were Europe's "New Poor," whose interest and involvement in the New Europe as we have been discussing it is, needless to say, also virtually nil.

Consider the following: in 1975, the EC Commission estimated that about 38.5 million citizens of member countries lived below the poverty line, meaning that their incomes amounted to fifty percent or less of the national average. A decade later, the most recent period for which figures are available, the total number of Europe's poor and, increasingly, homeless, had risen to nearly 44 million, roughly 8 percent of the total population, and growing. In what was being characterized as a "two-speed" Europe, Portugal, Greece, Ireland, and Spain were at the bottom of the list, with the proportion of those living below the poverty line varying between 28 percent and 20 percent, followed by France, Denmark, Britain, and Italy, while Belgium, the Netherlands, Luxembourg, and Germany had the best record, with less than 10 percent living below the poverty line.

Even the poorest European cities cannot match the misery, distress, poverty, and suffering found in New York City, Washington, D.C., and Chicago. But British social workers believe there are as many as one million homeless people in Britain; several thousand can be seen in London's cardboard cities, sprawling under bridges close to the city center, and in the South Bank arts complex near the Thames River. In Paris, to the embarrassment of the Socialist government, the numbers of *nouveaux pauvres* have grown so rapidly that new charities have sprung up to help them find food, jobs, and housing, as they have come to take their places alongside the Parisian *clochards,* or hobos, still drawing comfort from cheap wine and the warmth of the city's Métro system.

Munich, Germany's wealthy, posh, cultural and high-tech capital, counted 10,000 homeless; half its 200,000 low-rent homes were to be turned over to private buyers within five years, as German social-welfare experts estimated that the new influx of immigrants from the East has drained resources to care for the nation's total homeless of some 100,000 people. In Italy, where there are no official figures, the poor and homeless can be seen in Florence, Rome, Milan, Turin, sleeping in railroad stations and churches, and asking for handouts in virtually every downtown shopping area; many are destitute blacks from Africa.

WHY NO REVOLUTION?

To their credit, every EC member country was creating jobs—7 million between 1985 and 1989. Another one million jobs were projected for 1990 to 1992. Smith Barney's Horne commented that this level of job creation in the Common Market was "quite extraordinary" because it represented a rate of expansion of 1 percent per year, one of the highest levels among Western nations. But the numbers hid the character of the jobs being created: nearly half were temporary, or part time, often in the services sector, such as fast-food restaurants. In addition, more than half of the jobs were being filled by young newcomers to the job market, often women, and thus not making a dent in the ranks of the chronically unemployed, who continued drawing benefits from generous but gradually dwindling payments from government-backed insurance plans.

Government payments to the Community's unemployed, while they vary in size and scope from country to country, represent, above all, a safety valve, partly explaining why, with thirteen million people out of work, Europe had not exploded with more numerous demonstrations, strikes, and protests. In other words, as jobs continued being created in industry throughout the early 1990s, there was a general consensus in the Community that it was better to maintain high levels of subsidies and government unemployment payments and, where necessary, protectionism in order to keep redundant workers and farmers reasonably comfortable, but, above all, off the streets.

Thus Philips, as part of its major restructuring and laying-off of about 57,000 workers in 1991 and 1992, was forced reluctantly to absorb more than $700 million in payments to those being laid off or retired early, for a third of the company's projected record-breaking loss of $2.4 billion in 1990. "You think twice before firing people with those kinds of cost pressures," a company official in Eindhoven said, while a Dutch union official countered, "The problem is, we have no real say—the crisis at Philips has brought home to us that very grim reality." But signs of change are stirring, which might eventually change worker-employee relations.

THE "SOCIAL DIMENSION" REEMERGES

As part of an EC Commission–led effort to establish new rules for worker-employer relationships, another major confrontation was beginning to emerge as Europe approached its December 31, 1992, deadline. Influential centrist and leftist leaders, led by Mitterrand, Kohl, Gonzáles, Gianni De Michelis of Italy, and Delors, echoing the increasingly vocal views of moderate union leaders, argued that something was still missing in the 1992 program—a "European social dimension." Those opposed to the proposals put forward in late 1990, notably powerful business lobbies and the British government, angrily dismissed the idea as "European-style social engineering."

As debate heated up in 1991 over efforts to "harmonize" labor relations, the protagonists repeatedly accused each other of being "anti-European," of violating both the letter and spirit of the 1992 program.

Gavin Laird, since 1982 general secretary of Britain's powerful Amalgamated Engineering Union, represents three-quarters of a million workers in manufacturing industries throughout the United Kingdom. Tenacious, exuding good humor, with a gruff Scottish brogue, Laird has spent virtually his entire career in Britain's trade-union movement—and is an ardent supporter of the 1992 program. "We want to see Europe based on successful, profitable companies, and we want to see an end to unemployment," he told an *International Herald Tribune* conference in mid-June 1990, but he quickly added that union leaders throughout the Community also wanted something in return for the greater freedom and prosperity accruing to EC-based business as barriers are dismantled with enthusiastic EC and governmental support. That "something" involved an ambitious

agenda by European labor groups and their allies, which would guarantee that, as Laird pledged, a Europe, Inc. was not simply built at the
expense of "every working man and woman in Europe, union member, or not."

The EC Commission has a highly controversial agenda, inspired
by Delors and drafted largely by Greece's dark-eyed, moody Socialist
Vasso Papandreou, economist, former member of the Greek Parliament, and the industry minister prior to joining the Commission, in
charge of social matters. It includes new, Europe-wide rules for establishing everything from maternity leave, night work, minimum wages
to a system of worker representation on boards of every EC company
employing more than a thousand people, on the condition that the
company is established in more than one EC member country. The
new rules, as Mrs. Papandreou explained it, are to close the gap
between poorer EC member countries, such as Ireland, Spain, Portugal, and Greece, her own ailing country, and the wealthier members
to the north.

"The social dimension is not some kind of a 'sweet' to be offered
at the end of a meal," Mrs. Papandreou told our conference. "It must
not be pushed into second place as just one of the consequences of
the economic development of the internal market." She was convey-
ing precisely the same message Delors had expressed when he addressed—and was cheered by—Britain's TUC Congress meeting in
September 1988, and which so infuriated Mrs. Thatcher as we saw in
Chapter 1. But the former British leader, whose views on the "social
dimension" are widely shared by the Major government, was—and
is—by no means alone.

Zygmunt Tyszkiewicz is the Brussels-based general secretary of the
powerful Union of Industrial and Employers' Federations in Europe,
or UNICE. Called "Tish" by just about everyone, he is Polish-born, a
British citizen, and has previously worked for international companies throughout Europe, including Shell, the Anglo-Dutch oil giant.
UNICE, which resembles a mixture of the U.S. Chamber of Commerce
and the National Association of Manufacturers, represents tens of
thousands of companies and their federations in every Western European country. But, as Tyszkiewicz has noted, nine-tenths of UNICE's
work consists of "the regular, invisible interchange of ideas between
our experts and those of the Community" in the Commission, the
Parliament, and the Council. UNICE is concerned with every major
subject, including economic, monetary, regulatory, and research is-

sues and external relations, and one that UNICE has fought particularly hard—the EC Commission's proposals for worker representation on company boards.

In his slightly accented English and distinguished, even-keyed manner of speaking, Tish quickly gets emotional when you mention the issue, arguing vehemently that the "social dimension" would only add a new layer of red tape and bureaucracy in Brussels. It would compound company costs, such as shuttling employees and executives to meetings. Even worse, he maintains, it would cripple EC-based companies competing against American and particularly Japanese industries. UNICE and its parent organizations in every EC country have vowed to continue fighting. This was not the first time the issue had come to a boiling point. In the early 1980s, as now, UNICE was leading a coalition, including the influential American Chamber of Commerce, in Belgium, committed to blocking the so-called Vredeling Directive. And they succeeded.

Named after Henk Vredeling, a Dutch Socialist and a former EC commissioner, the plan closely resembled its successor, but with an important difference—it would have made consultations and worker membership on company boards mandatory, not voluntary, and might have provided employees inside looks at worldwide operations, including market strategies, new products, and technologies. A senior official of the European Trade Union Federation, representing national unions in EC member countries, described the lobbying by UNICE and its allies against the proposal as "brutal." Because Britain had—and still has—a veto power over Council of Ministers' decisions affecting social questions, the Vredeling proposal languished and died. "But the basic purpose—a greater role for workers—is very alive," said Laird. "We shall continue our efforts, including through the Labour party" in Britain.

Neil Kinnoch, the Labour Party leader most likely to face Major and conservatives in national elections scheduled to be held prior to June 1992, has already made it clear that, if elected, he will press for wider, greater rights for workers in the New Europe, along the lines the Commission has proposed. Kinnoch, who admires Delors for his audacity and pragmatism, also supports boosting the powers of the European Parliament, since 1989 controlled by Socialists and their left-wing allies. "We want a European Community in which the market works for the advantage of the people, rather than one in which the people are made to serve the convenience of the market," Kinnoch said. He and his advisers have repeatedly stressed that a Labour government would press for the extension of qualified majority voting to social issues in the Council of Ministers; under current procedures, social issues, questions related to taxation, security and foreign policy can only be approved by a unanimous vote in the council.

When Britain's foreign secretary, Douglas Hurd, in May 1991 rejected a Commission proposal to adopt majority voting on social and labor issues, declaring it "foolish," Delors exploded. "I feel like someone who at the start of this century heard people say that the abolition of child labor would cause the general collapse of the economy." Amid predictions by foreign ministers of Italy and Belgium that Britain would wind up isolated, the outlook is for more debate on the issue, but no action—until, of course, a Labour government is returned to power in London.

RACISM, GYPSIES, AND CORSICANS

For the most part, the people we have encountered so far are polite, civilized, who, fundamentally, accept the rules of the game, adhering to democratic, balanced, negotiated rules of conduct. Most of them are middle-class, establishment, "bourgeois," even if they are anti-European in that they oppose certain changes and resist attempts to shape their European economic and social environment. They are, above all, within the law, peaceful, nonviolent. Virtually all of them—Americans, Britons, Continental Europeans, Japanese—could, in an imaginary room, discuss their differences, sharing similar or common cultural values and heritage. They belonged, were "sensible," tolerant, within the law, and fair play counted for something.

But consider the following examples from the deeply disturbing darker, violent, blatantly criminal side of the Community's life.

■ Item: On a spring day in May 1990, a shocked France learned of one of the most appalling acts of anti-Semitism to have taken place in the country since the end of World War II. The night before, vandals had desecrated thirty-four graves, mutilated dead and buried bodies, and smashed marble headstones in a Jewish cemetery at Carpentras, a quiet, charming fourteenth-century town east of Avignon. During the next few days, a rash of similar incidents exploded around the country in what police said were deliberate imitations of the Carpentras attack.

On May 14, responding to the attacks, angry Jewish leaders organized a mass demonstration in Paris that drew eighty thousand demonstrators, including Mitterrand; it was the first time since the 1944 Liberation that a French president had marched in a street demonstration. Four young skinheads were arrested for the vandalism, all members of a neo-Nazi group. They were released. Jean-Marie Le Pen, leader of a far-right-wing party, the National Front, said that the hasty arrests and release amounted to "a macabre stage-managed scene" to discredit him and his followers. Mitterrand said the extreme right Le Pen movement, which was drawing 15–17 percent support in national surveys, exploited "anxieties," reflecting poor housing or homelessness, soulless neighborhoods, low salaries, unemployment, and more recently the upheavals in Eastern Europe and the Soviet Union.

■ Item: In late autumn 1989, at the site of a former concentration camp near Hamburg, Germany, about seventy Gypsies, occupying the camp museum since the start of the year, were expelled by police in an extraordinary move, highlighting a controversial dimension in West Germany's attitude toward East European immigrants. The Gypsies, among fifteen thousand of them living in Hamburg who had migrated from Poland, Romania, and Yugoslavia, were demanding a right to settle in Germany as a stateless people.

When I arrived at the site, I was told that local police had already warned them they would face expulsion, unless they accepted "social" integration, meaning sending their children to Hamburg schools, signing up for social security benefits, and so on. The Gypsies refused. "I am thirty-four, have lived here for thirty-two years, and I am not about to change my lifestyle. I don't have a passport, or a residence card, but I am here. . . . No one wants us, compared to other resident East Europeans who are welcomed," complained Rudko Kawczynski, their spokesman. "That is why we have picked this site to protest," he added, pointing to rows of double-decker wooden bunks, models of the originals, which had served the Neuengamme concentration camp, where 500 Gypsies were exterminated by the Nazis, out of a total 55,000 who perished there.

When I asked what European integration represented for him, Kawczynski said: "For me, and others here, 1992 means being sent back to Poland. We are an embarrassment. The

German people, for many reasons, still fear us. The Single Market, for us, means trouble." As I stood at a bus stop in the chill February sunshine, just outside the camp's stone walls, my eyes fixed on the glistening restored strands of barbed wire surrounding the camp, I asked a passerby in German if he knew the whereabouts of the Gypsies and the museum. He stared at me for half a second, a touch of puzzled annoyance crossing his face. He shrugged, and kept walking. I returned to Hamburg.

■ Item: In the spring of 1990, a Corsican businessman friend who lives near the city of Bastia in northern Corsica, was planning to build a small restaurant-café, which would offer disco-dancing evenings. In his early thirties, from a long-established Corsican family, he was visited at home one evening by several young bearded men whom he knew only slightly. Their message was chillingly simple: forget the café and go into some other form of business. Dancing, discos, and similar "entertainment" facilities were better left to those "qualified" to run them, otherwise, they warned, he might encounter "difficulties." My friend got the message and dropped the project. "We now get nearly a million Italians coming to Corsica, many on the new ferries, and there is new interest in Italian culture, and this is a positive aspect of Europeanization," he said, as we relaxed at a Bastia café overlooking the bustling port. His next project would be a camping site.

"But what happened to me reflected another dangerous side of 1992 here—the Corsican and Italian Mafia moving in, laundering drug money, buying up land and property, and, we fear, with some complicity of the FLNC," a reference to the Corsican National Liberation Front, an outlawed but highly active organization of militant autonomists. Within a year, a wave of violence and killings swept the scenic island, including the shooting of several leading Corsican political figures. My friend was shattered, convinced that any hopes for obtaining financing for his camping site were now doomed.

Following violent attacks on camping sites and bungalows at the end of May 1991, José Rossi, a centrist deputy from Ajaccio, the island's capital, told *Le Figaro* that Corsica was "drifting" toward chaos, and that it would take five to six years before life there returned to "normal."

THE MAFIA ALSO LIKES 1992

These seemingly disconnected incidents contributed an unwelcome chapter to the New Europe's economic and political agenda, comprising the following elements: right-wing, nationalistic xenophobia; the mounting waves of immigrants not only from Eastern Europe but from North Africa; and finally, drives into Europe by organized crime, spearheaded by Sicilian Italian and Latin American drug barons, who foresee profits through laundering illegal funds in the disappearance of controls and trade barriers. Drugs and crime, because of their scope, warrant a closer look for the grave dangers they represent in the New Europe.

The Sicilian Mafia's presence in Europe, dating back to the mid-1860s, is hardly news. But perceptions changed quickly when the highly respected governor of Italy's central bank, Carlo Azeglio Ciampi, in 1989, became the nation's first establishment figure to warn about the new danger of mounting crime in Europe, declaring bluntly that "the Mafia bosses in their dark double-breasted suits are getting ready for 1992. . . . Banking structures and requirements must be unified throughout Europe to prevent the Mafiosi from laundering their money."[8] He and officials from the Italian secret service and customs police disclosed to Italian parliamentary investigators that the recycled funds, because of their origin, posed threats to the banking system, Italy's stock exchange, interest rates, and government bonds as the 1992 program went forward. A year later, Milan police, in a spectacular example, cracked down on a Mafia gang planning to issue bogus European securities.

At about the same time, Prime Minister Andreotti called in the heads of police and specialized anticrime squads from across Italy, and ordered a renewed campaign against the Mafia, partly to avoid unfair accusations from EC partners. Underworld gang wars had left their highest death tolls in nearly a decade, prompting the prime minister to comment: "This is not the Italy that Europe should find in 1993." American diplomats in Rome and Madrid remained skeptical over how much could be accomplished, warning that new underworld economic wealth and power were proliferating not only in Italy but throughout the Common Market, particularly as the 1992 program went forward.

CENIS, the Italian Center for Social Research in Rome, has estimated that recycled Mafia-generated money flowing into the Milan stock exchange now totals around $15 billion annually, a staggering 15 percent of the daily turnover of Italy's largest exchange. Additional untraceable funds of equally large magnitude are being funneled into other West European financial centers, most likely in Geneva, Zürich, Vienna, Paris, Amsterdam, and London, researchers said.

Thus, the case cited by my Corsican friend was perhaps small, yet it illustrates how unsavory local and Mafia racketeering can exploit existing rivalries and tensions. As a result, many genuine investments for building up Corsica's vast potential for tourism and agriculture have been placed in danger. Banks, French and foreign, were simply scared off, waiting skeptically for the calm to return. Some of my oldest Corsican friends said in early 1991 that, for the first time in their lives, they were considering leaving the island, fearful of the violence and that the Mafia would wind up controlling large segments of the local economy, particularly hotels, restaurants, golf courses, and leisure boating facilities.

Estimates vary greatly, but some experts cite figures showing that the annual take of the Mafia in Italy in 1990 had swelled to about $75 billion, equal to about 12 percent of Italy's GNP. And the revenues were rising dramatically because of expanded—and, of course, illegal—drug business growing throughout Western Europe and being extended into Eastern Europe. Drug users in Poland alone have been estimated at about 200,000. European police explain that because of heavily saturated markets and crackdowns in the United States and Latin America, drug operations began moving into the Community on a large scale around 1988. Two years later, cocaine was selling at five to six times the street price in the United States, and climbing. According to knowledgeable friends in Budapest, a heroin hit cost $90 in Hungary, a cocaine fix cost about $150. Cocaine, which in 1990 sold for around $11,000 a kilo in New York City, went for $50,000 in Turin, Rome, and Milan.

Although Western Europe, including Britain, has traditionally been a larger consumer of heroin and hashish, primarily shipped from Southwest Asia and the Middle East, Interpol, the Lyon-based international police agency, reported that cocaine trafficking had made the Community not only a major consumer of all hard drugs, but a center of production, transshipments, and money laundering— and not only in Italy. Testimony by a U.S. State Department official to a House of Representatives narcotics-control task force, described illegal drug operations flourishing in Belgium, France, Germany, Greece, Italy, the Netherlands, Portugal, Spain, and Britain, but she quickly added: "No assessment can be made of supply and demand without taking into account not only increased European consumption of heroin and cocaine, but also recognizing the strong drug control programs in many European countries."[9]

Yet, despite increased, occasionally spectacular drug seizures, tightened controls at borders and banks, coordination by European institutions, such as the Strasbourg-based Council of Europe, and law-enforcement agencies, an estimated 80 percent of the drugs shipped to EC countries have been getting through, and are being consumed. Claire Stirling, in her superb book on the Mafia, *Octopus*, published in 1990, showed that police seizures of heroin were seven times as high in Western Europe as in the United States.

Western intelligence analysts reported that in 1984, a year before the 1992 program was launched, Western Europe consumed about 10 percent of the cocaine smuggled from Latin America. By the middle of 1991, the proportion of shipments had risen to well over 40 percent, and was growing steadily.

In an effort to cope with the influx of illegal drugs, the European Community in mid-1991 began establishing a European Central Drug Intelligence Unit to exchange information and coordinate training programs for narcotics agents operating in Eastern and Western Europe. But there was wide agreement that Europe lacked the means to cope effectively and would remain vulnerable. *Newsweek*, in a 1990 report, noted that the Hungarian police had only four drug-sniffing dogs available for controls at its borders.

ESTABLISHING A EUROPEAN FBI

Since 1988, EC officials and government leaders of member countries have repeatedly discussed the possibility of establishing a law-enforcement body similar to the U.S. Federal Bureau of Investigation, a European FBI. Chancellor Kohl, who first floated the idea, backed by Prime Minister González, sought establishment of a specialized multilingual and multinational force to prevent not only drug dealers but other criminals, terrorists, and illegal immigrants from taking advantage of a borderless Europe. The basic idea was to shift some controls away from the EC member states' internal police to a new, supranational agency, an approach repeatedly rejected by Britain on the grounds that it would dilute and hamper law enforcement.

Kohl and Mitterrand, in a joint proposal to the December 1990 EC summit meeting, suggested establishment of a council of EC justice and interior ministers to deal with the worsening problem of drugs and other crimes, immigration, and the issue of asylum rights. But Major balked, as Mrs. Thatcher before him had, suggesting efforts already underway should be pursued; consequently, the French-German initiative was shelved.

A major breakthrough had already been achieved in mid-1990 with a 142-article treaty signed by five of the twelve EC members: France, Belgium, the Netherlands, Luxembourg, and West Germany. It is known as the Schengen agreement, for the quaint sixteenth-century Luxembourg village where the signing took place and where in 1985 the first draft agreement on border controls was hammered out. The five governments agreed that their police forces would cooperate more closely than ever before; that a computerized central data bank would be established in Strasbourg; that laws and regulations governing visas, extradition, and "hot pursuit" of suspects by police across borders would be harmonized and tightened.

In a move that triggered immediate outrage and controversy, a list was drawn up of 114 countries in Asia, Africa, the Middle East, and Latin America, whose nationals would henceforth require visas to enter "Schengenland." Signatories described it as a "laboratory" for the Community; a senior German official said the plan represented "a big step in the direction of a united Europe . . . our attempt to hit back at the criminal anti-Europeans."

Not everyone agreed. Some human-rights groups and leftist political parties denounced the agreement as "a fortress." A Dutch Socialist declared: "Schengen is fantastic if you're white and if you have a fresh haircut and a well-filled wallet,"[10] referring to the widely held view among leftist groups that the agreements were designed mainly for controlling immigration.

Were these latter groups, among others, being anti-European? Consider the following:

- The problems with the extradition provisions had less to do with the ability of negotiators to hammer out agreements than with incompatible police and legal procedures, vigorously defended by government officials in member countries and even civil rights groups. In cases of suspects or criminals crossing borders, an agreement was reached by the Schengen signatories that allow police to pursue and arrest as far as ten kilometers within a neighboring country—except in France; there, foreign police were allowed to pursue but not arrest suspects. Civil rights groups in Holland and Germany challenged the setting up of a data bank as an unacceptable invasion of privacy.

Meantime, fears were repeatedly expressed by unions representing tens of thousands of officials whose jobs were threatened. They were identified by the Royal Institute of International Affairs as customs officials, immigration officers, and police employed on border-control duties throughout the Community. Many, like Jean-Jacques, the frontier policeman we met on the TEE train in Chapter 1, would be transferred to the Community's external borders; others would take early retirement.

■ Italy, Spain, and Portugal joined later in 1991, but Denmark, which also planned to join, feared jeopardizing its long-established travel-free zone with its Nordic neighbors—Norway, Sweden, Iceland, and Finland. Spain was attacked by Latin American countries for having established controls and insisting that visitors from former colonies in the Western Hemisphere arrive with two-way, prepaid airline tickets. Meantime, although none of the governments would say so publicly, Spain, Portugal, and Greece had been kept at arm's length by the original five Schengen signatories because their borders were considered "porous" and "vulnerable" on the EC's southern flank, largely because their coastlines were poorly patrolled. But that hardly explained the underlying fear of EC governments and Brussels authorities—uncontrolled immigration.

REVERSING THE AMERICAN DREAM

Who earlier in this century imagined, much less predicted, the very substantial wave of foreigners—many of them affluent—seeking refuge in Western Europe?

Most of us grew up with the idea that the Europeans went West, and indeed they did—forty-five million in the nineteenth century alone, settling mainly in the United States and Latin America. In the mid-1960s, as migration toward the Americas slowed and the EC economies boomed, workers from throughout the Mediterranean area, Africa, the Caribbean region, and Asia began pouring into EC member countries, often performing the menial and poorly paid jobs. The collapse of communism, starting in late 1989, added to the flow, mainly from East Germany, with the result that by 1991 the Community counted about 8.2 million immigrants, not counting at least 4 million without valid papers, nor 400,000, such as ethnic Germans, who emigrated from the Soviet Union.

France had the highest proportion of legally registered immigrants among EC member countries; (6.5 percent of the total population), followed by West Germany (5.3 percent), Britain (4 percent), Holland (3.6 percent), Belgium (3.4 percent), Luxembourg (3 percent), Denmark (2 percent), Italy (1 percent), Portugal (0.6 percent), Ireland (0.5 percent), Spain (0.3 percent), and Greece (0.3 percent). But these numbers are, in reality, much higher when illegal immigrants are counted—more than an estimated 2 million in France alone, mainly from French-speaking Africa. No one has reliable statistics. But the trends are clear, as are the threats and warnings from right-wing groups throughout Eastern and Western Europe clamoring for controls on the newcomers, particularly as the Community braced for new waves of demands for visas from North African countries whose citizens sought escape from the wake of a resurgence of Islamic fundamentalism and worsening poverty.

EC Commission, United Nations, and World Bank reports agree that, in the years ahead, population growth in the region will far exceed economic expansion, meaning that standards of living in North Africa will continue to fall, greatly increasing pressures for migration. EC and UN studies show that the population of only three neighboring North African countries—Algeria, Morocco, and Tunisia—will rise from their total 1989 level of around 58 million people to around 108 million by the year 2025.

In Spain, for example, immigration officials were fearful that Morocco, just fifteen miles across the Straits of Gibraltar, was fast becoming to Spain what Mexico had become to the United States. In neighboring Algeria, Western diplomats were declaring that the country already is the "Mexico of the Mediterranean," citing the teeming, poverty-stricken rural areas and its overpopulated cities.

Meantime, as an abundant number of reports from demographers have demonstrated, Europe will need new, younger blood as its birthrates fall, life expectancy grows, and its populations rapidly aged.

One study, published by the International Institute for Applied Systems Analysis in Austria, showed that, by the year 2050, the number of Europeans over the age of sixty will comprise nearly half of the continent's total population.

Aside from moves to restrict immigration temporarily, fueled by growing impatience, hostility and violence, few EC governments had an answer to the prospects of coping with the emerging waves of North Africans, Soviets and East Europeans—possibly one million per year—who would be seeking refuge and jobs in the New Europe throughout the 1990s as their economies failed and as Moscow continued cracking down on independence movements in Soviet republics, such as the Ukraine and the Baltic states.

Most EC member governments were moving to establish strict quotas to limit the flows, while gradually cutting back on granting entry visas. Shrill, harsh answers were also being voiced in some quarters, notably by the New Europe's extreme right-wing groups, which, although they were out of line with what the majority of Europeans seemed to want, threatened the Community's peaceful, democratic efforts to build unity and prosperity through reforms.

One of the best examples is Jean-Marie Le Pen, a burly fair-haired former paratroop officer, who served in Indochina, Egypt, and Algeria. He is a trained lawyer and a politician, with seats in both the National Assembly in France and the European Parliament in Strasbourg. Two weeks before an election in France in 1988, his former wife, Pierrette, accused him in two magazine interviews of being anti-Semitic and said that his anti-immigration stance stemmed from his racial sentiments. Le Pen, who brushed off the allegations as "fantasies," has repeatedly asserted in public that immigration from developing countries presents France a "source of criminality, aggravates unemployment, and brings national identity into question. . . . We want a policy of return for immigrants."[11]

President of the National Front, which he founded in 1979, Le Pen was conspicuously absent from the Paris protest march following the Carpentras cemetery incident. Many of the demonstrators, despite his vehement protests, charged that Le Pen was at least indirectly responsible for the desecration, and had certainly contributed to the anti-Jewish and racist sentiment in France. Some recalled how in a 1987 radio interview he described the gas chambers in Nazi concentration camps as "a mere detail in the history of the Second World War," which triggered widespread outrage. In May 1990 he was ordered by a civil court to pay one franc in damages to groups who sued him over the statement; the one franc reflected the court's feeling that the complaint was justified but its inability to evaluate the damage.

Le Pen's popularity—and he has regularly scored between 15 and 17 percent in national polls—is largely based on anxieties in France about immigration from North Africa, fueled by unemployment and his flair for appealing to France's deep sense of nationalism. Right-wing movements are flourishing in Italy, Belgium, and Germany, whose leaders have regularly won seats in the European Parliament. Le Pen and Germany's Schoenhuber formed a loose alliance in the Parliament, and they have cooperated in trying to build links to right-wing groups in cities throughout East Germany. The chances are slight that these groups will ever become powerful, but their ideas about the future of Europe—violently critical—appeal to many people and weaken support for European unity. Le Pen, if ever he were to become more powerful in France, would certainly be tough on immigrants and expect his EC partners to follow suit. He has always emphasized that he favors a Europe of nations, in which independence and sovereignty matter the most, and that he firmly opposes the establishment of a "superpower" in Brussels, operated by what he described as "an irresponsible bureaucracy."

CONCLUDING

Clearly Japan remains determined to target and dominate West European markets in key strategic as well as mature industrial sectors throughout the 1990s. Japan will also, it appeared, continue receiving encouragement and financing from individual EC member states, and possibly the Commission, because Japan is also creating jobs and prosperity in the New Europe.

Consequently, the European Community appears destined to remain plagued by a dilemma—how to be both global and "European" at the same time. That paradoxical situation will be accompanied by new pressures for reform and protectionism because, as many observers believe, Japan is Europe's greatest economic and industrial challenger and danger.

But intense U.S. government pressures for trade liberalization and, from within, by the EC Commission, are succeeding in weakening some of the protectionist forces. As we shall see in Chapter 9, a new, revived transatlantic partnership with Washington, despite strains, and skirmishing over Airbus and farm subsidies, is also emerging.

In contrast, state-controlled sectors of business, banking, and industry are strong, determined to resist change, as is the Community's heavily subsidized, relatively small, but highly influential farm sector. In other words, the struggle for a more open, deregulated EC economy will be slow and difficult and continue to be internationally controversial.

Meantime, a "social dimension" to Europe's new growth also faces an uphill struggle, unless unions and left-wing governments intensify their pressures on policy-makers in their national capitals and in Brussels. It is an open question just how determined they will prove themselves in a showdown.

Crime and drug use are spreading, yet increased enforcement coordination at the Community level may provide an effective counterweight to groups like the Mafia. This assumes, however, that governments toughen their collective stance, and EC institutions are granted more powers; this, too, has been happening, but slowly.

Finally, right-wing groups will retain a minority, and influential position, in the Community's political life, but will not, it seems, ever again obtain a significant political role. Le Pen, for example, in some ways sounds like the EC figure he said he admired most—Mrs. Thatcher. But did their views really coincide? It is time to turn to the political life and institutions of the New Europe, to examine how they evolved into their contemporary form and in what direction they are heading.

The Dream of Political Federalism: Dissipating Mrs. Thatcher's Nightmare

> We have reached a major milestone on the way to one of the great dreams of our century—political union on a federal basis.
>
> —HELMUT KOHL

We had been waiting half an hour for Chancellor Kohl in a movie house in downtown Rome, temporarily converted for his wrap-up news conference. In the nearby seventeenth-century gilded Montecitorio Palace, Kohl and eleven other heads of EC member governments were still putting finishing touches on a twenty-four-page document. Their goal: attaining one of Europe's most cherished and illusive goals—transforming the Community into a federated group of states, sharing greatly reinforced economic and political powers. As Kohl, surrounded by aides, swept into the hall, complained about the blinding television lights, and looked out at gathered newsmen from behind a table, he seemed delighted with the results of the two-day summit meeting of EC leaders that had just ended. It was December 15, 1990.

"Not every meeting of this kind can be described as historic," Kohl began exuberantly, "but this one has taken us to a decisive phase . . . the ideas of President Mitterrand and myself were positively taken up here." He went on to emphasize that "the best dream of this century" was in the process of being realized; it would, once and for all, place much of Europe's economic, monetary, and key political decision-making under a unified, federalized political system, probably sometime in 1993. Meantime, in another building nearby, Mitterrand, calm and relaxed, told French newsmen that, as a result of the summit meeting, the Community's "very nature" would be changed, while downstairs, in the same building, a tense Delors praised the agreement for setting Europe's "rendezvous with history."

However, not every leader attending the summit meeting, notably Britain's new prime minister John Major, wanted Europe's future federal system defined—certainly not yet. But all twelve EC member countries, for the first time since the signing of the Rome Treaty, had taken a momentous, irreversible step: they had ordered the immediate start of two intergovernmental conferences attended by every member country. Their mandate: to complete negotiations on establishing the Community's political union, as well as economic and monetary union, so that the two agreements being hammered out in parallel would be ready for ratification by every EC national parliament by December 31, 1992, thus coinciding with the completion of the Community's plan for its Single Market.

CHARTING A NEW COURSE

The follow-up negotiations, which began immediately in Rome, and continued nonstop in Brussels throughout most of 1991, amid obstacles and complex difficulties, were aimed at drafting amendments to the 1957 Rome Treaty. When completed and ratified, they would significantly reinforce the political powers of the Community's three institutions, particularly the Council, but also of the Commission and to a lesser degree of the European Parliament. We shall return to these bodies shortly. The negotiations also edged the Community toward establishing its first common, unified economic and monetary system, including a European Central Bank and a single currency, which we have already examined in Chapter 6.

Were these conference negotiations, as some euphoric observers believed, Europe's modern equivalent of America's Philadelphia Federal Constitutional Convention, which in 1787 drafted the U.S. Constitution? Or was this like the 1815 Congress of Vienna, reorganizing Europe after Napoleon's defeat? Some visionary delegates compared the Rome meeting to the Congress of Europe held in the Hague in 1948, the first postwar attempt to unite Europe, which was chaired by Winston Churchill and recommended establishment of a European Assembly, a loose grouping of existing European parliaments.

One of Kohl's closest advisers on Europe in the chancellery, Joachim Bitterlich, made the best comparison with an earlier historic gathering—the meeting in early June 1955 of six EC foreign ministers in the Sicilian port town of Messina. That meeting, for the first time, called not only for the "establishment of a united Europe" but for adoption of a blueprint for a Common Market, inspired directly by Monnet's ideas and his intense behind-the-scenes lobbying. As a result of the Messina meeting, the six participating governments—France, Germany, Italy, the Netherlands, Belgium, and Luxembourg—ordered the start-up of the marathon negotiations that led to the signing of the Rome Treaty two years later.

Most historians, like Bitterlich, have concluded that the Rome Treaty is the Community's rough equivalent of the American Constitution, for it vastly expanded the 1951 treaty establishing the Common Market's fledgling organization, the European Coal and Steel Community. As we have already seen in Chapter 2, it sketched Europe's first embryo federal system of government, including executive, legislative, and judicial branches.

But as Mitterrand, among others, has noted, without Messina there would never have been a Treaty of Rome and, therefore, no Community in its contemporary form. It was one of those coincidences of history that the ceremonies for the Rome Treaty signing took place in the city hall, a short walk from the Montecitorio Palace. The date: March 25, 1957.

WHY REVISE THE ROME TREATY?

The basic assumptions underlying the proposed Rome Treaty amendments were related: First, that sovereign nation states acting on their own would never be strong enough to guarantee Europe's stability and security, and that reliance on the nation state would, ultimately, encourage nationalistic, protectionist forces, which had so tragically marked Europe's history in two preceding centuries. Mitterrand, a fierce partisan of this idea, is fond of recalling that he was a delegate to the Hague Congress, which failed to unite Europe amid worsening East-West tensions and the gripping effects of the Cold War, highlighted by the spectacular U.S.-led allied airlift to West Berlin. He frequently refers to the 1948 conference, when speaking of his vision for a united Europe, as a tragic missed opportunity.

The second assumption is that Europe's economies, too, will be strong only if their vast, disparate human, technological, and research resources are more closely integrated, and used collectively wherever possible. We have seen in previous chapters how European political and business leaders, since the mid-1980s, made enormous, dramatic strides in causing Europe's economic revival, allowing them to challenge successfully the United States and Japan in a wide range of sectors by following this cooperative approach.

At the time of the EC Rome summit meeting, business leader Wisse Dekker told a group of students from Leyden University that he firmly believed Europe was at last embarking on a "new, difficult path" to political union, following the completion of the 1992 program. "This last phase . . . will be difficult, with many obstacles, but an important start has been made, and we welcome it," Dekker said, summing up the opinion of most European multinational companies, many of whose leaders agreed with him that, for the first time, political union and economic, social, and monetary union have become inextricably linked.

Thus in Rome, beginning on the evening of December 13, 1990, as delegates arrived for a gala performance of Puccini's opera *Tosca*, opening the summit, a crucial, indispensable start had been made in bridging what Delors had described as Europe's economic "renaissance" and a unique form of European federal government. As the summit ended on Saturday afternoon, December 15, ending six months of hectic, nonstop preparations, led by Italy's Prime Minister Andreotti and Foreign Minister De Michelis, every delegate had expressed satisfaction at the outcome as a clearer picture emerged of what the new political Europe probably will look like in the early 1990s:

- A new governmental system in which members are increasingly sharing political sovereignty and responsibilities—in those areas they feel are best handled jointly, on a shared, agreed-upon basis. Member governments will have not surrendered power or sovereignty to a nonelected bureaucratic body as some leaders feared. The new system, in other words, will not have evolved into a supranational body, or superstate, run by the EC Commission as Mrs. Thatcher warned. Rather than resembling the United States, as many visionaries of federalism had hoped, the new political Europe more closely resembles Canada, Switzerland, Belgium, and other loosely federated states, comprising a new edifice called the European Union.

- A more powerful set of EC institutions. The Community will have reinforced powers. However, the main decision-making body, or as EC leaders in Rome concluded "the one" center of power will be the European Council—heads of member governments who have been elected in their home countries. Its role will be increased, so that it will be empowered to unify and direct the Community's approach to foreign policy and military-defense matters; it will be granted its own secretariat. The Commission also will emerge stronger, with new rights to initiate policy proposals in foreign policy and security matters, but shared with, and under the direction of, the Council. The European Parliament will also be playing a far more active role in the streamlined process, but not with greatly increased powers. A European citizenship will be established.

- France and Germany, the so-called "alliance within the Alliance," having jointly launched the movement toward political union in the spring of 1990, will continue to shape its direction. French leaders, determined to bring Germany into monetary union, and an assertive Bonn, determined to bring France into political union, will jointly continue providing the momentum for the Community's drive for cohesion. This alliance vividly recalls that of Adenauer and de Gaulle three decades earlier. But this time Bonn and Paris will not be dominating everything. Smaller countries, such as Italy, the Netherlands, Belgium, and Spain, fearful of a "triumvirate" of France, Germany, and Britain, have won acceptance for greater use of majority voting in the Council.

- Finally, foreign governments will find the new, reinforced powers of the Community a source of friction and deep concern, particularly in Washington and Tokyo. Dealing with the Community over issues in the Middle East, Latin America, and particularly in Eastern Europe and the Soviet republics will become more difficult as the powers of the Community are extended and as it increasingly speaks with a single, more autonomous voice, backed by stronger institutions commanding wider popular support in every member country. The addition of several new members will further reinforce the Community's world role.

Fanciful projections?

Several moments after reading the final communiqué in the crowded, noisy Rome press center, I asked a senior American diplomat how he thought Washington would react, particularly in light of the heated exchanges between Brussels and Washington over their differing approaches to the GATT-sponsored trade negotiations. "The Europeans, once again, have us off balance, and it is very, very scary," the diplomat, a seasoned European expert, told me. "Because they are moving much faster than we had ever imagined—in trade, and now into political decision-making, with implications for NATO, the future defense of Europe, and so on. Reacting to this moving target called Europe is painful, difficult, perplexing and, yes, you could say they are scaring the pants off of us." Clearly, as on past occasions, the Community was capturing the world's attention.

THE PREDICTION THAT CAUSED AN UPROAR

Another media event related to the Community's political future was triggered by a single phrase uttered by Delors while briefing the European Parliament on a warm July 6, 1988, in Strasbourg. Only a week earlier, EC leaders at their summit meeting in Hannover, Germany, had moved forward on drafting plans for economic and monetary union, which Delors had correctly surmised would eventually confront EC politicians with a disquieting prospect—loss of their national sovereignty. Few observers, including diplomats, paid more than passing attention.

The phrase uttered by Delors, well in the middle of the speech, said the following: "In ten years' time, 80 percent of economic legislation and perhaps social and tax legislation will be of Community origin."

The five hundred deputies gathered in the modern spacious hall vigorously applauded the message as a promise of new legislative powers. After all, many members had for months been urging that the Parliament should be given a far wider role in shaping EC legislation. Most European leaders thought, however, that Delors was deliberately exaggerating how far the Community's powers might actually be extended within a decade. Some agreed with his basic message—namely, that traditionally national powers were gradually shifting to Community institutions. The EC has a long way to go before accounting for 80 percent of all key economic and social legislation, but it has been moving in that direction. Only one major leader thought differently and said so: Mrs. Thatcher.

Two weeks later, commenting on a BBC radio show, clearly irritated, she snapped that when it came to speaking about the Community's political future Delors had gone "over the top," and that his ideas about shifts in future decision-making in the Community were "airy fairy" and "absurd." The fifty-minute interview was but an opening round in a series of attacks that would earn her epithets from hostile critics ranging from "Britain's de Gaulle" to "Elephant in the China Shop of Europe." But she had correctly sensed what was happening—European Community legislative powers had indeed been growing since the 1992 program had begun. And it was encroaching on national parliaments and governments, owing largely to the fact that many decisions relating to deregulation, harmonization, and other aspects of the plan had been taken on the basis of qualified majority voting for well over a year.

Delors, therefore, had touched a live nerve, deliberately exposing a trend she was determined to halt, certainly to shape, in keeping with her strong views regarding the need to defend Britain's vital, sovereign interests at home and abroad. Just under two years later, facing a revolt within her Conservative party, Mrs. Thatcher resigned as prime minister, stunning her friends and colleagues, including her forty-seven-year-old chancellor of the Exchequer, who would succeed her: John Major. He and Douglas Hurd, who remained in his post as foreign secretary, had persuaded her to take Britain into the Community's Exchange Rate Mechanism and they came to the Rome summit with a decidedly conciliatory, friendlier approach to EC union.

But Major also emphasized in Rome that it was his government's style and tone that may have changed from his predecessor's approach and that Britain would be submitting its own reform plans for the Community, which immediately triggered an angry outburst from Delors. Reflecting his deep, traditionally French suspicion of Britain's approach to monetary union, a European central bank, and a single currency, he told newsmen that if Britain accepts the final goal of a single currency and a single central bank, "then we can work as twelve. But if they divert us . . . then the answer is no . . . and if we have to provoke a political crisis, then so be it."

Major replied that compromises were inevitable, comparing the mandate for the two intergovernmental conferences to a menu. "Our favorite dishes are on that menu, and so are the favorite dishes of others, and the Community has not yet determined what orders to place." Throughout most of 1991, British officials and conservative members of the British Parliament made it clear they would continue to defend energetically many of Mrs. Thatcher's basic ideas about Europe and, they recalled, Britain could, and might, cast its veto over the treaty amendments under negotiation.

SPEAKING IN BRUGES

Mrs. Thatcher's most basic, eloquent approach to the Community—reflecting her skepticism and hostility—erupted in a speech to the College of Europe in the seventeenth-century, canal-lined Belgian town of Bruges. It was September 20, 1988.

She stepped up to the rostrum, determined to stake out her ground in what was to become a long, complex, embittered debate over what form the Community's future political structures would take. Above all, she was determined to defend nationhood and British institutions, which she considered endangered—and which, she said, included the British monarchy, along with five other kings and queens still on thrones in other EC member states. She was also confident that her political situation at home could not have been stronger. It was still more than a year until her supporters began to complain openly about her hostility to Europe and until her Chancellor of the Exchequer, Nigel Lawson, who disagreed with her approach to EC monetary union, resigned.

Only two months before her Bruges speech, in a move that left even many of her supporters stunned and disappointed, she had refused to reappoint Lord Cockfield, "Mr. 1992," to a second term as Britain's senior British EC commissioner. She explained that

Europe's future was to be found in fewer regulations and power centers, not more. It was clear whom she was aiming at, for Delors, in the meantime, was already beginning to propose what he termed "balanced" expansion of EC powers, fearful that the 1992 Single Market program was becoming little else than a deregulatory, supply-side industrial recovery program for business. He had already irritated her greatly with his much-applauded call for a "social dimension" in the Community's evolution toward unity at the TUC Congress in Bournemouth, England, several weeks earlier. And so it seemed an ideal moment for her to assert her views about Europe—in public.

The speech began by outlining Britain's historic ties to the rest of Europe, dating back to "our ancestors," the Celts, Saxons, Danes, and the Romans, who, she said, reflected "our common experience."[1] But over the centuries Britain has fought to "prevent Europe from falling under the dominance of a single power. We have fought and we have died for her freedom," she said, recalling Britain's involvement in this century's two world wars and its military commitment to Europe during the postwar era. Gradually, she warmed up to the main thrust of her speech.

"Britain does not dream of some cozy, isolated existence on the fringes of the European Community . . . the Community is not an end in itself." The first, guiding principle for building a successful Community, Mrs. Thatcher declared, was "willing and active cooperation between independent, sovereign states." She then dropped her bombshell: "Europe will be stronger precisely because it has France as France, Spain as Spain, Britain as Britain, each with its own customs, traditions, and identity. It would be folly to try to fit them into some sort of 'identikit' European personality." Here was a clear, unequivocal call for national independence and the primacy of the nation state over federalism—in any form—and a commitment to fight for it.

Continuing as a cool, tense atmosphere began settling over the hall, she reaffirmed her commitment to European efforts to promote global cooperation in trade, defense, and foreign policy, and quickly zeroed in on her target, recalling nearly a decade of Thatcherism in Britain. "We have not successfully rolled back the frontiers of the state in Britain only to see them reimposed at a European level with a European superstate, exercising a new dominance from Brussels." Her target was clearly the Commission, which she described as "an appointed bureaucracy" and Delors, whom she did not name. Definitely not needed, she emphasized, was the extension of Community powers by treaty revisions and new conferences, such as those that began in December 1990 following the Rome summit meeting.

Regarding monetary issues, she continued, "the key issue is not whether there should be a European Central Bank," but rather the acceleration of the free movement of capital and the deregulation of markets, while protectionism is scaled back. Indeed, encouraging enterprise to compete more effectively within the Community and in world markets should remain the EC's predominant goal, as defined in the 1992 program. There was no reason, either, to abolish frontier controls if, as she declared, "we are also to protect our citizens from crime and stop the movement of drugs, of terrorists and illegal immigrants."

As for Delors's call for enhanced, harmonized rules for workers and a greater role in corporate decision-making, she adamantly warned: "We certainly do not need new regulations, which raise the cost of employment and make Europe's labor market less flexible and less competitive with overseas suppliers." Here was the answer to Delors's proposed strengthening of workers' role in the business life of the Community, which was already being vociferously opposed by business groups, such as UNICE, as we saw in Chapter 7.

In conclusion, she returned to her main message, urging that Europe "be a family of nations, understanding each other better . . . but relishing our national identity no less than our common European endeavor." The *Sunday Times* of London summed up her speech with a blunt headline: "Non! to the Nightmare."

In the uproar and heated debate that followed, it became clear that in simple, direct, eloquent terms she had posed—and partly answered—a central question: should EC institutions be strengthened, and if so, how? She was the first major EC leader to oppose aggressively any significant enlargement of the powers of the Commission, her *bête noire*. The prospect of a more powerful European Council bothered her less; she felt more comfortable with the Council, because it was composed of elected officials like herself, and was, therefore, democratic. She did not mention the European Court of Justice or the Parliament, but it certainly looked at the time as if she and her successor would resist increasing their powers in a substantial way.

Finally, in a related vein, she had raised an even more fundamental question, which was still on the table as EC leaders, including her successor, met for their Rome summit gathering: what would be the future relations between these institutions, their national governments and parliaments? And if they were streamlined, or changed, for what purpose? Certainly not, her colleagues in the Conservative Party agreed, to build a "Socialist Europe." So what had she accomplished at Bruges, she was asked later. "Making people think," she said.

Delors said he had a similar thought in mind when he made his equally famous "80 percent speech" predicting the shift of political power to Community institutions. "It was a provocation, a deliberate attempt to get leaders to think about the process we were getting involved in . . . the percentage figure [which drew considerable media attention] was not important, but the process, and that was my point."[2] Delors made it perfectly clear that he hoped the Commission would evolve into a stronger, executive branch of the Brussels machinery, with broader powers to initiate and implement legislation, along with a greater say in the Community's conduct of foreign policy, and defense matters.

Before continuing, let us, briefly, examine the institutions, where they are and how they operate.

THE EXECUTIVE BRANCH

The chart on page 253 shows how the three main EC bodies—the Commission, the Council, and the Parliament—now arrive at decisions. The European Court of Justice, a fourth important institution, which we will not discuss in this chapter, rules on the interpretation and application of Community laws. Based in Luxembourg, it has thirteen judges, appointed for six years by agreement among EC member governments; the judges have created a body of EC law, on which they can—and regularly do—override decisions of national courts. But the starting point for legislative action, and the "guardian" of the Community's basic laws, is the Commission, based in the condemned star-shaped Berlaymont and headed, temporarily, to other buildings on or near Schuman Square in Brussels until a new headquarters is built.

Every Wednesday morning at around 9:30, a group of about twenty men and women have filed into their thirteenth-floor conference room in the Berlaymont, greeted one another, and settled around a spacious, wood table, and brought to order by their president, Delors. Thus begins a typical Wednesday in the weekly life of the EC Commission, composed of seventeen men and women, whose main responsibility is proposing Community policy and legislation. They are also responsible for implementing decisions taken by the Council and running the Community on a day-to-day basis. This is the Community's combination of an appointed civil service and a U.S.-style executive branch, yet lacking full decision-making powers, which belong to the Council, comprising EC member governments.

Here, too, is the organization Mrs. Thatcher scathingly denounced as the "appointed bureaucracy," her "nightmare." But she is by no means alone in questioning the role of the Commission, which has been described by other EC leaders as "an embryo government" and as "Delors's European superstate." Both Kohl and Mitterrand, among others, have been reluctant to give the organization sweeping additional powers.

"The charisma of Delors, his power and talent, overshadows, hides, and covers the weaknesses of the Commission as an institution," an Élysée Palace adviser said, explaining the president's personal assessment. "In fact, the President [Mitterrand] is not at all comfortable with the Commission in its present form, and, we might add, some of its members. . . . There are ways in which the body acts, independently, which disturbs us." The French leader had touched on the very essence of the Commission's unique mission—maintaining relative independence of national governments.

TAKING A SOLEMN VOW

The seventeen commissioners, including Delors as we saw in Chapter 1, are nominated by their governments and appointed by the Council of Ministers to four-year terms; the president and five vice presidents are chosen nominally for two years, but these terms are almost always extended to cover the full term. Once they are appointed, a solemn swearing-in ceremony takes place in the modern headquarters building of the European Court, located on the rolling hills of the Plateau de Kirchberg in Luxembourg. It is there that a unique oath is administered to every incoming commissioner.

Depicted in a 1987 novel, *The Commissioner*, by Stanley Johnson, a British writer, the oath is taken by every incoming commissioner, who promises to act "in complete independence and in the general interest of the Communities."[3] Appearing separately before the Court president, the incoming commissioners solemnly swear to refuse to accept, or solicit, instructions from any government or outside body, and to refrain from trying to influence other members. Johnson, a longtime insider, who has served as a member of the European Parliament and adviser to the Commission, describes what many of us have seen and heard about commissioners once they have taken the oath—namely, the oath is painfully difficult to carry out in practice.

Driving back to Brussels from Luxembourg, the ambitious and sophisticated American wife of James Morton, an incoming British commissioner and the main character in Johnson's book, thought to herself, after hearing the oath, that it sounded like "trite formulae, part of the rigmarole which Europeans always seemed to think were so important. But for Morton, they appeared to matter . . . whatever others might think of his Brussels assignment, it was clear Morton was going to give it a go." Morton goes on to become a highly successful, controversial commissioner in what Roy Jenkins and others have described as a highly readable and accurate account of life on the Commission. What it lacks, understandably, is detailed description of the day-to-day, often dreary routine of those once described in a superb *Financial Times* headline as "The Faceless Men Shaping Europe's Destiny."

These are the 12,000 permanent, full-time employees of the Commission, comprising a bureaucracy that, like the commissioners for whom they work, and like their counterparts in most Western governments, attract most of the lobbying attention. Within their senior ranks, numbering several thousand, are the "Eurocrats," the professional, experienced officials from the Community's member countries grouped into twenty-three directorate generals, or divisions, each responsible for separate areas. Thus, for example, DG 1 is in charge of external relations, DG 3 of the internal market, DG 4 of competition, DG 6 of agriculture, DG 12 of science and R&D, DG 15 of financial institutions, DG 17 of energy, and so on, roughly comparable to ministerial or cabinet posts in Western-style governments. Like the commissioners, they, too, are committed to the Community's ideals and goals, and so conflicts with national or corporate interests can—and do—arise all the time. Because in many key areas, such as competition policy, the Commission has real power and uses it.

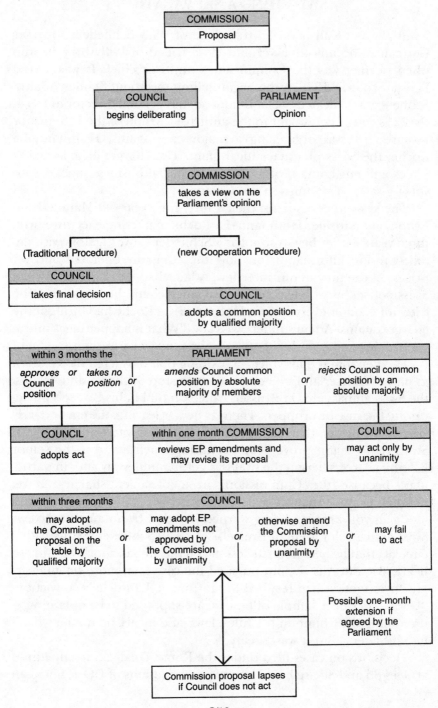

COMMISSION
Proposal

COUNCIL	PARLIAMENT
begins deliberating	Opinion

COMMISSION
takes a view on the Parliament's opinion

(Traditional Procedure)   (new Cooperation Procedure)

COUNCIL	COUNCIL
takes final decision	adopts a common position by qualified majority

within 3 months the	PARLIAMENT	
approves or *takes no* Council *position* or position	*amends* Council common position by absolute majority of members	or *rejects* Council common position by an absolute majority

COUNCIL	within one month COMMISSION	COUNCIL
adopts act	reviews EP amendments and may revise its proposal	may act only by unanimity

within three months	COUNCIL		
may adopt the Commission proposal on the table by qualified majority	or may adopt EP amendments not approved by the Commission by unanimity	or otherwise amend the Commission proposal by unanimity	or may fail to act

Possible one-month extension if agreed by the Parliament

Commission proposal lapses if Council does not act

SWITCHING A SKI VACATION

I will always recall being in the office of Willy Schlieder, a former German trade union lawyer and close friend of Willy Brandt, who when we met was the Commission's antitrust chief. It was a cold February day in 1976, as he began telling me about Stanley Adams. Schlieder, a dedicated Social Democrat and general director of DG 4, the EC's rough equivalent to the antitrust division of the U.S. Justice Department, was organizing a major case against Hoffmann–La Roche, the Swiss pharmaceutical giant. The charge: illegally fixing prices and engaging in other allegedly illegal business practices involving sales of vitamins in the Community.

The key witness: Adams, then a forty-nine-year-old Maltese-born Briton and a former Hoffmann–La Roche marketing executive, who three years earlier began supplying Schlieder's investigators with detailed inside information on how the company operated and set prices. At the time of our interview, Adams had been arrested by the Swiss police, his wife had committed suicide, and he was soon to be tried for economic espionage; Hoffmann–La Roche had brought the charges against Adams under Swiss law. "What is happening is outrageous," Schlieder said, "because he was our key witness."

He then lowered his voice, explaining that only a few days earlier, as part of Switzerland's determination to stop Schlieder and Adams, the Swiss ambassador in Brussels called on him in his Brussels office, urging the case be dropped. Then, as he was leaving, the envoy darkly warned Schlieder that taking his winter skiing-vacation holiday in Switzerland might prove "compromisingly delicate" for the senior EC official, considering the trial was getting underway and, in particular, because the Commission, in a precedent-shaking move, planned to post Adams's bail.

"Can you imagine being warned like that by an ambassador? A Swiss ambassador, here in Brussels?" I recall Schlieder saying, with a chuckle, that he had, nevertheless, taken the ambassador's warning to heart, skied in Austria, but pursued the case even more relentlessly. His investigation had resulted in Hoffmann–La Roche's conviction. "It was a perfect example of how we are supposed to be operating— upholding the Community's rules, laws, and ideals, no matter what," he said later. "But it wasn't easy."

Decisions on cases filed under the Rome Treaty anticompetition articles 85 and 86 are based on recommendations of DG 4; fines can be imposed—of up to 10 percent of a company's worldwide sales. But usually, as in the case of Hoffmann–La Roche, the penalties recommended are considerably less. Thus, in December 1990, a proposed fine of nearly $70 million against three chemical companies for allegedly operating an illegal cartel in the soda-ash market—Belgium's Solvay, Britain's Imperial Chemical Industries, and an affiliate of Germany's BASF—was the largest in the Community's history. Decisions by the Commission, however, are not easily reached, and for a fundamental reason: each commissioner has but one vote; approval requires a simple majority. Lobbying is always intensive in such cases. All three companies involved in the soda-ash case tried for several weeks to convince the Commission that their rebating system was perfectly legal; they also vowed to challenge the decision in the European Court of Justice.

Understandably, when such cases come up in the Commission, the discussions can be relaxed, or tense, boring, technically complex, or explosive. The chemical case went relatively smoothly, because as Commission officials explained, there was a "wide consensus" that the high fines were needed to reflect the determination of the Commission to make sure industrial companies refrain from flouting strict and clear competition rules. But things do not always go smoothly when the fifteen men and two women commissioners are sitting around the table in camera.

"Delors can blow up, and does, and so do others, because we are so different in our backgrounds, interests, and approach, with the result that some meetings are nasty indeed," said one Commission official, "and the fireworks can occur in the thirteenth-floor conference room, or in the corridors, but fireworks there are." For example, in early December 1990, when it became clear that the Community was being singled out for the impending failure of the Uruguay Round of trade-liberalization talks, the tough-talking Irish commissioner of agriculture Raymond MacSharry clashed frequently with Frans Andriessen, the cerebral, aloof former Dutch finance minister, who as head of DG 1 was responsible for the negotiations. Andriessen, as we shall see in Chapter 9, is also known for his liberal, free-trading views and determined to make the Community more open to outside competition.

But MacSharry, whose critics described him as obstinate, abrasive and friendly to farm interests, pushed successfully for a hard line on maintaining EC farm-support programs—greatly angering Bush administration negotiators—while Andriessen, with backing from a few others, urged a more conciliatory approach to trade liberalization. Consequently, the Commission often looked as if it were in total disarray—and often it was—as EC officials criticized each other for having been repeatedly blamed by Washington for the failure of the negotiations to break the transatlantic deadlock.

Another example of how awkward and dispute-prone the system is: Early in 1990, the senior German commissioner triggered a flap by unexpectedly announcing to a news conference that he was establishing a committee to report weekly on the impact of German unification on the Community. The Commission had, in fact, decided to discuss the unification study informally and possibly study it, but no one could recall anything's being decided about a permanent committee and, certainly not about its being chaired by a fellow commissioner. Andriessen immediately complained about the intrusion on his turf—external relations. Now meet the German commissioner, Martin Bangemann.

Ebullient, impetuous, politically ambitious, Bangemann surprised everyone by announcing that he was resigning as West German economics minister in the spring of 1988—to seek the presidency of the EC Commission. Many political observers immediately thought, mistakenly, a crisis was brewing in Brussels and that Delors might be planning something, even though he certainly seemed determined to remain in his post until the end of his term, December 31, 1992. The fifty-four-year-old German lawyer and former member of the European Parliament had been appointed by Kohl to the commission, responsible for the internal market and industrial affairs, succeeding Lord Cockfield. Since then Bangemann has made no secret of his ambition: to succeed Delors. But Bangemann's clash with Andriessen in 1990 ended in a compromise because the Dutchman knew his way around Brussels far better, having just successfully completed a four-year term as EC agriculture commissioner.

A combination of Delors's guidance and skillful, behind-the-scenes maneuvering by his troubleshooter Lamy—known around the thirteenth floor as "Delors's Exocet" missile—led to Bangemann's being assigned to head a task force to monitor the impact of German unification on the 1992 program. Andriessen was asked to assess the foreign-policy aspects of German unification, while Delors would supervise both operations. It was a typical EC Commission compromise. No one resigned. No one was fired. No one lost much face. Indeed, it is virtually impossible to remove a commissioner; that is a prerogative of the European Parliament, which has been brandished, but never used. And in the end everyone agreed on the settlement. Why?

Because as Lamy, who has studied the Community's decision-making system, has concluded, the key to understanding how the Commission works is what he refers to as the three Cs: conciliation, compromise, and consensus. "I like to think of the Commission as a board of directors of a company—free of political restraints felt at home in governments," says Lamy, himself a former French finance ministry official, ranked *inspecteur des finances,* one of the elite corps of the ministry, who trace their origins to Charlemagne. "It may not be very exciting for outsiders, but that is the way it works here . . . to get votes, you need to win agreement first." In other words, Delors cannot simply decide and then, impose what he wants. Not only has he lost bouts within the Commission, but, in fact, there are two other centers of Community power.

WELCOME TO STRASBOURG

Driving or walking out of town from the historic center of Strasbourg, dominated by its awesome thirteenth-century cathedral, via the Quai des Pêcheurs, you cannot miss the sprawling modern white building known as the Palais de l'Europe. Flying outside at the entrance are 25 flags of West and East European countries and of Turkey, Cyprus, and Malta. Welcome to the Council of Europe, Western Europe's oldest institution, founded in 1949 as an assembly of representatives from parliaments of member countries and best known for the European Rights Convention and the European Court of Human Rights, whose rulings are binding on members.

But something is wrong. Isn't this the European Parliament? The answer is both no and yes. This is the Council of Europe's headquarters, but in it the European Parliament also has been holding monthly plenary meetings since the building went up in 1977—temporarily, until a permanent headquarters is someday designated. Adding to the confusion is the fact that the blue gold-star-studded flag of the European Community, adopted in 1986, has been the Council of Europe's emblem since 1955. Understandably, many of the 100,000 annual visitors, particularly Americans and Japanese tourists, depart in confusion. So what exactly is it?

First, the European Parliament is the EC's only directly elected body; its 518 members are elected every five years by universal suffrage in every member state. Second, despite repeated demands for more power, the European Parliament wields far less power than national legislatures and it is by far the weakest of the major EC institutions. Nevertheless, following ratification of the Single European Act in 1987, which granted new political powers to EC institutions to implement the 1992 program, the Parliament somewhat increased its powers over new Community legislation in what is known as "the new Cooperation Procedure." This is outlined on the chart on page 253. The aim is to allow the Parliament to propose amendments to draft directives suggested by the Commission, after the Council has taken positions but before the directives are formally adopted as EC law. The Parliament's approval is not a prerequisite for adoption, however.

Finally, there is no parliament quite like it from a cultural and operational point of view, which may explain some of the biting epithets heard over the years—"expensive joke," a "resting place for windbags," a "talking shop," a "gravy train," and "cloud-cuckoo land."

Indeed, few parliamentary bodies in the West have been so misunderstood, mistrusted, and ignored by large segments of European public opinion, including French, and yet have remained unique and potentially influential. Operating in nine official EC languages, in three different cities—Strasbourg, Luxembourg, and Brussels—the European Parliament is a traveling road show. The plenary sessions, which last about a week each month, are held in Strasbourg. But all committee meetings are held in Brussels, which remains the Parliament's favorite city for a new headquarters, considering that the new and larger parliament building in Brussels will be ready for occupancy in mid-1992, as we have seen in Chapter 1. However, France has strenuously fought the proposed move in order to keep the parliament's plenary sessions in Strasbourg and threatened to veto designation of other cities for several EC agencies being created until agreement is reached to designate Strasbourg the Parliament's "permanent" home. Meantime, the Parliament's administrative headquarters remains in Luxembourg.

The costs of simply transporting lawmakers, their staffs, secretaries, files, and furniture from one site to another costs the Parliament an estimated $50 million a year. And that, concluded Derek Prag, a British Conservative party deputy, whose committee studied the issues, is wasteful, absurd, and unprecedented among Western democracies. The main problem facing the Parliament is its future powers, particularly with regard to national parliaments. What powers? To do what? Let us meet a few of its key figures:

- Enrique Baron Crespo is a dapper, dark-eyed Spanish Socialist, who was elected president of the Parliament by a very small margin at the age of forty-five, the first Spaniard ever to have headed a major Community institution. A lawyer and an economist, fluent in six languages, and previously a member of the Spanish parliament and government, Crespo is low-key, somewhat thin-skinned. His critics argue he has not pressed hard enough for new powers, which his predecessors have sought since 1969. Crespo argues somewhat defensively that he has obtained "constituent and satisfactory" powers for the Parliament and will continue pressing for a "determining" role in the intergovernmental conference on political union in Brussels.
- Jean-Pierre Cot is an outspoken French Socialist, law professor, and former minister for overseas development. He was fifty-two when elected president of the Socialists in the 1989 elections, the largest among the Parliament's eleven major political groups, around which the body is organized and votes; they are similar to U.S.-style caucuses. A longtime supporter of former French Prime Minister Michel Rocard, Cot has repeatedly attacked Delors for being too weak in promoting the cause of Europe's "social dimension." Like most of his colleagues, Cot wants the Parliament to appoint, or at least to be involved in the appointment of, EC commissioners and their president, and urges the right of "codecision" with the Council in approving legislation.
- Otto von Habsburg is the mustached scion of the Austro-Hungarian Empire, which ruled Central Europe until its collapse with the outbreak of World War I. A lawyer, he was reelected to the Parliament at the age of seventy-seven as a conservative from Upper Bavaria in Germany, where he lives in a modest villa. Months before the Berlin Wall collapsed in 1989, von Habsburg was urging that Hungary and possibly other East European countries seek full EC membership. He also was among the first European leaders to suggest that an upper house be established to complement the Parliament, even if,

initially, as he told John Templeman of *Business Week,* it resembled a weak version of England's House of Lords.[4] The archduke also advocates a strong, U.S.-style European presidency.

■ James Elles is a good example of Britain's young and bright "European" conservatives. Although respectful of Mrs. Thatcher's domestic policies, he is more in tune with the conciliatory approaches of other Tory leaders, like John Major. Elles has a friendly, outgoing manner; his wife is French. Reelected at the age of thirty-nine, Elles is uncomfortable with Delors's interest in expanding the powers of the Commission without control by the European Parliament. But he also believes Mrs. Thatcher deliberately, harmfully exaggerated its emerging role. He would like to see the Council made more open to the Parliament's scrutiny in the legislative process and strongly favors economic and monetary union. He urges caution on the speed of political union and EC enlargement through new members, recalling that it took 170 years, from 1789, before Hawaii became America's fiftieth state—in 1959.

What these four members of the European Parliament share with many of their 514 colleagues, is their belief that the Parliament deserves better treatment; that it could someday become a world-class legislature; but that for the foreseeable future its prospects for obtaining substantial new powers are slim. I recall, painfully, listening to Crespo telling a news conference in Rome, on the opening day of the EC summit, of his hopes for closely "associating" the Parliament with the work of the intergovernmental conferences and for having a say in the proposed amendments before they are submitted to national parliaments for ratification. But that idea has stirred little interest.

Exasperated with the constant assertions that the Parliament is the Community's only "democratic" organization, Mitterrand told fellow heads of government that true democracy was "in this room" where they were meeting, emphasizing they, too, were elected officials. Kohl has led the movement within the Council to grant the Parliament the right to initiate legislation and veto power over new Commission proposals—powers the Parliament does not currently possess.

The European Parliament is hardly considered powerless, however, for as Britain's Lord Plumb, Crespo's predecessor, has boasted:

"They all come down here to Strasbourg, or to Brussels, to consult us, to lobby us, to influence us . . . the Commission, the Americans and the Japanese," and, as his aides have emphasized, many world leaders have come to Strasbourg to deliver important speeches, including President Reagan, Pope John Paul II, Yasir Arafat, and Soviet leader Mikhail Gorbachev. The Brussels-based lobbyists, whom we have described in Chapter 1, also flock to Strasbourg regularly to influence the Parliament as it amends pending legislation or directives submitted by the Commission. "You certainly cannot ignore the Parliament—they are a very important player," insists Eamonn Bates, a Brussels-based consultant, and formerly chief lobbying strategist for American companies at the American Chamber of Commerce in the Belgian capital.

Example: Throughout 1989, the Parliament mobilized heavy pressure on the Commission to seek tighter reciprocity restrictions on foreign banks and financial institutions planning to establish operations within the EC after 1992. The Commission resisted the pressure; EC finance ministers were split on how tough the Community should be with American and Japanese banks, amid intensive lobbying by the U.S. and Japanese governments, warning that such further drifting toward Fortress Europe would lead to retaliation. In the end, a compromise was reached, but as Brussels insiders noted, the pressures exerted demonstrated that Parliament's new powers were to be reckoned with; they stemmed from a provision in the Single Act of 1987 allowing the Parliament to veto a Council position, but only on the basis of an absolute majority. Largely because of that power, in the first twelve months of the reformed system the Commission accepted 79 percent of the Parliament's amendments on a first reading, and 56 percent on a second reading, following the procedure shown on the chart on page 253.

Pierre Pflimlin was extraordinary for his eighty-one years when I met him in his Strasbourg office in the Parliament building—and upbeat about the future. It was January 19, 1989. In his younger days, Pflimlin had seen it all and known them all—Schuman, Monnet, Adenauer, Italy's foreign minister Alcide de Gasperi. A former premier of France, mayor of Strasbourg and president of the European Parliament between 1984 and 1987, Pflimlin wanted to speak English, in his German-sounding Alsatian accent. "As far as I am concerned, after Messina and Rome, adoption of the Single Act was the truly significant beginning of the unification of Europe," Pflimlin said as he moved around his office, gesturing with his hands. He emphasized that he was referring to the provisions establishing qualified majority voting for the 1992 program, thus weakening any single government's veto power, and the reinforcing of the powers of the Parliament, which he said he also welcomed. "We have had many difficulties, but we have come a long way," he said, "including here in this Parliament, which many of your Americans ignore, but it exists, it will become stronger. . . . Why you ask? Because Europe exists," he said.

ULTIMATE POWER

Let us suppose Pflimlin's prediction comes true—that the Parliament's powers, and perhaps those of the Commission, will be increased substantially sometime in 1993. Will it matter? There has never been any doubt—going back to Monnet's days—where power is concentrated. Amid all the talk and movement toward what Kohl at his Rome news conference termed "political union on a federal basis," he never really defined what he had in mind. Nor did Mitterrand, nor De Michelis, and certainly not Major. Yes, everyone agreed, the Community's "finality" was federalism, just as Mitterrand had stated on previous occasions. But when the drafters of the final communiqué had to write down what they had in mind under the heading "institutional framework," they concluded that for the foreseeable future there would be but "one ultimate decision-making center, namely the Council."

And just in case someone missed the point, another paragraph was inserted emphasizing that the Council alone would provide the Community its "fundamental political momentum," and that this role would be reinforced through the creation of its own secretariat—meaning yet another set of eyes and ears in Brussels. What exactly is the Council?

Here is another uniquely European and highly complex executive body, which confuses outsiders. It comprises ministers or heads of EC member governments and, therefore, is the apex of power in the Community. True, the Commission alone has had the right to initiate and propose policy, as can be seen in the chart on page 253, and thus the Commission also has exercised an executive function. But the

Council decides; it is the Community's prime, ultimate decision-making body. When meeting at the level of heads of government during summits, the group is known by its full name—the European Council established in 1974.

In an unusual twist to keep everyone happy, thanks to its main architect, Giscard D'Estaing of France, the presidency of the Council rotates every six months. This allows every member country, in alphabetical order, to preside temporarily not only over the summit meetings but over regular gatherings of ministers from member countries. "This is where the action is, where the power is, and where Europe comes together—at the top," a senior EC Commission official explained, "demonstrating that while we, here at the Commission, have powers to initiate, they—over there—decide."

My source was gesturing to a nondescript concrete, high-rise office building adjacent to the Berlaymont, known as the Charlemagne Building. It is here where some 2,000 "Eurocrats," including translators and interpreters, work, including the COREPER, the Committee of Permanent Representatives, which includes the ambassadors of EC member countries; they are responsible for preparing decisions for the Council, based on Commission recommendations. The COREPER, comprising ambassadors, take their orders from national governments.

But national veto power has diminished and will weaken even more as the Council extends a system of majority voting—a major innovation of the 1987 Single Act amending the Rome Treaty. The new system, designed to speed up implementation of the 1992 program, by eliminating unanimous voting on some issues, extended majority voting to most areas—with the exception of taxation, social and workers' rights, the status of immigrants, and foreign policy. This means, for example, any EC member can still block admission of a new member. The intergovernmental conference on political union was, in fact, seeking to extend majority voting into some of these areas, but kept the relative weights of members in the Council voting unchanged. Thus the four largest countries—Germany, France, Italy, and Britain—have ten votes each. Spain has eight votes. Belgium, Greece, the Netherlands, and Portugal each has five votes; Denmark and Ireland three each; and Luxembourg, the EC's smallest country, two votes.

What this means, in pure mathematical terms, is the following: a total of 54 votes constitutes a qualified majority out of a total of 76.

But a coalition of the five largest EC members cannot obtain more than 48 votes, and thus cannot impose their will on the other seven. Similarly, according to the rules, any two of the Big Four, plus any of the smaller countries—with the exception of Luxembourg—can block any proposal before the Council. "It certainly is more democratic than the old veto-power system and allows us more flexibility in getting proposals through," commented Lamy, adding, however, that ultimately the Community's political power for decision-making rests with heads of EC governments. This was the essence of the European Union being established. Making it work will be something else again.

THE ALLIANCE WITHIN THE ALLIANCE

It was one of those routine French–West German summit meetings in 1985, and we had gathered for a routine, late-afternoon news conference at the Élysée Palace. As the questions and answers droned on, Mitterrand casually grasped Kohl's wrist, glanced at the chancellor's watch, and told startled reporters that the hour had grown late and that Kohl should catch his plane back to Bonn. It is no secret that the French president never wears a watch, but the gesture, in front of reporters, followed the earlier, much-publicized hand-holding by Mitterrand and Kohl during commemorative ceremonies at the World War I battlefield site of Verdun in eastern France. Both gestures demonstrated the strong political and personal bonds between the two leaders and their countries, which Robert Picht, director of the German-French Institute in Ludwigsburg, Germany, termed "the alliance within the Alliance." As we were leaving the palace, a French official commented: "Can you imagine Mitterrand holding hands with Ronald Reagan, or grasping Mrs. Thatcher's wrist—in front of reporters?"

The French-German alliance has had its ups and downs, but from the beginning it has been known as the "locomotive driving Europe." And that power stems from basic assumptions—and tradeoffs—shared by French and German leaders going back to Adenauer and de Gaulle and directly influenced by Monnet, who provided many of the ideas for converting the ideas into reality. The most fundamental idea, shared by leaders on both sides of the Rhine, was that France and Germany, in order to avoid future conflicts, must cement their reconciliation in a permanent, concrete manner. Thus in 1951 the European Coal and Steel Community was established, first of all to bring both countries' coal and steel industries under a single authority and to open the organization to membership by other Europeans. Nine years later the Common Agricultural Policy was established, also reflecting a tradeoff—France would obtain German-backed protection and subsidized support for its farm products, while Germany, with France's support, obtained preferential treatment by the Community for its manufacturing industries. But there was more to come.

Irritating Washington and London, Adenauer and de Gaulle, with much fanfare, signed their first postwar treaty of cooperation in Paris Jan. 22, 1963, which eventually extended into many areas: political cooperation, defense, economic and trade policy, investments, culture, tourism, science and technology. Airbus Industrie, for example, was started by the Germans and the French; Britain only joined several years later. Eureka, while initially a French idea, was launched with Germany. The two countries established Europe's first, joint military brigade in 1988 and planned to merge several embassies in Africa and Outer Mongolia. Under the impetus of Giscard d'Estaing and Schmidt, respectively president of France and German chancellor, the European Monetary System was established, as we saw in Chapter 6. For ten years longer—specifically until the collapse of the Berlin Wall and Germany's subsequent reunification—many observers were convinced that West Germany's ties with France would eclipse Bonn's traditional alliance and friendship with Washington.

THE BERLIN WALL COLLAPSES

No event so shocked the world—and traumatized France—as the destruction of the Berlin Wall, beginning around midnight on November 9, 1989. Amid the cacophony of honking horns, fireworks, and shouts of happy Berliners, many triumphantly waving champagne glasses and loose chunks of the Wall to television cameras, it suddenly became clear to most of the world that the most decisive step of the postwar era had been taken in ending the cold War and the Soviet Union's grip over all of Central Europe. France took the news particularly hard.

For several years, tensions, jealousies, backbiting, and rivalries had been building between France and West Germany. Businessmen on both sides of the Rhine criticized each other's protective attitudes toward everything from beer (Germany's) to high-speed trains (France's). Germans delighted in pointing out that it was France that blocked, and then withdrew from, the European Fighter Aircraft program in 1985. The French delighted in pointing out how powerful Frankfurt banks deliberately, hypocritically blocked foreign acquisitions in West Germany. And despite heavily supported student exchange programs, and the fact that the two countries are each other's largest trade partners, only about one in a hundred French and German citizens manages well in each other's language. The Wall's collapse dramatically intensified France's suspicions of its neighbor and threatened nearly three decades of officially-inspired friendship and cooperation. With some reason.

In Bonn and Brussels, exuberant West German government officials said they now wanted to lead the Western Alliance in Central Europe the way America leads in Latin America. Berlin would soon be reestablished as the capital in a reunited Germany, many Germans boasted, and although West Germany already had the Community's largest, most prosperous economy and was the largest exporter, it now looked as if it were about to become a superpower. "A Germany Too Big for Us," headlined a cover story by France's *Le Point* weekly news magazine nearly a year after the Wall collapsed. French cartoonists depicted Kohl strutting around Europe, wearing a spiked German World War I helmet. In Brussels, Martin Bangemann warned the Community to avoid asking his country to choose between unification and further EC integration. Former French Defense Minister Jean-Pierre Chevènement was quoted as predicting that the main victim of German reunification would be Delors, while Mitterrand appeared worried, confused, and groping for answers.

In an interview with American colleagues, several weeks after the Wall's destruction, Mitterrand concluded that the Community was now at a historical crossroad and warned that if EC integration— economic, monetary, and political—was not accelerated, all of Continental Europe might fall back into warring, splintered, nationalistic rivalries.[5] The French leader was caught in a painful dilemma—how to maintain his prestige and image of world leader at home while bolstering the French-German relationship, at a time when West Germany was totally absorbed, driving headlong toward unification with East Germany. That would not only add 16.7 million people and 108,000 square kilometers of territory, but, for another century at least, would assure Germany's role as Europe's premier economic and industrial power. Was Germany also seeking to revive its earlier, frightening ambitions to dominate Europe politically and if so, how? Helmut Schmidt, among others, predicted that Bonn's preoccupation with unification and its political future in Europe would, in any case, slow the speed of EC integration.

But Schmidt, among others, was to be proven wrong, because a new political tradeoff between Germany and France was already in the making, which was to place Europe back on the track Schmidt and Giscard d'Éstaing had set for Europe a decade earlier. The first component of the arrangement involved obtaining Germany's support for a single currency and a single central bank, the Eurofed, which we have already examined in Chapter 6. For France, economic and monetary union would increase its own weight and influence within the Community, while preventing a mightier Germany from totally dominating—and eventually weakening—European monetary unity and, possibly along with it, the franc. Overriding fierce opposition and deep skepticism from his finance ministry, the Bundesbank, and other conservative groups in his coalition government, who feared a weakened Deutsche mark, Kohl pressed for agreement with Mitterrand. But there was a catch.

In return for moving forward with economic and monetary union and for finally committing himself to the January 1, 1994, date for the start-up of Stage Two, Kohl demanded wholehearted French support for political union. For the German chancellor that also entailed specific commitments—reinforcing the powers of the European Parliament prior to the next elections in 1994; extending EC decision-making into the realms of foreign policy and security matters, meaning the military-defense realm. Kohl and his hard-driving, influential foreign minister, Hans-Dietrich Genscher, also pressed for the extension of Council majority voting to issues of great interest to Germany: environment, health, social policy, energy, research, technology, and the rights of consumers. Mitterrand, keeping his part of the bargain, agreed. The result was a four-page letter, signed by Kohl and Mitterrand, committing themselves to all of these points, among others, and sent to Andreotti, who was the presiding Council President, a week prior to the opening of the December summit meeting in Rome.

Tough bargaining lay ahead, amid strong fears by smaller EC countries that France and Germany were back at their old habits of seeking to dominate Europe—allegations brushed off by Mitterrand and Kohl, who noted that extending majority voting and increasing the Parliament's powers were hardly antidemocratic. Holland's prime minister, Ruud Lubbers, in a December 12, 1990, letter to Andreotti, which was also made public just prior to the summit, attacked the Kohl-Mitterrand letter for neglecting to endorse a reinforced role for the Commission, and for having decided to "elevate the European Council to a position of preeminence within European Political Union." What France and Germany were suggesting, Lubbers argued, "could easily put at risk the institutional balance within the Community" between the Council, the Commission, and the Parliament.

What became clear after that historic Rome summit meeting was that the Community was rapidly moving forward toward both economic-monetary and political union, and that with Mrs. Thatcher gone, and Major sounding far more conciliatory and cooperative, Britain, too, would now become an active participant in the intergovernmental conferences. But what kind of a role would Britain play, particularly as it slipped deeper into recession amid worsening unemployment? As I sat in the last row of the chartered Air France press plane, heading from the Rome summit to Paris, my thoughts went to a talk I had with Lord Carrington, the wise, humorous, deeply cultivated former British foreign secretary and member of the Conservative party who had broken with Mrs. Thatcher over the Falklands War in 1982.

As we sipped coffee in his cozy, well-appointed office in downtown London, he talked about Britain's role in the New Europe, or, rather, its lack of a role. It was November 23, 1989, and German-French relations were on our minds following the collapse of the Berlin Wall earlier in the month.

The Community, in its present form, had been shaped without Britain, Carrington began, "without our voice being heard, but rather to suit, protect, and advance the interests of France and Germany, but mainly France. This analysis, which Carrington had also made in his autobiography, *Reflecting on Things Past,* published a year earlier, contrasted sharply with the 1988 Bruges speech of Mrs. Thatcher, who, he declared without hesitating, "has Europe wrong."

Carrington predicted, rightly as it turned out, any future Conservative government would be forced to play a far more "constructive" role in EC affairs, because the parallel processes of German and

Community integration were going forward at an ever-accelerating speed. But, above all, this former Grenadier Guards officer said, the Community must take responsibility for its collective security matters and foreign policy. "It has never been clear to me how a Community so increasingly close, economically and politically, can exclude security from its thinking and, most important, from its authority," he said. Just over a year later, in the midst of the Gulf crisis, he reaffirmed this view, stating it was more important than ever for the Community to adopt a common security policy.

As we were talking in London, the world was just over eight months away from the sudden early-morning strike against Kuwait by Iraq's dictatorial leader, Saddam Hussein, which, as Italy's De Michelis noted with his usual flair and enthusiasm, galvanized the Community into action on what he described as "a more unified political structure." Few if any observers knew yet what he meant, or what he and other EC leaders had in mind, but a new beginning in Europe's approach to foreign policy was being started—with dazzling speed, determination, and characteristically divided sentiments among EC member governments.

The New European Diplomacy: Trying to Speak and Act with a Single Voice

> The contribution which an organized and vigorous
> Europe can make to civilization is indispensable for
> peace.
>
> ROBERT SCHUMAN

That terse sentence by France's foreign minister appears as the second, visionary paragraph of the Schuman Plan announced with great fanfare in Paris on May 9, 1950. The plan not only launched the European Coal and Steel Community established a year later, but for the first time in the postwar era marked Europe's resolve to play an active, united role in world affairs. Six weeks later, North Korea attacked South Korea, and several European countries, responding separately, committed military support to a U.S.-led, sixteen-nation United Nations force to support a war that would last three years. The European involvement was small and symbolic, but set a goal that many observers at the time considered purely utopian.

The more immediate impact of the Korean War was to strengthen further the realization on both sides of the Atlantic that Europe, too, was vulnerable to a Communist attack. The response by American and European policy-makers was to support creation of a European army that would include a rearmed West Germany. Following long and difficult negotiations, enthusiastic backing both from the Eisenhower administration and the six governments of the fledgling European Coal and Steel Community, a treaty establishing a European Defense Community, with its own armed forces, was signed in 1952. But one key country—France—refused to ratify the agreement; on August 30, 1954, the French National Assembly rejected the plan, largely because of fears of a rearmed Germany, and because the proposed European army would be under American, not European, command. Thus the plan died. Reminiscing in Strasbourg, Pflimlin, pointing to the visionary 1950 declaration, said somewhat sadly, "The EDC failure, our vision for a common defense and foreign policy for a federated Europe was, unfortunately, not yet ripe politically, but the idea remained alive."[1]

TORN BY THE GULF WAR

Thirty-seven years later, embroiled in the war against Iraq, with several of its members suffering light casualties, popular opinion deeply divided, amid escalating financial costs of the war and political disarray, the European Community faced the very same tough question: Would Europe ever be speaking and acting with a single, coherent voice in foreign and military affairs, and if so, how and in what regions of the world? Or, as one of the Bush administration's most perceptive European strategists, the State Department's Undersecretary of State for Economic Affairs Robert Zoellick, put it two months after the war began: Will the New Europe's future role in the world be insular, itinerant, or international?[2] The Gulf War had forced the question into the open once again—in sudden, dramatic, tragic terms—without providing a satisfactory answer.

Thus, as we have seen in previous chapters, though European economies, with the exception of Britain, were bouncier than America's, their best technologies competing successfully against American and Japanese industries in world markets, and despite progress being made toward greater financial, industrial, monetary, and political integration, the Community member states still lacked a common, single operational approach to foreign affairs and security policy. Collectively, the twelve EC nations entered 1991 lacking consensus on how to act in a war being largely waged on their behalf. In Brussels, there was neither an EC foreign minister nor an EC defense minister, much less a Community decision-making body with independent, supranational powers. More fundamentally, the twelve EC member governments, for historical and immediate economic and strategic reasons, did not yet share the same assessment of their responsibilities in the Middle East.

In other words, there still was insufficient collective political will to translate the Schuman Plan declaration into action during a time of crisis. As the *International Herald Tribune* editorialized at the end of January 1991, we were still confronted with a "hesitant, haggling Europe," in which member countries held tightly to their "own instincts about foreign policy."

Two days after the initiation of Desert Storm by America, *Le Monde* editorialized that we were viewing *"L'Europe absente,"* and noted, bitingly, that Europe's efforts to form a consensus was dealt a severe blow by Mitterrand's playing *cavalier seul.*[3] This was the widely used French phrase for Mitterrand's repeated, last-ditch—and unsuccessful—attempts to win support for a Middle East peace plan—a plan he announced in Paris but without first consulting other EC leaders, most notably Britain's Major, who lunched with the French leader at the Élysée Palace January 14, only hours before the plan was unveiled at the United Nations in New York. Major returned to London apparently unaware of Mitterrand's plan, which included a UN Middle East conference to settle the Palestinian problem, among other issues, and a fence-mending trip to Baghdad by Roland Dumas, France's foreign minister, which also had been planned but was dropped.

The French initiative, later backed by Germany, Spain, Italy, and Greece, was rejected angrily by officials in Washington and London, and arrogantly brushed off by Baghdad—within hours of the launching of the first military strikes against Iraq by the U.S.-led coalition of twenty-eight nations, beginning in the early-morning hours of January 17, 1991.

Nevertheless, putting their differences aside, ten EC members joined the 28-nation coalition as Britain, France, and Italy immediately—and separately—sent some fifty thousand troops, plus fighter planes, ships, and tanks, the largest contingent among the non-U.S. participants. Belgium, Spain, the Netherlands, Portugal, Denmark,

Greece, and Germany sent token forces, with strict limitations on their use. The only precedents in this century for European military intervention outside the NATO area were the sending of token forces to the 1950–53 Korean War and the German-led expeditionary force of French, Italian, British, Russian, Japanese, and American troops sent to Peking to put down the Boxer Rebellion in 1900. The notable exception this time was Germany, the Community's largest, most economically powerful member, whose active armed forces at the time of the outbreak of the war totaled 590,000 men and women, including 100,000 military personnel stationed in the former East Germany.

Indeed, Germany, which only a few months earlier was being portrayed as a modern, revitalized Fourth Reich with global ambitions, declined to send its troops, ground and air forces to the Gulf, citing constitutional prohibitions against involvement in military action outside NATO. But there was more to Germany's lack of response. Deeply rooted in the complex, confusing character of the New Germany was a mixture of fear, distrust, pacifism, anti-Americanism, a preoccupation with wealth and comfort, and, above all, indifference, fueled by a profound sense of drift and searching for its role in the postwar Europe. This was succinctly described in a short, penetrating book, *Le Vertige Allemand*, by Brigitte Sauzay, an official interpreter for Kohl and Mitterrand, published in 1985. Week after week, countrywide protests attacked not only the war but German industry's illegal sales of technology and equipment to produce chemical, nuclear, and biological weapons to Iraq, which only added to the national discomfort, considering that Iraq was repeatedly using its Western-supplied arsenal to attack Israel.

Bonn did, however, pledge $11 billion to help America and its allies pay the staggering costs of the war, and it stationed eighteen aging French-German-made Alpha jets and six hundred soldiers, in Turkey, a NATO member. This, however, did little to blunt intense, angry criticism in Washington and London that Germany, as a major European power, was shirking its responsibilities.

Meantime, Belgium refused to supply Britain with ammunition, amid widely conflicting, contradictory, and constantly shifting results of public-opinion surveys in many EC countries, in favor of and opposed to the war. Terrorist attacks and antiwar demonstrations erupted throughout Europe and North Africa, as hundreds of thousands of students, labor leaders, environmentalists, and average citizens, particularly Arabs, vented their frustration and anger at the United States rather than Iraq. Many EC coalition governments were deeply divided; France's Socialist defense minister, Jean-Pierre Chevènement, opposed to Mitterrand's policy of pursuing the war in Iraq, resigned January 29, the first high official in any EC-member government to have broken ranks. The European Parliament, following nearly three hours of intense, heated debate on January 23, 1991, was unable to muster a majority vote for any of ten proposed resolutions on the war.

Further damaging the Community's credibility and, possibly, its longer-range capacity to forge a united stand, was a disheartened voice from within the European Council—that of Britain's Prime Minister Major. Reflecting the views of many conservatives and certainly of Mrs. Thatcher, Major told the House of Commons on January 22 that "political union and a common foreign and security policy in Europe would have to go beyond statements and extend to action. . . . Clearly, Europe is not ready for that and we should not be too ambitious when it comes to the intergovernmental conference on political union," which had already started its preliminary meetings in Brussels, following the mid-December Rome EC summit meeting.

Thus, an annoyed and frustrated Major was signaling his EC partners, primarily those who had refused to make a heavy military commitment to winning the war, such as Germany and Belgium, that Britain did not consider them ready for political union, which only several weeks earlier in Rome had been solemnly agreed upon as a major goal for the Community in the 1990s.

Several days later in Strasbourg, Delors conceded that, being "brutally honest, public opinion sensed that Europe was rather ineffectual," and that the Community's divided reactions "have highlighted Europe's shortcomings."

SIGNS OF A NEW BEGINNING

Was the Community's capacity to speak with a single voice on foreign affairs only rhetoric, an empty dream? The answer, despite the disarray we have just been describing, is No—a qualified No. The Gulf War ended any lingering hopes that Europe would become a global superpower in this century. The image of a "Grand European Colossus" was, in any case, greatly exaggerated. And yet, in all fairness to the Community, its collective response to what began as a regional conflict was widely admired as far as it went, demonstrating there is considerable potential for European unity amid the flaws and faults.

Consider the first few days of the Gulf crisis. In an unprecedented move, within two days after Hussein's strike against Kuwait on August 2, EC foreign ministers jointly announced their governments would immediately embargo purchases of Iraqi and Kuwaiti oil, freeze Iraqi assets, and protect Kuwaiti assets from Iraq; ban all further sales of arms to Baghdad, and suspend all its preferential trading arrangements between Iraq and the Community. "We did our best, swiftly, under difficult circumstances," a Commission official commented, noting that President Bush telephoned Andreotti, then presiding over the Council of Ministers, warmly praising the Community effort. Compared to the Community's reaction to other crises, the speed of the response was remarkable, U.S. and EC officials said, considering that it took the Community several weeks to formulate and agree on a joint reaction condemning the Soviet Union's invasion of Afghanistan in 1979.

In the weeks following the invasion and occupation of Kuwait, the Commission and the Council met regularly, coordinating their embargo against Iraq and building support for the U.S.-sponsored resolutions in the United Nations. The Community granted $600 million in financial assistance to neighboring countries hard hit by the crisis, notably Egypt, Jordan, and Turkey; aid was increased several months later. France, Germany, the Commission, and later Britain repeatedly urged that the allies focus on what the French called the *après crise* period—the negotiated settlements that would follow the war and in which the Community was determined to play a role. As Community leaders recalled, the EC had been the first among the Western allies to recognize the Palestinian question as more than a refugee problem and urged it in its June 1980 so-called Venice Declaration, negotiated at an EC summit meeting in the Italian city. The declaration, which greatly irritated Washington, urged that the Palestine Liberation Organization "will have to be associated with the negotiations" on any future settlements in the region.

During the December summit meeting in Rome, an upbeat De Michelis predicted a "more unified political structure" emerging for the Community as a result of the Gulf crisis, which accurately reflected the euphoric mood at the conference. The conviction that the European Community had learned its lesson, prompted EC leaders to provide their negotiators a clear mandate to establish a common approach to foreign affairs and security matters. Among the proposed Rome Treaty amendments was "the gradual extension" of the Community's competence in a range of new areas—UN peacekeeping operations, coordination of armaments developments and exports, disarmament, nonproliferation—and its participation in future collective security arrangements in Europe, most likely through some form of link with the Western Europe Union, a nine-nation consultative body of NATO members established after the rejection of the proposed European Defense Community in 1954. The WEU is Western Europe's only forum for coordinating defense questions, grouping every EC member, except Denmark, Greece, and Ireland. But it has remained moribund, virtually powerless; WEU is not a European Community organization even though it was established in the postwar era, along with the European Coal and Steel Community, as a way of facilitating the rearmament of West Germany.

The Gulf crisis revived strong interest in strengthening WEU, its supporters urging that it become a revitalized "European pillar" within the NATO alliance and, more specifically, by being merged, or brought under the European Community—a plan ardently supported by Kohl, Mitterrand, De Michelis, and Delors. Already, during the Iran-Iraq War in 1987, WEU had supervised protection of oil tankers headed for European ports, and it coordinated member-nation logistics and naval operations during the Gulf War, a modest role at best. "It is too early to talk of conclusions," De Michelis told newsmen during the Rome summit, "but it is now clear that we are embarking on a new path. . . . The Gulf crisis is galvanizing us to move forward in foreign policy—a subject, a few weeks ago, we couldn't even talk about. It is a beginning."

Within several weeks following the outbreak of the war, French, British, and Italian political leaders—including Socialists and conservatives in the ranks of the opposition—began urging a coordinated European Community role in the postwar period. "We cannot have the United States speaking and acting eternally on our behalf . . . and France and Britain cannot do it all alone," said Édouard Balladur, France's former finance minister under the neo-Gaullist government of Jacques Chirac, defeated by Mitterrand in 1988.[4] The Gulf crisis has shown, Balladur said, that European cooperation must now be pursued more actively than ever before, including establishment of a future European military force under its own command.

Robert Hunter, foreign affairs adviser to former U.S. President Jimmy Carter, who became vice president of the Washington-based Center for Strategic and International Studies, told my colleague Joseph Fitchett a month following Iraq's invasion of Kuwait that it was "critically important" for the Community to seize on the Gulf crisis as a way of helping the West prepare militarily for handling "Third World contingencies."[5]

And several months before Iraq invaded Kuwait, reflecting his decidedly similar conclusions based on long reflection, Delors proposed that the Community develop its own conventional, multinational, military force for use outside the NATO region. He did not repeat his suggestion as the crisis worsened throughout the year and into 1991; however, European public opinion overwhelmingly supported the idea. According to an opinion poll published by the Commission December 11, 1990, nearly 70 percent of those interviewed in ten EC member countries said they favored a common EC defense policy, and said the best response to the Gulf crisis would be a common European defense organization.

As the Gulf War began, according to the Institute for Strategic Studies in London, 2.5 million men and women from EC member countries, with the exception of neutral Ireland, were serving in their respective armed services grouped in the NATO alliance. That figure compared with 326,000 U.S. military personnel stationed in the European area, but whose numbers were diminished as some combat units, mainly in Germany, were sent to Saudi Arabia. The surprisingly large European contingent prompted many observers to suggest that the Community's impact would have been far greater had, say, even fifty thousand European troops been dispatched to the Gulf under a unified, possibly a WEU command. That never happened, of course, and was, as far as could be determined, never suggested by anyone in a position of power.

Nevertheless, the prospects of as many as 200,000 U.S. troops being withdrawn from their European bases, primarily in Germany, prompted new questioning in European capitals over how the gap would be filled and whether the European Community was now prepared to build its own security organization—within or alongside NATO. Most observers predicted such a plan would emerge before the end of 1992.

Defense ministers of the North Atlantic Treaty Organization in late May 1991 were putting finishing touches on plans to establish a multinational force of some 70,000 NATO-controlled troops capable of responding rapidly to military crises affecting the territories of member states. U.S. and French, EC and Italian officials, among others, were unable to resolve the question of whether, as the United States suggested, the European force should be under NATO or, as Mitterrand, Delors, and other EC leaders argued, it should be under the European Council, linked to WEU. That could mean, of course, the European contingent would be virtually independent of NATO and the United States and, thus, unacceptable to Washington. Britain, not surprisingly, remained the United States' staunchest ally in the simmering debate.

Item: It is late afternoon January 17, 1991, in the Kléber international conference center near the Arch of Triumph in a fashionable section of Paris's 16th arrondisement. U.S. and allied bombing of Iraq has been underway for several hours, as the twelve EC foreign ministers end their fourth special meeting on the Gulf crisis in two weeks. Presiding is the white-haired, slim, and soft-spoken Jacques Poos, Luxembourg's foreign minister, who had taken over as president of the EC Council of Ministers from De Michelis. Flanked by Delors, Poos, noting calmly that "since this morning arms are talking," and that virtually all the allies, notably Britain and France, had joined the U.S.-led military effort to defeat Iraq, he shifts to the measures that might be taken in the aftermath of the war.

"The twelve have not stopped functioning, trying for solutions which are not purely military," Poos said, pledging the Community's support for full participation in a Middle East conference once hostilities ended; for expanding economic aid programs to the region, in what Chancellor Kohl had already described as a new Marshall Plan; and for helping guarantee future security in the Mediterranean region. Advisers to both Kohl and Mitterrand told me repeatedly as the war unfolded that the French-German alliance was as strong as ever, and that the two leaders would continue supporting the move toward political union launched in Rome. "Unlike the British, who have good reason to be upset with the Germans for their behavior in the Gulf, we understand the German position, and live with it," a Mitterrand adviser commented, noting, "It must be stated that for years we have been telling them to abstain from any form of military initiative . . . what do you expect?"

Meantime, reflecting the dazzling speed with which events were moving—and the shifting moods in national capitals—Britain's foreign secretary Douglas Hurd and France's foreign minister Roland Dumas on January 24 began their first discussions since the war started, aimed at preparing for an international peace conference. Hurd made it clear that Britain, although it has key strategic, economic, and trade interests in Saudi Arabia and neighboring Arab states, was not contemplating stationing troops in the region on a permanent basis. France, which like Britain is a member of the UN Security Council and a nuclear power, appeared ready to join Britain in a renewed initiative, which a spokesman for Dumas added would "inevitably" be organized with participation by the Community in order to provide the broadest possible support.

THE SOVIET UNION, EFTA, AND OTHER AGENDA ITEMS

Looking drawn, disappointed, and grim at the January 17 news conference, Delors declared that "for us, there is no question of a pause," emphasizing the Commission would remain committed to seeking long-term solutions in neighboring Arab countries, which he said would mean proposing a new "international order" in the region stretching from the Gulf to Gibraltar. The Commission had already started drafting programs aimed at providing the Community a key role in future economic-development programs in the area, similar to the Community's role in helping finance the reconstruction of Eastern Europe and the Soviet Union. At the same time, Delors also emphasized the Commission fully intended to pursue other major items on its foreign-affairs agenda, on which there was wide agreement—and more coherence—than in the Community's response to the Gulf crisis.

The agenda items—demonstrating that when, and only when, consensus existed, the Community could function in a unified, coherent manner—included the following:

- Strengthening trade, investment, and political ties with Eastern Europe and the Soviet Union, despite grave reservations expressed repeatedly by the Bush administration. Leading the EC initiative were Kohl, Mitterrand, and Delors. Most EC governments remained strongly committed to Soviet leader Gorbachev and his reforms, despite a Soviet military crackdown in the Baltic states and Washington's reservations about providing subsidized aid without promises from Moscow to genuinely reform and privatize the Soviet economy, which were repeated following the failure of the spectacular surprise coup against Gorbachev in August 1991.

- Widening the EC, mainly by expanding ties with the seven remaining members of the European Free Trade Association. EFTA was founded in 1960 as a British-led, free-trade union, also including Austria, Denmark, Liechtenstein, Portugal, Sweden, and Switzerland. Successful completion of negotiations to establish an EC-EFTA agreement in 1992 would create a new trading bloc—the so-called European Economic Area, as EFTA members adopted EC rules, with full access to Community markets. Meantime, Austria, Sweden, and Norway were seeking, or planning to request, full EC membership, whose terms were expected to be negotiated during 1993.

- Expanding financial aid, trade, and training assistance to Third World countries, notably in Africa and Central America, under the umbrella of long-established multibillion-dollar programs. The biggest is the Lomé Convention, under which sixty-six developing countries are receiving nearly $14 billion in aid over ten years, starting in 1990. But urgent appeals have been sent to Brussels from Latin America and Africa for more EC funds, investments, and aid. European Community officials in Brussels found they were becoming overwhelmed by aid requests from Eastern Europe, the Soviet Union and, most recently, the Middle East.

- Expanding and improving relations with the United States, which have frequently been strained; they have traditionally been focused on trade-related matters, as we saw in Chapters 4–7. The focus gradually shifted to such questions as: Should Washington and Brussels act jointly in foreign policy? How? In mid-November 1990, a joint declaration was issued establishing a procedure by which the U.S. president and the presidents of the Commission and Council will meet twice a year to discuss foreign policy, security issues, terrorism, drug trafficking, and other noneconomic issues. The agreement was seen as a first step toward creating higher-level "political dialogue." The first such U.S.-EC summit held in Washington April 11, 1991 was rated highly successful by both sides.

- Finally, forging a coherent internal organization to handle foreign policy, meaning establishment of the equivalent of a European foreign ministry. The present system, dividing responsibility between the Council and the Commission, has been described as "complex and untidy" and in dire need of streamlining.[6] Blueprints for reform were placed on the negotiating table during the intergovernmental talks on political union held in Brussels throughout most of 1991, calling for the reinforcement of the powers of both the Council and the Commission, and more majority voting in the Council.

ANDRIESSEN'S WORLD OF "EURODIPLOMACY"

No amount of organizational, bureaucratic reform in Brussels will ever provide a substitute for political will by national governments. And yet, in all fairness to the Commission, there is no denying that it lacks material resources, managerial and diplomatic talent, and, most important, a clear, unequivocal mandate from member governments to act in the foreign-policy arena—beyond trade-related issues. Indeed, until the eruption of crises in the Soviet Union, Eastern Europe, and the Gulf, the Commission was, technically and legally speaking, prohibited from even discussing political and security matters in its regular meetings. Since the 1960s, through the Gulf War, coordination of member countries' foreign policy has been the responsibility of the EC Council of Ministers, grouping member governments, under an informal procedure known as European Political Cooperation, EPC, in which the Commission now participates actively; we shall return to EPC later.

Until 1977, under the presidency of Roy Jenkins, the Commission was not allowed to attend the annual meetings of the seven major industrialized nations, represented by their heads of state or government. And even then, as Jenkins recalls half-jokingly, at the final wrap-up news conference of his first summit meeting in London May 8, 1977, British officials failed to provide him with a microphone. More embarrassing was the abrupt manner in which Delors, nine years later, was refused a seat in the Group of Seven finance ministers during the summit meeting of heads of state and government held in Tokyo, primarily because of U.S. intransigence. Gradually, Washington's attitude toward the Commission and Delors changed for the better, and we shall return to this later, but there was no denying that the Community's diplomatic machinery was cumbersome and ill-suited for the tasks looming ahead in the 1990s.

Consider Andriessen, "The Flying Dutchman," the EC's longest-serving commissioner, who came as close as Brussels has yet come to producing its own foreign minister. The "ministry" over which he presides from the thirteenth floor of the Berlaymont is small by world standards—employing a total of 1,056 men and women, which includes those assigned to Brussels and to about 90 permanent representative offices throughout the world. This number compares to roughly five times as many, or 4,700 men and women, assigned to comparable jobs in Britain's Foreign Office in London, for example. Yet, DG 1, the Commission's Directorate General for External Relations, is the Community's permanent, professional diplomatic organization, operating under Delors's direction; it is still a long way from being what former EC envoy to Washington Denman has urged—a "European Foreign Office."

In fact, DG 1 more closely resembles a trade ministry than a full-fledged diplomatic service. It represents the Community in all international trade negotiations, such as the GATT-sponsored Uruguay Round of trade liberalization, and in administering multibillion-dollar aid programs to Eastern Europe and the Soviet Union. The Commission also represents the Community in the work of the OECD and maintains observer status at the UN and other specialized agencies; and Delors was a full-fledged delegate to the Conference on Security and Cooperation in Europe and one of the thirty-five signatories to its Charter of Paris on November 21, 1990. The CSCE, as it is known, is a forum on European security, including the United States, the Soviet Union and Western Europe.

The new role has placed the Commission and, more directly, Andriessen and Delors in the center of many world events—and in the heart of lively, cantankerous discussions over policy within the Commission. We have already seen how difficult it is to obtain a consensus within the Commission, and touched on Andriessen's conflicts with fellow commissioners, notably with Ireland's MacSharry over reforming the Community's agricultural subsidy programs. Similarly, in the Commission's debates over how to respond to the Soviet Union's crackdown in the Baltic republics in early 1991, Andriessen found himself on a collision course with fellow commissioners over whether or not to delay, or cancel, the Community's $1 billion aid program to Moscow; Andriessen, backed by Delors, argued successfully for a delay on the grounds that it was important to keep channels of communication open to Gorbachev.

As the Community's involvement in world affairs grew, and more nations looked to it for financial assistance, market access, and, in several cases, full membership, Andriessen's tasks become more demanding and complex. The Commission's decidedly thin resources have been succinctly described by Peter Ludlow of the Centre for European Policy Studies in Brussels as lacking most in the intangible area of "political culture."[7] Ludlow was referring to the Commission's widely recognized handicap of being almost totally focused on trade-related issues and clearly understaffed for taking on wider responsibilities. As a remedy, Ludlow and former French ambassador Henri Froment Meurice recommended, in a critical report they co-authored in 1989, that some two hundred additional, senior diplomatic officials should be assigned to DG 1.

Although EC leaders at the December 1990 Rome summit declined to recommend such specific institutional reform measures, they clearly intended to provide the Commission with what they described as "a reinforced role" in foreign and security policy. The reorganization was also expected to lead to the Commission's sharing of the right to initiate ideas and programs with the Council of Ministers, a crucial, difficult interlocking relationship, to which we shall return.

This is not to say that Andriessen, a former Dutch finance minister, was unable to function in the present setup. At sixty-one, serving his third term as commissioner, energetic, prickly, but well liked by fellow ministers, he appeared to be everywhere at once throughout most of 1990, traveling more than any other commissioner, including Delors. Responsible for the EC's multifaceted trade negotiations with the world's major blocs, he visited Japan, South Korea, Hong Kong, South Africa, Mexico, South Carolina, Washington, Boston, San Francisco, and Dublin during one month of hectic traveling in the spring of 1990. Several EC ministers and fellow commissioners asked openly whether he wasn't stretched too thin, suggesting he should be spending more time in Brussels, concentrating on only crucial EC interests, such as the GATT negotiations.

But Andriessen repeatedly brushed off these suggestions, insisting that being widely seen and active was also crucial for the Commission's credibility, even if its powers were limited. "We do the best we can under difficult circumstances, but then with good plane connections, particularly in Asia, you can cover a lot of ground," said Andriessen's gregarious Dutch spokesman, Nico Wegter. "It may be an exaggerated, overly optimistic view, but there are many countries extremely interested, and, in some cases, almost desperate to do business with us." The *Washington Post*'s prize-winning columnist, Jim Hoagland, put it more succinctly at the end of June 1991, observing the Community "has become the magnet around which the entire Continent is organizing."

HELPING THE RUSSIANS

A major goal of most foreign countries has been to gain access to the Community's markets, protected by external trade restrictions, such as quotas and the like, and to obtain EC-backed financial credits and other forms of development assistance, including, in the case of the Soviet Union for example, joint exploitation of energy and mineral resources. On the opening day of the EC summit meeting in Rome, December 14, 1990, prior to discussing their future unity, EC leaders spent several hours discussing their expanding ties with the Soviet Union, and by evening announced a $1 billion package of emergency food aid, as a signal of strengthened Community support for Gorbachev. That was a moderate contribution, considering that in a visit to European capitals in the weeks before the summit, the Soviet leader had obtained pledges totaling $12 billion in financial credits from Germany, Italy, France, and Spain. But it was a sign of the Community's growing role in forming ties with the Soviet Union, now a beleaguered power, desperate for help, and determined to build more and sturdier bridges to Brussels.

West European business had already captured the largest share of the trade and investments and many of the contracts in the Soviet Union and Eastern Europe. With the help of the Community, the Europeans intended to maintain and expand these advantages—even if the main competitors, the United States and Japan, reacted with annoyance and frustration.

Item: It was a warm spring day in June 1989, and my first trip back to Moscow in fifteen years. Exactly one year earlier, the Soviets had dropped their long hostility to the Community and their portrayal of it as an extension of NATO, clearing the way for establishing full diplomatic relations between Brussels and members of the Council for Mutual Economic Assistance, COMECON, the Moscow-dominated trading bloc of Communist countries. Everybody was talking about Gorbachev's call for establishment of a "common European home," a phrase first uttered not by the Soviet leader, as is often thought, but by his foreign minister, Andrei Gromyko, in Bonn on January 18, 1983.

But Gorbachev made the image his, using it in dozens of speeches in Moscow and in the West, including at the European Parliament in Strasbourg. It gradually came to mean strengthened economic, trade, political, cultural, and technological links between the Soviet Union and Eastern and Western Europe.[8] The notion seemed vague and utopian in talks with Russians in the Soviet capital, where my emotional, depressing discussions focused instead on the excruciating slowness with which the Gorbachev regime was implementing economic and political reforms; the rampant corruption, astronomical prices, black marketeering, unemployment, and the ultimate humiliation for many over forty-eight years of age, food rationing, which had become part of daily life for the first time since World War II. For those in power, including Gorbachev's economic advisers, the European Community's plans for economic and monetary union were, above all, looming as an attractive way of gaining access to the Community's markets in order to sell Soviet products—and much more.

"Look, you can see how really bad things are here now," a senior Soviet official in the foreign ministry told me. "We now want to be part of this EC 1992 exercise, to participate in getting trade advantages and access to big high-tech projects and drawing EC investments here," one of his colleagues added, during a surprisingly frank two-hour discussion at the ministry.[9] These officials, all in their thirties, experts on Europe and enthusiastic supporters of Gorbachev, were particularly worried about being excluded from the Commission's plans for common external tariffs and other trade restrictions; from common licensing agreements, harmonization of standards and new technologies, such as high definition television, advanced telecommunications, and new high-speed train networks; and Eureka research programs. The new interest in the EC was also being actively pursued in Brussels, where Soviet ambassador Vladimir Shemiatenkov met regularly with Andriessen and occasionally Delors, particularly with regard to gaining access to EC-directed aid programs and to financing of the EBRD development bank, which was preparing to begin lending to the Soviets in 1991, assuming the promised economic reforms went forward.

But strains were developing. Within two years, with COMECON disbanded, Gorbachev had lost control over increasingly violent independence movements within key republics and, in response, cracked down in the Baltic republic of Lithuania in early January 1991. In Brussels, the Commission and the Council concluded that it had no choice but to follow Washington's lead in applying sanctions against Moscow. But, as in the case of Europe's mixed reaction to the Gulf War, EC members responded with degrees of harshness. Thus, although France and Germany joined the EC and NATO in warning Moscow of new repression and in suspending some aid programs, they urged Gorbachev to settle his conflicts through negotiation. Kohl even went so far as to urge Baltic leaders to show restraint in their struggles with Gorbachev. It was not difficult to understand why. Consider some of the stakes.

Since the world economic summit in July 1989, the Commission has been responsible for coordinating a massive financial-aid program to Eastern Europe on behalf of twenty-four leading industrialized nations, which by the spring of 1991 had committed $38 billion to the region. Despite pressures to apply sanctions to the Soviets, Andriessen, a year later, warned that "there can be no question of allowing external shocks or uncertainties to jeopardize prospects for reform in Central and Eastern Europe," referring to Soviet actions in the Baltic states and to the Gulf War.

Meantime, by early 1991, several thousand joint ventures among American, European, and Soviet groups were just getting started, or were under negotiation; billions of dollars in debt were not being repaid to Western European, and particularly to German banks; confusion about Soviet decision-making was rampant throughout most of early 1991, amid expectations by EC officials, businessmen, and bankers that Gorbachev's reforms would be slowed, if not halted, as the economy slipped further into paralysis. And yet European business leaders were quick to reassure their Soviet hosts, their shareholders back home, and Brussels that, whatever their U.S. competitors decided, they had no immediate intentions of pulling out, and would continue to welcome government and EC Commission support for their ventures.

Some examples: Fiat's $5 billion project to build car plants;

Daimler's to build a bus factory; France's Alcatel's plan to install telephone switching equipment in a $2.8 billion venture, among others. German and Italian banks supplied more than $20 billion in commercial credits to the Soviets through 1992, although as the crisis worsened they simply stopped lending. Some Western investors told *Business Week* correspondents they thought a crackdown might even help the economy, by restoring authority and a more simplified, centralized approach to negotiations, including those with the Community.[10] More than anything else, the Europeans were determined not to lose their advantages to the Americans, and were counting heavily on support from both the Commission and the Council, even if many business leaders and bankers remained confused about their exact roles.

THE COUNCIL OF MINISTERS HAS THE POWER

When assessing the "Community," quite apart from national differences, there is yet another generally misunderstood and confusing institutional phenomenon, which we dealt with briefly in Chapter 8—the structure, role, and emerging powers of the Council of Ministers, and EPC, the procedure under which EC member governments consult and coordinate their foreign policy. Functioning as a consortium of representatives of member states, supported logistically by their permanent Brussels-based representatives in COREPER, the Council resembles a small parliament. Located in the Charlemagne building, next door to the Berlaymont, the Council has its own secretariat, permanent working groups, and a confidential telex system linking the twelve member countries' foreign ministries. It is COREPER and EC ambassadors, not the Commission, who play the key role in helping the Council president prepare decisions, although there is permanent coordination with the Commission—for example, on how to approach the GATT negotiations, aid to the Soviet Union, applications for EC membership, declarations on human-rights violations, and the like.

The predominant decision-making role of the Council explains why the larger, more powerful EC member governments—usually France—become annoyed and jealous when an accessible EC Commission president becomes too prominently featured by the media, recalling the shattering demise of Hallstein under the determined pressure of de Gaulle, as we saw in Chapter 2. Valéry Giscard d'Estaing, then President of France, according to French officials, exploded with anger when he saw the photograph on the cover of the February 1979 magazine *Europe,* published by the EC delegation in Washington, showing Jimmy Carter and Jenkins talking over the headline TWO PRESIDENTS. It created the impression that Jenkins also was a head of state, on a par with the most powerful executive in the world. And Mitterrand has occasionally commented icily on Delors's frequent, well-covered contacts with the press, reflecting the dual, overlapping nature of the foreign-policy mechanism. In 1987, under the Single Act amendment, a new, innovative approach to streamlining the process was launched—the troika.

Item: Reporters are gathered in the air-conditioned VIP departure lounge of Israel's airport on July 24, 1990. Foreign Minister David Levy has just politely, firmly brushed off the latest European Community plea for including the PLO in a future Middle East conference dealing with the 1967-occupied territories and other issues involving Arab countries and Israel. What startled the uninitiated was not Israel's repetition of its well-known position on the Palestinian question, but the attention accorded to—and the composition of—the departing EC delegation: a troika of foreign ministers, comprising Italy's De Michelis, Ireland's Gerry Collins, and Luxembourg's Poos. En route to Tunis as part of a swing to Arab capitals, the three-man delegation was representing "Europe's voice" in foreign affairs, using a plan under which the foreign minister whose government holds the rotating Council presidency is joined by his or her predecessor and successor. An EC commissioner, often Andriessen, is almost always present, providing a permanent link.

Within their tightly knit communities around the world, and particularly in moments of crisis or tensions involving Europe, diplomats from EC member countries act as something of a club. They consult frequently among themselves, and where a permanent EC representative is on the scene—in roughly ninety countries—he is always included. "Because of the rotating chairmanship, the local EC Commission representative, because he is generally present at all the meetings, remains at the center," said Philippe de Suremain, a seasoned French diplomat who served as the embassy's political counselor in Israel until 1989, before being reassigned to the ministry responsible for European issues, and who was named France's first postwar ambassador to Lithuania in September 1991. "Our regular meetings, which focus on trade but also on political-strategic issues, usually are held twice a month, with an agenda. . . . There is always a sense of cohesion, rarely seen or understood, by those outside, but it certainly has helped provide Europe a single voice in foreign policy."[11]

FRUSTRATING KISSINGER

Dealing with the Commission and the Council has, however, frustrated many U.S. administrations and frequently troubled one of America's best-informed critics and statesmen—Henry Kissinger. No former diplomat summed up the Community's dilemma better than his written accounts of the second administration of President Richard Nixon and, specifically, of its "Year of Europe" initiative in 1973. Proclaiming 1973 as the Year of Europe had a purpose: to work out what Kissinger describes as a "new Atlantic Charter," which would enshrine a visionary and pragmatic declaration of common purpose in such areas as defense, trade, and East-West relations, as part of a "reinvigorating" of the Alliance.[12]

Yet, as attempts were made to organize a meeting between President Nixon and European heads of government in connection with a NATO summit meeting that year, it became obvious to Kissinger and Nixon that such a meeting would make it "procedurally impossible" in terms of protocol to discuss the United States relationship with the Community. Why? Because some EC members, such as Ireland, did not belong to NATO, while some NATO members, such as Turkey, were not EC members. Chancellor Willy Brandt, suggested that Nixon meet with the EC foreign ministers, which, Kissinger recalled, the Americans found unacceptable, considering that the heads of NATO governments also would be in Brussels.

Kissinger's conclusion was disturbingly clear: "Since no European political institution yet existed, there was no focal point for contact with Europe. Brandt in fact faced us with a Catch-22 dilemma: If every European leader was a spokesman for Europe but could not represent it, and those who represented Europe were civil servants with no authority to negotiate, who then could act authoritatively?" In the end, the Community's heads of government simply avoided responding to the initiative, hiding, Kissinger wrote, "behind their experts, and the experts procrastinated in glacial procedures."[13]

When I called on Kissinger in his Park Avenue office in New York in the spring of 1990, he readily conceded that the Community had made—and was making—progress since his and Nixon's ill-fated initiative, which, it should be recalled, came in the midst of the Watergate scandal. The daily revelations and resignations of Nixon's closest advisers in Washington did not help on the diplomatic front in his talks with the allies. So how did the Commission and the Council strike him now, nearly two decades later, as the EC strove to move from a collection of disparate, sovereign states to a more united political entity, trying to speak and act with a single voice on foreign policy and security issues?

"They are somewhere in between the two extremes you have mentioned, and they are making progress," he said, but emphasized that many of the same problems he painfully encountered in the 1970s remained. "They are economically stronger, and I consider Delors a man of vision. . . . I like him." But, he urged, a "more effective, permanent, consultative mechanism was needed" of the kind both Nixon and, before him, President John Kennedy had sought to establish with the Community. And Kissinger made it clear that he was speaking of the European Council. "We are still excluded from their deliberations, including the vital defense and foreign-policy issues," he continued, and when I asked why, Kissinger came up with one of the best answers I have ever heard. "They do not want to be dominated."[14]

At the time of our talk in New York, the Bush administration was, in fact, negotiating what evolved into the Transatlantic Declaration on EC-U.S. relations signed in Paris during the CSCE Conference, but not made public until several days later on November 23, 1990. After dropping several provisions unacceptable to both sides, which related to liberalizing world trade (a U.S. idea) and supporting world financial stability (an EC suggestion), a new consulting arrangement finally emerged. It establishes twice-yearly meetings between the U.S. president, the secretary of state, and other cabinet officers on the one hand, and the presiding EC Council president, EC members' foreign ministers, the EC Commission president and his fellow commissioners, on the other. Meetings alternate between Brussels and Washington.

The step is regarded as symbolically important, and was widely regarded on both sides of the Atlantic as an improvement over the previous system of consultation, under which the U.S. secretary of state and cabinet officers responsible for trade and commerce met with the EC Commission president and commissioners, usually following the annual December NATO summit meeting in Brussels, which U.S. officials were attending anyway. But this awkward procedure failed to address, much less resolve, transatlantic tensions and conflicts over agricultural trade, foreign investments. Needed most was some permanent, high-level mechanism by which the United States and the Community could consult and act together in times of crisis, such as the Gulf War.

DELORS FEELS "HUMILIATED"

The obstacles in establishing institutional links, as Kissinger noted, were only some among many obstacles, not the least of which involved personalities in Brussels and Washington. Consider that Delors's outspoken, abrupt style never went down well in Washington, while he was finance minister in the early 1980s, particularly with Donald Regan, the equally blunt and temperamental U.S. Treasury secretary; or with James A. Baker III, who was President Ronald Reagan's chief of staff and replaced Regan at Treasury. Regan had clashed with Delors as early as the 1982 Versailles summit meeting over European participation in building the controversial Siberian gas pipeline, over East-West trade, and over what Delors had mistakenly thought was U.S. agreement to participate in a European proposal for concerted intervention in world currency markets. Neither Delors nor Baker and Regan ever forgot the incident.

Similarly, at the world economic summit meeting in Tokyo in 1986, Baker personally blocked the determined bid of Delors to obtain a seat for the Commission at the table of the then Group of Five, which had just been expanded to seven members with the entry of Canada and Italy. The so-called G7 group comprises finance ministers and central bankers, who meet regularly to discuss and coordinate monetary and economic policy; this group should not be confused with the seven heads of state and government, plus the EC Commission president, who participate in the annual world economic summit meetings.

Brushed aside by Baker at the Tokyo gathering, and in the absence of active support by the key G7 members, notably Britain,

France, and Germany, Delors felt "humiliated," a senior Commission official who accompanied him on the trip said. He added that Delors, embittered, vowed he would never attend another world summit meeting. Some thought it was pure Delors theatrics and that he might have overdone it. "There was no humiliation—except in Delors's mind," recalled Philippe Sassier, the perceptive French television economics commentator, who covered the Tokyo summit, adding, "The Americans felt, perhaps rightly, that there would be too many Europeans in G7, considering that France, Britain, Germany, and now Italy were in the club." Later, a senior U.S. diplomat explained that "Jim Baker simply did not consider the Commission a European government—not yet, and in any case, considering the lukewarm attitude of the other Europeans, why should the American government have been out front?"

THE COLD SHOULDER IN WASHINGTON

Thus Delors was hardly surprised when he first began sounding out American officials on how he would be received during his second visit to Washington as Commission president, planned for 1989. Through intermediaries, his overtures were politely brushed off. And there was a reason. Obsessed by the barely lukewarm reception accorded him by President Ronald Reagan during his first visit as Commission president four years earlier, Delors was demanding that this time he would get "official," head-of-state, red-carpet treatment. Under the best of Washington scenarios, this meant a twenty-one-gun salute and a military review upon arrival; lodging at Blair House, the official U.S. residence reserved for heads of state and government; addressing a joint session of Congress, and, of course, wining and dining at the White House, the State Department, and other agencies and organizations, plus plenty of media exposure.

There were precedents, which Delors had carefully studied. Heads of the Common Market, going back to the Eisenhower administration, have generally received VIP treatment. Delors's model was the highly publicized four-day visit to the United States by Roy Jenkins in December 1978, which included separate meetings with President Jimmy Carter, Vice President Walter Mondale, and other cabinet officers; an honorary degree from Michigan University; a speech to the National Press Club; and plenty of news coverage. The cover story in *Europe* magazine, which angered Giscard d'Estaing was precisely the pro-European stance Washington sought to convey during Jenkins's trip—at the instigation of Carter himself and one of his key aides, Robert Hunter.

The Reagan administration would have none of Delors's plan, nor, initially, would President-elect Bush. "They were still gazing to the Pacific. Europe was not on their screens—yet. But it had been very much on ours," recalled Hunter, who had helped organize Jenkins's U.S. trip while a senior member of Carter's National Security Council. "It was our policy to promote and support Europe," Hunter said, adding that Carter was also the first U.S. president to have officially visited the Commission headquarters in Brussels.

Thus, throughout late 1988 and early 1989, U.S. diplomats in Brussels and administration officials in Washington told their EC counterparts that the White House was perfectly willing to hold talks with Delors, but the visit would have to be informal, focused largely on trade, and that meant being classified "private," meaning no VIP treatment. U.S. officials tried explaining that there was no way he could be ranked on the same level as a head of state or government. In terms of protocol, they said, he was the equivalent of the head of an international organization, such as OECD and the IMF.

Annoyed, embittered, persuaded that he would again waste his time in Washington, Delors was about to drop the whole idea of visiting the United States. First, however, he decided to float an idea with the Bush administration. He granted an interview to the *Wall Street Journal,* published February 13, in which he proposed a "new partnership" with the Bush administration in which political and security issues would be discussed and, for the first time in the postwar era, elevated to the same level as trade. "We must try to place relations on a political level, including trade affairs. . . . If we have a purely commercial relationship, it's unacceptable," he said. Delors also urged that Washington actively support the 1992 program, and that Brussels and Washington should coordinate their loan policies with regard to Eastern Europe and the Soviet Union. There was no immediate response from Washington, as a morose, disappointed Delors decided to cancel the trip.

PRESIDENT BUSH CHANGES COURSE

What Delors and other EC leaders did not realize was that Bush was already deeply engrossed in completely reshaping his administration's approach to the Community and, more broadly, the Atlantic Alliance. The first hint of the change came at Boston University on May 21. Flanked by Mitterrand, who had just visited Bush at his summer home in Kennebunkport, Maine, the president declared that the United States "welcomes the emergence of Europe as a partner in world leadership," and stands ready to develop with the EC "new mechanisms of consultation and cooperation on political and global issues." This was definitely new, and was meant to respond to Delors. In the strongest terms yet uttered by a U.S. leader about 1992 and the community's emerging role in world affairs, Bush went on to say that "we believe a strong, united Europe means a strong America . . . a resurgent Western Europe is an economic magnet, drawing Eastern Europe closer, toward the commonwealth of free nations."

A new note was struck and Delors was somewhat encouraged. But what about the trip to Washington? Just over a week later, Bush was in Brussels, winding up a highly successful fortieth-anniversary celebration of NATO's founding. A visit to the thirteenth floor of the Berlaymont had been organized. What no one knew in advance was how the easygoing U.S. president would entice the touchy EC Commission president to come to Washington on a visit still being billed "private."

The scene was the EC Commission conference room in the Berlaymont. As Kingon, the former U.S. ambassador, recalled it, "he [Delors] still did not want to go to the United States at that point . . . he was resisting. We had made it clear that there was no way we wanted Blair House, a joint session of Congress. . . . I had briefed the president before we went into the meeting room. Everything was ready."

Settled into their seats, Bush, Delors, and several other EC commissioners and the Commission spokesman Ehlermann were somewhat startled as Bush casually pulled a sheet of paper out of his pocket, Kingon recalled, looked at it, and turned to Delors. "We are going to see you in Washington on June 15—isn't that right, Mr. President?" Kingon recalls Bush saying. Startled, Delors said, "That is up to you, Mr. President." Then came the answer that sprang the trap. "Well, you are coming, we hope . . . for lunch, at the White

House," said Bush. According to Kingon, that "sealed it. . . . Delors was stuck. Would he refuse a lunch invitation from the president of the United States?" Another U.S. official recalls Bush's stepping into his limousine in front of the Berlaymont, and casually, with a smile and a wave to Delors, saying, "See you in Washington in the middle of next month." And that, chuckled the delighted diplomat, "was it. Delors now had to go."

A month later, the lunch at the White House not only went smoothly but marked a turning point, setting the United States and the Community on a new course of vastly improved relations. On the U.S. side were Bush; Baker; Carla Hills, the U.S. trade representative; U.S. Ambassador-designate Thomas Niles, Kingon's replacement. Delors was accompanied by Lamy and Roy Denman, the outgoing EC ambassador in Washington. The talk focused largely on transatlantic trade and events in Eastern Europe, particularly how multibillion-dollar aid programs for Hungary, Poland, and other Eastern European countries could be coordinated by Washington and the Community. What emerged one month later was a new role for the Commission in managing the aid programs on behalf of twenty-four industrialized countries; the task was assigned to Delors during the world economic summit in Paris in July 1989.

Yet, as Delors readily conceded, without Bush's support it would never have worked. "From his earliest days as vice president, Bush has understood the importance of Europe, and it was he, as president, who moved to change the spirit of our relations," Delors told me afterward. "And from that point on, my relations began to improve with Secretary Baker, who had always mistrusted me, I had the feeling."

Within weeks, with Bush's agreement, the administration moved to enhance the Community's position and prestige by a seemingly minor but highly symbolic gesture: upgrading the diplomatic status of the EC Commission office in the U.S. capital. This meant that from then on permanent EC representatives would, like all other ambassadors, be accredited to the White House instead of to the State Department. No longer would the Commission be ranked, as it had been since 1958, alongside international organizations such as the IMF, the World Bank, and the OECD. Allied countries, notably Japan, which had been quietly studying the U.S. attitude as it evolved, followed suit. "Japan has gradually come to understand—and be fascinated by—what we are doing within the Community, and they spend a lot of time studying us," commented former Dutch prime minister Andries van Agt, who presented his credentials as the new EC ambassador to Bush in January 1990, after serving as head of the EC Commission in Tokyo for nearly three years.

While on a trip in November 1989 to Tokyo, where I first met van Agt, I asked a senior Japanese foreign-ministry official what the U.S. move would mean. "It was different with us, considering that it is our emperor who is the main accrediting figure, but the American example changed our approach to also take account of the EC's new stature and its emerging power," he said, adding that "we, too, as you can see by the activities of our private companies and banks, are taking the EC seriously . . . very seriously, and we ask, how big will it become?"

Recognition that Tokyo anticipated "big" growth indeed came during an official state visit to Japan in May 1991 by the Commission president and his key aides. Both Delors and his wife were entertained at lunch by the emperor and the empress in the Japanese capital, a courtesy reserved for heads of state or government. "The lunch was not only delicious, but, in protocol terms, symbolized an important event because it meant we had arrived there—in power terms," a Delors adviser said upon his return to Brussels.

"WIDENING" OR "DEEPENING"?

As the Community's diplomatic relations with Japan and the United States were being upgraded and improved, lively interest was also stirring in a new development being pursued by Brussels—"widening." This was EC shorthand for new relations being forged with governments in Eastern and Western Europe. The Bush administration was drawn to this idea, which not only involved the twelve EC countries completing their market integration, but included new-comers. It was, therefore, viewed in Washington as an opportunity for opening even more markets for American products, technology, and investments, and providing an economically strong, market-oriented zone that would replace the formerly Soviet-dominated COMECON trading bloc of Communist countries.

Such a geographically wider, possibly united Europe would encompass an additional dozen countries, creating a vast, stable, perhaps demilitarized and prosperous area, with a population approaching 500 million people. Names were being invented to describe the new European architecture. Delors spoke of a "Europe of concentric circles," with Brussels at its center. Diplomats increasingly referred to a "European Economic Area" when talking of negotiations aimed at linking the Community with the seven-nation EFTA bloc. Mitterrand occasionally referred to a "European Confederation" as an objective for East and West Europe, inspired, he said, by the visionary objectives laid down at the 1948 Hague Conference of Europe, which he attended as a delegate. Similarly, Kohl urged the establishment of a"peaceful, pan-European order," guaranteeing freedom, security, and prosperity. He and Mitterrand cited the Conference on Security and Cooperation in Europe and the Council of Europe in Strasbourg as participants in the new order.

Addressing the CSCE summit meeting in Paris, the Council of Europe's secretary general, Catherine Lalumière, pointed out that since the Strasbourg-based organization of twenty-five European nations was founded in 1949, Communist countries had always refused any involvement. But in the post–Berlin Wall era, she said, the Council was already becoming an organization for "pan-European cooperation," in areas such as human rights, culture, communications, environment, and legal cooperation. Hungary had just become its twenty-fourth member, followed by Czechoslovakia, as cooperation agreements were signed by the Council of Europe with Yugoslavia, Bulgaria, Romania, and the Soviet Union.

Regional variants of European architecture also began to surface. Italy's De Michelis, for example, sought to build interest in a trading bloc, which he called "Pentagonale," and which, strangely, resembled the former Austro-Hungarian Empire. If it ever materializes, this bloc would be dominated by Italy, encompassing Austria and most of its neighbors in Eastern Europe, linked by joint investments, energy, and regional transport networks. The problem was that most of these blueprints, like Mitterrand's confederation, remained deliberately vague, reflecting hopes for the future. Some of Europe's leaders have outlined their blueprints in separate declarations appearing in the final chapter of this book.

The European Community would, in any event, remain the nucleus, or what Kohl in his statement described as the "foundation for the unification of the whole of Europe," a message that came through as the post-1992 era approached. A widely divergent group of countries were seeking full membership or associate relationships with Brussels. They included Austria, Czechoslovakia, Hungary, Poland, and Turkey in the east; Norway, Sweden, Finland, and Iceland in the north; and neighboring Switzerland, Cyprus, and Malta.

However, responding to requests and applications for full membership, the Commission and the Council, speaking and acting with a single voice, had a simple, firm answer: no membership applications would be considered until the end of 1992 at the earliest. Internal development, or "deepening," must take priority over enlargement or "widening." It was an old debate, which, as Helen Wallace of the Royal Institute of International Affairs has noted, "haunted" Community leaders.[15]

Thus, within two years after the founding of the Community in 1958, Britain, having rejected the Treaty of Rome's goals and obligations, led the way in establishing EFTA, which, basically, is a loose, Geneva-based trading association, whose initial members also included Austria, Denmark, Norway, Portugal, Sweden, and Switzerland; a decade later, Iceland joined, as did Finland and Liechtenstein. By remaining outside the fledgling Community, Britain committed the first in a series of disastrous mistakes, according to Roy Jenkins. He cited successive British governments' refusal to join the European Coal and Steel Community, the Common Market, and, initially, the ERM of the European Monetary System, even though, in 1973, Britain became a full member, along with Ireland and Denmark. As Jenkins colorfully put it: "We stood on a railway platform, more or less benevolently waving goodbye as the train pulled out, and then had to decide whether to run after it and try to clamber aboard with such dignity and comfort as we could subsequently muster."[16]

But as EC integration and the movement toward monetary and political union accelerated among the twelve EC members, most of the remaining seven EFTA members began to look at new scenarios, fearful that they risked winding up in a "no-man's land" isolated from the developments sweeping neighboring Community countries. Thus, despite the prospects of difficult, painful adjustments required by full EC membership, Austria submitted its application in 1989, the first European member to take that step, following Turkey's application for membership submitted two years earlier. Malta and Cyprus followed suit in 1990.

More surprising, in December of that year the Swedish parliament gave the Social Democratic government a mandate to apply in 1991; as Carl Bildt, chairman of the conservative Moderate Party and the leading contender to become prime minister in a new conservative government, declared, "The die is cast. There is no turning back now." It was a most surprising development, considering that under decades of Social Democratic rule the prevailing majority view in Sweden was that its sacred neutrality would conflict with EC membership. Sweden's foreign minister Sten Andersson went so far as to suggest that the three major Nordic countries—Norway, Sweden, and Finland—apply together, a clear response to their economic needs and a recognition that the longtime advocates of EC membership— the Nordic business-community leadership—had been right all along. A year earlier, following lunch in his cozy, well-appointed dining room in downtown Stockholm, Peter Wallenberg, who with his family controls Sweden's largest constellation of industrial companies, told us that Sweden had no choice, that it suffered from an "island mentality," and would, by necessity, wind up submitting a bid for full membership. Bildt predicted Sweden would be a member by January 1, 1995.

Even with new bids coming into Brussels, the negotiations to strongly link the EC and EFTA moved forward, the idea being to extend some fourteen hundred Community rules and regulations to EFTA countries, thus greatly liberalizing the flow of people, goods, services, and capital in the eighteen-nation area. The agreement was to take effect on January 1, 1993, following ratification by every EC and EFTA member parliament. But this represented only a free-trade arrangement, with a common external tariff, not a merger of the two regions; Austria pressed its membership bid and the others planned to follow, for, as virtually every EC leader told potential newcomers, there could be no free ride. Obligations and loss of sovereignty to EC institutions went with full membership.

Everywhere I went in the region, and in Eastern Europe, enthusiasm for EC membership was high, and not only among the business elite. I recall vividly the quip of a forty-six-year-old Oslo taxi driver named Knut, during my visit to Norway in the spring of 1989. "What would Common Market membership mean to me, you ask?" he said as we wound our way through the crowded downtown traffic. "Not that much, but my friends and relatives in farming and fishing will feel it. . . . And yet, though it may not be heaven being in, remaining outside will be hell. Norway would be lost up here, cut off, in the cold, and that just isn't much of a future for a country of our size." Norway narrowly rejected EC membership in a nationwide referendum in

1972; 46% of Norwegians supported membership and 53% were opposed. Starting in the late 1980s, national support gradually swung behind the view expressed by Knut amid widespread expectations that Oslo would renew its bid by 1992 at the latest, following Sweden's bid submitted July 1, 1991.

Therefore, looking ahead into the 1990s, it appeared that the Community would simultaneously deepen and widen itself, but only with regard to Europe. This meant that neighboring developing countries, including those that had previously applied for membership—Turkey and Morocco—would be forced to negotiate new types of arrangements with Brussels. In other words, there were definite limits on how far the EC's reach could extend in this century. That message finally penetrated in Turkey, following the Commission's decision in February 1990 to postpone further action on Ankara's pending membership bid. "Turkey is a European, Mediterranean, Balkan, and Middle Eastern country, all at once," conceded Turkey's foreign minister during a conference in Istanbul in November 1990.

In a major shift from Turkey's long insistence that it was "European" and deserved full membership, and having faced repeated, polite rebuffs by Andriessen and other EC leaders, the foreign minister, Kurtcebe Alptemuçin, said his government was shelving its bid and "the endless discussions" about what it would do for Turkey and would, instead, expand its economic, political, and trade ties with its other neighbors—the Soviet Union, the Balkan states, and those in the Middle East. "We are not letting the EC bid drop, it is important, but we should not allow it to be made into the vital issue it was," Cem Boyner, chairman of the Turkish Industrialists' and Businessmen's Association, told the same conference.

The so-called "magnet effect" extended well beyond Europe. The accomplishments of the Common Market, particularly since 1985, were regarded as a model by Third World leaders, notably throughout Africa, the North African countries, and in Latin America. As we have seen in Chapter 5, EC corporations and banks have been actively establishing trade beachheads in such sectors as telecommunications. The Community was also contributing its modest part. Abel Matutes, the EC commissioner responsible for North-South relations, travels extensively to the Mediterranean countries and Latin America, frequently calming the anxieties of leaders convinced that Europe will turn its attention to Eastern Europe and the Gulf region—at their expense.

Matutes, who is Spanish, a former professor of economics at the University of Barcelona, a businessman, and leader of the highly conservative Alliance opposition party in Spain, tells his Latin American colleagues repeatedly that the Community had only modest financial aid at its disposal for them, but that the Commission would continue its aid programs. For example, EC foreign ministers in December 1990 agreed on a development aid package, running from 1991 to 1995, providing Latin America and Asia a total of nearly $4 billion, along with improved trade concessions. On the same day, the Council approved grants of $6 billion in aid and low-interest loans to fourteen Mediterranean countries from 1992 to 1996. Both packages were modest by world standards.

The largest single aid package the Community has offered to the Third World is known as the Lomé Convention, named for the capital of Togo in Africa, where the first such program was launched in 1975. Under the fourth Lomé Convention, ratified in 1990, a total of sixty-six poor African, Caribbean, and Pacific nations will receive nearly $14 billion in aid over ten years. African leaders in particular have repeatedly complained that such amounts are woefully inadequate for helping save their countries from worsening economic decay, staggering debt, drought, waste, corruption, and political instability.

Such statements dismay EC officials, who insist that the Community's powers and resources are something of an optical illusion, often appearing larger than they are in reality the farther one moves from Brussels. But the Community's increasingly active role in the world was only beginning to take shape. Let us, therefore, in the concluding chapter, turn to several pivotal European capitals and their leaders in order to understand better their vision of the New Europe as we approach the year 2000.

The Future of Europe:
Answering a Single Question

Asking knowledgeable sources to predict the future some ten years hence is a difficult chore even under the best of circumstances. Asking contemporary actors or actresses who control the instruments of political power to assess the future is plainly hazardous. And the chances of accuracy shrink dramatically when cast against the backdrop of the tumultuous, unpredictable events of the 1980s and the early 1990s, some of which we have covered in previous chapters.

Nevertheless, because the idea was novel and the challenge intriguing, I decided in the late summer of 1990 to put one question— and only one—to several EC heads of state and government. The question: What is your vision of Europe in the year 2000—what will it be, what will it not be?

What follow are their responses, each drafted, reviewed, and updated by some authors several times, and presented in the order in which they were completed and made available.

MARGARET THATCHER, Prime Minister of Britain (1979–90)

My Vision of Europe

You invite me to set out my views on Europe in the year 2000: what it will be, and what it will not be. Recent events have underscored the dangers of prediction. None of us foresaw the speed and suddenness of communism's collapse in Eastern Europe and the Soviet Union. We were caught unawares by Iraq's murder of Kuwait. The chances of predicting successfully how Europe will look in the year 2000 must be small. But I can say something about the Europe I *would like to see* by the end of the millennium.

As you point out, I set out my hopes for Europe quite fully in a speech at the College of Europe in Bruges. That was rather over two years ago. But in their essence they have not changed. Europe's achievements down the ages have been those of proud and independent states, each with its own history and traditions. At the time when the world was divided into great empires—Sung China, the Ottoman Empire, the Mogul Empire—Europe developed the small states, sometimes based on the city, sometimes on the kingdom. While the empires imposed a uniform system on their peoples, it was the diversity of the small states that accounted for Europe's great artistic and intellectual renaissance, its inventiveness, its industrial revolution. That is the foundation on which we have to build. We have the raw material there in the shape of our individual nations, now enlarged by the return to Europe of those Eastern European countries who, for forty years, were cut off by the Iron Curtain. Our task as governments is to ensure successful cooperation among them, so as to enhance the future prosperity and security of our peoples in an intensely competitive world. We shall not achieve that by trying to force them into a straitjacket. We have to preserve the different traditions, the parliamentary powers, and the sense of national pride which have been the source of Europe's vitality through the centuries. The conclusion which I drew at Bruges—and of which I am no less convinced today— is that the best way to build a *successful European Community is through willing and active cooperation between independent sovereign states.*

Indeed, my vision of Europe is reinforced by what has happened in these last twelve months in Eastern Europe and by other world events. The revolutions of 1989 in Eastern Europe have shown how strong the feeling of nationhood is. As the people of Eastern Europe detach themselves from the aberration that is communism, they look to their own country as the focus of their loyalty and their sovereignty. So too—quite naturally—do the people of the newly united Germany. They talk of their sovereignty and independence. To take another example: when it came to sending forces to the Gulf, it was not WEU which first responded, it was the independent nations—above all Britain and France—which took rapid and decisive action.

Europe cannot be built successfully by ignoring or suppressing this sense of nationhood, or by trying to treat sovereign nations as no more than regions controlled by a central body in Brussels. There is sometimes talk of trying to achieve federation by stealth. It won't work because it runs against the grain of history.

So my vision is of a Europe where increasingly we speak with a single voice: where we work more closely on the things we can do better together than alone: and where the concept that the Community does those things—but *only* those things—which cannot better be done by individual nations is rigorously observed. Europe is stronger when we act in this way, whether it be in trade, in defense or in our relations with the rest of the world. I want Europe to be more united and have a greater sense of common purpose. But it must be on the basis that we work *with* the grain of history and *with* the feelings of people. That is the way to achieve results.

That is my first point. My second is that Europe does not consist only of the twelve nations of the existing European Community. The new democracies of Eastern Europe want to join the institutions of Western Europe and we should encourage them. Some are already in the process of entering the Council of Europe, which we very much welcome. I have proposed that the *European Community should declare unequivocally that it is ready to accept all the countries of Eastern Europe* as members, provided that democracy has taken root and their economies are capable of sustaining membership. The association agreements which we have offered are only intermediate steps. The option of eventual membership must be clearly, openly, and generously on the table. We cannot say in one breath that these countries are part of Europe and in the next that our European Community club is so exclusive that we will not admit them. In considering plans for European integration we should hesitate before doing anything that would make it more difficult for the countries of Eastern Europe. Just as the Community reached out in the seventies to strengthen democracy in Greece, in Spain, and in Portugal by offering them membership with long transitional periods, so in the nineties it should be ready to open its doors to all the countries of Europe who want to join. I hope that by the end of the decade we shall be well down that road.

My third point concerns the *economics of Europe.* I do not want Europe to be a tight little inward-looking, protectionist group, which would induce the rest of the world to form itself into similar blocs. That could all too easily happen: indeed, we are already seeing some signs of it. It will be much better to create an outward-looking Europe, to reduce regulation and remove the constraints on trade, to allow the market to work and adopt policies which encourage enterprise.

The Single Market program will take us a major step toward that. But there is still a very long way to go before we have genuinely fair competition in the European Community, with the present disparities in subsidies and state aids removed. And we cannot allow the distortions and the damage to world trade caused by the CAP (Common Agricultural Policy) to continue for another decade. The Treaty of Rome (1957) was intended as a charter for economic liberty: and it should be our aim to make Europe by the year 2000 a model of what free trade and open markets can achieve—and therefore an example to the rest of the world.

My fourth point is that we should concentrate on the *practical measures* which appeal, above all, to young people and will bring home to them the benefits of a more united Europe. We should make it easier to move around Europe, whether on business or for pleasure, with a minimum of inconvenience (while maintaining basic checks which are necessary against drugs, crime, and terrorism). We should increase exchanges of young people. The best example of what I have in mind is the Channel Tunnel, due to be completed in 1993. By making trade and travel easier, it will bring Britain and the rest of Europe together in a very practical way.

My fifth point is that we should *not make the mistake of seeing Europe as the creation or the preserve of the Treaty of Rome.* If we really want to unite Europe, we need a wider vision. We should strengthen and extend the Helsinki process, first to entrench basic human rights, and second to enlarge political consultation throughout the whole of Europe. The CSCE is the only body which brings together all the European countries as well as the United States and the Soviet Union: and we should fashion it into an institution where regular political consultation takes place, not only about Europe's problems but those of the wider world as well. Our aim should be to create, by the end of the century, a great area of democracy stretching from the west coast of the United States right across to the Soviet Far East.

That leads me on to my sixth and last point, which concerns *the defense of Europe.* Some people talk of establishing collective security structures for Europe on the model of the League of Nations. But that sort of body will in reality function only if nations behave so virtuously as to make collective security unnecessary anyway. That is why I do not believe we should look for CSCE to offer a defense for Europe. Security is founded not only on ideals, but on the will and the capacity to defend them with adequate military strength. And for that we in Europe shall continue to rely on NATO, which has proved its worth.

The partnership with the United States will remain just as essential as it has been these last forty years. But we cannot look to the Americans to display the same degree of commitment unless we Europeans take a greater share of defense burdens, not only in Europe but out-of-area as well. That was one reason why it was so important for European countries to respond quickly to the crisis in the Gulf and to send adequate forces to stand alongside the United States and the Arab nations to resist aggression. After all Europe is much more dependent than the United States on oil from the Gulf for its industries and its prosperity: we should be no less stalwart in defending our shared interests. That is the lesson which Europe will have to learn and where our performance will need to improve dramatically over the next decade.

One has to be selective in a short article and I have said nothing, for example, about the passionate wish of Europe's people for a cleaner and safer environment, or about our responsibility toward the developing countries, above all to keep our markets open to them.

But the essence of my vision of Europe in the year 2000 is here. I have not spoken—as I am sure other contributors will—of political or economic or monetary union, or of integration, or of a federal Europe. They are labels. What matters is the reality:

- that the countries of our continent should be united by their commitment to democracy, the rule of law, and a market economy;
- that they should remain proud, independent nations within a broad framework of cooperation;
- that by acting together they should ensure that the influence

which our history, our experience, and our civilization have given us ensure that Europe's influence matches that of other great world powers;

- and that we should always act in close partnership with the great United States.

HELMUT KOHL, Chancellor of Germany (Since 1982)

Europe's Future

I

Today, forty-five years after the Second World War, we are witnessing dramatic political, economic, and social changes in Central, Eastern, and Southeastern Europe. The nations of Europe are overcoming the painful, unnatural division of our continent. Germany has regained its unity in freedom.

Europe is now entering a new era and is thus at a decisive stage of its development, which requires all of us to display courage, determination, and foresight. This historic opportunity is mainly attributable to three factors:

- Western unity and cohesion in fundamental matters and during crucial tests;
- the regained momentum of European unification, which acquired new thrust and appeal through the program for completing the Single Market and through the reforms set out in the Single Act, which has become for all European nations a model of evolution toward a community marked by political and economic solidarity and stability;
- the processes of reform in the countries of Central, Eastern, and Southeastern Europe, involving the quest for democracy and freedom as well as the introduction of a new liberal economic system.

Cooperation, partnership, and integration are therefore the key concepts for shaping the future architecture of Europe on the threshold to a new millennium.

We shall not be able to frame this architecture overnight, but must proceed patiently and resolutely. To do so, we need a clear vision of what we want to achieve and initiate in the years ahead.

II

I am convinced that overcoming the division of Germany will be a gain not only for the Germans but for all Europeans and will decisively assist European unification. Following the momentous changes, we now have a greater opportunity than ever before in Europe to attain the goal defined in the preamble to the German constitution: the creation of a united Europe.

Only the European Community can serve as the strong, dynamic nucleus and foundation of pan-European unification. It alone appears capable of giving Europe this quality, speaking with one voice in the world for the whole of Europe and adequately bringing this continent's weight to bear. To this end we must, however, endow it with the requisite structures and instruments. It is therefore essential to realize the vision of the founding fathers and develop the Community into a European Union.

The single European market, to be completed by December 31, 1992, is an important stage—albeit only an intermediate one—on this route.

On the basis of the initiative that I launched with President Mitterrand of France on April 18, 1990, two intergovernmental conferences on economic and monetary union as well as political union were started at Rome on December 15, 1990. The aim is to conclude these conferences in good time so that their results can be ratified by the parliaments of EC countries by the end of 1992.

Only if these reforms reach a successful conclusion will the European Community be able to meet the challenges facing it internally and externally and to shoulder its share of political and economic responsibility for the whole of Europe and toward its partners in the world.

What are the main objectives?

First: In view of the next European elections, in 1994, we must considerably strengthen the rights and powers of the European Parliament. In keeping with our democratic principles, we are prepared to transfer further rights of national parliaments and governments to European institutions if distinct parliamentary controls simultaneously exist at the European level. We therefore need a stronger European Parliament, with powers increasingly similar to those of our national parliaments. For example, in future the European Parliament should participate in electing the president and members of the Commission. But above all we must clear the way for the European Parliament's genuine involvement in legislation.

Second: We must greatly increase the efficiency of the Community's institutions. This undoubtedly includes streamlining the working methods and decision-making processes of the Commission, Council, and Parliament. But the status and functions of the European Council, as laid down especially in the 1983 Solemn Declaration of Stuttgart, should also be codified and developed further in the treaties.

Third: We must frame a true common foreign and security policy, which must include development policy. It remains our conviction that unification is incomplete without fully including security policy and hence defense matters in the long term. Particularly the events of recent months have made it clear to us that we need an effective set of instruments in order to bring our common interests to bear even better in the world.

Fourth: We must as a matter of priority impart a new quality to cooperation in key areas of police and judicial action. The gradual abolition of border checks makes it essential to develop new forms of closely coordinated action in central fields, such as combatting terrorism, drugs, and organized international crime, which we can counter but inadequately with the existing tools.

Fifth: We seek the elaboration of a common economic, financial, and monetary policy. On the basis of the guidelines provided by the Delors Committee and by the European Council in Rome at the end of October 1990, we want to achieve European economic and monetary union. The core must be an independent European system of central banks which—like the German Central Bank—is committed to ensuring monetary stability as a priority goal. The path must lead to a European currency that is as strong and widely accepted as the German mark.

Sixth: Despite all the foregoing we definitely do not seek more centralism in Europe, but a citizen's Europe, which respects and preserves regional features and traditions. This requires codifying the basic principles of a reasonable balance between the powers of the Community and those of its members: federalism, subsidiarity, and regard for regional interests are essential structural principles of the future European architecture.

To us Germans, concurrence of the two intergovernmental conferences is of fundamental importance: Now, as before, our central objective is the political unification of Europe; though highly important in itself, economic and monetary union will remain fragmentary if we fail to achieve political union at the same time. An inextricable link therefore exists between political union and economic and monetary union.

My basic aim is to help "place the European train on the tracks leading to the right destination," so that, concurrently with the introduction of a common European currency, the political foundations are laid for the United States of Europe.

Only a European Community that is internally strengthened in this way can become a decisive factor of stability on our continent, which will for a long time to come undergo far-reaching changes in the political, economic, and security sectors and which is seeking a peaceful pan-European order that guarantees freedom, security, and prosperity for everyone.

Europe does not end at the rivers Oder and Neisse. The people in Poland, Czechoslovakia, Hungary, and the other countries of Central and Southeastern Europe need a clear European perspective. The same applies to the EFTA nations, with whom we already cooperate closely and are jointly seeking to create a European economic area that could ultimately become a model for the whole of Europe.

In future the European Community must therefore view itself even more as the nucleus and foundation for the unification of the whole of Europe. Thus it must continue to be open to other European countries.

The aim, however, cannot be to admit as many countries as possible into the European Community. It would not survive such an exertion unscathed in institutional or structural terms because of the major disparities in the level of development of many countries.

There would also be a danger—and this is the decisive consideration—of the European Community being reduced to an elevated free-trade area. Precisely this has never been our aim in unifying Europe. Those who seek the political unification of Europe must first consolidate and enhance the Community so that it can remain an anchor and driving force for the whole of Europe.

We definitely do not want to exclude our European neighbors or let them become or stay "second-class Europeans." On the contrary, the European Community must and will make energetic efforts to support the successful continuation of reforms in Central, Eastern, and Southeastern Europe and to raise cooperation with those countries and the EFTA onto a new plane. The cooperation agreements and the envisaged association agreements are essential tools toward this aim.

One of the greatest challenges is to involve the Soviet Union ever more closely in the coming years in the task of shaping Europe's future architecture—politically, economically, culturally, and in matters of security. However, this is only possible if the Soviet Union systematically continues its policy of reform in both domestic and foreign affairs. Decades of East-West conflict have caused many to forget that numerous peoples in the Soviet Union are closely linked to Europe, not just geographically but through their history and culture. Now at last we want to turn these links to political benefit.

The understanding that we seek for the whole of Europe also requires the creation of overarching cooperative structures and the consolidation of security and stability.

The process of security and cooperation in Europe, the CSCE, has been of inestimable value in overcoming the divisions on our continent and in building a roof under which all nations of Europe can live and work together in guaranteed security and common freedom.

We must therefore devote particular attention to further expanding the CSCE. But we should not forget the Council of Europe, which in the course of the past year has already opened up to the young democracies of Central Europe—I need only mention Hungary's recent admission. The Council of Europe has over the last forty years made valuable contributions toward protecting human and civil rights and has permitted major progress to be made in cultural cooperation, environmental protection, and other fields.

Such an overall structure could be termed a "European confederation"—to use the concept introduced by President Mitterrand—in which all countries of our continent participate on equal terms.

At the same time we must strive to develop further, in a spirit of genuine partnership in all fields, the ties between the merging Europe and North America, which have played a decisive part in guaranteeing our security and freedom. The Transatlantic Declarations adopted on our initiative indicate the path to follow.

III

I am convinced that in the years ahead we shall make substantial progress toward realizing the vision of a European Union, in other words toward a united Europe. In this way, we are making a crucial contribution toward a new and strong Europe, to a common European future in peace and freedom, in prosperity and security. Germany, united in freedom, is conscious of its responsibility for a Europe whole and free and will continue to gear its policies to this goal.

JACQUES DELORS, President of the EC Commission (Since 1985)

The Global Challenge Facing Europe

Will the nineties be Europe's decade, as some of our leaders claim? The tremendous hopes that have blossomed since the collapse of the Communist system and the refound dynamism of the European Community would seem to support this view.

But there are many imponderables. Will the countries of Central and Eastern Europe succeed in the twofold task of democratizing their societies and modernizing their economies? Will the Soviet Union manage to surmount economic chaos and nationalist tensions? Will the European Community make sufficient progress toward its own twin goals of political union and economic and monetary union between now and 1995 to make the integration process irreversible? Will it even raise its ambitions to the point of sharing the burden of worldwide responsibilities with the United States?

As one who has witnessed the revitalization of the European venture at first hand since 1985 and helped to reconcile differences of opinion between twelve member states, I am well aware of the scale of the task before us.

Let us start, then, with the Community of Twelve—a Community respected and sometimes envied by the rest of Europe. By the end of the century it will have to prove that it has made the most, in economic and social terms, of its opportunities as a single economic area with a population of somewhere between 340 and 450 million, depending on whether it admits new members or not. If it can develop internally, it will be in an even better position to help resolve the world's problems: monetary disorder, debt, underdevelopment, protection of the environment, and the scourges assailing society. But this presupposes a single currency and the ability to promote the convergence of national economies toward its ambitious goals of economic and social development.

The Community will continue to be motivated by the legacy of its founding fathers, but it will be guided by necessity too, conscious of its importance for those around it. How could the Community enjoy its prosperity if instability and uncertainty were to weigh on Eastern Europe, if underdevelopment and burgeoning population growth were to exacerbate tensions to the south? To counter these threats the Community will have to take the lead in development aid and in international action to combat pollution and the destruction of nature.

Of course, everything comes down to politics in the end. That is why political integration has to proceed in parallel with economic, monetary, and social union. The Twelve are expected to play a role on the international stage, to speak with a single voice, to act in concert. After what is bound to be a long learning process, the Community will develop a common foreign policy. It will have to be cautious in its approach, gradually working to reconcile rather different traditions and geopolitical viewpoints. Here, too, necessity will be the mainspring of action.

Logically, too, the twelve will not be able to separate foreign policy from security forever. Tensions and conflicts will not vanish overnight with the ending of the Cold War. But with a European military force within an Atlantic Alliance adapted to the new situation, the Community could help to guarantee respect for international law. There is also the hope—albeit somewhat fragile in the summer of 1991—of a stronger role for the United Nations as a mediator in conflict and arbiter for respect of the elementary rules underpinning peace.

None of this, to be sure, will be possible without gradual reform of the Community's institutions, its decision-making processes, and its means of action. The prospects I have just outlined clearly imply a transfer of sovereignty from the nation states to the Community. Let me stress, yet again, the two prerequisites for success. First, the approach must be gradual, with progress being determined by the strength of our conviction that joint action is more effective. Second, a balance must be struck between integration and cooperation between nations—so that ultimately people will feel a need to be Europeans while nevertheless retaining a sense of pride in being English, German, Italian, or French.

The Community's institutions will have to be adapted in line with these two imperatives. A sound institutional structure is essential. Getting it to work is even more important. Institutions are there to uphold the law and the rules of "living together." Those at the helm must seek to identify the essential interests shared by the peoples and states of the Community and to translate that consensus into action.

The great achievement of the authors of the Treaty of Rome was that they devised a system that has stood the test of time. The underlying spirit must be preserved as the Community's powers and responsibilities expand.

The Court of Justice will become a constitutional court too; the European Parliament will assume the role of legislator in Community matters; the Commission will continue to be the prompter, the initiator of action, though it will have to share the right of initiative in foreign-policy matters with the Council; and the Council will retain the final say in major decisions. The new structure, then, will be similar in inspiration to the one we know today. It will simply have to shoulder wider responsibilities.

The picture would be very different indeed if the Community had to absorb twelve to fifteen new members. In that event, the Commission would have to secure much wider executive powers to avoid the very real danger of decision-making's getting bogged down. In return, powers of censure would be extended from the European Parliament to the European Council (the heads of state and government, who meet regularly twice to four times a year).

But the institutional approach will not solve the central problem of how to organize a "greater Europe." To my mind the historic challenge facing the Community is to come up with blueprints for a new architecture and make them a reality. The most realistic scenario, I believe, is François Mitterrand's idea of a loosely structured Confederation, which would nevertheless provide an adequate framework for developing political, economic, and cultural exchanges among all the nations of Europe. So what shape will this wider European structure have taken by the year 2000?

A common market; a monetary system—rather like the present

European Monetary System—with a single common currency based on the ECU; practical cooperation in specific areas (environment, infrastructures, research and technology, cultural matters); a Political Cooperation Council involving regular meetings of the foreign ministers; a delegation of national parliaments. . . .

We need then to be cautious in our assessments. We need to be ready, willing and above all able to cope with unexpected problems and tensions. In political terms this means reconciling the Community's advance toward its own ambitious goals with participation by all the countries of Europe in a single enterprise founded on common values and interests. This would guarantee respect for diversity—whether in terms of economic situations, basic foreign policy approaches or views on the respective roles of the nation-state and the European entity.

A greater Europe along these lines might be looked at askance, particularly by the United States and Canada, which could, quite rightly, fear the emergence of a new imbalance. Hence the need, in parallel with any such developments, to pursue the Helsinki process, in which both countries are major players. Under the auspices of the Conference on Security and Cooperation in Europe, trade and cooperation could extend from San Francisco to Vladivostok. Nor, I believe, can we exclude the growing economic might of Japan. This dynamic and competitive country must assume its share of the burden of responsibility for world developments.

It is perhaps unwise to attempt to answer every question that the next ten years will raise. It is perhaps shortsighted to reflect on "a greater Europe" in a world that is growing more interdependent day by day. And this perhaps explains my repeated insistence on the global challenge and the worldwide responsibilities facing the Community.

FRANÇOIS MITTERRAND, President of France (Since 1981)

The Europe We Want

The major enterprise of my generation, since the end of World War II, has been, and indeed still is, to free Europeans from the shackles of hatred and the inevitability of decline, to restore Europe to its rightful place, and to build a new kind of community with the free consent of the reconciled peoples of Europe.

It is now some years since Europe started along the road leading to the return of its reality, identity, and power.

There have been many stages along the way to this rebirth: the creation of the European Coal and Steel Community (ECSC) in 1951; the signing of the Treaty of Rome on March 25, 1957; the entry of Great Britain and Ireland in 1973; the establishment of the European Council in 1975; the decision to create the European Monetary System (EMS) in 1979; and the election of the European Parliament by universal suffrage in 1979. The Common Agricultural Policy, put in place during the sixties, gave European agriculture a shot in the arm. From six member states in 1957, to nine in 1972, to ten in 1981, the European Economic Community became a reality.

The signing of the Franco-German Treaty in 1963 and its renewal in 1983 consolidated the European edifice, turning one-time adversaries into partners whose initiatives have proven essential in the construction of Europe.

But beginning in the late 1970s, difficulties and disputes began to accumulate, blocking further progress. There were sixteen such problems, of varying importance. The most significant of these had to do with the British contribution; this came at a time, in the first half of 1984, when the presidency of the European Council was my responsibility. Something had to be done. We managed to resolve this situation at the European Council meeting at Fontainebleau in June 1984, thanks to solid Franco-German understanding, a softening of the British position, and the contributions of the chairman of the EC Commission, Jacques Delors.

Once over that obstacle, we were able to resume the construction of Europe . . . and we have not stopped since. The entry into the EEC of Spain and Portugal, which I viewed as indispensable, brought the number of member states to twelve. To promote research and development of the very latest in technology, Eureka was officially established by eighteen countries on July 17, 1985.

The European Council, meeting in Milan in June 1985, decided to create a great internal market within Europe by December 31, 1992. This would require the adoption of some three hundred directives. From that date on, if we accomplish what we have set out to do, people, merchandise, and capital will be able to circulate freely in

Europe, without technical, regulatory, or taxation barriers.

Another major advance, what was called the Single European Act, was agreed on at the European Council meeting in Strasbourg in December 1985. Its objectives were to update the Treaty of Rome, which had created the three European communities in 1957, and to facilitate Community decision-making by a more frequent resort to majority voting. It was also intended to improve cooperation among the twelve on foreign-policy matters.

Since that time, and despite some very real (if foreseeable) difficulties, there has been true progress toward economic and monetary union as well as political union.

In Hannover, in June 1988, the twelve gave themselves one year to examine the means of achieving economic and monetary union. At the end of that year, Jacques Delors presented a report in June 1989 in Madrid. And, finally, it was under French presidency in December 1989 that the decision was made to convene an Intergovernmental Conference on Economic and Monetary Union by the end of 1990.

Before the European Council meeting in Dublin, in April 1990, Chancellor Kohl and I agreed that at this point in its development, and in parallel with its monetary ambitions, the Community should reaffirm its goal of political union—in the spirit of the 1985 Single European Act—and should give itself the means of achieving that goal.

We proposed to our ten partners that we move in four directions: (1) to ensure the unity and coherence of action by the Union in the economic, monetary, and political domains; (2) to make our institutions more efficient; (3) to reinforce the democratic legitimacy of the union; and (4) to define and implement a common policy on foreign affairs and security. The Community would thus become an agent for peace and development in the world.

At the two Dublin summit meetings, the twelve embraced these objectives and decided that the two intergovernmental conferences, on economic and monetary union and on political union, should be opened before the end of 1990, should be carried through to a successful conclusion, and should see the fruits of their efforts ratified by all member states before December 31, 1992.

Before the European Council meeting in Rome, Chancellor Kohl and I addressed our partners, in the same spirit, with more precise proposals to help the conference on political union get off to a good start: (1) to deepen and widen the Union's powers in many fields; (2)

to establish a true European citizenship, to strengthen the powers of the Parliament in the direction of co-decision-making, and to bring the national parliaments into association with the union; (3) to enlarge the role of the European Council, which, in our eyes, must be at the same time arbitrator, guarantor, and promoter of a consistent deepening of integration on the way to European Union; (4) to draw up a common policy on foreign affairs and security which would be extended progressively into every domain. We also called for the establishment of a true European citizenship, as urged by Felipe González. These two conferences opened as scheduled in Rome in December. They have one year to carry out their work.

Our economic and monetary goal is to achieve in three phases—we are now in the first—a common monetary policy, irrevocably fixed parities, and, ultimately, a single currency, at which point monetary policy and the single currency would be administered by a European system of central banks.

Our political objective is to transform the Economic Community into an entity with all the attributes of a union of states. Between the Europe of nation-states, which soon comes up against the limits set by the egotism of our old nations, and a supranational Europe, a generous utopia but without political reality, a more pragmatic path is now widely open to us: that of a Europe respectful of the identities of its constituent nations, but capable of overcoming their differences and particularisms in order to construct a political entity the like of which history has never known. A political and economic entity which has shown itself since 1957 to be an unfailing source of prosperity and progress, not only for the inhabitants of the twelve member states but for those of the sixty-nine countries linked to it by the Lomé accords; and it will be even more so once we have reached our objectives.

Recent changes and events in the world have given rise to a wind of skepticism in Europe over the construction of the Community. Yet I would point out that the process of German unification took place, and was completed on October 3, 1990, just as the European Council had urged and requested on December 8 and 9, 1989, in Strasbourg: democratically and peacefully, respecting the agreements, treaties, and principles set out in the Helsinki Final Act; and in a context of European integration.

More generally, I would observe that the collapse of all barriers between the countries of Western Europe and those of Eastern

Europe (once again referred to as Central and Eastern Europe), has done nothing to lessen the validity of the Community idea. The twelve reacted promptly to the new situation. Aid and cooperation agreements have been signed with Poland, Hungary, Czechoslovakia, Bulgaria, Romania, and the Soviet Union. New negotiations are under way to yet further strengthen relations with these countries in the framework of agreements of association, which will improve trade relations, develop cooperation, and establish real political dialogue.

There has been criticism in certain circles that Europe as such had not been capable of taking diplomatic initiatives to reestablish the sovereignty of Kuwait and preserve the peace.

I would recall that, the day after the invasion of Kuwait by Iraq, the Community issued an unqualified condemnation of the aggressor and decided to implement an embargo; and that, under the aegis of the Western European Union, the navies of several European nations coordinated their actions.

I would add that if political union, and notably a common policy on foreign affairs and security, was one of the new objectives set by the twelve in 1990, it was precisely because in these domains ultimate authority lies with the individual states and with them alone. The Community acted within the framework of its jurisdiction. It could neither exceed its powers nor go beyond the limits of its authority.

After January 1, 1993, the time will come for a strengthened and more coherent European Community to examine the applications for membership lodged by a number of countries. Under the Treaty of Rome, every democratic country in Europe has a vocation to join. But this also requires a commitment to observe all Community rules. Clearly, this will have to be done in stages. The many applications for membership, some of them already received and others foreseeable, are in themselves a tribute to the success we have had in the construction of Europe.

But does this mean we will have to wait eighteen more months before organizing relations between the European Community and the rest of Europe? Certainly not. As of now, my purpose is that this Community of twelve nations' citizens—and I am not the only one acting toward this goal—be the driving force of a more united, stronger, and more democratic Europe. It was in this spirit that I proposed on December 31, 1989, that the countries of Europe begin, without delay, planning the confederation that in due course will unite them on an equal footing. It is for the same reasons that, as early as December 1989, I supported President Gorbachev's proposal to move up to 1990 the summit meeting of the countries of the Conference on Security and Cooperation in Europe, which normally should have been held in 1992.

That meeting, which took place in Paris on November 20 and 21, 1990, provided a stage for the signing of the first treaty on conventional disarmament between the members of the Atlantic alliance, on the one side, and the former member states of the Warsaw Pact, on the other; it also adopted a declaration in which the same twenty-one countries declared that they were no longer adversaries; and it took a number of other decisions that reinforced the CSCE in terms of security and cooperation among its thirty-four member states. On that day, the Cold War truly ended.

There have been times when faith in Europe seemed to waver. And yet it has always stood up against unfavorable winds and overcome seemingly insuperable obstacles. Today we sometimes hear concerns voiced in certain countries of the Community about their sovereignty. How far will all this take us? It is true that we cannot build Europe without delegating more sovereignty, but it should also be pointed out that there have been many occasions in the past where this has occurred with democratic consent, and broad acceptance.

It is not a question of each of our member states giving up, and thereby losing, part of its sovereignty, or of being stripped of its sovereignty by a rival power, as might have happened in earlier times. Rather, it is a matter of each state sharing certain elements of its sovereignty with the European Community of tomorrow, a Community that we want to be strong, coherent, and democratic, that is, under the control of the peoples of Europe. The European Union tomorrow will not make nations disappear. It will permit them to exist in a world where the nation can no longer be—is no longer—the only dimension of sovereignty. I refuse to oppose the idea of the nation to that of Europe.

Let us then stay on course and prepare for the future while keeping in mind our rich history and civilization, but also the pain and discord of the past. Let us build the Europe that our Community foreshadows: the Europe of history and geography.

JUDGING FIVE COMMON THREADS

Let us briefly examine five underlying threads of broad agreement, which emerge from a careful reading of these texts:

- All of the leaders share a common visionary goal: to establish a prosperous, stable, more open European Community. They clearly agree on wanting for the Community a more respected, powerful force in world affairs by the year 2000, and, if possible, earlier. There is a striking absence of any de Gaulle-like visions of Western Europe, evoking strident nationalism.
- Each agrees on the urgent need to build political, technological and financial ties with Eastern Europe and the Soviet Union. They identify the region's reconstruction as one of the key foreign-policy goals for the Community as a way of preparing the transition to democracy and privatized, capitalistic economies, notably in Eastern Europe, with privileged EC links.
- Each actively supports economic power as the vital ingredient underpinning the primary goal. Sharing advanced technology is widely viewed by all as the key to European strength and its capacity to compete in world markets. The examples cited, reflecting their personal EC success stories, range from the Channel Tunnel cited by Mrs. Thatcher to Eureka cited by Mitterrand.
- Each fully supports the need for the Community to forge a common defense and foreign policy, extending to fighting terrorism and organized crime. Control is viewed as belonging under the auspices of the Council of Ministers, not the Commission or the Parliament. Meantime, each acknowledges U.S. power and influence in Europe, and the need for the Atlantic Alliance in some form.
- Each supports the strengthening of EC political institutions, enabling the combined weight of their shared sovereignty to provide "a single voice" in the economic area, as well as in such sectors as the environment. Although they avoid committing themselves to specific decision-making structures, the leaders agree to establish common, efficient power-sharing machinery.

FIVE DIFFERING SHADES IN OUTLOOK

However, there are areas of disagreement and shades of difference on a wide range of issues.

- Britain and Mrs. Thatcher, backed by smaller countries, view the future EC as a model of economic liberty and free trade above all. Delors, Mitterrand, and Kohl reflect a more visionary approach, which places political and monetary union on the same level of importance, to avoid the EC's evolving into simply what Kohl describes as an "elevated free-trade area."
- Mitterrand calls for a "Union of States," Kohl a "United States of Europe" and Mrs. Thatcher warns of "federation by stealth." Clearly, the EC's three main powers diverge on how much sovereignty should be shifted to the new decision-making body, and on which EC institutions should be granted new powers to implement common programs in areas like security.
- How far, how quickly to expand EC membership—notably to EFTA and Eastern Europe—has remained controversial. Thatcher and her supporters want quick, full membership for Czechoslovakia, Hungary, and Poland. Mitterrand, backed by Kohl and Delors, prefers establishing a "European Confederation," a loosely organized body, which would keep Brussels at the center, and in charge.
- The extent to which the United States should be associated with the Community's new security organization divides Europe. For Thatcherites and others, NATO must remain the cornerstone. Delors proposes the creation of a "European" military force. Kohl, among others, urges expanding the CSCE process, as one important, loose way of keeping the United States in Europe.
- Kohl—and only he—strongly urges that the European Parliament should be greatly strengthened, anticipating the 1994 elections, with powers resembling national Parliaments. Mitterrand favors expanding the powers of the Council, a view shared by Delors, who urges that if the EC absorbs a dozen or so new members, the Commission will require "much wider" executive powers.

CONCLUSIONS

My thoughts have often gone back to my first encounter with Jan Linschoten, the Philips engineer, on that 1981 spring morning in Eindhoven. A decade later, his vision of a reinvigorated Europe and of his ailing company were once again big news, amid persistent, unconfirmed rumors that Philips would disappear as Europe's largest electronics company. If this were to happen, it would represent a shattering blow to the Community's drive to become a major industrial force in world affairs. Yet financial difficulties, Japanese takeovers, and failures there will be. Examples drawn from multinational business, however, do not tell the whole story; they are neither conclusive nor comprehensive. The following, then, are my ten conclusions as we look to the future.

- Spurred by the failures of the early 1980s, the EC has set into motion a historical process that is irreversible. Thus, throughout the 1990s, the EC member governments will increasingly combine their resources and pursue common policies, but only in those areas where they agree. The most promising areas will be increasingly subsidized high technology, trade, and monetary policy.
- Europe's new political architecture, once established, will be unique by world standards; more closely resembling Switzerland and Belgium than the United States. Loosely structured, alongside national governments, and based in Brussels, the European Council will be at the apex. But it will be sharing power, increasingly, with the Commission, the new Eurofed, and the Parliament.
- Although EC economies slumped in 1990 and only piecemeal recovery started in 1991, the Community's growth rates will outpace those of the United States, and somewhat trail Japan in the 1990s. A new mood of "Eurorealism" will now guide EC expansion and monetary and fiscal policy. Meantime, investments from Japan and the United States will continue being drawn to EC countries.
- Jacques Delors will go down in history as the man who did more for European unity than any other leader in the postwar era, with the notable exception of Jean Monnet. Delors's vision and leadership will remain a crucial reference for future genera-

tions of students of European history, seeking to understand the tortuous efforts to build EC strength, global reach, and influence.

- Meantime, the French-German "alliance within the Alliance" will remain the crucial political driving force for the emergence of political, economic, and monetary union. Even when Kohl and Mitterrand are no longer in power, the Paris-Bonn axis will continue as Europe's pillar; if these ties were to break, European unity would disintegrate.

- The United States and Japan will be actively sought out as equal partners, but the process will be marked, increasingly, by tensions and conflict. Washington and Tokyo may well be eased or shunted aside, as European political unity gathers momentum. Yet, paradoxically, Europe will continue seeking U.S. military protection and Japan's investment and technology.

- In the 1990s, Britain will be the new active player in Community affairs—fearful that Mrs. Thatcher's hardline approach has isolated the country. London will pursue reinforcement of its position as the EC's financial hub, amid countervailing drives for dominance by Frankfurt and Paris. The pro-European stance will be pursued by future conservative and labor governments.

- The opponents of European integration will also gather momentum and power, fueled by chronic unemployment. Protectionism, crime, drug use, and racism, marked by anti-Semitism and anti-Arab protests, will continue to spread, along with extreme-right-wing and extreme-left-wing movements. Threats of large-scale migration from the Soviet Union could accelerate dramatically, bolstering East-West cooperation.

- Offsetting forces will be increasingly mobilized through structured cooperation between EC law-enforcement agencies and interior and justice ministries. Crackdowns on drugs, organized crime, and illegal government subsidies will be accelerated, along with EC-wide restrictions on immigration. European business leaders will become increasingly supportive of EC political union.

- Finally, young people, representing a new generation of Europeans, will provide much of the popular support for the stronger, internationalized New Europe. Youthful business leaders, workers, and intellectuals will increasingly seek their professional identities and sense of purpose in cross-border endeavors in a European context, including exchanges of all kinds.

Item: On a sunny, chill morning in April 1991, my wife and I were visiting the twelfth-century Norman cathedral of Cefalù on the northern coast of Sicily. Suddenly, we found ourselves surrounded by more than twenty students, all in their early teens, who came from a small town near Catania on the east coast of the island. Not only was it their first visit to this seaside resort, but it was a first encounter of this sort with foreigners.

Staring at us, then whispering and giggling, they gradually became bolder, trying their rudimentary French with my wife and halting, American-accented English with me. For nearly a half hour, as we sat pinned in a pew and as other tourists, somewhat baffled, strolled by, the students peppered us with questions. How could an American and a Frenchwoman actually live together? Were we also married? What did we think of Italian soccer players and sports-car drivers? Where, outside of Italy, could they study other European languages? Did we consider Sicily part of Europe? It reminded us of similar encounters as we traveled through the Soviet Union in the early 1970s.

Quietly, their bearded, youthful teacher moved forward. "Please excuse them," he said in French, "but you must understand we are a bit isolated here, and they very much want to be part of what is going on in the rest of Europe. . . . You are helping in that process by just talking with them in your own languages." As we slipped out of the cathedral, I concluded that we had glimpsed a part of the future and that, despite all the obstacles—and with some luck—the 1990s would indeed prove to be the Decade of Europe.

Epilogue

The spectacular, dizzying, violent upheavals in the Soviet Union and in Yugoslavia were the more notable events that erupted during the late summer of 1991 as this book was being readied for publication. While these events did not fundamentally change contemporary Europe's determined effort to become a more powerful and united force in world affairs, they certainly provided unexpected headaches, threats, complications, and distraction from much of the business at hand as described in previous chapters.

The political turmoil in the Soviet Union and Eastern Europe brought into stark perspective the fault lines among major EC powers—primarily France, Germany, Britain, and Denmark—as they rushed to respond, often in differing, conflicting ways, and so appeared to lack a common sense of purpose. With the notable exception of Jacques Delors, no single leader could claim to be responding with a "European voice." HANDWRINGING. HESITATION BLUES. UNITY THREATENED. UNDIRECTED POWER. Such headlines bitingly described the EC's latest identity crisis, which came just four months before the planned completion of agreements to forge EC political, monetary, and economic union.

And yet, in sharp contrast to the Community's humiliating disarray during the Gulf War, there were also positive signs of unity amid widespread consensus that the picture was by no means entirely bleak and might prove temporary. Consider the following:

- EC foreign ministers, meeting in Brussels on August 27, 1991, in a surprising display of unity and despite expressions of con-

327

cern in Washington, voted unanimously to recognize the Baltic states of Estonia, Latvia, and Lithuania as independent countries. "It is now time, after more than fifty years [since being forcibly incorporated into the Soviet Union] that these states resume their rightful place among the nations of Europe," the twelve ministers said in a joint communiqué. Accompanied by promises of development aid and encouragement for EC private investments, the Community was thus staking a major claim to bringing former Soviet Union republics into an enlarged "European Economic Area" as discussed in Chapter 9 and Chapter 10.

- On the same day, amid hectic preparations for all-out war in Croatia and the looming disintegration of Yugoslavia as a nation, EC governments agreed unanimously to intensify their diplomatic efforts that had begun several months earlier so as to arrange a durable ceasefire. Although as during the Gulf War, the EC lacked an independent military force, the EC Council dispatched an unarmed fifty-member team to the region during the summer, and a troika of EC foreign ministers traveled to Yugoslavia, threatening sanctions and pressing for a durable settlement based on an EC peace plan. Luxembourg's Foreign Minister Poos, in sharp contrast to the Community's posture during the Gulf crisis, declared euphorically: "This is the hour of Europe, not the hour of the Americans."

- Amid the humiliating defeat of the old-line Communists in Moscow and the emergence of reform-minded politicians, the German and French stock markets surged in response to a wave of new investor confidence. Europe's revived bullishness about the former Soviet Union was based on the prospects of new, private investments in independent republics, stretching from the Baltic states to the Ukraine, Moldavia, and Russia, including Siberia. Leading the investor interest were companies and banks in Germany, France, Italy, and Britain, including EC-based subsidiaries of American and Japanese companies and banks. The EBRD's chairman, Jacques Attali, prepared the fledgling bank for major lending operations; Kohl, Mitterrand, and Delors urged greatly expanding EC development aid programs in the former Soviet republics.

These three examples only highlighted two unresolved dilemmas on the Community's agenda: First, how to successfully conclude the negotiations aimed at bolstering and deepening the twelve-nation bloc economically and politically, while managing insistent demands for full EC membership, or some meaningful associate status, from its neighbors, thus widening the bloc. Second, closer to home, how to close the gap between the Community's established, unified trade policy and its weaker, disparate approach to foreign policy now being shaped increasingly by outside forces beyond Europe's control. Delors urged member governments to display "a lot of will and courage," warning that "you cannot shed tears of joy for the people of Eastern Europe one day, and the next say to them you will not buy their products."

Indeed, stark protectionist reminders of how daunting the task Delors suggested it would be surfaced immediately, triggered by strong, defensive reactions from some of the Community's powerful lobbies. In Paris, 150,000 farmers and their supporters marched in protest, and the Cresson government warned that a flood of agricultural products from the East would endanger EC farm subsidy programs; southern European and African countries feared their EC aid programs and their exports would now be sacrificed; and increasingly vocal, extreme right and even moderate conservative groups throughout the Community, warning of new flows of immigrants from the East and the South, called for stricter border controls in order to stem the tide.

The grim, shocking scene in mid-August of Italian police using truncheons and tear gas to quell thousands of poor, hungry Albanians seeking refuge in the Adriatic port of Bari reminded everyone that many neighboring people were desperate to settle in Western Europe at the very same time that its welcome mat was shrinking fast. The Italian government's exasperated reaction was to forcibly expel the Albanians via military airlifts and to warn the government in Tirana that in the future they must prevent Albanians from fleeing across the Adriatic Sea. Pope John Paul II implicitly criticized the government's handling of the incident, while *Le Monde,* in a front-page editorial August 12, termed Italy's behavior as "*La honte de l'Europe,*" the shame of Europe.

Despite new figures from the International Labor Organization showing that Italy and Germany had the highest numbers of illegal immigrants (600,000 and 400,000, respectively), the consensus was that the Community would be forced to show more flexibility, more willingness to open itself to inflows of people, commodities, and industrial products from the East—eventually. The short-term scenario, however, was for completion and ratification of the new agreements on political and monetary union among the twelve EC members by 1993 and for tightening of border controls. This would coincide with the opening of negotiations with potential, full-fledged EC members, notably Austria and Sweden. Within three years, negotiations would be underway with other EFTA members for full membership, possibly Norway, Finland, and Switzerland, as well as with Eastern European countries, including possibly Albania and former Soviet republics, each seeking associate status.

In other words, the twelve-nation bloc was expected to remain the political and economic core of the New Europe until 1995 and then gradually expand. Meantime, many officials, academics, and diplomats remained deeply skeptical about what the association agreements with Eastern neighbors would mean in concrete economic terms. "We are looking at many months of chaos in the East," commented a senior French foreign ministry official shuttling between the Baltic states, adding, "although we want to support their aspirations here in Paris and in Brussels, our collective (economic aid) resources remain limited, stretched thin . . . there are limits on what Europe can accomplish."

Indeed, of the three small Baltic states, only Estonia, with a population of 1.6 million and with historically close ties to nearby Finland across the narrow Baltic Sea, could boast a Western-style economy that had already attracted modest investments from Finland and to a lesser degree from Sweden. The economies of Latvia and Lithuania, with populations of 2.7 million and 3.7 million, were ranked as highly fragile and far weaker than neighboring Poland and Czechoslovakia, handicapped by their heavy dependence on Moscow for raw materials, energy, and monetary stability. "No one is going to rush in to invest there massively . . . not just yet," commented a senior Swedish investment banker in Stockholm.

In the United States, the prospects of only a very slow economic recovery in 1992 and a relatively low dollar cast uncertainties over Europe's economic outlook. Exports from EC member countries fell as domestic American markets shrank; two of the weakest players, France's Peugeot group and the American subsidiary of Britain's Rover group, announced in August they were definitely abandoning the U.S. automobile market. At home, EC carmakers warned that tens of thousands of jobs would be lost to Japanese competition unless the Community acted. Action on July 1, 1991, took the form of a long-awaited agreement between Tokyo and Brussels freezing Japanese imports of cars and light trucks in the Community at their current levels through 1999, accompanied by a gradual easing of import quotas in France, Italy, Spain, Portugal, and Britain.

Many questions were left unanswered by the sheltering accord, but not the impression that, once again, the Community was prepared to resort to government-inspired protection of key industries when necessary and certainly until a strong recovery was under way. This attitude fueled simmering anger and fears in Washington and Tokyo that, despite President Bush's exhortations, there now was virtually no hope of completing a meaningful GATT trade liberalization agreement prior to the U.S. presidential election in 1992.

Gradually, policymakers in Western capitals realized that despite the problems, perhaps because of them, improving relations between the world's three major trading blocs—North America, Europe, and Asia—was going to be longer and prove more difficult than had been previously imagined. In one of his final speeches before departing for Washington, U.S. ambassador Niles told the American Chamber of Commerce in France that dealing with the Community had indeed become much more like managing "a relationship with a country," than with a dozen disparate nations. This, he concluded, reflected the Community's success in forging greater unity and raised "a host of problems."

One of those problems will be dealing with the successor to Jacques Delors who planned stepping down as commission president in early 1993. Several candidates were already positioning themselves, including two EC commissioners and three prime ministers of EC member countries. Mitterrand's prediction that Delors's destiny lay in Brussels, not Paris, was rapidly becoming obsolete. Would the distinguished son of a minor bank employee run for the French presidency? Although Delors had not announced his intentions, he clearly was positioning himself to fight for the candidacy, encouraged by steady, high popularity among France's left-wing and centrist groups and, increasingly, among young people. With the French socialist party in disarray, unemployment rising, and even with other candidates also preparing themselves, notably former Prime Minister Michel Rocard, Delors's chances seemed far better than average. And if he succeeds in winning the Elysée Palace in 1995, most observers agreed, Delors will be in a new, perhaps even stronger, position to work for a united Europe.

Notes*

Introduction

1. Interview with the author, Eindhoven, April 30, 1981.
2. *Europe—A History of Its Peoples,* by Jean-Baptiste Duroselle, translated by Richard Mayne, Penguin Group, London, 1990, page 109.
3. *La Grande Illusion,* by Alain Minc, Bernard Grasset, Paris, 1989.
4. Interview with Folkhard Oelwein, director of public affairs, German Aerospace Industries Association, BDLI, in Bonn, February 28, 1989.
5. *The American Challenge,* by Jean-Jacques Servan-Schreiber, Hamish Hamilton, London, 1968.
6. *Fire in the Ashes,* by Theodore H. White, William Sloane Associates, New York, 1953, page 14.

Chapter 1

1. Interview with the author in Brussels, March 24, 1989.
2. Interview with the author in Brussels, March 24, 1989.
3. Interview with the author in Paris, December 10, 1989.
4. *Memoirs,* by Jean Monnet, Fayard, Paris, 1976, pages 540–41.
5. "The Czar of Brussels," cover story, *Newsweek,* Atlantic edition, by Scott Sullivan, February 6, 1989.
6. *Jacques Delors,* by Gabriel Milesi, Pierre Belfond, 1985, page 14.
7. This incident has been recounted by several French authors in their biographies of Delors, and to this author in several conversations with those involved, including Delors. The biographies include:
   La Decennie Mitterrand, by Pierre Favier and Michel Martin-Roland, Seuil, Paris, 1990.

*Sources of quotes and interviews are indicated in the notes and, wherever possible, in the text. Also, because of international or Atlantic editions of U.S. and European newspapers and magazines, which could cause confusion with regard to pages on which articles appear, I have identified articles by their headlines, along with the dates of publication. In selected cases for the convenience of the reader, I have grouped books on a subject in the notes, as well as in the bibliography.

Le Président, by Franz-Olivier Giesbert, Seuil, Paris, 1990.

Le Noir et le Rouge, by Catherine Nay, Grasset, Paris, 1984.

8. Interview with Delors, *International Herald Tribune*, in the first installment of a special series of supplements, "1992: The World's Rendezvous with Europe," March 25, 1988.

9. Interview with the author in Brussels, July 28, 1989.

10. Interview with the author in Paris, September 26, 1989.

11. Milesi, pages 108–109.

12. Interview with the author in London, November 22, 1989.

13. "Delors Presses Award of CGCT to Siemens AG," *International Herald Tribune*, March 16, 1987.

Chapter 2

1. *Napoleon and Hitler: A Comparative Biography*, by Desmond Seward, Harrap, London, 1988.

2. The following are several of the most important works consulted that deal with the life of Charlemagne:

    Einhard and Notker the Stammerer. Two Lives of Charlemagne, translated with an Introduction by Lewis Thorpe, Penguin, London, 1987.

    L'Empire Carolingien, by Henri Fichtenau, Payot, 1958.

    Charlemagne et L'Empire Carolingien, by Louis Halphen, Albin Michel, Paris, 1949.

3. *L'Histoire*, Number 124, July-August 1989, Paris, page 7.

4. Einhard, ibid, page 77.

5. *La Construction de l'Europe*, by Pierre Gerbet, Imprimerie Nationale, Paris, 1983, page 19.

6. Seward, *Napoleon and Hitler*, page 217.

7. *L'Histoire*, page 61.

8. *Actes et Paroles*, Imprimerie Nationale, August 21, 1849.

9. "La Naissance du Marché Commun," Pierre Gerbet, Éditions Complexe, Brussels, 1987, page 23.

10. *Orient Express*, by Jean des Cars and Jean-Paul Caracalla, Denoel, Paris, 1984, page 21.

11. *Recollections of Werner von Siemens. Inventor and Entrepreneur*, Lund Humphries, London, Prestel Verlag, Munich, 1983.

12. *The Economist*, April 22, 1989, page 28.

13. *The Rise and Fall of the Third Reich*, by William L. Shirer, Pan Books, London, 1960, page 13.

14. *Architekt der Welt Herrschaft Die Endziele Hitlers*, by Jochen Thies, Atheneum/Droste Taschenbucher Geschichte, Düsseldorf, 1980.

15. Interview with the author in Paris, February 9, 1990.

16. As compiled by Hans Ephraimson-Abt, of Saddle River, New Jersey, a selected list of works dealing with the German-American Bund includes the following:

    "The German American Bund," by Marion Mann, Thesis, City College, New York, 1970.

    National Socialist Principles, Their Application by the Nazi Party's Foreign Orga-

nizations and Use of German Nazi Aims Abroad, U.S. Printing Office, Washington, D.C., 1943.

   Deutschtum of Nazi Germans and the United States, by Arthur Smith, Putnam, New York, 1941.

   Die Auslandsorganisation der NSDAP, by Emile Ehrich, Juenker & Dunnehapt, 1937.

17. The following are some of the most revealing books and articles dealing with the role of the Nazis in Latin America:

   Le 4e Reich: Martin Borman et Les Rescapes Nazis en Amérique du Sud, by Ladislas Farago, Belfond, 1974, Translated from *Aftermath, Martin Borman and the Fourth Reich,* Simon and Schuster, New York, 1975.

   Autopsia de Perón. Balance Del Peronismo, by Louis Mercier Vega, Tusquets Editor, Barcelona, 1974.

   "Les Filières d'Évasion Nazies," *Historama,* Hors Serie No. 28, Neuilly, France.

18. *Wenn Hitler den Krieg Gewonnen Hatte,* by Ralph Giordano, Rasch and Roehring, Hamburg, 1989.

19. *Wall Street Journal,* European edition, July 24, 1989.

20. Monnet, *Memoirs,* page 320.

21. Interview with the author, Lausanne, September 29, 1989.

22. White, *Fire in the Ashes,* page 367.

23. *Memoirs. From Stalin to Gorbachev,* by Andrei Gromyko, Arrow Books, London, 1989, page 171.

24. White, *Fire in the Ashes,* page 71.

25. *Collision in Brussels: The Common Market Crisis of 30 June 1965,* by John Newhouse, W. W. Norton, New York, 1967, page 24.

26. Ibid., page 21.

27. Monnet, *Memoirs,* page 724.

Chapter 3

1. *The Rise and Fall of the Great Powers,* by Paul Kennedy, Hyman, London, 1988, page 473.

2. *The Europeans,* by Luigi Barzini, Penguin Books, London, 1983, page 30.

3. Interview with the author in Luxembourg, July 27, 1989.

4. Interview with the author in Eindhoven, April 10, 1989.

5. Interview with the author in Paris, March 29, 1990.

6. *1992: The External Dimension,* by David Henderson, The Group of Thirty, New York and London, 1989.

7. The following are among the best books on 1992:

   The 1992 Challenge from Europe: Development of the European Community's Internal Market, by Michael Calingaert, National Planning Association, Washington, D.C., 1989.

   Europe Without Frontiers—Completing the Internal Market, Office for Official Publications of the Communities, Luxembourg, 1988.

   Beyond 1992 Europe and Its Western Partners, by Peter Ludlow, Centre for European Policy Studies, Brussels, 1989.

The Times Guide to 1992. Britain in a Europe Without Frontiers, by Richard Owen and Michael Dynes, Times Books, London, 1989.

8. *Europower. The Essential Guide to Europe's Transformation in 1992,* by Nicholas Colchester and David Buchan, The Economist Books–Random House, New York, 1990, page 31.

   1992—Le Défi, by Pablo Cecchini, Flammarion, Paris, 1988.

   1992 Implications and Potential, by James Elles, Bow, London, 1988.

   1992 Eurospeak Explained, by Stephen Crampton, Rosters, London,

9. *Europe's Not So Bad Off,* by J. Paul Horne, Smith Barney international research report, January 15, 1985.

10. "De Benedetti: Lower Borders in a Bold Bid," by Steven Greenhouse, New York Times Service, in the *International Herald Tribune,* January 21, 1988.

11. Among the best articles on the battle are the following:

    "Altogether Now," *The Economist,* January 20, 1990.

    "End of an Era. De Benedetti's Raid Disrupts Aristocracy of a Quiet Kingdom," by Mark Nelson, *European Wall Street Journal,* March 30, 1988.

    "How De Benedetti Botched the Battle of Belgium." *Business Week,* International Edition, March 7, 1988.

    "More Than One Man Can Do," by Alan Friedman, *Financial Times,* April 25, 1988.

    "De Benedetti Picks Up the Pieces," by Jane Sasseen, *International Management,* April 1989.

12. "American Tips for Europeans on Warding Off Raiders," by Eric Patel, *European Wall Street Journal,* October 17, 1989.

13. Interview with the author in Munich, December 15, 1989.

14. Speech by Horne to Harvard Club, January 11, 1990.

15. IHT 1992 series, "The World's Rendezvous with Europe."

Chapter 4

1. "Le Scandale des Espions Francais," by Jean Lesieur and Jean-Marc Gonin, *L'Express,* May 18, 1990. "When 'Friends' Become Moles," by Jay Peterzell, *Time,* International Edition, May 28, 1990. "FBI Confirms French Spying," by Michael Wines, New York Times Service, in *International Herald Tribune,* November 19, 1990.

2. "India Alleges Airbus Bribed Officials to Cancel $1.2 billion Boeing Deal," by Steven Coll, Washington Post Service, in the *International Herald Tribune,* March 30, 1990.

3. "U.S. Studies Airbus Sales Practices," by Warren Getler, *International Herald Tribune,* October 31, 1985.

4. Interview with the author in Bonn, February 23, 1989. For a comparison, contained in an authoritative account of the American F-16 several decades earlier, I suggest *Arms Deal. The Selling of the F-16* by Ingemar Dorfer, Praeger, New York, 1983.

5. At ceremonies marking the delivery of fifty Ariane launchers, at Évry, France, February 15, 1989.

6. "Mitsubishi Warns Spain on $1 Billion Contract," by Peter Bruce, *Financial Times,* November 18, 1988.

7. Foreign Corrupt Practices Act as amended in 1988. Public Law 100-418. (H.R. 4848), August 23, 1988.
8. "Deal Makers Are Burning Up the Phone Lines," *Business Week*, International Edition, March 13, 1989.
9. Readers Report, *Business Week*, International Edition, April 10, 1989.
10. *International Herald Tribune*, December 24–25, 1990.
11. *Outlook Report, Organization for Economic Cooperation and Development*, Number 48, Paris, December 1990.
12. "Wary Hope on Eastern Europe," *Fortune*, International Edition, January 29, 1990.

Chapter 5

1. *Buying into America: How Foreign Money Is Changing the Face of Our Nation*, by Martin and Susan Tolchin, Times Books, New York, 1988. *The New Competitors: How Foreign Investors Are Changing the U.S. Economy*, by Norman J. Glickman and Douglas P. Woodward, Basic Books, New York, 1989. *Foreign Direct Investment in the United States*, by Edward M. Graham and Paul R. Krugman, Institute for International Economics, Washington, D.C., 1989.
2. Interview with the author in New York City, May 7, 1990.
3. "The Selling of Arkansas: It Isn't Easy," by Nina Martin, *International Herald Tribune*, April 11, 1987. Interview with the author, Brussels, July 10, 1990.
4. *The Germans. Rich, Bothered and Divided*, by David Marsh, Century, London, 1989.
5. "Culture Shock at Home: Working for a Foreign Boss," *Business Week*, International Edition, December 17, 1990.
6. Graham and Krugman. *Foreign Direct Investment*, page 84.
7. Interview with the author, Cambridge, Massachusetts, March 14, 1989.
8. "U.S. Scrutinizing Foreign Investment," by Clyde Farnsworth, New York Times Service, in the *International Herald Tribune*, July 24, 1990.
9. *The American Challenge* by Jean-Jacques, Servan-Schreiber, Hamish Hamilton, London, 1968.
10. Interview with the author in Paris, December 15, 1986.
11. "Brits Buy Up the Ad Business," by Randall Rothenberg, *New York Times Magazine*, July 2, 1989.
12. Interview in "1992—The World's Rendezvous with Europe" series, December 14, 1989.
13. "The Blossoming of Bertelsmann," *Business Week*, International Edition, November 5, 1990.
14. Interview with the author in Frankfurt, April 26, 1990.
15. Interview with the author in Great Neck, Long Island, New York, May 4, 1990.
16. Interview with the author in Princeton, New Jersey, May 1, 1990.
17. Interview with the author in East Hartford, Connecticut, May 3, 1990.
18. "Banks Warn Latin America That East Europe Is a Rival," by Reuters, in *International Herald Tribune*, April 2, 1990.
19. Interview with the author in Madrid, December 10, 1988.
20. "The ITT Wars," by Rand V. Araskog, Henry Holt, New York, 1989, page 39.
21. "Telefónica's Tough Talking Socialist Chief Preaches Profit Motive as Firm Modernizes," by Nicholas Bray, *European Wall Street Journal*, July 4, 1989.

22. Speech by Jacques de Larosière, International Conference Center, Bercy, Paris, November 23, 1990.

Chapter 6

1. Speech to the European Parliament, Strasbourg, January 17, 1989.
2. Interview with the author in Luxembourg, July 27, 1989.
3. "European TV Picture Is Slow to Focus," by Raymond Snoddy, *Financial Times*, June 1, 1990.
4. "Fulbright Urges Wider Educational Exchanges with East," by Barry James, *International Herald Tribune*, June 11, 1990.
5. "International Satellite Broadcasting" special supplement, *Financial Times*, May 29, 1990.
6. Interview with the author in Lille, November 30, 1988.
7. Interview with the author in Gleneagles, Scotland, May 31, 1989.
8. *Proposals for a European High-Speed Network*, by Community of European Railways, Brussels, January 1989.
9. "Not in My Backyard," by Robin Smyth, *London Observer*, May 13, 1990.
10. Interview with the author in Zürich, October 20, 1989.
11. Interview with the author in Frankfurt April 26, 1990.
12. Speech in Brussels, May 17, 1990.
13. "Greenbacks and ECUs. An Historical Perspective on the Emergence of Unified Currency Systems," by Jeffrey R. McCord, *UK and USA Magazine*, London, Autumn 1989.
14. Interview with the author in Brussels, July 28, 1989.
15. Interview with the author in Rhodes, October 14, 1988.
16. Interview with the author in London, June 1, 1990.
17. Interview with the author in London, November 22, 1989.
18. Interview with the author in Rotterdam, October 21, 1988.

Chapter 7

1. "The War Started a Long time Ago," *Der Spiegel*, November 6, 1989.
2. Interview with the author in Tokyo, November 7, 1989.
3. "The View from France: French CEOs Look Ahead," The McKinsey Quarterly, Autumn 1989.
4. "A Strong Europe—A Competitive Industry," speech to the European Parliament by Cesare Romiti, March 7, 1989.
5. Interview with the author in Bad Oldesloe, Germany, February 27, 1989.
6. "Les PME et L'Europe," by Edith Cresson, *Le Nouvel Économiste*, June 29, 1990.
7. "Illusion and Reality in International Trade Negotiations," by C. Ford Runge, Department of Agriculture and Applied Economics, University of Minnesota, St. Paul, Minn., November 1990.
8. "Europe in 1992: Wide Open Market for Mafia, Inc.," by Jennifer Parmelee, Washington Post Service, in *International Herald Tribune*, May 20–21, 1989.
9. Testimony by Assistant Secretary of State Ann Wrobleski, to House of Representatives Task Force on International Narcotics Control, Washington, D.C., in USIA Wireless File, March 23, 1989.

10. "European Border Controls: Who Needs Them?" by Alain Butt Philip, The Royal Institute of International Affairs, London, 1989.
11. "France's Campaign/Jean-Marie Le Pen," by Julian Nundy, *International Herald Tribune*, April 16, 1988.

Chapter 8

1. Transcript produced by London Press Service, Central Office of Information, September 20, 1988.
2. Interview with the author in Brussels, July 28, 1989.
3. *The Commissioner* by Stanley Johnson, Century Hutchinson, London, 1987. For an inside analysis of the EC bureacracy, comparing British and French approaches: *Choses Vues d'Europe—Pascal Lamy*, by Denis Olivennes, Foundation Saint Simon, Paris, May 1990.
4. "Visionaries to Watch in the Europarliament," by John Templeman, *Business Week*, International Edition, June 12, 1989.
5. "Decisive Times. France's Mitterrand Sees European Nations at Risky Crossroads," by Karen Elliott House and E. S. Browning, *European Wall Street Journal*, November 22, 1989.

Chapter 9

1. Interview with the author, January 19, 1989.
2. "The New Europe in a New Age: Insular, Itinerant or International? Prospects for an Alliance of Values," by Robert B. Zoellick, U.S. State Department, address in Annapolis, Maryland, September 21, 1990.
3. "L'Europe Absent," *Le Monde*, January 17, 1991.
4. Interview with Jean-Pierre ElKabach, Europe-1 radio station, Paris, January 21, 1991.
5. "A Carter Aide's View of the Gulf" by Joseph Fitchett, *International Herald Tribune*, September 17, 1990.
6. "Towards a European Foreign Policy," by Henri Froment Meurice and Peter Ludlow, Centre for European Policy Studies, Brussels, November 29–December 1, 1989, page 6.
7. Ibid, page 19.
8. *The Common European House*, by François Heisbourg, Director of the International Institute for Strategic Studies, London, May 16, 1990.
9. Interview with the author in Moscow, June 9, 1989.
10. "Investors Are Shaken—But Nobody's Packing," *Business Week, International Edition* January 28, 1991, page 33.
11. Interview with the author, Tixier, France, December 31, 1990.
12. *Years of Upheaval*, by Henry Kissinger, Little Brown, Boston, 1982.
13. Ibid, page 157.
14. Interview with the author in New York, May 8, 1990.
15. *Widening and Deepening: The European Community and the New European Agenda*, by Helen Wallace, Royal Institute of International Affairs, London, 1989.
16. "European Unity and National Sovereignty," by Roy Jenkins, address in Amsterdam, September 23, 1988.

Bibliography

The following is a selective list of books I have consulted, I consider them of high value for anyone seeking to understand the New Europe.

General History

Barzini, Luigi, *The Europeans*, Penguin Books, London, 1984.

Benda, Julien, *Discours à la Nation Européene*, Gallimard, Paris, 1933.

Caracalla, Jean-Paul, and des Cars, Jean, *Orient Express*, Denoel, Paris, 1984.

Duroselle, Jean-Baptiste, *Europe, a History of Its People*, translated by Richard Mayne, Penguin Books, London, 1990.

Einhard and Notker the Stammerer, *Two Lives of Charlemagne*, Penguin Books, London, 1969.

Enzenberger, Hans Magnus, *Europe, Europe*, Pantheon Books, New York, 1989.

Fichtenau, Henry, *L'Empire Carolingien*, Payot, Paris, 1958.

Giordano, Ralph, *Wenn Hitler den Krieg Gewonnen hatte*, Rasch und Roehring, Hamburg, 1989.

Gunther, John, *Inside Europe Today*, Harper & Brothers, New York, 1961.

Halphen, Louis, *Charlemagne et l'Empire Carolingien*, Albin Michel, Paris, 1949.

Kennedy, Paul, *The Rise and Fall of the Great Powers*, Unwin Hyman, London, 1988.

Kramer, Jane, *Europeans*, Penguin Books, London, 1990.

Lewis, Flora, *Europe, a Tapestry of Nations*, Simon and Schuster, New York, 1987.

Seward, Desmond, *Napoleon and Hitler*, Harrap, London, 1988.

Shirer, William L., *The Rise and Fall of the Third Reich*, Pan Books, London, 1960.

Thies, Jochen, *Architekt der Welt Herrschaft Die Endziele Hitlers*, Atheneum/Droste Taschenbucher Geschichte, Düsseldorf, 1980.

Vassiltchikov, Marie "Missie" *The Berlin Diaries*, Mandarin, London, 1990.

White, Theodore H., *Fire in the Ashes*, William Sloane, New York, 1953.

Brussels, Washington, and the European Community

Babb, Laura Longley, *The Washington Post Guide to Washington*, Bicentennial Edition, McGraw-Hill, New York, 1976.

Calingaert, Michael, *The 1992 Challenge from Europe*, National Planning Association, Library of Congress, Washington, 1988.

Cecchini, Pablo; Catinat, Michel; and Jacquemin, Alexis, *1992–Le Défi*, Flammarion, Paris, 1988.

Colchester, Nicholas, and Buchan, David, *Europower*, Times Books/Random House, New York, 1990.

Crampton, Stephen, *1992, Eurospeak Explained*, Rosters, London.

Curzon Price, Victoria, *1992—Europe's Last Chance?* Institute of Economic Affairs for the Wincott Foundation, London, 1988.

Elles, James, *1992 Implications and Potential*, Bow Publications, London, 1988.

Ewing, Charles, *Yesterday's Washington, D.C.*, E. A. Seemann Publishing, Miami, Florida, 1976.

Froncek, Thomas, *The City of Washington. An Illustrated History*, Knopf, New York, 1977.

Gerbet, Pierre, *La Naissance du Marche Commun*, Éditions Complexe, Brussels, 1987.

——, *La Construction de l'Europe*, Imprimerie Nationale, 1983, Paris.

Johnson, Stanley, *The Commissioner*, Century Hutchinson, London, 1987.

Ludlow, Peter, *Beyond 1992. Europe and Its Western Partners*, Centre for European Policy Studies, Brussels, 1989.

Milesi, Gabriel, *Jacques Delors*, Pierre Belfond, Paris, 1985.

Monnet, Jean, *Mémoires*, Fayard, Paris, 1976.

Morris, Brian; Boehm, Klaus; and Oeller, Maurice, *The European Community 1991-2. The Professional Reference Book for Business, Media and Government*, MacMillan Press and Walter De Grayton, Berlin, 1991.

Newhouse, John, *Collision in Brussels: The Common Market Crisis of 30 June 1965*, W. W. Norton, with the Twentieth Century Fund, New York, 1967.

Owen, Richard, and Dynes, Michael, *The Times Guide to 1992*, Times Books, London, 1989.

Pratte, Alain, *Quelle Europe?*, Commentaire Julliard, Paris, 1991.

Schwok, René, *Horizon 1992—La Suisse et le Grand Marché* Européen," Georg Éditeur and Institut Universitaire d'Études Européenes, Geneva, 1989.

Aviation and the Aerospace Industry

Dorfer, Ingemar, *Arms Deal—The Selling of the F-16*, Praeger, New York, 1983.

Europe's Future in Space, Joint Policy Report, Routledge & Kegan Paul, London, 1988.

Lacoste, Beatrice, *Europe: Stepping Stones to Space*, Obric, Bedfordshire, Great Britain, 1990.

Newhouse, John, *The Sporty Game*, Knopf, New York, 1982.

Picq, Jean, *Les Ailes de l'Europe—l'Aventure de l'Airbus*, Fayard, Paris, 1990.

Schmitz, Arno L., *Take Off—The Book of German Aerospace*, in cooperation with the Federal Association of the West German Aerospace Industry (BDLI) Monch, Bonn, 1978.

Multinationals

Agnelli, Susanna, *We Always Wore Sailor Suits*, Corgi Books, Weidenfeld & Nicholson, London, 1976.

Arakskog, Rand V., *The ITT Wars*, Henry Holt, New York, 1989.

Cayez, Pierre, *Rhône-Poulenc, 1895–1975* Armand Colin/Masson, Paris, 1988.

Fredet, Jean-Gabriel and Denis Pingaud, *Les Patrons Face à la Gauche*, Ramsay, Paris, 1982.

Friedman, Alan, *Agnelli and the Network of Italian Power*, Harrap, London, 1988.

Hamon, Maurice, *Du Soleil à la Terre—Une Histoire de Saint-Gobain*, Lattes, Paris, 1988.

Humphries, Lund, *Recollections of Werner von Siemens*, Presetel Verlag, Munich, 1983.

Overkleeft, D. and Grossman, L. E., *The Dekker Perspective*, Graham & Trotman, London, 1988.

Philips, Frederick, *45 Years with Philips*, Blandford Press, Poole Dorset, Britain, 1978.

Robinson, John, *Multinationals and Political Control*, Gower, London, 1983.

Sampson, Anthony, *The Arms Bazaar*, Hodder and Stoughton, London, 1977.

Sautter, Christian, *Les Dents du Géant*, Olivier Orban, Paris, 1987.

Sobel, Robert, *ITT the Management of Opportunity*, Truman Talley Books, New York, 1982.

Trade, Investment, and Foreign Policy

Aho, C. Michael and Aronson, David Jonathan, *America Better Listen*, Council on Foreign Relations, New York, 1985.

Brock, William, and Hormats, Robert, *The Global Economy*, W. W. Norton, New York, 1990.

Carrington, Peter, *Reflecting on Things Past*, Bessie Books/Harper & Row, New York 1988.

Glickman, Norman J., and Woodward, Douglas P., *The New Competitors: How Foreign Investors Are Changing the U.S. Economy*, Basic Books, New York, 1989.

Graham, Edward M., and Krugman, Paul R., *Foreign Direct Investment in the United States*, Institute for International Economics, Washington, D.C., 1989.

Kissinger, Henry, *Years of Upheaval*, Little Brown, Boston, 1982.

Landau, George W.; Feo, Julio; and Hosono Akio, *Latin America at a Crossroads: The Challenge to the Trilateral Countries*, Trilateral Commission, New York, Paris and Tokyo, 1990.

Manfrass, Klaus, *Paris-Bonn*, Jan Thorbecke Verlag, Sigmaringen, Germany, 1984.

Marsh, David, *The Germans—The Pivotal Nation*, St. Martin's Press, New York, 1990.

Meyer, Michel, *Le Mal Franco-Allemand*, Denoel, 1979.

Pfaff, William, *Barbarian Sentiments: How the American Century Ends*, Hill & Wang, a division of Farrar Straus & Giroux, New York, 1989.

Picht, Robert, *Das Bundnis im Bundnis*, Guadriga (Severin und Siedler) Berlin, 1982.

Prestowitz, Jr., Clyde V.; Morse, Ronald A.; and Tonelson, Alan, *Powernomics*, Madison Books, Lanham, Md., 1991.

Sauzay, Brigitte, *Le Vertige Allemand*, Olivier Orban, Paris, 1985.

Servan-Schreiber, Jean-Jacques, *The American Challenge*, Hamish Hamilton, London, 1968.

Tolchin, Martin and Susan, *Buying Into America: How Foreign Money Is Changing the Face of Our Nation*, Times Books, New York, 1988.

Index

345

About the Author

Axel Krause is the corporate editor of the *International Herald Tribune* in Paris. An American citizen, he has been reporting on Europe for nearly three decades and is a regular contributor to European periodicals, radio, and television programs. From 1962, he was senior correspondent for McGraw-Hill Publications, including *Business Week*, in Paris, Moscow, and Washington, becoming the *International Herald Tribune*'s first European economics correspondent in 1979.

Born in Berlin, he immigrated to the United States in 1940 with his mother and younger brother and grew up in Yonkers, New York. He graduated with honors in history from Colgate University in 1956 and two years later from Princeton University's Woodrow Wilson School of Public and International Affairs. His journalistic career began as a staff reporter for the Plainfield *Courier News,* United Press International, and the *Wall Street Journal,* prior to accepting his first post as foreign correspondent for *Business Week* in Paris.

As economics correspondent for the *International Herald Tribune,* he covered European business, world trade, and economics, including the aerospace industry, the European Community, and Japan's worldwide economic expansion. Since 1987, as corporate editor, he has been supervising a series of continuing *IHT* supplements assessing the EC's 1992 program and is a regular contributor to *Europe* magazine in the United States, and to *European Affairs,* published in Amsterdam. He also is a member of the advisory board of the European Community Studies Association in the United States. He lives in Paris with his wife and two children. This is his first book.